C++ FOR
EVERYONE

C++ FOR EVERYONE

SECOND EDITION

Cay Horstmann

San Jose State University

WILEY

John Wiley & Sons, Inc.

VICE PRESIDENT AND EXECUTIVE PUBLISHER	Don Fowley
EXECUTIVE EDITOR	Beth Lang Golub
EDITORIAL PROGRAM ASSISTANT	Michael Berlin
PRODUCTION SERVICES MANAGER	Dorothy Sinclair
SENIOR PRODUCTION EDITOR	Janet Foxman
EXECUTIVE MARKETING MANAGER	Christopher Ruel
MARKETING ASSISTANT	Diana Smith
CREATIVE DIRECTOR	Harry Nolan
SENIOR PHOTO EDITOR	Lisa Gee
SENIOR DESIGNER	Madelyn Lesure
EXECUTIVE MEDIA EDITOR	Tom Kulesa
PRODUCTION SERVICES	Cindy Johnson
COVER PHOTO	© Ricardo Azoury/iStockphoto

This book was set in Stempel Garamond by Publishing Services, and printed and bound by RRD Jefferson City. The cover was printed by RRD Jefferson City.

This book is printed on acid-free paper. ∞

Founded in 1807, John Wiley & Sons, Inc. has been a valued source of knowledge and understanding for more than 200 years, helping people around the world meet their needs and fulfill their aspirations. Our company is built on a foundation of principles that include responsibility to the communities we serve and where we live and work. In 2008, we launched a Corporate Citizenship Initiative, a global effort to address the environmental, social, economic, and ethical challenges we face in our business. Among the issues we are addressing are carbon impact, paper specifications and procurement, ethical conduct within our business and among our vendors, and community and charitable support. For more information, please visit our website: *www.wiley.com/go/citizenship*.

Library of Congress Cataloging in Publication Data:
Horstmann, Cay S., 1959-
  C++ for everyone / Cay S. Horstmann. -- 2nd ed.
    p. cm.
  Includes index.
   ISBN 978-0-470-92713-7 (pbk.)
  1. C++ (Computer program language) I. Title.
  QA76.73.C153H6685 2010
  005.13'3--dc22
                    2010039907

ISBN   978-0-470-92713-7 (Main Book)
ISBN   978-0-470-92092-3 (Binder-Ready Version)

Printed in the United States of America

10 9 8 7 6 5 4 3 2

PREFACE

This book is an introduction to C++ and computer programming that focuses on the essentials—and on effective learning. The book is designed to serve a wide range of student interests and abilities and is suitable for a first course in programming for computer scientists, engineers, and students in other disciplines. No prior programming experience is required, and only a modest amount of high school algebra is needed. Here are the key features of this book:

Guidance and worked examples help students succeed.

Beginning programmers often ask "How do I start? Now what do I do?" Of course, an activity as complex as programming cannot be reduced to cookbook-style instructions. However, step-by-step guidance is immensely helpful for building confidence and providing an outline for the task at hand. "Problem Solving" sections stress the importance of design and planning. "How To" guides help students with common programming tasks. Additional Worked Examples are available online.

Practice makes perfect.

Of course, programming students need to be able to implement nontrivial programs, but they first need to have the confidence that they can succeed. This book contains a substantial number of self-check questions at the end of each section. "Practice It" pointers suggest exercises to try after each section. At the end of each chapter, you will find a great variety of programming assignments, ranging from simple practice problems to realistic applications.

Teach computer science principles, not just C++ or object-orientation.

This book uses the C++ programming language as a vehicle for introducing computer science concepts. A substantial subset of the C++ language is covered, focusing on the modern features of standard C++ that make students productive. The book takes a traditional route, stressing control structures, procedural decomposition, and array algorithms, before turning to the design of classes in the final chapters.

A visual approach motivates the reader and eases navigation.

Photographs present visual analogies that explain the nature and behavior of computer concepts. Step-by-step figures illustrate complex program operations. Syntax boxes and example tables present a variety of typical and special cases in a compact format. It is easy to get the "lay of the land" by browsing the visuals, before focusing on the textual material.

Visual features help the reader with navigation.

Focus on the essentials while being technically accurate.

An encyclopedic coverage is not helpful for a beginning programmer, but neither is the opposite—reducing the material to a list of simplistic bullet points. In this book, the essentials are presented in digestible chunks, with separate notes that go deeper into good practices or language features when the reader is ready for the additional information. You will not find artificial over-simplifications that give an illusion of knowledge.

New to This Edition

Problem Solving Strategies

This edition adds practical, step-by-step illustrations of techniques that can help students devise and evaluate solutions to programming problems. Introduced where they are most relevant, these strategies address barriers to success for many students. Strategies included are:

- Algorithm Design (with pseudocode)
- First Do It By Hand (doing sample calculations by hand)
- Flowcharts
- Test Cases
- Hand-Tracing
- Storyboards
- Reusable Functions
- Stepwise Refinement
- Adapting Algorithms
- Discover Algorithms by Manipulating Physical Objects
- Draw a Picture (pointer diagrams)
- Tracing Objects (identifying state and behavior)
- Discovering Classes

Optional Engineering Exercises

End-of-chapter exercises have been enhanced with problems from scientific and engineering domains. Geared to students learning C++ for a technical major, the exercises are designed to illustrate the value of programming in those fields. Additional exercises are available on the book's companion web site.

New and Reorganized Topics

All chapters were revised and enhanced to respond to user feedback and improve the flow of topics. Loop algorithms are now introduced explicitly in Chapter 4. Debugging is now introduced in a lengthy Worked Example in Chapter 5. Arrays are covered before vectors are introduced in Chapter 6, and a new section on vector algorithms builds on the array algorithms presented earlier in the chapter. A new optional section on structure types is now in Chapter 7. New example tables, photos, and exercises appear throughout the book.

A Tour of the Book

The core material of the book is:

Chapter 1. Introduction
Chapter 2. Fundamental Data Types
Chapter 3. Decisions
Chapter 4. Loops
Chapter 5. Functions
Chapter 6. Arrays and Vectors

In a course for engineers with a need for systems and embedded programming, you will want to cover Chapter 7 on pointers. Sections 7.1 and 7.4 are sufficient for using pointers with polymorphism in Chapter 10.

File processing is the subject of Chapter 8. Section 8.1 can be covered sooner for an introduction to reading and writing text files. The remainder of the chapter gives additional material for practical applications.

Chapters 9 and 10 introduce the object-oriented features of C++. Chapter 9 introduces class design and implementation. Chapter 10 covers inheritance and polymorphism.

✚ Four additional chapters are available on the Web. They can be used individually for a capstone chapter, or they can be combined for teaching a two-semester course. (They can also be incorporated into a custom print version of the text; ask your Wiley sales representative for details.)

Chapter 11. Recursion
Chapter 12. Sorting and Searching
Chapter 13. Lists, Stacks, and Queues
Chapter 14. Sets, Maps, and Priority Queues

Figure 1 shows the dependencies between the chapters.

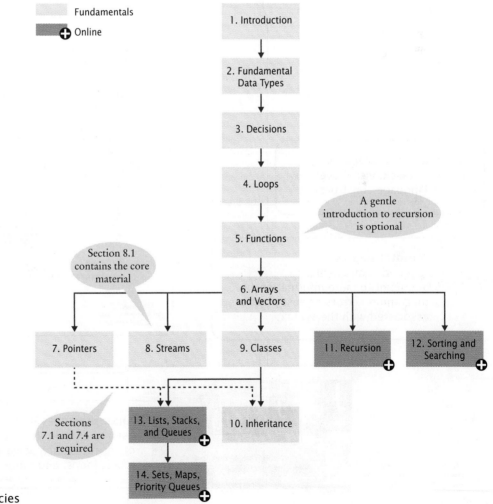

Figure 1
Chapter Dependencies

A Walkthrough of the Learning Aids

The pedagogical elements in this book work together to focus on and reinforce key concepts and fundamental principles of programming, with additional tips and detail organized to support and deepen these fundamentals. In addition to traditional features, such as chapter objectives and a wealth of exercises, each chapter contains elements geared to today's visual learner.

Throughout each chapter, **margin notes** show where new concepts are introduced and provide an outline of key ideas.

Annotated **syntax boxes** provide a quick, visual overview of new language constructs.

Annotations explain required components and point to more information on common errors or best practices associated with the syntax.

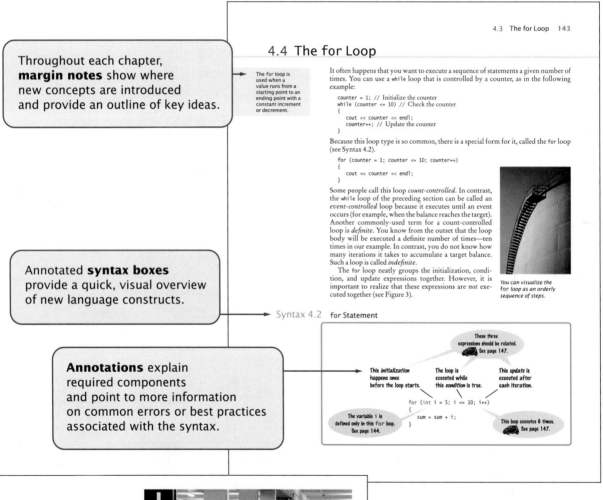

4.3   The for Loop   143

4.4 The for Loop

The for loop is used when a value runs from a starting point to an ending point with a constant increment or decrement.

It often happens that you want to execute a sequence of statements a given number of times. You can use a while loop that is controlled by a counter, as in the following example:

```
counter = 1; // Initialize the counter
while (counter <= 10) // Check the counter
{
    cout << counter << endl;
    counter++; // Update the counter
}
```

Because this loop type is so common, there is a special form for it, called the for loop (see Syntax 4.2).

```
for (counter = 1; counter <= 10; counter++)
{
    cout << counter << endl;
}
```

Some people call this loop *count-controlled*. In contrast, the while loop of the preceding section can be called an *event-controlled* loop because it executes until an event occurs (for example, when the balance reaches the target). Another commonly-used term for a count-controlled loop is *definite*. You know from the outset that the loop body will be executed a definite number of times—ten times in our example. In contrast, you do not know how many iterations it takes to accumulate a target balance. Such a loop is called *indefinite*.

The for loop neatly groups the initialization, condition, and update expressions together. However, it is important to realize that these expressions are *not* executed together (see Figure 3).

You can visualize the for loop as an orderly sequence of steps.

Syntax 4.2   for Statement

These three expressions should be related. See page 147.

This *initialization* happens once before the loop starts.

The loop is executed while this *condition* is true.

This *update* is executed after each iteration.

```
for (int i = 5; i <= 10; i++)
{
    sum = sum + i;
}
```

The variable i is defined only in this for loop. See page 144.

This loop executes 6 times. See page 147.

Like a variable in a computer program, a parking space has an identifier and a contents.

Analogies to everyday objects are used to explain the nature and behavior of concepts such as variables, data types, loops, and more.

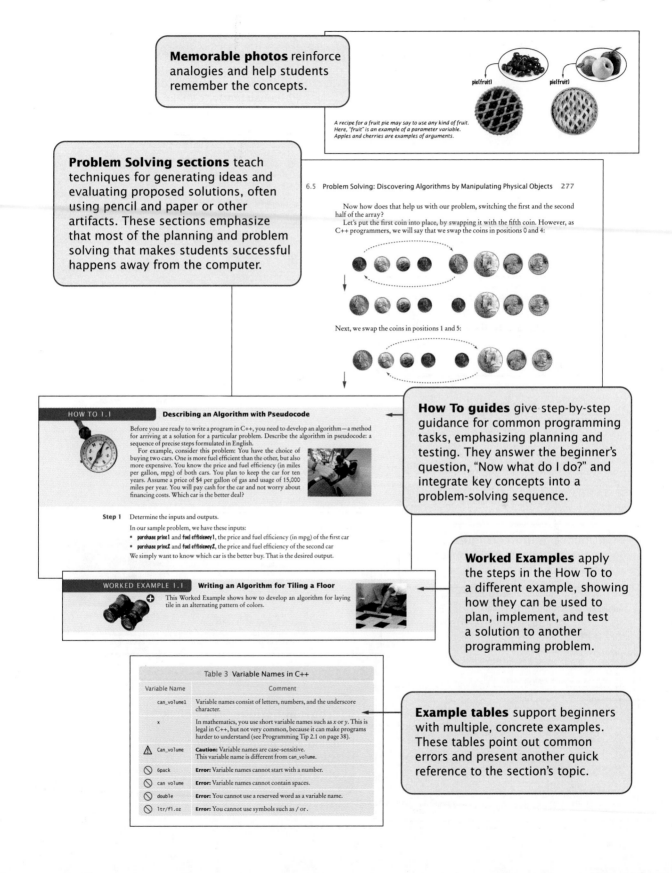

Memorable photos reinforce analogies and help students remember the concepts.

A recipe for a fruit pie may say to use any kind of fruit. Here, "fruit" is an example of a parameter variable. Apples and cherries are examples of arguments.

pie(fruit)   pie(fruit)

Problem Solving sections teach techniques for generating ideas and evaluating proposed solutions, often using pencil and paper or other artifacts. These sections emphasize that most of the planning and problem solving that makes students successful happens away from the computer.

6.5 Problem Solving: Discovering Algorithms by Manipulating Physical Objects   277

Now how does that help us with our problem, switching the first and the second half of the array?

Let's put the first coin into place, by swapping it with the fifth coin. However, as C++ programmers, we will say that we swap the coins in positions 0 and 4:

Next, we swap the coins in positions 1 and 5:

HOW TO 1.1   **Describing an Algorithm with Pseudocode**

Before you are ready to write a program in C++, you need to develop an algorithm—a method for arriving at a solution for a particular problem. Describe the algorithm in pseudocode: a sequence of precise steps formulated in English.

For example, consider this problem: You have the choice of buying two cars. One is more fuel efficient than the other, but also more expensive. You know the price and fuel efficiency (in miles per gallon, mpg) of both cars. You plan to keep the car for ten years. Assume a price of $4 per gallon of gas and usage of 15,000 miles per year. You will pay cash for the car and not worry about financing costs. Which car is the better deal?

Step 1   Determine the inputs and outputs.

In our sample problem, we have these inputs:
- **purchase price1** and **fuel efficiency1**, the price and fuel efficiency (in mpg) of the first car
- **purchase price2** and **fuel efficiency2**, the price and fuel efficiency of the second car
We simply want to know which car is the better buy. That is the desired output.

How To guides give step-by-step guidance for common programming tasks, emphasizing planning and testing. They answer the beginner's question, "Now what do I do?" and integrate key concepts into a problem-solving sequence.

Worked Examples apply the steps in the How To to a different example, showing how they can be used to plan, implement, and test a solution to another programming problem.

WORKED EXAMPLE 1.1   **Writing an Algorithm for Tiling a Floor**

This Worked Example shows how to develop an algorithm for laying tile in an alternating pattern of colors.

Table 3 Variable Names in C++	
Variable Name	Comment
can_volume1	Variable names consist of letters, numbers, and the underscore character.
x	In mathematics, you use short variable names such as x or y. This is legal in C++, but not very common, because it can make programs harder to understand (see Programming Tip 2.1 on page 38).
⚠ Can_volume	**Caution:** Variable names are case-sensitive. This variable name is different from can_volume.
🚫 6pack	**Error:** Variable names cannot start with a number.
🚫 can volume	**Error:** Variable names cannot contain spaces.
🚫 double	**Error:** You cannot use a reserved word as a variable name.
🚫 ltr/fl.oz	**Error:** You cannot use symbols such as / or .

Example tables support beginners with multiple, concrete examples. These tables point out common errors and present another quick reference to the section's topic.

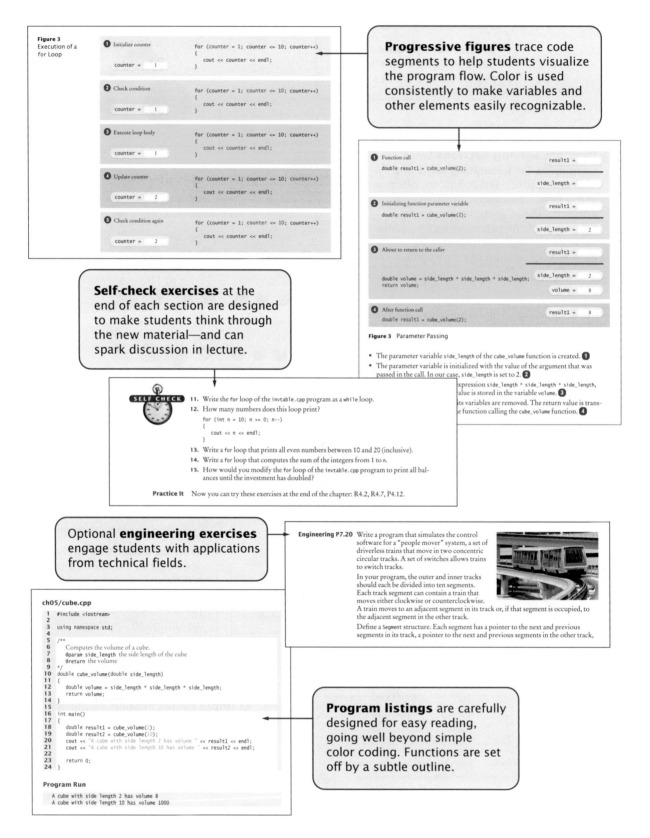

Figure 3
Execution of a
for Loop

❶ Initialize counter

```
for (counter = 1; counter <= 10; counter++)
{
    cout << counter << endl;
}
```

counter =   1

❷ Check condition

```
for (counter = 1; counter <= 10; counter++)
{
    cout << counter << endl;
}
```

counter =   1

❸ Execute loop body

```
for (counter = 1; counter <= 10; counter++)
{
    cout << counter << endl;
}
```

counter =   1

❹ Update counter

```
for (counter = 1; counter <= 10; counter++)
{
    cout << counter << endl;
}
```

counter =   2

❺ Check condition again

```
for (counter = 1; counter <= 10; counter++)
{
    cout << counter << endl;
}
```

counter =   2

Progressive figures trace code
segments to help students visualize
the program flow. Color is used
consistently to make variables and
other elements easily recognizable.

❶ Function call

```
double result1 = cube_volume(2);
```

result1 =

side_length =

❷ Initializing function parameter variable

```
double result1 = cube_volume(2);
```

result1 =

side_length =   2

❸ About to return to the caller

```
double volume = side_length * side_length * side_length;
return volume;
```

result1 =

side_length =   2

volume =   8

❹ After function call

```
double result1 = cube_volume(2);
```

result1 =   8

Figure 3 Parameter Passing

- The parameter variable side_length of the cube_volume function is created. ❶
- The parameter variable is initialized with the value of the argument that was passed in the call. In our case, side_length is set to 2. ❷
- ...expression side_length * side_length * side_length, ...value is stored in the variable volume. ❸
- ...its variables are removed. The return value is trans-...e function calling the cube_volume function. ❹

Self-check exercises at the
end of each section are designed
to make students think through
the new material—and can
spark discussion in lecture.

SELF CHECK

11. Write the for loop of the invtable.cpp program as a while loop.
12. How many numbers does this loop print?

```
for (int n = 10; n >= 0; n--)
{
    cout << n << endl;
}
```

13. Write a for loop that prints all even numbers between 10 and 20 (inclusive).
14. Write a for loop that computes the sum of the integers from 1 to n.
15. How would you modify the for loop of the invtable.cpp program to print all balances until the investment has doubled?

Practice It Now you can try these exercises at the end of the chapter: R4.2, R4.7, P4.12.

Optional **engineering exercises**
engage students with applications
from technical fields.

Engineering P7.20 Write a program that simulates the control
software for a "people mover" system, a set of
driverless trains that move in two concentric
circular tracks. A set of switches allows trains
to switch tracks.

In your program, the outer and inner tracks
should each be divided into ten segments.
Each track segment can contain a train that
moves either clockwise or counterclockwise.
A train moves to an adjacent segment in its track or, if that segment is occupied, to
the adjacent segment in the other track.

Define a Segment structure. Each segment has a pointer to the next and previous
segments in its track, a pointer to the next and previous segments in the other track,

ch05/cube.cpp

```
1   #include <iostream>
2
3   using namespace std;
4
5   /**
6       Computes the volume of a cube.
7       @param side_length the side length of the cube
8       @return the volume
9   */
10  double cube_volume(double side_length)
11  {
12      double volume = side_length * side_length * side_length;
13      return volume;
14  }
15
16  int main()
17  {
18      double result1 = cube_volume(2);
19      double result2 = cube_volume(10);
20      cout << "A cube with side length 2 has volume " << result1 << endl;
21      cout << "A cube with side length 10 has volume " << result2 << endl;
22
23      return 0;
24  }
```

Program listings are carefully
designed for easy reading,
going well beyond simple
color coding. Functions are set
off by a subtle outline.

Program Run

```
A cube with side length 2 has volume 8
A cube with side length 10 has volume 1000
```

Common Errors describe the kinds of errors that students often make, with an explanation of why the errors occur, and what to do about them.

Common Error 2.1

Using Undefined Variables

You must define a variable before you use it for the first time. For example, the following sequence of statements would not be legal:

```
double can_volume = 12 * liter_per_ounce;
double liter_per_ounce = 0.0296;
```

In your program, the statements are compiled in order. When the compiler reaches the first statement, it does not know that liter_per_ounce will be defined in the next line, and it reports an error.

Programming Tips explain good programming practices, and encourage students to be more productive with tips and techniques such as hand-tracing.

Programming Tip 3.6

Hand-Tracing

A very useful technique for understanding whether a program works correctly is called *hand-tracing*. You simulate the program's activity on a sheet of paper. You can use this method with pseudocode or C++ code.

Get an index card, a cocktail napkin, or whatever sheet of paper is within reach. Make a column for each variable. Have the program code ready. Use a marker, such as a paper clip, to mark the current statement. In your mind, execute statements one at a time. Every time the value of a variable changes, cross out the old value and write the new value below the old one.

For example, let's trace the tax program with the data from the program run on page 95. In lines 13 and 14, tax1 and tax2 are initialized to 0.

Hand-tracing helps you understand whether a program works correctly.

```
6  int main()
7  {
8      const double RATE1 = 0.10;
9      const double RATE2 = 0.25;
10     const double RATE1_SINGLE_LIMIT = 32000;
11     const double RATE1_MARRIED_LIMIT = 64000;
12
13     double tax1 = 0;
14     double tax2 = 0;
15
```

tax1	tax2	income	marital status
0	0		

In lines 18 and 22, income and marital_status are initialized by input statements.

```
16     double income;
17     cout << "Please enter your income: ";
18     cin >> income;
19
20     cout << "Please enter s for single, m for married: ";
21     string marital_status;
22     cin >> marital_status;
23
```

tax1	tax2	income	marital status
0	0	$0000	m

Because marital_status is not "s", we move to the else branch of the outer if statement (line 36).

Special Topics present optional topics and provide additional explanation of others.

Special Topic 6.2

A Sorting Algorithm

A *sorting algorithm* rearranges the elements of a sequence so that they are stored in sorted order. Here is a simple sorting algorithm, called **selection sort**. Consider sorting the following array values:

[0] [1] [2] [3] [4]
11 9 17 5 12

An obvious first step is to find the smallest element. In this case the smallest element is 5, stored in values[3]. You should move the 5 to the beginning of the array. Of course, there is already an element stored in values[0], namely 11. Therefore you cannot simply move values[3] into values[0] without moving the 11 somewhere else. You don't yet know where the 11 should end up, but you know for certain that it should not be in values[0]. Simply get it out of the way by *swapping it* with values[3]:

5 9 17 11 12

Now the first element is in the correct place. In the foregoing figure, the darker color indicates the portion of the array that is already sorted.

Next take the minimum of the remaining entries values[1]...values[4]. That minimum value, 9, is already in the correct place. You don't need to do anything in this case, simply extend the sorted area by one to the right:

5 9 17 11 12

Repeat the process. The minimum value of the unsorted region is 11, which needs to be swapped with the first value of the unsorted region, 17:

5 9 11 17 12

Random Facts provide historical and social information on computing—for interest and to fulfill the "historical and social context" requirements of the ACM/IEEE curriculum guidelines.

Random Fact 4.1 **The First Bug**

According to legend, the first bug was found in the Mark II, a huge electromechanical computer at Harvard University. It really was caused by a bug—a moth was trapped in a relay switch.

Actually, from the note that the operator left in the log book next to the moth (see the photo), it appears as if the term "bug" had already been in active use at the time.

The pioneering computer scientist Maurice Wilkes wrote, "Somehow, at the Moore School and afterwards, one had always assumed there would be no particular difficulty in getting programs right. I can remember the exact instant in time at which it dawned on me that a great part of my future life would be spent finding mistakes in my own programs."

The First Bug

Appendices

Appendix A contains a programming style guide. Using a style guide for programming assignments benefits students by directing them toward good habits and reducing gratuitous choice. The style guide is available in electronic form so that instructors can modify it to reflect their preferred style.

Appendices B and C summarize C++ reserved words and operators. Appendix D lists character escape sequences and ASCII character code values. Appendix E documents all of the library functions and classes used in this book.

Additional appendices available from the book's companion web site include an expanded version of Appendix E that includes the functions and classes used in the four optional chapters, 11–14, plus appendices that cover number systems, bit and shift operations, and a comparison of C++ and Java.

Student and Instructor Resources

The following resources for students and instructors can be obtained by visiting www.wiley.com/college/horstmann. Two companion web sites accompany the book—one for students, and a password-protected site for instructors only.

- Additional exercises geared to the scientific and engineering problem domains
- Worked Examples that apply the problem-solving steps in the book to other realistic examples (identified in the book by an icon, ✚)
- Source code for all examples in the book
- Solutions to all review and programming exercises (for instructors only)
- Lecture presentation slides (in PowerPoint format) that summarize each chapter and include code listings and figures from the book (for instructors only)
- A test bank that focuses on skills, not just terminology (for instructors only)
- Four additional chapters on recursion, sorting and searching, and data structures
- The programming style guide in electronic form

Pointers in the book describe what students will find on the Web.

WORKED EXAMPLE 2.1   **Computing Travel Time**

In this Worked Example, we develop a hand calculation to compute the time that a robot requires to retrieve an item from rocky terrain.

Visit the *C++ for Everyone* companion web sites at www.wiley.com/college/horstmann.

Acknowledgments

Many thanks to Beth Golub, Tom Kulesa, Andre Legaspi, Elizabeth Mills, Michael Berlin, and Lisa Gee at John Wiley & Sons, and to the team at Publishing Services for their hard work and support for this book project. An especially deep acknowledgment and thanks to Cindy Johnson, who, through enormous patience and attention to detail, made this book a reality. We would also like to thank Jonathan Tolstedt, North Dakota State University, for his high-quality solutions; Brent Seales, University of Kentucky, for revising and enhancing the test bank; and to Evan Gallagher, Polytechnic Institute of New York University, for his creative PowerPoint slides.

We are very grateful to the many individuals who reviewed and/or class tested this and the first edition of the book. We value their many valuable suggestions for improvement. They include:

Charles D. Allison, *Utah Valley State College*

Fred Annexstein, *University of Cincinnati*

Stefano Basagni, *Northeastern University*

Noah D. Barnette, *Virginia Tech*

Susan Bickford, *Tallahassee Community College*

Ronald D. Bowman, *University of Alabama, Huntsville*

Peter Breznay, *University of Wisconsin, Green Bay*

Richard Cacace, *Pensacola Junior College, Pensacola*

Kuang-Nan Chang, *Eastern Kentucky University*

Joseph DeLibero, *Arizona State University*

Subramaniam Dharmarajan, *Arizona State University*

Mary Dorf, *University of Michigan*

Marty Dulberg, *North Carolina State University*

William E. Duncan, *Louisiana State University*

John Estell, *Ohio Northern University*

Waleed Farag, *Indiana University of Pennsylvania*

Stephen Gilbert, *Orange Coast Community College*

Kenneth Gitlitz, *New Hampshire Technical Institute*

Daniel Grigoletti, *DeVry Institute of Technology, Tinley Park*

Barbara Guillott, *Louisiana State University*

Charles Halsey, *Richland College*

Jon Hanrath, *Illinois Institute of Technology*

Neil Harrison, *Utah Valley University*

Jurgen Hecht, *University of Ontario*

Steve Hodges, *Cabrillo College*

Jackie Jarboe, *Boise State University*

Debbie Kaneko, *Old Dominion University*

Mir Behrad Khamesee, *University of Waterloo*

Sung-Sik Kwon, *North Carolina Central University*

Lorrie Lehman, *University of North Carolina, Charlotte*

Cynthia Lester, *Tuskegee University*

Yanjun Li, *Fordham University*

W. James MacLean, *University of Toronto*

LindaLee Massoud, *Mott Community College*

Charles W. Mellard, *DeVry Institute of Technology, Irving*

Ethan V. Munson, *University of Wisconsin, Milwaukee*

Philip Regalbuto, *Trident Technical College*

Don Retzlaff, *University of North Texas*

Jeff Ringenberg, *University of Michigan, Ann Arbor*

John P. Russo, *Wentworth Institute of Technology*

Kurt Schmidt, *Drexel University*

Brent Seales, *University of Kentucky*

William Shay, *University of Wisconsin, Green Bay*

Michele A. Starkey, *Mount Saint Mary College*

William Stockwell, *University of Central Oklahoma*

Jonathan Tolstedt, *North Dakota State University*

Boyd Trolinger, *Butte College*

Muharrem Uyar, *City College of New York*

Mahendra Velauthapillai, *Georgetown University*

Kerstin Voigt, *California State University, San Bernardino*

David P. Voorhees, *Le Moyne College*

Salih Yurttas, *Texas A&M University*

A special thank you to all of our class testers:

Pani Chakrapani and the students of the University of Redlands

Jim Mackowiak and the students of Long Beach City College, LAC

Suresh Muknahallipatna and the students of the University of Wyoming

Murlidharan Nair and the students of the Indiana University of South Bend

Harriette Roadman and the students of New River Community College

David Topham and the students of Ohlone College

Dennie Van Tassel and the students of Gavilan College

CONTENTS

⊕ Available online at www.wiley.com/college/horstmann.

✚ Available online at www.wiley.com/college/horstmann.

ALPHABETICAL LIST OF   SYNTAX BOXES

⊕ Available online at www.wiley.com/college/horstmann.

Available online at www.wiley.com/college/horstmann.

➕ Available online at www.wiley.com/college/horstmann.

➕ Available online at www.wiley.com/college/horstmann.

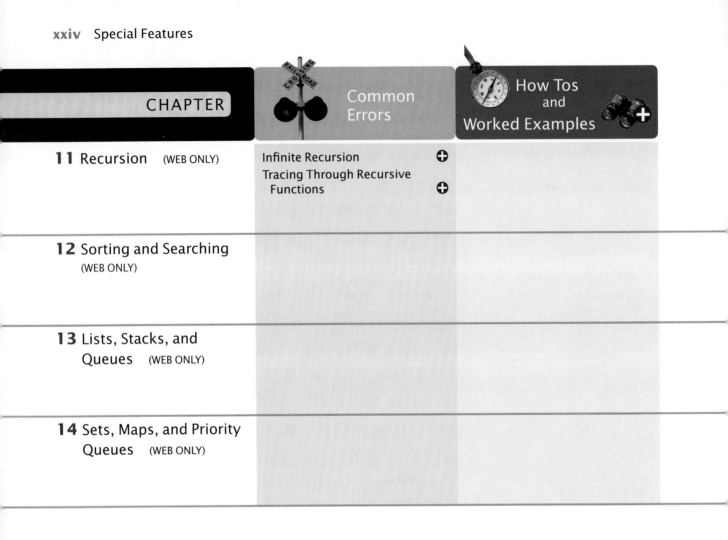

CHAPTER	Common Errors	How Tos and Worked Examples
11 Recursion (WEB ONLY)	Infinite Recursion ✚ Tracing Through Recursive Functions ✚	
12 Sorting and Searching (WEB ONLY)		
13 Lists, Stacks, and Queues (WEB ONLY)		
14 Sets, Maps, and Priority Queues (WEB ONLY)		

Programming Tips	Special Topics	Random Facts
Library Functions for Sorting and Binary Search ⊕	The Quicksort Algorithm ⊕ Defining an Ordering for Sorting Objects ⊕	Cataloging Your Necktie Collection ⊕
		Reverse Polish Notation ⊕
	Defining an Ordering for Container Elements ⊕ Constant Iterators ⊕ Discrete Event Simulations ⊕	

⊕ Available online at www.wiley.com/college/horstmann.

CHAPTER 1

INTRODUCTION

To learn about the architecture of computers

To learn about machine languages and higher-level programming languages

To become familiar with your compiler

To compile and run your first C++ program

To recognize compile-time and run-time errors

To describe an algorithm with pseudocode

To understand the activity of programming

Just as you gather tools, study a project, and make a plan for tackling it, in this chapter you will gather up the basics you need to start learning to program. After a brief introduction to computer hardware, software, and programming in general, you will learn how to write and run your first C++ program. You will also learn how to diagnose and fix programming errors, and how to use pseudocode to describe an algorithm—a step-by-step description of how to solve a problem—as you plan your programs.

1.1 What Is Programming?

Computers execute very basic instructions in rapid succession.

You have probably used a computer for work or fun. Many people use computers for everyday tasks such as electronic banking or writing a term paper. Computers are good for such tasks. They can handle repetitive chores, such as totaling up numbers or placing words on a page, without getting bored or exhausted.

The flexibility of a computer is quite an amazing phenomenon. The same machine can balance your checkbook, print your term paper, and play a game. In contrast, other machines carry out a much narrower range of tasks; a car drives and a toaster toasts. Computers can carry out a wide range of tasks because they execute different programs, each of which directs the computer to work on a specific task.

A computer program is a sequence of instructions and decisions.

The computer itself is a machine that stores data (numbers, words, pictures), interacts with devices (the monitor, the sound system, the printer), and executes programs. A *computer program* tells a computer, in minute detail, the sequence of steps that are needed to fulfill a task. The physical computer and peripheral devices are collectively called the *hardware*. The programs the computer executes are called the *software*.

Today's computer programs are so sophisticated that it is hard to believe that they are composed of extremely primitive operations. A typical operation may be one of the following:

- Put a red dot at this screen position.
- Add up these two numbers.
- If this value is negative, continue the program at a certain instruction.

The computer user has the illusion of smooth interaction because a program contains a huge number of such operations, and because the computer can execute them at great speed.

Programming is the act of designing and implementing computer programs.

The act of designing and implementing computer programs is called *programming*. In this book, you will learn how to program a computer—that is, how to direct the computer to execute tasks.

To write a computer game with motion and sound effects or a word processor that supports fancy fonts and pictures is a complex task that requires a team of many highly skilled programmers. Your first programming efforts will be more mundane. The concepts and skills you learn in this book form an important foundation, and you should not be disappointed if your first programs do not rival the sophisticated software that is familiar to you. Actually, you will find that there is an immense thrill even in simple programming tasks. It is an amazing experience to see the computer precisely and quickly carry out a task that would take you hours of drudgery, to make small changes in a program that lead to immediate improvements, and to see the computer become an extension of your mental powers.

1. What is required to play music on a computer?
2. Why is a CD player less flexible than a computer?
3. What does a computer user need to know about programming in order to play a video game?

Practice It   Now you can try these exercises at the end of the chapter: R1.1, R1.4.

1.2 The Anatomy of a Computer

To understand the programming process, you need to have a rudimentary understanding of the building blocks that make up a computer. We will look at a personal computer. Larger computers have faster, larger, or more powerful components, but they have fundamentally the same design.

At the heart of the computer lies the **central processing unit** (CPU) (see Figure 1). It consists of a single *chip*, or a small number of chips. A computer chip (integrated circuit) is a component with a plastic or metal housing, metal connectors, and inside wiring made principally from silicon. For a CPU chip, the inside wiring is enormously complicated. For example, the Pentium chip (a popular CPU for personal computers at the time of this writing) is composed of several million structural elements, called *transistors*.

The central processing unit (CPU) performs program control and data processing.

The CPU performs program control and data processing. That is, the CPU locates and executes the program instructions; it carries out arithmetic operations such as addition, subtraction, multiplication, and division; it fetches data from external memory or devices and stores data back.

Storage devices include memory and secondary storage.

The computer stores data and programs. There are two kinds of storage. *Primary storage* is made from memory chips: electronic circuits that can store data, provided they are supplied with electric power. *Secondary storage*, usually a *hard disk*, provides less expensive storage that persists without electricity. A hard disk consists of rotating platters, which are coated with a magnetic material, and read/write heads, which can detect and change the magnetic flux on the platters (see Figure 2).

Figure 1
Central Processing Unit

Figure 2
A Hard Disk

Programs and data are typically stored on the hard disk and loaded into memory when the program starts. The program then updates the data in memory and writes the modified data back to the hard disk.

To interact with a human user, a computer requires peripheral devices. The computer transmits information (called *output*) to the user through a display screen, speakers, and printers. The user can enter information (called *input*) by using a keyboard or a pointing device such as a mouse.

Some computers are self-contained units, whereas others are interconnected through *networks*. Through the network cabling, the computer can read data and programs from central storage locations or send data to other computers. For the user of a networked computer it may not even be obvious which data reside on the computer itself and which are transmitted through the network.

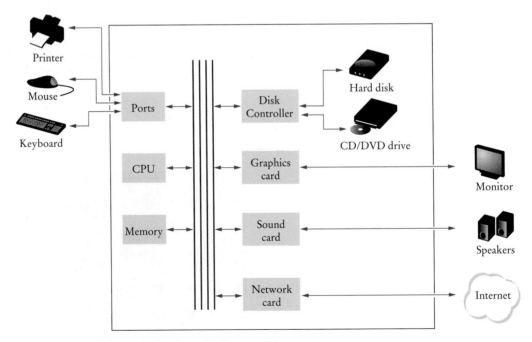

Figure 3   Schematic Design of a Personal Computer

Figure 3 gives a schematic overview of the architecture of a personal computer. Program instructions and data (such as text, numbers, audio, or video) are stored on the hard disk, on an optical disk such as a DVD, or elsewhere on the network. When a program is started, it is brought into memory, where the CPU can read it. The CPU reads the program one instruction at a time. As directed by these instructions, the CPU reads data, modifies it, and stores it. Some program instructions will cause the CPU to place dots on the display screen or printer or to vibrate the speaker. As these actions happen many times over and at great speed, the human user perceives images and sound. Some program instructions read user input from the keyboard or mouse. The program analyzes the nature of these inputs and then executes the next appropriate instruction.

SELF CHECK

4. Where is a program stored when it is not currently running?
5. Which part of the computer carries out arithmetic operations, such as addition and multiplication?

Practice It Now you can try these exercises at the end of the chapter: R1.2, R1.3.

Random Fact 1.1 The ENIAC and the Dawn of Computing

The ENIAC (electronic numerical integrator and computer) was the first usable electronic computer. It was designed by J. Presper Eckert and John Mauchly at the University of Pennsylvania and was completed in 1946—two years before transistors were invented. The computer was housed in a large room and consisted of many cabinets containing about 18,000 vacuum tubes (see Figure 2). Vacuum tubes burned out at the rate of several tubes per day. An attendant with a shopping cart full of tubes constantly made the rounds and replaced defective ones. The computer was programmed by connecting wires on panels. Each wiring configuration would set up the computer for a particular problem. To have the computer work on a different problem, the wires had to be replugged.

Work on the ENIAC was supported by the U.S. Army, which was interested in computations of ballistic tables that would give the trajectory of a projectile, depending on the wind resistance, initial velocity, and atmospheric conditions. To compute the trajectories, one must find the numerical solutions of certain differential equations; hence the name "numerical integrator". Before machines like the ENIAC were developed, humans did this kind of work, and until the 1950s the word "computer" referred to these people. The ENIAC was later used for peaceful purposes, such as the tabulation of U.S. Census data.

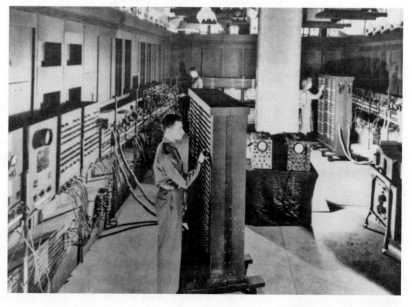

Figure 4 The ENIAC

1.3 Machine Code and Programming Languages

On the most basic level, computer instructions are extremely primitive. The processor executes *machine instructions*. A typical sequence of machine instructions is

1. Move the contents of memory location 40000 into the CPU.
2. If that value is > 100, continue with the instruction that is stored in memory location 11280.

> Computer programs are stored as machine instructions in a code that depends on the processor type.

Actually, machine instructions are encoded as numbers so that they can be stored in memory. On a Pentium processor, this sequence of instruction is encoded as the sequence of numbers

$$161 \ 40000 \ 45 \ 100 \ 127 \ 11280$$

On a processor from a different manufacturer, the encoding would be different. When this kind of processor fetches this sequence of numbers, it decodes them and executes the associated sequence of commands.

How can we communicate the command sequence to the computer? The simplest method is to place the actual numbers into the computer memory. This is, in fact, how the very earliest computers worked. However, a long program is composed of thousands of individual commands, and it is a tedious and error-prone affair to look up the numeric codes for all commands and place the codes manually into memory. As already mentioned, computers are really good at automating tedious and error-prone activities. It did not take long for computer scientists to realize that the computers themselves could be harnessed to help in the programming process.

Computer scientists devised *high level programming languages* that allow programmers to describe tasks, using a syntax that is more closely related to the problems to be solved. In this book, we will use the C++ programming language, which was developed by Bjarne Stroustrup in the 1980s.

> C++ is a general-purpose language that is in widespread use for systems and embedded programming.

Over the years, C++ has grown by the addition of many features. A standardization process culminated in the publication of the international C++ standard in 1998. A minor update to the standard was issued in 2003, and a major revision is expected to come to fruition around 2011. At this time, C++ is the most commonly used language for developing system software such as

Bjarne Stroustrup

databases and operating systems. Just as importantly, C++ is increasingly used for programming "embedded systems", small computers that control devices such as automobile engines or cellular telephones.

Here is a typical statement in C++:

```
if (int_rate > 100) { cout << "Interest rate error"; }
```

This means, "If the interest rate is over 100, display an error message". A special computer program, a compiler, translates this high-level description into machine instructions for a particular processor.

> High-level programming languages are independent of the processor.

High-level languages are independent of the underlying hardware. C++ instructions work equally well on an Intel Pentium and a processor in a cell phone. Of course, the compiler-generated machine instructions are different, but the programmer who uses the compiler need not worry about these differences.

6. Is the compiler a part of the computer hardware or software?

7. Does a person who uses a computer for office work ever run a compiler?

8. What are the most important uses for C++?

Practice It   Now you can try these exercises at the end of the chapter: R1.5.

Random Fact 1.2 **Standards Organizations**

Two standards organizations, the American National Standards Institute (ANSI) and the International Organization for Standardization (ISO), have jointly developed the definitive standard for the C++ language.

Why have standards? You encounter the benefits of standardization every day. When you buy a light bulb, you can be assured that it fits in the socket without having to measure the socket at home and the bulb in the store. In fact, you may have experienced how painful the lack of standards can be if you have ever purchased a flashlight with nonstandard bulbs. Replacement bulbs for such a flashlight can be difficult and expensive to obtain.

The ANSI and ISO standards organizations are associations of industry professionals who develop standards for everything from car tires and credit card shapes to programming languages. Having a standard for a programming language such as C++ means that you can take a program that you developed on one system with one manufacturer's compiler to a different system and be assured that it will continue to work.

1.4 Becoming Familiar with Your Programming Environment

> Set aside some time to become familiar with the programming environment that you will use for your class work.

Many students find that the tools they need as programmers are very different from the software with which they are familiar. You should spend some time making yourself familiar with your programming environment. Because computer systems vary widely, this book can only give an outline of the steps you need to follow. It is a good idea to participate in a hands-on lab, or to ask a knowledgeable friend to give you a tour.

Step 1   Start the C++ development environment.

Computer systems differ greatly in this regard. On many computers there is an **integrated development environment** in which you can write and test your programs. On other computers you first launch an *editor*, a program that functions like a word processor, in which you can enter your C++ instructions; then open a con*sole window* and type commands to execute your program. You need to find out how to get started with your environment.

Step 2   Write a simple program.

The traditional choice for the very first program in a new programming language is a program that displays a simple greeting: "Hello, World!". Let us follow that tradition. Here is the "Hello, World!" program in C++:

```
#include <iostream>

using namespace std;

int main()
{
    cout << "Hello, World!" << endl;
    return 0;
}
```

We will examine this program in the next section.

No matter which programming environment you use, you begin your activity by typing the program statements into an editor window.

> An editor is a program for entering and modifying text, such as a C++ program.

Create a new file and call it `hello.cpp`, using the steps that are appropriate for your environment. (If your environment requires that you supply a project name in addition to the file name, use the name `hello` for the project.) Enter the program instructions *exactly* as they are given above. Alternatively, locate an electronic copy in the source files for the programs in this book and paste it into your editor.

> C++ is case sensitive. You must be careful about distinguishing between upper- and lowercase letters.

As you write this program, pay careful attention to the various symbols, and keep in mind that C++ is **case sensitive**. You must enter upper- and lowercase letters exactly as they appear in the program listing. You cannot type MAIN or Endl. If you are not careful, you will run into problems—see Common Error 1.2 on page 16.

Step 3 Compile and run the program.

> The compiler translates C++ programs into machine code.

The process for building and running a C++ program depends greatly on your programming environment. In some integrated development environments, you simply push a button. In other environments, you may have to type commands. When you run the test program, the message

```
Hello, World!
```

will appear somewhere on the screen (see Figures 5 and 6).

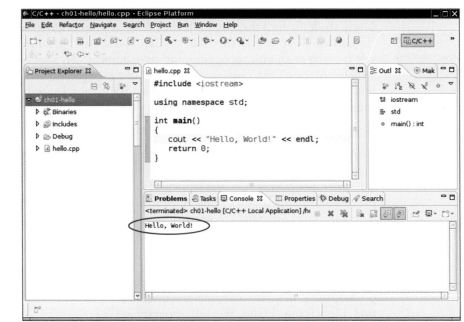

Figure 5
Running the `hello` Program in an Integrated Development Environment

Figure 6
Compiling and
Running the hello
Program in a
Console Window

```
Terminal
File  Edit  View  Terminal  Help
~$ cd cs1/bookcode/ch01
~/cs1/bookcode/ch01$ g++ -o hello hello.cpp
~/cs1/bookcode/ch01$ ./hello
Hello, World!
~/cs1/bookcode/ch01$ 
```

It is useful to know what goes on behind the scenes when your program gets built. First, the compiler translates the C++ *source code* (that is, the statements that you wrote) into machine instructions. The machine code contains only the translation of the code that you wrote. That is not enough to actually run the program. To display a string on a window, quite a bit of low-level activity is necessary. The implementors of your C++ development environment provided a library that includes the definition of cout and its functionality. A **library** is a collection of code that has been programmed and translated by someone else, ready for you to use in your program. (More complicated programs are built from more than one machine code file and more than one library.) A program called the **linker** takes your machine code and the necessary parts from the C++ library and builds an **executable file**. (Figure 7 gives an overview of these steps.) The executable file is usually called hello.exe or hello, depending on your computer system. You can run the executable program even after you exit the C++ development environment.

> The linker combines machine code with library code into an executable program.

Step 4   Organize your work.

As a programmer, you write programs, try them out, and improve them. You store your programs in *files*. Files have names, and the rules for legal names differ from one system to another. Some systems allow spaces in file names; others don't. Some distinguish between upper- and lowercase letters; others don't. Most C++ compilers require that C++ files end in an **extension** .cpp, .cxx, .cc, or .C; for example, test.cpp.

Files are stored in **folders** or **directories**. A folder can contain files as well as other folders, which themselves can contain more files and folders (see Figure 8). This hierarchy can be quite large, and you need not be concerned with all of its branches.

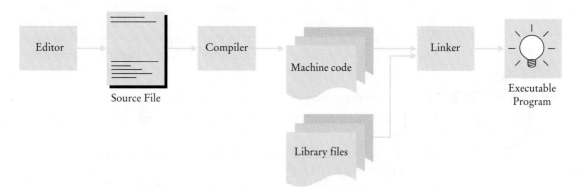

Figure 7   From Source Code to Executable Program

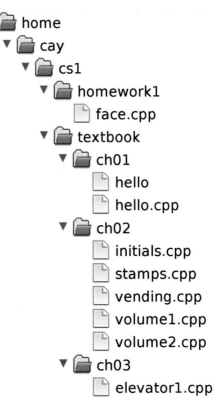

Figure 8 A Folder Hierarchy

However, you should create folders for organizing your work. It is a good idea to make a separate folder for your programming class. Inside that folder, make a separate folder for each assignment.

Some programming environments place your programs into a default location if you don't specify a folder yourself. In that case, you need to find out where those files are located.

Be sure that you understand where your files are located in the folder hierarchy. This information is essential when you submit files for grading, and for making *backup* copies.

You will spend many hours creating and improving C++ programs. It is easy to delete a file by accident, and occasionally files are lost because of a computer malfunction. To avoid the frustration of recreating lost files, get in the habit of making backup copies of your work on a memory stick or on another computer.

Develop a strategy for keeping backup copies of your work before disaster strikes.

SELF CHECK

9. How are programming projects stored on a computer?
10. What do you expect to see when you load an executable file into your text editor?
11. What do you do to protect yourself from data loss when you work on programming projects?

Practice It Now you can try these exercises at the end of the chapter: R1.6.

Programming Tip 1.1

Backup Copies

Backing up files on a memory stick is an easy and convenient storage method for many people. Another increasingly popular form of backup is Internet file storage. Here are a few pointers to keep in mind.

- *Back up often.* Backing up a file takes only a few seconds, and you will hate yourself if you have to spend many hours recreating work that you could have saved easily. I recommend that you back up your work once every thirty minutes.

- *Rotate backups.* Use more than one directory for backups, and rotate them. That is, first back up onto the first directory. Then back up onto the second directory. Then use the third, and then go back to the first. That way you always have three recent backups. If your recent changes made matters worse, you can then go back to the older version.

- *Pay attention to the backup direction.* Backing up involves copying files from one place to another. It is important that you do this right—that is, copy from your work location to the backup location. If you do it the wrong way, you will overwrite a newer file with an older version.

- *Check your backups once in a while.* Double-check that your backups are where you think they are. There is nothing more frustrating than to find out that the backups are not there when you need them.

- *Relax, then restore.* When you lose a file and need to restore it from backup, you are likely to be in an unhappy, nervous state. Take a deep breath and think through the recovery process before you start. It is not uncommon for an agitated computer user to wipe out the last backup when trying to restore a damaged file.

1.5 Analyzing Your First Program

In this section, we will analyze the first C++ program in detail. Here again is the source code:

ch01/hello.cpp

```
1   #include <iostream>
2
3   using namespace std;
4
5   int main()
6   {
7      cout << "Hello, World!" << endl;
8      return 0;
9   }
```

The first line,

```
#include <iostream>
```

tells the compiler to include a service for "stream input/output". You will learn in Chapter 8 what a stream is. For now, you should simply remember to add this line into all programs that perform input or output.

Syntax 1.1 C++ Program

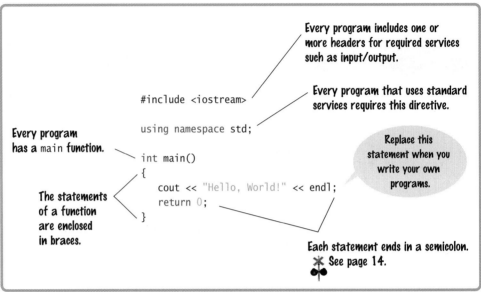

The next line,

```
using namespace std;
```

tells the compiler to use the "standard namespace". Namespaces are a mechanism for avoiding naming conflicts in large programs. You need not be concerned about namespaces. For the programs that you will be writing in this book, you will always use the standard namespace. Simply add using namespace std; at the top of every program that you write, just below the #include directives.

The construction

```
int main()
{
    ...
    return 0;
}
```

> Every C++ program contains a function called main.

defines a *function* called main that "returns" an "integer" (that is, a whole number without a fractional part, called int in C++) with value 0. This value indicates that the program finished successfully. A **function** is a collection of programming instructions that carry out a particular task. Every C++ program must have a main function. Most C++ programs contain other functions besides main, but it will take us until Chapter 5 to discuss functions and return values.

For now, it is a good idea to consider all these parts as the plumbing that is necessary to write a simple program. Simply place the code that you want to execute inside the braces of the main function. (The basic structure of a C++ program is shown in Syntax 1.1.)

> Use cout and the << operator to display values on the screen.

To display values on the screen, you use an entity called cout and the << operator (sometimes called the *insertion* operator). For example, the statement

```
cout << 39 + 3;
```

displays the number 42.

Syntax 1.2   Output Statement

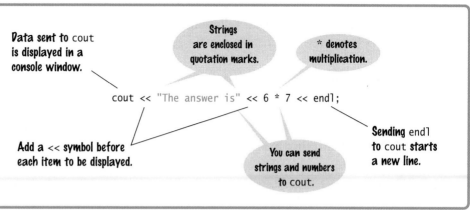

Data sent to cout **is displayed in a console window.**

Strings are enclosed in quotation marks.

* **denotes multiplication.**

```
cout << "The answer is" << 6 * 7 << endl;
```

Add a << **symbol before each item to be displayed.**

You can send strings and numbers to cout.

Sending endl **to** cout **starts a new line.**

Enclose text strings in quotation marks.

The statement

```
cout << "Hello";
```

displays the **string** Hello. A string is a sequence of characters. You must enclose the contents of a string inside quotation marks so that the compiler knows you literally mean the text "Hello" and not a function with the same name.

Use + to add two numbers and * to multiply two numbers.

You can send more than one item to cout. Use a << before each one of them. For example,

```
cout << "The answer is " << 6 * 7;
```

displays The answer is 42 (in C++, the * denotes multiplication).

Send endl **to** cout **to end a line of displayed output.**

The endl symbol denotes an *end of line* marker. When this marker is sent to cout, the cursor is moved to the first column in the next screen row. If you don't use an end of line marker, then the next displayed item will simply follow the current string on the same line. In this program we only printed one item, but in general we will want to print multiple items, and it is a good habit to end all lines of output with an end of line marker.

End each statement with a semicolon.

Finally, note that each statement in C++ ends in a semicolon, just as every English sentence ends in a period.

SELF CHECK

12. How do you modify the hello.cpp program to greet you instead?

13. What is wrong with this program?

```
#include <iostream>
using namespace std;
int main()
{
    cout << Goodbye, World! << endl;
    return 0;
}
```

14. What does the following sequence of statements print?

```
cout << "Hello";
cout << "World";
```

15. What does the following statement print?

```
cout << 2 * 2 << 2;
```

16. What does the following statement print?

```
cout << "Hello" << endl << endl << "World";
```

Practice It   Now you can try these exercises at the end of the chapter: R1.7, P1.1, P1.2.

Common Error 1.1

Omitting Semicolons

In C++ every statement must end in a semicolon. Forgetting to type a semicolon is a common error. It confuses the compiler because the compiler uses the semicolon to find where one statement ends and the next one starts. The compiler does not use line ends or closing braces to recognize the ends of statements. For example, the compiler considers

```
cout << "Hello, World!" << endl
return 0;
```

a single statement, as if you had written

```
cout << "Hello, World!" << endl return 0;
```

and then it doesn't understand that statement, because it does not expect the word return in the middle of an output command. The remedy is simple. Just scan every statement for a terminating semicolon, just as you would check that every English sentence ends in a period.

Special Topic 1.1

Escape Sequences

How can you display a string containing quotation marks, such as

```
Hello, "World"
```

You can't use

```
cout << "Hello, "World"";
```

As soon as the compiler reads "Hello, ", it thinks the string is finished, and then it gets all confused about World. Compilers have a one-track mind, and if a simple analysis of the input doesn't make sense to them, they just refuse to go on, and they report an error. In contrast, a human would probably realize that the second and third quotation marks were supposed to be part of the string.

Well, how do we then display quotation marks on the screen? The designers of C++ provided an escape hatch. Mark each quotation mark with a backslash character (\), like this:

```
cout << "Hello, \"World\"";
```

The sequence \" denotes a literal quote, not the end of a string. Such a sequence is called an *escape sequence*.

There are a few other escape sequences. If you actually want to show a backslash on the display, you use the escape sequence \\. The statement

```
cout << "Hello\\World";
```

prints

```
Hello\World
```

Finally, the escape sequence \n denotes a **newline** character that starts a new line on the screen. The command

```
cout << "Hello, World!\n";
```

has exactly the same effect as

```
cout << "Hello, World!" << endl;
```

1.6 Errors

Programming languages follow very strict conventions. When you talk to another person, and you scramble or omit a word or two, your conversation partner will usually still understand what you have to say. But when you make an error in a C++ program, the compiler will not try to guess what you meant. (This is actually a good thing. If the compiler were to guess wrongly, the resulting program would do the wrong thing—quite possibly with disastrous effects.) In this section, you will learn how to cope with errors in your program.

Experiment a little with the hello.cpp program. What happens if you make a typing error such as

Programmers spend a fair amount of time fixing compile-time and run-time errors.

```
cot << "Hello, World!" << endl;
cout << "Hello, World! << endl;
cout << "Hollo, World!" << endl;
```

> A compile-time error is a violation of the programming language rules that is detected by the compiler.

In the first case, the compiler will complain that it has no clue what you mean by cot. The exact wording of the error message is dependent on the compiler, but it might be something like "Undefined symbol cot". This is a **compile-time error** or **syntax error**. Something is wrong according to the language rules, and the compiler finds it. When the compiler finds one or more errors, it will not translate the program to machine code, and as a consequence there is no program to run. You must fix the error and compile again. It is common to go through several rounds of fixing compile-time errors before compilation succeeds for the first time.

If the compiler finds an error, it will not simply stop and give up. It will try to report as many errors as it can find, so you can fix them all at once. Sometimes, however, one error throws it off track. This is likely to happen with the error in the second line. Since the programmer forgot the closing quote, the compiler will keep looking for the end of the string. In such cases, it is common for the compiler to emit bogus error reports for neighboring lines. You should fix only those error messages that make sense to you and then recompile.

The error in the third line is of a different kind. The program will compile and run, but its output will be wrong. It will print

```
Hollo, World!
```

> A run-time error causes a program to take an action that the programmer did not intend.

This is a **run-time error**. The program is syntactically correct and does something, but it doesn't do what it is supposed to do. The compiler cannot find the error, and it must be flushed out when the program runs, by testing it and carefully looking at its output. Because run-time errors are caused by logical flaws in the program, they are often called **logic errors**. Some kinds of run-time errors are so severe that they generate an **exception**: a signal from the processor that aborts the program with an error message. For example, if your program includes the statement cout << 1 / 0; your program may terminate with a "divide by zero" exception.

During program development, errors are unavoidable. Once a program is longer than a few lines, it requires superhuman concentration to enter it correctly without slipping up once. You will find yourself omitting semicolons or quotes more often than you would like, but the compiler will track down these problems for you.

Run-time errors are more troublesome. The compiler will not find them—in fact, the compiler will cheerfully translate any program as long as its syntax is correct— but the resulting program will do something wrong. It is the responsibility of the program author to test the program and find any run-time errors. Program testing is an important topic that you will encounter many times in this book.

> The programmer is responsible for inspecting and testing the program to guard against run-time errors.

SELF CHECK

17. Suppose you omit the () characters after main from the hello.cpp program. Will you get a compile-time error or a run-time error?

18. When you used your computer, you may have experienced a program that "crashed" (quit spontaneously) or "hung" (failed to respond to your input). Is that behavior a compile-time error or a run-time error?

19. Why can't you test a program for run-time errors when it has compiler errors?

Practice It   Now you can try these exercises at the end of the chapter: R1.10, R1.11.

Common Error 1.2

Misspelling Words

If you accidentally misspell a word, strange things may happen, and it may not always be completely obvious from the error messages what went wrong. Here is a good example of how simple spelling errors can cause trouble:

```
#include <iostream>

using namespace std;

int Main()
{
   cout << "Hello, World!" << endl;
   return 0;
}
```

This code defines a function called Main. The compiler will not consider this to be the same as the main function, because Main starts with an uppercase letter and the C++ language is **case-sensitive**. Upper- and lowercase letters are considered to be completely different from each other, and to the compiler Main is no better match for main than rain. The compiler will compile your Main function, but when the linker is ready to build the executable file, it will complain about the missing main function and refuse to link the program. Of course, the message "missing main function" should give you a clue where to look for the error.

If you get an error message that seems to indicate that the compiler is on the wrong track, it is a good idea to check for spelling and capitalization. In C++, most names use only lowercase letters. If you misspell the name of a symbol (for example out instead of cout), the compiler will complain about an "undefined symbol". This error message is usually a good clue that you made a spelling error.

1.7 Problem Solving: Algorithm Design

You will soon learn how to program calculations and decision making in C++. But before we look at the mechanics of implementing computations in the next chapter, let's consider the planning process that precedes implementation.

Finding the perfect partner is not a problem that a computer can solve.

You may have run across advertisements that encourage you to pay for a computerized service that matches you up with a love partner. Think how this might work. You fill out a form and send it in. Others do the same. The data are processed by a computer program. Is it reasonable to assume that the computer can perform the task of finding the best match for you? Suppose your younger brother, not the computer, had all the forms on his desk. What instructions could you give him? You can't say, "Find the best-looking person of the opposite sex who likes inline skating and browsing the Internet". There is no objective standard for good looks, and your brother's opinion (or that of a computer program analyzing the digitized photo) will likely be different from yours. If you can't give written instructions for someone to solve the problem, there is no way the computer can magically solve the problem. The computer can only do what you tell it to do. It just does it faster, without getting bored or exhausted.

Now consider the following investment problem:

> You put $10,000 into a bank account that earns 5 percent interest per year. How many years does it take for the account balance to be double the original?

Could you solve this problem by hand? Sure. You figure out the balance as follows:

year	interest	balance
0		10000
1	10000.00 x 0.05 = 500.00	10000.00 + 500.00 = 10500.00
2	10500.00 x 0.05 = 525.00	10500.00 + 525.00 = 11025.00
3	11025.00 x 0.05 = 551.25	11025.00 + 551.25 = 11576.25
4	11576.25 x 0.05 = 578.81	11576.25 + 578.81 = 12155.06

You keep going until the balance is at least $20,000. Then the last number in the year column is the answer.

Of course, carrying out this computation is intensely boring to you or your younger brother. But computers are very good at carrying out repetitive calculations quickly and flawlessly. What is important to the computer is a description of the steps for finding the solution. Each step must be clear and unambiguous, requiring no guesswork. Here is such a description:

Start with a year value of 0, a column for the interest, and a balance of $10,000.

year	interest	balance
0		10000

Repeat the following steps while the balance is less than $20,000
    Add 1 to the year value.
    Compute the interest as balance x 0.05 (i.e., 5 percent interest)
    Add the interest to the balance.

year	interest	balance
0		10000
1	500.00	10500.00
14	942.82	19799.32
(15)	989.96	20789.28

Report the final year value as the answer.

Of course, these steps are not yet in a language that a computer can understand, but you will soon learn how to formulate them in C++. This informal description is called **pseudocode**.

There are no strict requirements for pseudocode because it is read by human readers, not a computer program. Here are the kinds of pseudocode statements that we will use in this book:

Pseudocode is an informal description of a sequence of steps for solving a problem.

- Use statements such as the following to describe how a value is set or changed:

  total cost = purchase price + operating cost

  or

  Multiply the balance value by 1.05.

  or

  Remove the first and last character from the word.

- You can describe decisions and repetitions as follows:

  If total cost 1 < total cost 2
  While the balance is less than $20,000
  For each picture in the sequence

  Use indentation to indicate which statements should be selected or repeated:

  For each car
      operating cost = 10 x annual fuel cost
      total cost = purchase price + operating cost

  Here, the indentation indicates that both statements should be executed for each car.

- Indicate results with statements such as:

  Choose car 1.
  Report the final year value as the answer.

The exact wording is not important. What is important is that pseudocode describes a sequence of steps that is

- Unambiguous
- Executable
- Terminating

Figure 9
The Software Development Process

Understand
the problem

Develop and
describe an
algorithm

Test the
algorithm with
simple inputs

Translate
the algorithm
into C++

Compile and test
your program

A method is *unambiguous* when there are precise instructions for what to do at each step and where to go next. There is no room for guesswork or creativity. A method is *executable* when each step can be carried out in practice. Had we asked to use the actual interest rate that will be charged in years to come, and not a fixed rate of 5 percent per year, our method would not have been executable, because there is no way for anyone to know what that interest rate will be. A method is *terminating* if it will eventually come to an end. In our example, it requires a bit of thought to see that the method will not go on forever: With every step, the balance goes up by at least $500, so eventually it must reach $20,000.

An algorithm is a recipe for finding a solution.

An algorithm for solving a problem is a sequence of steps that is unambiguous, executable, and terminating.

A sequence of steps that is unambiguous, executable, and terminating is called an **algorithm**. We have found an algorithm to solve our investment problem, and thus we can find the solution by programming a computer. The existence of an algorithm is an essential prerequisite for programming a task. You need to first discover and describe an algorithm for the task that you want to solve before you start programming (see Figure 9).

SELF CHECK

20. Suppose the interest rate was 20 percent. How long would it take for the investment to double?

21. Suppose your cell phone carrier charges you $29.95 for up to 300 minutes of calls, and $0.45 for each additional minute, plus 12.5 percent taxes and fees. Give an algorithm to compute the monthly charge from a given number of minutes.

22. Consider the following pseudocode for finding the most attractive photo from a sequence of photos:

> Pick the first photo and call it "the best so far".
> For each photo in the sequence
>   If it is more attractive than the "best so far"
>   Discard "the best so far".
>   Call this photo "the best so far".
> The photo called "the best so far" is the most attractive photo in the sequence.

Is this an algorithm that will find the most attractive photo?

23. Suppose each photo in Self Check 22 had a price tag. Give an algorithm for finding the most expensive photo.

24. Suppose you have a random sequence of black and white marbles and want to rearrange it so that the black and white marbles are grouped together. Consider this algorithm:

> **Repeat until sorted**
>   **Locate the first black marble that is preceded by a white marble, and switch them.**

What does the algorithm do with the sequence ○●○○●●? Spell out the steps until the algorithm stops.

25. Suppose you have a random sequence of colored marbles. Consider this pseudocode:

> **Repeat until sorted**
>   **Locate the first marble that is preceded by a marble of a different color, and switch them.**

Why is this not an algorithm?

Practice It   Now you can try these exercises at the end of the chapter: R1.13, R1.14.

HOW TO 1.1   **Describing an Algorithm with Pseudocode**

Before you are ready to write a program in C++, you need to develop an algorithm—a method for arriving at a solution for a particular problem. Describe the algorithm in pseudocode: a sequence of precise steps formulated in English.

For example, consider this problem: You have the choice of buying two cars. One is more fuel efficient than the other, but also more expensive. You know the price and fuel efficiency (in miles per gallon, mpg) of both cars. You plan to keep the car for ten years. Assume a price of $4 per gallon of gas and usage of 15,000 miles per year. You will pay cash for the car and not worry about financing costs. Which car is the better deal?

Step 1   Determine the inputs and outputs.

In our sample problem, we have these inputs:

- **purchase price1** and **fuel efficiency1**, the price and fuel efficiency (in mpg) of the first car
- **purchase price2** and **fuel efficiency2**, the price and fuel efficiency of the second car

We simply want to know which car is the better buy. That is the desired output.

Step 2   Break down the problem into smaller tasks.

For each car, we need to know the total cost of driving it. Let's do this computation separately for each car. Once we have the total cost for each car, we can decide which car is the better deal.

> The total cost for each car is **purchase price + operating cost.**

We assume a constant usage and gas price for ten years, so the operating cost depends on the cost of driving the car for one year.

> The operating cost is **10 x annual fuel cost.**
> The annual fuel cost is **price per gallon x annual fuel consumed.**

The annual fuel consumed is **annual miles driven / fuel efficiency.** For example, if you drive the car for 15,000 miles and the fuel efficiency is 15 miles/gallon, the car consumes 1,000 gallons.

Step 3   Describe each subtask in pseudocode.

In your description, arrange the steps so that any intermediate values are computed before they are needed in other computations. For example, list the step

> total cost = purchase price + operating cost

after you have computed **operating cost**.

Here is the algorithm for deciding which car to buy:

> For each car, compute the total cost as follows:
>   annual fuel consumed = annual miles driven / fuel efficiency
>   annual fuel cost = price per gallon x annual fuel consumed
>   operating cost = 10 x annual fuel cost
>   total cost = purchase price + operating cost
> If total cost1 < total cost2
>   Choose car1.
> Else
>   Choose car2.

Step 4   Test your pseudocode by working a problem.

We will use these sample values:

> Car 1: $25,000, 50 miles/gallon
> Car 2: $20,000, 30 miles/gallon

Here is the calculation for the cost of the first car:

> annual fuel consumed = annual miles driven / fuel efficiency = 15000 / 50 = 300
> annual fuel cost = price per gallon x annual fuel consumed = 4 x 300 = 1200
> operating cost = 10 x annual fuel cost = 10 x 1200 = 12000
> total cost = purchase price + operating cost = 25000 + 12000 = 37000

Similarly, the total cost for the second car is $40,000. Therefore, the output of the algorithm is to choose car 1.

WORKED EXAMPLE 1.1      **Writing an Algorithm for Tiling a Floor**

This Worked Example shows how to develop an algorithm for laying tile in an alternating pattern of colors.

CHAPTER SUMMARY

Define "computer program" and programming.

- Computers execute very basic instructions in rapid succession.
- A computer program is a sequence of instructions and decisions.
- Programming is the act of designing and implementing computer programs.

Describe the components of a computer.

- The central processing unit (CPU) performs program control and data processing.
- Storage devices include memory and secondary storage.

➕ Available online at www.wiley.com/college/horstmann.

Describe the process of translating high-level languages to machine code.

- Computer programs are stored as machine instructions in a code that depends on the processor type.
- C++ is a general-purpose language that is in widespread use for systems and embedded programming.
- High-level programming languages are independent of the processor.

Become familiar with your C++ programming environment.

- Set aside some time to become familiar with the programming environment that you will use for your class work.
- An editor is a program for entering and modifying text, such as a C++ program.
- C++ is case sensitive. You must be careful about distinguishing between upper- and lowercase letters.
- Develop a strategy for keeping backup copies of your work before disaster strikes.

- The compiler translates C++ programs into machine code.
- The linker combines machine code with library code into an executable program.

Describe the building blocks of a simple program.

- Every C++ program contains a function called main.
- Use cout and the << operator to display values on the screen.
- Enclose text strings in quotation marks.
- Use + to add two numbers and * to multiply two numbers.
- Send endl to cout to end a line of displayed output.
- End each statement with a semicolon.

Classify program errors as compile-time and run-time errors.

- A compile-time error is a violation of the programming language rules that is detected by the compiler.
- A run-time error causes a program to take an action that the programmer did not intend.
- The programmer is responsible for inspecting and testing the program to guard against run-time errors.

Write pseudocode for simple algorithms.

- Pseudocode is an informal description of a sequence of steps for solving a problem.
- An algorithm for solving a problem is a sequence of steps that is unambiguous, executable, and terminating.

REVIEW EXERCISES

R1.1 Explain the difference between using a computer program and programming a computer.

R1.2 Which parts of a computer can store program code? Which can store user data?

R1.3 Which parts of a computer serve to give information to the user? Which parts take user input?

R1.4 A toaster is a single-function device, but a computer can be programmed to carry out different tasks. Is your cell phone a single-function device, or is it a programmable computer? (Your answer will depend on your cell phone model.)

R1.5 Explain two benefits of using C++ over machine code.

R1.6 On your own computer or on your lab computer, find the exact location (folder or directory name) of
   a. The sample file hello.cpp (after you saved it in your development environment).
   b. The standard header file <iostream>.

R1.7 What does this program print?

```cpp
#include <iostream>
using namespace std;
int main()
{
   cout << "6 * 7 = " << 6 * 7 << endl;
   return 0;
}
```

R1.8 What does this program print?

```cpp
#include <iostream>
using namespace std;
int main()
{
   cout << "Hello" << "World" << endl;
   return 0;
}
```

Pay close attention to spaces.

R1.9 What does this program print?

```cpp
#include <iostream>
using namespace std;
int main()
{
   cout << "Hello" << endl << "World" << endl;
   return 0;
}
```

R1.10 Write three versions of the hello.cpp program that have different compile-time errors. Write a version that has a run-time error.

R1.11 How do you discover compile-time errors? How do you discover run-time errors?

R1.12 Write an algorithm to settle the following question: A bank account starts out with $10,000. Interest is compounded monthly at 6 percent per year (0.5 percent per month). Every month, $500 is withdrawn to meet college expenses. After how many years is the account depleted?

R1.13 Consider the question in Exercise R1.12. Suppose the numbers ($10,000, 6 percent, $500) were user selectable. Are there values for which the algorithm you developed would not terminate? If so, change the algorithm to make sure it always terminates.

R1.14 In order to estimate the cost of painting a house, a painter needs to know the surface area of the exterior. Develop an algorithm for computing that value. Your inputs are the width, length, and height of the house, the number of windows and doors, and their dimensions. (Assume the windows and doors have a uniform size.)

R1.15 You want to decide whether you should drive your car to work or take the train. You know the one-way distance from your home to your place of work, and the fuel efficiency of your car (in miles per gallon). You also know the one-way price of a train ticket. You assume the cost of gas at $4 per gallon, and car maintenance at 5 cents per mile. Write an algorithm to decide which commute is cheaper.

R1.16 You want to find out which fraction of your car use is for commuting to work, and which is for personal use. You know the one-way distance from your home to your place of work. For a particular period, you recorded the beginning and ending mileage on the odometer and the number of work days. Write an algorithm to settle this question.

R1.17 In the problem described in How To 1.1 on page 20, you made assumptions about the price of gas and the annual usage. Ideally, you would like to know which car is the better deal without making these assumptions. Why can't a computer program solve that problem?

R1.18 The value of π can be computed according to the following formula:

$$\frac{\pi}{4} = 1 - \frac{1}{3} + \frac{1}{5} - \frac{1}{7} + \frac{1}{9} - \cdots$$

Write an algorithm to compute π. Because the formula is an infinite series and an algorithm must stop after a finite number of steps, you should stop when you have the result determined to six significant digits.

R1.19 Suppose you put your younger brother in charge of backing up your work. Write a set of detailed instructions for carrying out his task. Explain how often he should do it, and what files he needs to copy from which folder to which location. Explain how he should verify that the backup was carried out correctly.

Engineering R1.20 The San Francisco taxi commission set the following rates for 2010:

- First 1/5th of a mile: $3.10
- Each additional 1/5th of a mile or fraction thereof: $0.45
- Each minute of waiting or traffic delay: $0.45

The charge for "waiting or traffic delay" applies instead of the mileage charge for each minute in which the speed is slower than the break-even point. The break-even point is the speed at which 1/5th of a mile is traversed in one minute.

Develop an algorithm that yields the fare for traveling a given distance in a given amount of time, assuming that the taxi moves at a constant speed.

Engineering R1.21 Suppose you know how long it takes a car to accelerate from 0 to 60 miles per hour. Develop an algorithm for computing the time required to travel a given distance (for example 5 miles), assuming that the car is initially at rest, accelerates to a given speed (for example 25 miles per hour), and drives at that speed until the distance is covered. *Hint:* An object that starts at rest and accelerates at a constant rate a for t seconds travels a distance of $s = \dfrac{1}{2}at^2$.

PROGRAMMING EXERCISES

P1.1 Write a program that prints a greeting of your choice, perhaps in another language.

P1.2 Write a program that prints the message, "Hello, my name is Hal!" Then, on a new line, the program should print the message "What would you like me to do?" Then it's the user's turn to type in an input. You haven't yet learned how to do it—just use the following lines of code:

```
string user_input;
getline(cin, user_input);
```

Finally, the program should ignore the user input and print the message "I am sorry, I cannot do that."

This program uses the string data type. To access this feature, you must place the line

```
#include <string>
```

before the main function.

Here is a typical program run. The user input is printed in color.

```
Hello, my name is Hal!
What would you like me to do?
Clean up my room
I am sorry, I cannot do that.
```

When running the program, remember to press the Enter key after typing the last word of the input line.

P1.3 Write a program that prints out a message "Hello, my name is Hal!" Then, on a new line, the program should print the message "What is your name?" As in Exercise P1.2, just use the following lines of code:

```
string user_name;
getline(cin, user_name);
```

Finally, the program should print the message "Hello, *user name*. I am glad to meet you!" To print the user name, simply use

```
cout << user_name;
```

As in Exercise P1.2, you must place the line

```
#include <string>
```

before the main function.

Here is a typical program run. The user input is printed in color.

```
Hello, my name is Hal!
What is your name?
Dave
Hello, Dave. I am glad to meet you!
```

P1.4 Write a program that prints the sum of the first ten positive integers, $1 + 2 + \ldots + 10$.

P1.5 Write a program that prints the product of the first ten positive integers, $1 \times 2 \times \ldots \times 10$. (Use * for multiplication in C++.)

P1.6 Write a program that prints the balance of an account that earns 5 percent interest per year after the first, second, and third year.

P1.7 Write a program that displays your name inside a box on the terminal screen, like this:

```
 -------
| Dave |
 -------
```

Do your best to approximate lines with characters such as | - +.

P1.8 Write a program that prints your name in large letters, such as

```
*    *   **    ****    ****   *   *
*    *  *  *   *   *   *   *   *   *
*****   *    *  ****    ****    * *
*    *  ******  *   *   *   *     *
*    *  *    *  *   *   *   *     *
```

P1.9 Write a program that prints a face similar to (but different from) the following:

```
   /////
  +-----+
 (|  o o  |)
  |   ^   |
  |  '-'  |
  +-----+
```

P1.10 Write a program that prints a house that looks exactly like the following:

```
    /\
   /  \
  +----+
  | .-.|
  | | ||
  +-+-++
```

P1.11 Write a program that prints an animal speaking a greeting, similar to (but different from) the following:

```
 /\_/\     -----
( ' ' )  / Hello \
(  -  ) <  Junior |
 | | |   \ Coder!/
(_|_)     -----
```

P1.12 Write a program that prints three items, such as the names of your three best friends or favorite movies, on three separate lines.

P1.13 Write a program that prints a poem of your choice. If you don't have a favorite poem, search the Internet for "Emily Dickinson" or "e e cummings".

P1.14 Write a program that prints an imitation of a Piet Mondrian painting. (Search the Internet if you are not familiar with his paintings.) Use character sequences such as @@@ or ::: to indicate different colors, and use - and | to form lines.

P1.15 Write a program that prints the United States flag, using * and = characters.

Engineering P1.16 The atmospheres of the gas giant planets (Jupiter, Saturn, Uranus, and Neptune) are mostly comprised of hydrogen (H_2) followed by helium (He). The atmospheres of the terrestrial planets are mostly comprised of carbon dioxide (CO_2) followed by nitrogen (N_2) for Venus and Mars, and for Earth, mostly Nitrogen (N_2) followed by Oxygen (O_2). Write a program that outputs this information in a chart with four columns for the type of planet, the name of the planet, its primary atmospheric gas, and secondary atmospheric gas.

Engineering P1.17 Write a program that displays the following image, using characters such as / \ - | + for the lines. Write Ω as "Ohm".

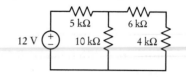

ANSWERS TO SELF-CHECK QUESTIONS

1. A program that reads the data on the CD and sends output to the speakers and the screen.
2. A CD player can do one thing—play music CDs. It cannot execute programs.
3. Nothing.
4. In secondary storage, typically a hard disk.
5. The central processing unit.
6. Software.
7. No—a compiler is intended for programmers, to translate high-level programming instructions into machine code.
8. System software and embedded systems
9. Programs are stored in files, and files are stored in folders or directories.
10. You will see a seemingly random sequence of characters and symbols.
11. You back up your files and folders.
12. Replace "World" with your name, for example:

    `cout << "Hello, Harry!" << endl;`
13. There are no quotes around `Goodbye, World!`.
14. It prints `HelloWorld`, without a space or comma.
15. `42`, without a space.
16. `Hello`

    `World`

    with a blank line between the two words.
17. A compile-time error.
18. It is a run-time error. After all, the program had been compiled in order for you to run it.
19. When a program has compiler errors, no executable file is produced, and there is nothing to run.

20. 4 years:

0 10,000

1 12,000

2 14,400

3 17,280

4 20,736

21. Is the number of minutes at most 300?

a. If so, the answer is $29.95 × 1.125 = $33.70.

b. If not,

1. Compute the difference: (number of minutes) – 300.

2. Multiply that difference by 0.45.

3. Add $29.95.

4. Multiply the total by 1.125. That is the answer.

22. No. The step **If it is more attractive than the "best so far"** is not executable because there is no objective way of deciding which of two photos is more attractive.

23. **Pick the first photo and call it "the most expensive so far".**
For each photo in the sequence
   If it is more expensive than "the most expensive so far"
      Discard "the most expensive so far".
      Call this photo "the most expensive so far".
The photo called "the most expensive so far" is the most expensive photo in the sequence.

24. The first black marble that is preceded by a white one is marked in blue:

○●○●●

Switching the two yields

●○○●●

The next black marble to be switched is

●○○●●

yielding

●○●○●

The next steps are

●●○○●

●●○●○

●●●○○

Now the sequence is sorted.

25. The sequence doesn't terminate. Consider the input ○●●●○. The first two marbles keep getting switched.

FUNDAMENTAL DATA TYPES

FLIGHT
DESTINATION
GATE #
742
LOS ANGELES
801
LONDON
485
MADRID
770
PARIS
54
TOKYO
753
HONG KONG
114
MIAMI
618
NEW YORK
24
RIO DEJANEIRO
454
SYDNEY
815
BANGKOK
787
MILAN

CHAPTER GOALS

To be able to define and initialize variables and constants

To understand the properties and limitations of integer and floating-point numbers

To write arithmetic expressions and assignment statements in C++

To appreciate the importance of comments and good code layout

To create programs that read and process input, and display the results

To process strings, using the standard C++ string type

CHAPTER CONTENTS

Numbers and character strings (such as the ones on this display board) are important data types in any C++ program. In this chapter, you will learn how to work with numbers and text, and how to write simple programs that perform useful tasks with them.

2.1 Variables

When your program carries out computations, you will want to store values so that you can use them later. In a C++ program, you use *variables* to store values. In this section, you will learn how to define and use variables.

To illustrate the use of variables, we will develop a program that solves the following problem. Soft drinks are sold in cans and bottles. A store offers a six-pack of 12-ounce cans for the same price as a two-liter bottle. Which should you buy? (12 fluid ounces equal approximately 0.355 liters.)

In our program, we will define variables for the number of cans per pack and for the volume of each can. Then we will compute the volume of a six-pack in liters and print out the answer.

What contains more soda? A six-pack of 12-ounce cans or a two-liter bottle?

2.1.1 Variable Definitions

The following statement defines a variable named cans_per_pack:

```
int cans_per_pack = 6;
```

A **variable** is a storage location in a computer program. Each variable has a name and holds a value.

> A variable is a storage location with a name.

A variable is similar to a parking space in a parking garage. The parking space has an identifier (such as "J 053"), and it can hold a vehicle. A variable has a name (such as cans_per_pack), and it can hold a value (such as 6).

Like a variable in a computer program, a parking space has an identifier and a contents.

Syntax 2.1   Variable Definition

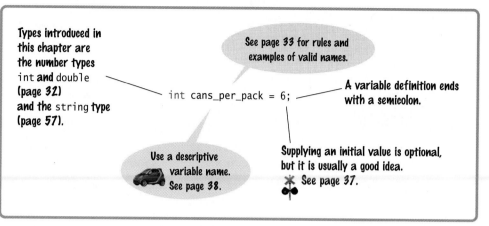

Types introduced in this chapter are the number types `int` and `double` (page 32) and the `string` type (page 57).

See page 33 for rules and examples of valid names.

```
int cans_per_pack = 6;
```

A variable definition ends with a semicolon.

Use a descriptive variable name. See page 38.

Supplying an initial value is optional, but it is usually a good idea. ✳ See page 37.

When defining a variable, you usually specify an initial value.

When defining a variable, you also specify the type of its values.

When defining a variable, you usually want to **initialize** it. That is, you specify the value that should be stored in the variable. Consider again this variable definition:

```
int cans_per_pack = 6;
```

The variable `cans_per_pack` is initialized with the value 6.

Like a parking space that is restricted to a certain type of vehicle (such as a compact car, motorcycle, or electric vehicle), a variable in C++ stores data of a specific **type**. C++ supports quite a few data types: numbers, text strings, files, dates, and many others. You must specify the type whenever you define a variable (see Syntax 2.1).

The `cans_per_pack` variable is an **integer**, a whole number without a fractional part. In C++, this type is called `int`. (See the next section for more information about number types in C++.)

Note that the type comes before the variable name:

```
int cans_per_pack = 6;
```

Table 1 shows variations of variable definitions.

Each parking space is suitable for a particular type of vehicle, just as each variable holds a value of a particular type.

Table 1 Variable Definitions in C++	
Variable Name	**Comment**
`int cans = 6;`	Defines an integer variable and initializes it with 6.
`int total = cans + bottles;`	The initial value need not be a constant. (Of course, `cans` and `bottles` must have been previously defined.)
🚫 `int bottles = "10";`	**Error:** You cannot initialize a number with a string.
`int bottles;`	Defines an integer variable without initializing it. This can be a cause for errors—see Common Error 2.2 on page 37.
`int cans, bottles;`	Defines two integer variables in a single statement. In this book, we will define each variable in a separate statement.
⚠ `bottles = 1;`	**Caution:** The type is missing. This statement is not a definition but an assignment of a new value to an existing variable—see Section 2.1.4 on page 34.

2.1.2 Number Types

Use the int type for numbers that cannot have a fractional part.

In C++, there are several different types of numbers. You use the *integer* number type, called `int` in C++, to denote a whole number without a fractional part. For example, there must be an integer number of cans in any pack of cans—you cannot have a fraction of a can.

Table 2 Number Literals in C++		
Number	**Type**	**Comment**
6	`int`	An integer has no fractional part.
-6	`int`	Integers can be negative.
0	`int`	Zero is an integer.
0.5	`double`	A number with a fractional part has type `double`.
1.0	`double`	An integer with a fractional part .0 has type `double`.
1E6	`double`	A number in exponential notation: 1×10^6 or 1000000. Numbers in exponential notation always have type `double`.
2.96E-2	`double`	Negative exponent: $2.96 \times 10^{-2} = 2.96 / 100 = 0.0296$
🚫 100,000		**Error:** Do not use a comma as a decimal separator.
🚫 3 1/2		**Error:** Do not use fractions; use decimal notation: 3.5.

Use the double type for floating-point numbers.

When a fractional part is required (such as in the number 0.355), we use **floating-point numbers**. The most commonly used type for floating-point numbers in C++ is called `double`. (If you want to know the reason, read Special Topic 2.1 on page 38.) Here is the definition of a floating-point variable:

```
double can_volume = 0.355;
```

When a value such as 6 or 0.355 occurs in a C++ program, it is called a number *literal*. Table 2 shows how to write integer and floating-point literals in C++.

2.1.3 Variable Names

When you define a variable, you should pick a name that explains its purpose. For example, it is better to use a descriptive name, such as `can_volume`, than a terse name, such as `cv`.

In C++, there are a few simple rules for variable names:

1. Variable names must start with a letter or the underscore (_) character, and the remaining characters must be letters, numbers, or underscores.

2. You cannot use other symbols such as $ or %. Spaces are not permitted inside names either. You can use an underscore instead, as in `can_volume`.

3. Variable names are **case-sensitive**, that is, `Can_volume` and `can_volume` are different names. For that reason, it is a good idea to use only lowercase letters in variable names.

4. You cannot use **reserved words** such as `double` or `return` as names; these words are reserved exclusively for their special C++ meanings. (See Appendix B.)

Table 3 shows examples of legal and illegal variable names in C++.

Table 3 Variable Names in C++	
Variable Name	Comment
can_volume1	Variable names consist of letters, numbers, and the underscore character.
x	In mathematics, you use short variable names such as x or y. This is legal in C++, but not very common, because it can make programs harder to understand (see Programming Tip 2.1 on page 38).
⚠ Can_volume	**Caution:** Variable names are case-sensitive. This variable name is different from `can_volume`.
🚫 6pack	**Error:** Variable names cannot start with a number.
🚫 can volume	**Error:** Variable names cannot contain spaces.
🚫 double	**Error:** You cannot use a reserved word as a variable name.
🚫 ltr/fl.oz	**Error:** You cannot use symbols such as / or .

2.1.4 The Assignment Statement

You use the **assignment statement** to place a new value into a variable. Here is an example:

```
cans_per_pack = 8;
```

The left-hand side of an assignment statement consists of a variable. The right-hand side is an expression that has a value. That value is stored in the variable, overwriting its previous contents.

There is an important difference between a variable definition and an assignment statement:

```
int cans_per_pack = 6; // Variable definition
...
cans_per_pack = 8; // Assignment statement
```

The first statement is the *definition* of cans_per_pack. It is an instruction to create a new variable of type int, to give it the name cans_per_pack, and to initialize it with 6. The second statement is an *assignment statement:* an instruction to replace the contents of the *existing* variable cans_per_pack with another value.

The = sign doesn't mean that the left-hand side is *equal* to the right-hand side. The expression on the right is evaluated, and its value is placed into the variable on the left.

Do not confuse this *assignment operation* with the = used in algebra to denote *equality*. The assignment operator is an instruction to do something, namely place a value into a variable. The mathematical equality states the fact that two values are equal.

For example, in C++, it is perfectly legal to write

```
total_volume = total_volume + 2;
```

It means to look up the value stored in the variable total_volume, add 2 to it, and place the result back into total_volume. (See Figure 1.) The net effect of executing this statement is to increment total_volume by 2. For example, if total_volume was 2.13 before execution of the statement, it is set to 4.13 afterwards. Of course, in mathematics it would make no sense to write that $x = x + 2$. No value can equal itself plus 2.

Syntax 2.2   Assignment

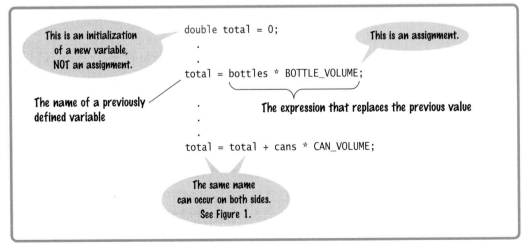

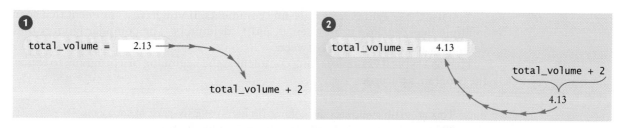

Figure 1 Executing the Assignment total_volume = total_volume + 2

2.1.5 Constants

When a variable is defined with the reserved word const, its value can never change. Constants are commonly written using capital letters to distinguish them visually from regular variables:

```
const double BOTTLE_VOLUME = 2;
```

It is good programming style to use named constants in your program to explain the meanings of numeric values. For example, compare the statements

```
double total_volume = bottles * 2;
```

and

```
double total_volume = bottles * BOTTLE_VOLUME;
```

A programmer reading the first statement may not understand the significance of the number 2. The second statement, with a named constant, makes the computation much clearer.

2.1.6 Comments

As your programs get more complex, you should add **comments**, explanations for human readers of your code. Here is an example:

```
const double CAN_VOLUME = 0.355; // Liters in a 12-ounce can
```

This comment explains the significance of the value 0.355 to a human reader. The compiler does not process comments at all. It ignores everything from a // delimiter to the end of the line.

Just as a television commentator explains the news, you use comments in your program to explain its behavior.

You use the // syntax for single-line comments. If you have a comment that spans multiple lines, enclose it between /* and */ delimiters. The compiler ignores these delimiters and everything in between.

Here is a typical example, a long comment at the beginning of a program, to explain the program's purpose:

```
/*
    This program computes the volume (in liters) of a six-pack of soda cans
    and the total volume of a six-pack and a two-liter bottle.
*/
```

We are now ready to finish our program. The following program shows the use of variables, constants, and the assignment statement. The program displays the volume of a six-pack of cans and the total volume of the six-pack and a two-liter bottle. We use constants for the can and bottle volumes. The total_volume variable is initialized with the volume of the cans. Using an assignment statement, we add the bottle volume.

ch02/volume1.cpp

```cpp
1   #include <iostream>
2
3   using namespace std;
4
5   /*
6       This program computes the volume (in liters) of a six-pack of soda
7       cans and the total volume of a six-pack and a two-liter bottle.
8   */
9   int main()
10  {
11      int cans_per_pack = 6;
12      const double CAN_VOLUME = 0.355; // Liters in a 12-ounce can
13      double total_volume = cans_per_pack * CAN_VOLUME;
14
15      cout << "A six-pack of 12-ounce cans contains "
16          << total_volume << " liters." << endl;
17
18      const double BOTTLE_VOLUME = 2; // Two-liter bottle
19
20      total_volume = total_volume + BOTTLE_VOLUME;
21
22      cout << "A six-pack and a two-liter bottle contain "
23          << total_volume << " liters." << endl;
24
25      return 0;
26  }
```

Program Run

```
A six-pack of 12-ounce cans contains 2.13 liters.
A six-pack and a two-liter bottle contain 4.13 liters.
```

SELF CHECK

1. Define a variable suitable for holding the number of bottles in a case.

2. What is wrong with the following variable definition?

```
int ounces per liter = 28.35
```

3. Define and initialize two variables, `unit_price` and `quantity`, to contain the unit price of a single bottle and the number of bottles purchased. Use reasonable initial values.

4. Use the variables defined in Self Check 3 to display the total purchase price.

5. Some drinks are sold in four-packs instead of six-packs. How would you change the `volume1.cpp` program to compute the total volume?

6. What is wrong with this comment?

```
double can_volume = 0.355; /* Liters in a 12-ounce can //
```

7. Suppose the type of the `cans_per_pack` variable in the `volume1.cpp` program was changed from `int` to `double`. What would be the effect on the program?

8. Why can't the variable `total_volume` in the `volume1.cpp` program be declared as `const`?

9. How would you explain assignment using the parking space analogy?

Practice It Now you can try these exercises at the end of the chapter: R2.1, R2.2, P2.1.

Common Error 2.1

Using Undefined Variables

You must define a variable before you use it for the first time. For example, the following sequence of statements would not be legal:

```
double can_volume = 12 * liter_per_ounce;
double liter_per_ounce = 0.0296;
```

In your program, the statements are compiled in order. When the compiler reaches the first statement, it does not know that `liter_per_ounce` will be defined in the next line, and it reports an error.

Common Error 2.2

Using Uninitialized Variables

If you define a variable but leave it uninitialized, then your program can act unpredictably. To understand why, consider what happens when you define a variable. Just enough space is set aside in memory to hold values of the type you specify. For example, with the definition

```
int bottles;
```

a block of memory big enough to hold integers is reserved. There is already *some* value in that memory. After all, you don't get freshly minted transistors—just an area of memory that has previously been used, filled with flotsam left over from prior computations. (In this regard, a variable differs from a parking space. A parking space can be empty, containing no vehicle. But a variable always holds some value.)

If you use the variable without initializing it, then that prior value will be used, yielding unpredictable results. For example, consider the program segment

```
int bottles; // Forgot to initialize
int bottle_volume = bottles * 2; // Result is unpredictable
```

There is no way of knowing what value will be computed. If you are unlucky, a plausible value will happen to appear when you run the program at home, and an entirely different result will occur when the program is graded.

Programming Tip 2.1

Choose Descriptive Variable Names

We could have saved ourselves a lot of typing by using shorter variable names, as in

```
double cv = 0.355;
```

Compare this definition with the one that we actually used, though. Which one is easier to read? There is no comparison. Just reading `can_volume` is a lot less trouble than reading `cv` and then *figuring out* it must mean "can volume".

In practical programming, this is particularly important when programs are written by more than one person. It may be obvious to *you* that `cv` stands for can volume and not current velocity, but will it be obvious to the person who needs to update your code years later? For that matter, will you remember yourself what `cv` means when you look at the code three months from now?

Special Topic 2.1

Numeric Types in C++

In addition to the `int` and `double` types, C++ has several other numeric types.

C++ has two floating-point types. The `float` type uses half the storage of the `double` type that we use in this book, but it can only store 6–7 digits. Many years ago, when computers had far less memory than they have today, `float` was the standard type for floating-point computations, and programmers would indulge in the luxury of "double precision" only when they needed the additional digits. Today, the `float` type is rarely used.

By the way, these numbers are called "floating-point" because of their internal representation in the computer. Consider numbers 29600, 2.96, and 0.0296. They can be represented in a very similar way: namely, as a sequence of the significant digits—296—and an indication of the position of the decimal point. When the values are multiplied or divided by 10, only the position of the decimal point changes; it "floats". Computers use base 2, not base 10, but the principle is the same.

Table 4 Number Types		
Type	Typical Range	Typical Size
`int`	–2,147,483,648 ... 2,147,483,647 (about 2 billion)	4 bytes
`unsigned`	0 ... 4,294,967,295	4 bytes
`short`	–32,768 ... 32,767	2 bytes
`unsigned short`	0 ... 65,535	2 bytes
`long long`	–9,223,372,036,854,775,808 ... 9,223,372,036,854,775,807	8 bytes
`double`	The double-precision floating-point type, with a range of about $\pm 10^{308}$ and about 15 significant decimal digits	8 bytes
`float`	The single-precision floating-point type, with a range of about $\pm 10^{38}$ and about 7 significant decimal digits	4 bytes

In addition to the int type, C++ has integer types short, long, and long long. For each integer type, there is an unsigned equivalent. For example, the short type typically has a range from −32,768 to 32,767, whereas unsigned short has a range from 0 to 65,535. These strange-looking limits are the result of the use of binary numbers in computers. A short value uses 16 binary digits, which can encode $2^{16} = 65,536$ values. Keep in mind that the ranges for integer types are not standardized, and they differ among compilers. Table 4 contains typical values.

Special Topic 2.2

Numeric Ranges and Precisions

Because numbers are represented in the computer with a limited number of digits, they cannot represent arbitrary integer or floating-point numbers.

The int type has a *limited range:* On most platforms, it can represent numbers up to a little more than two billion. For many applications, this is not a problem, but you cannot use an int to represent the world population.

If a computation yields a value that is outside the int range, the result *overflows*. No error is displayed. Instead, the result is truncated to fit into an int, yielding a useless value. For example,

```cpp
int one_billion = 1000000000;
cout << 3 * one_billion << endl;
```

displays −1294967296.

In situations such as this, you can switch to double values. However, read Common Error 2.6 on page 45 for more information about a related issue: roundoff errors.

Programming Tip 2.2

Do Not Use Magic Numbers

A **magic number** is a numeric constant that appears in your code without explanation. For example,

```cpp
total_volume = bottles * 2;
```

Why 2? Are bottles twice as voluminous as cans? No, the reason is that every bottle contains 2 liters. Use a named constant to make the code self-documenting:

```cpp
const double BOTTLE_VOLUME = 2;
total_volume = bottles * BOTTLE_VOLUME;
```

There is another reason for using named constants. Suppose circumstances change, and the bottle volume is now 1.5 liters. If you used a named constant, you make a single change, and you are done. Otherwise, you have to look at every value of 2 in your program and ponder whether it means a bottle volume, or something else. In a program that is more than a few pages long, that is incredibly tedious and error-prone.

Even the most reasonable cosmic constant is going to change one day. You think there are seven days per week? Your customers on Mars are going to be pretty unhappy about your silly prejudice. Make a constant

```cpp
const int DAYS_PER_WEEK = 7;
```

2.2 Arithmetic

In the following sections, you will learn how to carry out arithmetic and mathematical calculations in C++.

2.2.1 Arithmetic Operators

Use * for multiplication and / for division.

C++ supports the same four basic arithmetic operations as a calculator—addition, subtraction, multiplication, and division—but it uses different symbols for multiplication and division.

You must write a * b to denote multiplication. Unlike in mathematics, you can not write a b, a . b or a × b. Similarly, division is always indicated with a /, never a ÷ or a fraction bar.

For example, $\frac{a+b}{2}$ becomes (a + b) / 2.

Parentheses are used just as in algebra: to indicate in which order the subexpressions should be computed. For example, in the expression (a + b) / 2, the sum a + b is computed first, and then the sum is divided by 2. In contrast, in the expression

    a + b / 2

only b is divided by 2, and then the sum of a and b / 2 is formed. Just as in regular algebraic notation, multiplication and division have a *higher precedence* than addition and subtraction. For example, in the expression a + b / 2, the / is carried out first, even though the + operation occurs further to the left. If both arguments of an arithmetic operation are integers, the result is an integer. If one or both arguments are floating-point numbers, the result is a floating-point number. For example, 4 * 0.5 is 2.0.

2.2.2 Increment and Decrement

The ++ operator adds 1 to a variable; the -- operator subtracts 1.

Changing a variable by adding or subtracting 1 is so common that there is a special shorthand for it, namely

    counter++;
    counter--;

The ++ increment operator gave the C++ programming language its name. C++ is the incremental improvement of the C language.

2.2.3 Integer Division and Remainder

If both arguments of / are integers, the remainder is discarded.

Division works as you would expect, as long as at least one of the numbers involved is a floating-point number. That is, 7.0 / 4.0, 7 / 4.0, and 7.0 / 4 all yield 1.75. However, if *both* numbers are integers, then the result of the division is always an integer, with the remainder discarded. That is,

    7 / 4

evaluates to 1 because 7 divided by 4 is 1 with a remainder of 3 (which is discarded). This can be a source of subtle programming errors—see Common Error 2.3 on page 43.

> The % operator computes the remainder of an integer division.

If you are interested in the remainder only, use the % operator:

```
7 % 4
```

is 3, the remainder of the integer division of 7 by 4. The % symbol has no analog in algebra. It was chosen because it looks similar to /, and the remainder operation is related to division. The operator is called **modulus**. (Some people call it *modulo* or *mod*.) It has no relationship with the percent operation that you find on some calculators.

Here is a typical use for the integer / and % operations. Suppose you have an amount of pennies in a piggybank:

```
int pennies = 1729;
```

You want to determine the value in dollars and cents. You obtain the dollars through an integer division by 100.

```
int dollars = pennies / 100;   // Sets dollars to 17
```

The integer division discards the remainder. To obtain the remainder, use the % operator:

```
int cents = pennies % 100;   // Sets cents to 29
```

Another common use of the % operator is to check whether a number is even or odd. If a number n is even, then n % 2 is zero.

Integer division and the % operator yield the dollar and cent values of a piggybank full of pennies.

2.2.4 Converting Floating-Point Numbers to Integers

> Assigning a floating-point variable to an integer drops the fractional part.

When a floating-point value is assigned to an integer variable, the fractional part is discarded:

```
double price = 2.55;
int dollars = price; // Sets dollars to 2
```

Discarding the fractional part is not always what you want. Often, you want to round to the *nearest* integer. To round a positive floating-point value to the nearest integer, add 0.5 and then convert to an integer:

```
int dollars = price + 0.5; // Rounds to the nearest integer
```

In our example, adding 0.5 turns all values above 2.5 into values above 3. In particular, 2.55 is turned into 3.05, which is then truncated to 3. (For a negative floating-point value, you subtract 0.5.)

Because truncation is a potential cause for errors, your compiler may issue a warning that assigning a floating-point value to an integer variable is unsafe. See Special Topic 2.3 on page 46 on how to avoid this warning.

2.2.5 Powers and Roots

In C++, there are no symbols for powers and roots. To compute them, you must call *functions*. To take the square root of a number, you use the sqrt function. For example, $\sqrt{x}$ is written as sqrt(x). To compute x^n, you write pow(x, n).

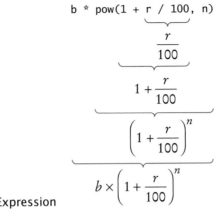

Figure 2
Analyzing an Expression

To use the sqrt and pow functions, you must place the line #include <cmath> at the top of your program file. The header file <cmath> is a standard C++ header that is available with all C++ systems, as is <iostream>.

As you can see, the effect of the /, sqrt, and pow operations is to flatten out mathematical terms. In algebra, you use fractions, exponents, and roots to arrange expressions in a compact two-dimensional form. In C++, you have to write all expressions in a linear arrangement. For example, the mathematical expression

$$b \times \left(1 + \frac{r}{100}\right)^n$$

becomes

```
b * pow(1 + r / 100, n)
```

Figure 2 shows how to analyze such an expression.

Table 5 Arithmetic Expressions

Mathematical Expression	C++ Expression	Comments
$\dfrac{x + y}{2}$	(x + y) / 2	The parentheses are required; x + y / 2 computes $x + \frac{y}{2}$.
$\dfrac{xy}{2}$	x * y / 2	Parentheses are not required; operators with the same precedence are evaluated left to right.
$\left(1 + \dfrac{r}{100}\right)^n$	pow(1 + r / 100, n)	Remember to add #include <cmath> to the top of your program.
$\sqrt{a^2 + b^2}$	sqrt(a * a + b * b)	a * a is simpler than pow(a, 2).
$\dfrac{i + j + k}{3}$	(i + j + k) / 3.0	If i, j, and k are integers, using a denominator of 3.0 forces floating-point division.

Table 6 Other Mathematical Functions	
Function	Description
sin(x)	sine of x (x in radians)
cos(x)	cosine of x
tan(x)	tangent of x
log10(x)	(decimal log) $\log_{10}(x)$, $x > 0$
abs(x)	absolute value $|x|$

Table 6 shows additional functions that are declared in the <cmath> header. Inputs and outputs are floating-point numbers.

SELF CHECK

10. A bank account earns interest of p percent per year. In C++, how do you compute the interest earned in one year? Assume variables p and balance of type double have already been defined.

11. In C++, how do you compute the side length of a square whose area is stored in the variable area?

12. The volume of a sphere is given by $V = \dfrac{4}{3}\pi r^3$.

    If the radius is given by a variable radius of type double, write a C++ expression for the volume. You may assume that π is defined by a constant PI.

13. What is the value of 1729 / 10 and 1729 % 10?

14. Suppose a punch recipe calls for a given amount of orange soda, measured in ounces.

    ```
    int amount = 32;
    ```

    We can compute the number of 12-ounce cans needed, assuming that the amount does not evenly divide into 12:

    ```
    int cans_needed = amount / 12 + 1;
    ```

    Use the % operator to determine how many ounces will be left over. For example, if 32 ounces are required, we need 3 cans and have 4 ounces left over.

Practice It Now you can try these exercises at the end of the chapter: R2.3, R2.5, P2.2.

Common Error 2.3

Unintended Integer Division

It is unfortunate that C++ uses the same symbol, namely /, for both integer and floating-point division. These are really quite different operations. It is a common error to use integer division by accident. Consider this segment that computes the average of three integers:

```
cout << "Please enter your last three test scores: ";
int s1;
int s2;
```

```
int s3;
cin >> s1 >> s2 >> s3;
double average = (s1 + s2 + s3) / 3; // Error
cout << "Your average score is " << average << endl;
```

What could be wrong with that? Of course, the average of s1, s2, and s3 is

$$\frac{s1+s2+s3}{3}$$

Here, however, the / does not mean division in the mathematical sense. It denotes integer division because both s1 + s2 + s3 and 3 are integers. For example, if the scores add up to 14, the average is computed to be 4, the result of the integer division of 14 by 3. That integer 4 is then moved into the floating-point variable average. The remedy is to make the numerator or denominator into a floating-point number:

```
double total = s1 + s2 + s3;
double average = total / 3;
```

or

```
double average = (s1 + s2 + s3) / 3.0;
```

Common Error 2.4

Unbalanced Parentheses

Consider the expression

```
(-(b * b - 4 * a * c) / (2 * a)
```

What is wrong with it? Count the parentheses. There are three (and two). The parentheses are *unbalanced*. This kind of typing error is very common with complicated expressions. Now consider this expression.

```
-(b * b - (4 * a * c))) / (2 * a
```

This expression has three (and three), but it still is not correct. In the middle of the expression,

```
-(b * b - (4 * a * c))) / (2 * a
                      ↑
```

there are only two (but three), which is an error. In the middle of an expression, the count of (must be greater than or equal to the count of), and at the end of the expression the two counts must be the same.

Here is a simple trick to make the counting easier without using pencil and paper. It is difficult for the brain to keep two counts simultaneously. Keep only one count when scanning the expression. Start with 1 at the first opening parenthesis, add 1 whenever you see an opening parenthesis, and subtract one whenever you see a closing parenthesis. Say the numbers aloud as you scan the expression. If the count ever drops below zero, or is not zero at the end, the parentheses are unbalanced. For example, when scanning the previous expression, you would mutter

```
-(b * b - (4 * a * c ) ) ) / (2 * a
 1         2           1 0 -1
```

and you would find the error.

Common Error 2.5

Forgetting Header Files

Every program that carries out input or output needs the <iostream> header. If you use mathematical functions such as sqrt, you need to include <cmath>. If you forget to include the appropriate header file, the compiler will not know symbols such as cout or sqrt. If the compiler complains about an undefined function or symbol, check your header files.

Sometimes you may not know which header file to include. Suppose you want to compute the absolute value of an integer using the abs function. As it happens, this version of abs is not defined in the <cmath> header but in <cstdlib>. How can you find the correct header file? You need to locate the documentation of the abs function, preferably using the online help of your development environment or a reference site on the Internet such as http://www.cplusplus.com (see Figure 3). The documentation includes a short description of the function and the name of the header file that you must include.

Figure 3 Online Documentation

Common Error 2.6

Roundoff Errors

Roundoff errors are a fact of life when calculating with floating-point numbers. You probably have encountered that phenomenon yourself with manual calculations. If you calculate $1/3$ to two decimal places, you get 0.33. Multiplying again by 3, you obtain 0.99, not 1.00.

In the processor hardware, numbers are represented in the binary number system, not in decimal. You still get roundoff errors when binary digits are lost. They just may crop up at different places than you might expect. Here is an example.

```
#include <iostream>

using namespace std;
```

```cpp
int main()
{
    double price = 4.35;
    int cents = 100 * price; // Should be 100 * 4.35 = 435
    cout << cents << endl; // Prints 434!
    return 0;
}
```

Of course, one hundred times 4.35 is 435, but the program prints 434.

Most computers represent numbers in the binary system. In the binary system, there is no exact representation for 4.35, just as there is no exact representation for 1/3 in the decimal system. The representation used by the computer is just a little less than 4.35, so 100 times that value is just a little less than 435. When a floating-point value is converted to an integer, the entire fractional part, which is almost 1, is thrown away, and the integer 434 is stored in cents. The remedy is to add 0.5 in order to round to the nearest integer:

```cpp
int cents = 100 * price + 0.5;
```

Programming Tip 2.3

Spaces in Expressions

It is easier to read

```cpp
x1 = (-b + sqrt(b * b - 4 * a * c)) / (2 * a);
```

than

```cpp
x1=(-b+sqrt(b*b-4*a*c))/(2*a);
```

Simply put spaces around all operators + - * / % =. However, don't put a space after a *unary* minus: a – used to negate a single quantity, such as -b. That way, it can be easily distinguished from a *binary* minus, as in a - b.

It is customary not to put a space after a function name. That is, write sqrt(x) and not sqrt (x).

Special Topic 2.3

Casts

Occasionally, you need to store a value into a variable of a different type. Whenever there is the risk of *information loss*, the compiler issues a warning. For example, if you store a double value into an int variable, you can lose information in two ways:

- The fractional part is lost.
- The magnitude may be too large.

For example,

```cpp
int n = 1.0E100; // NO
```

is not likely to work, because 10^{100} is larger than the largest representable integer.

Nevertheless, sometimes you do want to convert a floating-point value into an integer value. If you are prepared to lose the fractional part and you know that this particular floating-point number is not larger than the largest possible integer, then you can turn off the warning by using a **cast**. A cast is a conversion from one type (such as double) to another type (such as int) that is not safe in general, but that you know to be safe in a particular circumstance. You express a cast in C++ as follows:

```cpp
int cents = static_cast<int>(100 * price + 0.5);
```

Special Topic 2.4

Combining Assignment and Arithmetic

In C++, you can combine arithmetic and assignment. For example, the instruction

```
total += cans * CAN_VOLUME;
```

is a shortcut for

```
total = total + cans * CAN_VOLUME;
```

Similarly,

```
total *= 2;
```

is another way of writing

```
total = total * 2;
```

Many programmers find this a convenient shortcut. If you like it, go ahead and use it in your own code. For simplicity, we won't use it in this book, though.

Random Fact 2.1 The Pentium Floating-Point Bug

In 1994, Intel Corporation released what was then its most powerful processor, the Pentium. Unlike previous generations of its processors, it had a very fast floating-point unit. Intel's goal was to compete aggressively with the makers of higher-end processors for engineering workstations. The Pentium was a huge success immediately.

In the summer of 1994, Dr. Thomas Nicely of Lynchburg College, Virginia, ran an extensive set of computations to analyze the sums of reciprocals of certain sequences of prime numbers. The results were not always what his theory predicted, even after he took into account the inevitable roundoff errors. Then Dr. Nicely noted that the same program did produce the correct results when running on the slower 486 processor that preceded the Pentium in Intel's lineup. This should not have happened. The optimal round-off behavior of floating-point calculations were standardized by the Institute for Electrical and Electronic Engineers (IEEE) and Intel claimed to adhere to the IEEE standard in both the 486 and the Pentium processors. Upon further checking, Dr. Nicely discovered that there was a very small set of numbers for which the product of two numbers was computed differently on the two processors. For example,

$$4,195,835 - \left((4,195,835/3,145,727) \times 3,145,727 \right)$$

is mathematically equal to 0, and it did compute as 0 on a 486 processor. On his Pentium processor the result was 256.

As it turned out, Intel had independently discovered the bug in its testing and had started to produce chips that fixed it. The bug was caused by an error in a table that was used to speed up the processor's floating-point multiplication algorithm. Intel determined that the problem was exceedingly rare. They claimed that under normal use, a typical consumer would only notice the problem once every 27,000 years. Unfortunately for Intel, Dr. Nicely had not been a normal user.

Now Intel had a real problem on its hands. It figured that the cost of replacing all Pentium processors that it had sold so far would cost a great deal of money. Intel already had more orders for the chip than it could produce, and it would be particularly galling to have to give out the scarce chips as free replacements instead of selling them. Intel's management decided to punt and initially offered to replace the processors only for those customers who could prove that their work required absolute precision in mathematical calculations. Naturally, that did not go over well with the hundreds of thousands of customers who had paid retail prices of $700 and more for a Pentium chip and did not want to live with the nagging feeling that perhaps, one day, their income tax program would produce a faulty return. Ultimately, Intel caved in to public demand and replaced all defective chips, at a cost of about 475 million dollars.

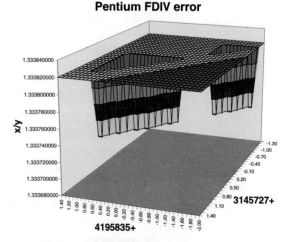

This graph shows a set of numbers for which the original Pentium processor obtained the wrong quotient.

2.3 Input and Output

2.3.1 Input

In this section, you will see how to place user input into a variable. Consider for example the `volume1.cpp` program on page 36. Rather than assuming that the price for the two-liter bottle and the six-pack of cans are identical, we can ask the program user for the prices.

When a program asks for user input, it should first print a message that tells the user which input is expected. Such a message is called a **prompt**.

```
cout << "Please enter the number of bottles: "; // Display prompt
```

Do not add an `endl` after the prompt. You want the input to appear after the colon, not on the following line.

Next, the program issues a command to read the input. The `cin` object reads input from the console window. You use the `>>` operator (sometimes called the *extraction* operator) to place an input value into a variable, like this:

> Use the `>>` operator to read a value and place it in a variable.

```
int bottles;
cin >> bottles;
```

When the program executes the input statement, it waits for the user to provide input. The user also needs to hit the Enter key so that the program accepts the input. After the user supplies the input, the number is placed into the `bottles` variable, and the program continues.

Note that in this code segment, there was no need to initialize the bottles variable because it is being filled by the very next statement. As a rule of thumb, you should initialize a variable when you declare it *unless* it is filled in an input statement that follows immediately.

You can read more than one value in a single input statement:

```
cout << "Please enter the number of bottles and cans: ";
cin >> bottles >> cans;
```

The user can supply both inputs on the same line:

```
Please enter the number of bottles and cans: 2 6
```

Alternatively, the user can press the Enter key after each input:

```
Please enter the number of bottles and cans: 2
6
```

Syntax 2.3   Input Statement

Don't use endl here.

Display a prompt in the console window. ———
```
cout << "Enter the number of bottles: ";
```
Define a variable to hold the input value. ——
```
int bottles;
cin >> bottles;
```
The program waits for user input,
then places the input into the variable.

2.3.2 Formatted Output

When you print the result of a computation, you often want some control over its appearance. For example, when you print an amount in dollars and cents, you usually want it to be rounded to two significant digits. That is, you want the output to look like

```
Price per ounce: 0.04
```

instead of

```
Price per ounce: 0.0409722
```

> You use manipulators to specify how values should be formatted.

The following command instructs cout to use two digits after the decimal point for all floating-point numbers:

```
cout << fixed << setprecision(2);
```

This command does not produce any output; it just manipulates cout so that it will change the output format. The values fixed and setprecision are called *manipulators*. We will discuss manipulators in detail in Chapter 8. For now, just remember to include the statement given above whenever you want currency values displayed neatly.

To use manipulators, you must include the <iomanip> header in your program:

```
#include <iomanip>
```

You can combine the manipulators and the values to be displayed into a single statement.

```
cout << fixed << setprecision(2)
    << "Price per ounce: "
    << price_per_ounce << endl;
```

There is another manipulator that is sometimes handy. When you display several rows of data, you usually want the columns to line up.

You use the setw manipulator to set the *width* of the next output field. The width is the total number of characters used for showing the value, including digits, the decimal point, and spaces. Controlling the width is important when you want columns of numbers to line up.

For example, if you want a number to be printed in a column that is eight characters wide, you use

```
cout << setw(8) << price_per_ounce;
```

You use manipulators to line up your output in neat columns.

This command prints the value price_per_ounce in a field of width 8, for example

```
       0 . 0 4
```

(where each ░ represents a space).

There is a notable difference between the setprecision and setw manipulators. Once you set the precision, that value is used for all floating-point numbers. But the width affects only the *next* value. Subsequent values are formatted without added spaces.

Our next example program will prompt for the price of a six-pack and the volume of each can, then print out the price per ounce. The program puts to work what you just learned about reading input and formatting output.

ch02/volume2.cpp

```cpp
1  #include <iostream>
2  #include <iomanip>
3
4  using namespace std;
5
6  int main()
7  {
8     // Read price per pack
9
10    cout << "Please enter the price for a six-pack: ";
11    double pack_price;
12    cin >> pack_price;
13
14    // Read can volume
15
16    cout << "Please enter the volume for each can (in ounces): ";
17    double can_volume;
18    cin >> can_volume;
19
20    // Compute pack volume
21
22    const double CANS_PER_PACK = 6;
23    double pack_volume = can_volume * CANS_PER_PACK;
24
25    // Compute and print price per ounce
26
27    double price_per_ounce = pack_price / pack_volume;
28
29    cout << fixed << setprecision(2);
30    cout << "Price per ounce: " << price_per_ounce << endl;
31
32    return 0;
33 }
```

Program Run

```
Please enter the price for a six-pack: 2.95
Please enter the volume for each can (in ounces): 12
Price per ounce: 0.04
```

Table 7 Formatting Output

Output Statement	Output	Comment
`cout << 12.345678;`	`12.3457`	By default, a number is printed with 6 significant digits.

`cout << fixed`
`    << setprecision(2)`
`    << 12.3;`
	`12.30`	Use the `fixed` and `setprecision` manipulators to control the number of digits after the decimal point.

`cout << ":" << setw(6)` `    << 12;`	`:    12`	Four spaces are printed before the number, for a total width of 6 characters.
`cout << ":" << setw(2)` `    << 123;`	`:123`	If the width not sufficient, it is ignored.
`cout << setw(6)` `    << ":" << 12;`	`     :12.3`	The width only refers to the next item. Here, the : is preceded by five spaces.

SELF CHECK

15. What is wrong with the following statement sequence?

```
cout << "Please enter the unit price: ";
double unit_price;
cin >> unit_price;
int quantity;
cin >> quantity;
```

16. What is problematic about the following statement sequence?

```
cout << "Please enter the unit price: ";
int unit_price;
cin >> unit_price;
```

17. What is the output of the following statement sequence?

```
double bottles = 10;
cout << "The total volume is" << 2 * bottles;
```

18. How do you print the floating-point variable `total_price` in dollars and cents, like this: `$1.22`?

19. Using the `setw` manipulator, improve the output statement

```
cout << "Bottles: " << bottles << endl
    << "Cans: " << cans << endl;
```

so that the output looks like this:

```
Bottles:       8
Cans:         24
```

The numbers to the right should line up. (You may assume that the numbers have at most 8 digits.)

Practice It Now you can try these exercises at the end of the chapter: R2.7, R2.8, P2.6, P2.7.

2.4 Problem Solving: First Do It By Hand

A very important step for developing an algorithm is to first carry out the computations *by hand*. If you can't compute a solution yourself, it's unlikely that you'll be able to write a program that automates the computation.

To illustrate the use of hand calculations, consider the following problem.

A row of black and white tiles needs to be placed along a wall. For aesthetic reasons, the architect has specified that the first and last tile shall be black.

Your task is to compute the number of tiles needed and the gap at each end, given the space available and the width of each tile.

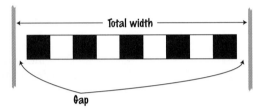

To make the problem more concrete, let's assume the following dimensions:

<aside>Pick concrete values for a typical situation to use in a hand calculation.</aside>

- Total width: 100 inches
- Tile width: 5 inches

The obvious solution would be to fill the space with 20 tiles, but that would not work—the last tile would be white.

Instead, look at the problem this way: The first tile must always be black, and then we add some number of white/black pairs:

The first tile takes up 5 inches, leaving 95 inches to be covered by pairs. Each pair is 10 inches wide. Therefore the number of pairs is 95 / 10 = 9.5. However, we need to discard the fractional part since we can't have fractions of tile pairs.

Therefore, we will use 9 tile pairs or 18 tiles, together with the initial black tile. Altogether, we require 19 tiles.

The tiles span 19 × 5 = 95 inches, leaving a total gap of 100 − 19 × 5 = 5 inches. The gap should be evenly distributed at both ends. At each end, the gap is (100 − 19 × 5) / 2 = 2.5 inches.

This computation gives us enough information to devise an algorithm with arbitrary values for the total width and tile width.

> number of pairs = integer part of (total width - tile width) / (2 x tile width)
> number of tiles = 1 + 2 x number of pairs
> gap at each end = (total width - number of tiles x tile width) / 2

As you can see, doing a hand calculation gives enough insight into the problem that it becomes easy to develop an algorithm.

SELF CHECK

20. Translate the pseudocode for computing the number of tiles and the gap width into C++.

21. Suppose the architect specifies a pattern with black, gray, and white tiles, like this:

Again, the first and last tile should be black. How do you need to modify the algorithm?

22. A robot needs to tile a floor with alternating black and white tiles. Develop an algorithm that yields the color (0 for black, 1 for white), given the row and column number. Start with specific values for the row and column, and then generalize.

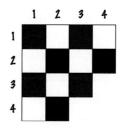

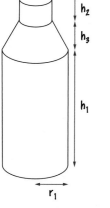

23. For a particular car, repair and maintenance costs in year 1 are estimated at $100; in year 10, at $1,500. Assuming that the repair cost increases by the same amount every year, develop pseudocode to compute the repair cost in year 3 and then generalize to year **n**.

24. The shape of a bottle is approximated by two cylinders of radius r_1 and r_2 and heights h_1 and h_2, joined by a cone section of height h_3.

Using the formulas for the volume of a cylinder, $V = \pi r^2 h$, and a cone section,

$$V = \pi \frac{\left(r_1^2 + r_1 r_2 + r_2^2\right) h}{3},$$

develop pseudocode to compute the volume of the bottle. Using an actual bottle with known volume as a sample, make a hand calculation of your pseudocode.

Practice It   Now you can try these exercises at the end of the chapter: R2.13, R2.15, R2.16.

WORKED EXAMPLE 2.1   **Computing Travel Time**

In this Worked Example, we develop a hand calculation to compute the time that a robot requires to retrieve an item from rocky terrain.

➕ Available online at www.wiley.com/college/horstmann.

HOW TO 2.1   Carrying out Computations

Many programming problems require that you carry out arithmetic computations. This How To shows you how to turn a problem statement into pseudocode and, ultimately, a C++ program.

For example, suppose you are asked to write a program that simulates a vending machine. A customer selects an item for purchase and inserts a bill into the vending machine. The vending machine dispenses the purchased item and gives change. We will assume that all item prices are multiples of 25 cents, and the machine gives all change in dollar coins and quarters. Your task is to compute how many coins of each type to return.

Step 1   Understand the problem: What are the inputs? What are the desired outputs?

In this problem, there are two inputs:
- The denomination of the bill that the customer inserts
- The price of the purchased item

There are two desired outputs:
- The number of dollar coins that the machine returns
- The number of quarters that the machine returns

Step 2   Work out examples by hand.

Let's assume that a customer purchased an item that cost $2.25 and inserted a $5 bill. The customer is due $2.75, or two dollar coins and three quarters.

That is easy for you to see, but how can a C++ program come to the same conclusion? The computation is simpler if you work in pennies, not dollars. The amount due the customer is 275 pennies. Dividing by 100 yields 2, the number of dollars. Dividing the remainder (75) by 25 yields 3, the number of quarters.

Step 3   Write pseudocode for computing the answers.

In the previous step, you worked out a specific instance of the problem. You now need to come up with a method that works in general.

Given an arbitrary item price and payment, how can you compute the coins due? First, compute the amount due in pennies:

amount due = 100 x bill value - item price in pennies

To get the dollars, divide by 100 and discard the remainder:

dollar coins = amount due / 100 (without remainder)

A vending machine takes bills and gives change in coins.

The remaining amount due can be computed in two ways. If you are familiar with the modulus operator, you can simply compute

amount due = amount due % 100

Alternatively, subtract the penny value of the dollar coins from the amount due:

amount due = amount due - 100 x dollar coins

To get the quarters due, divide by 25:

quarters = amount due / 25

Step 4   Define the variables and constants that you need, and specify their types.

Here, we have five variables:
- bill_value
- item_price
- amount_due
- dollar_coins
- quarters

Should we introduce constants to explain 100 and 25 as PENNIES_PER_DOLLAR and PENNIES_PER_QUARTER? Doing so will make it easier to convert the program to international markets, so we will take this step.

It is very important that amount_due and PENNIES_PER_DOLLAR are of type int because the computation of dollar_coins uses integer division. Similarly, the other variables are integers.

Step 5   Turn the pseudocode into C++ statements.

If you did a thorough job with the pseudocode, this step should be easy. Of course, you have to know how to express mathematical operations (such as powers or integer division) in C++.

```
amount_due = PENNIES_PER_DOLLAR * bill_value - item_price;
dollar_coins = amount_due / PENNIES_PER_DOLLAR;
amount_due = amount_due % PENNIES_PER_DOLLAR;
quarters = amount_due / PENNIES_PER_QUARTER;
```

Step 6   Provide input and output.

Before starting the computation, we prompt the user for the bill value and item price:

```
cout << "Enter bill value (1 = $1 bill, 5 = $5 bill, etc.): ";
cin >> bill_value;
cout << "Enter item price in pennies: ";
cin >> item_price;
```

When the computation is finished, we display the result. For extra credit, we use the setw manipulator to make sure that the output lines up neatly.

```
cout << "Dollar coins: " << setw(6) << dollar_coins << endl
     << "Quarters:     " << setw(6) << quarters << endl;
```

Step 7   Include the required headers and provide a main function.

We need the <iostream> header for all input and output. Because we use the setw manipulator, we also require <iomanip>. This program does not use any special mathematical functions. Therefore, we do not include the <cmath> header.

In the main function, you need to define constants and variables (Step 4), carry out computations (Step 5), and provide input and output (Step 6). Clearly, you will want to first get the input, then do the computations, and finally show the output. Define the constants at the beginning of the function, and define each variable just before it is needed.

Here is the complete program, ch02/vending.cpp:

```cpp
#include <iostream>
#include <iomanip>

using namespace std;

int main()
{
   const int PENNIES_PER_DOLLAR = 100;
   const int PENNIES_PER_QUARTER = 25;

   cout << "Enter bill value (1 = $1 bill, 5 = $5 bill, etc.): ";
   int bill_value;
   cin >> bill_value;
   cout << "Enter item price in pennies: ";
   int item_price;
   cin >> item_price;

   int amount_due = PENNIES_PER_DOLLAR * bill_value - item_price;
   int dollar_coins = amount_due / PENNIES_PER_DOLLAR;
   amount_due = amount_due % PENNIES_PER_DOLLAR;
   int quarters = amount_due / PENNIES_PER_QUARTER;

   cout << "Dollar coins: " << setw(6) << dollar_coins << endl
      << "Quarters:     " << setw(6) << quarters << endl;
}
```

Program Run

```
Enter bill value (1 = $1 bill, 5 = $5 bill, etc.): 5
Enter item price in pennies: 225
Dollar coins:      2
Quarters:          3
```

WORKED EXAMPLE 2.2   Computing the Cost of Stamps

This Worked Example uses arithmetic functions to simulate a stamp vending machine.

2.5 Strings

Strings are sequences of characters.

Many programs process text, not numbers. Text consists of **characters**: letters, numbers, punctuation, spaces, and so on. A **string** is a sequence of characters. For example, the string "Harry" is a sequence of five characters.

⊕ Available online at www.wiley.com/college/horstmann.

2.5.1 The string Type

You can define variables that hold strings.

```
string name = "Harry";
```

The string type is a part of the C++ standard. To use it, simply include the header file, <string>:

```
#include <string>
```

We distinguish between string variables (such as the variable name defined above) and string literals (character sequences enclosed in quotes, such as "Harry"). The string stored in a string variable can change. A string literal denotes a particular string, just as a number literal (such as 2) denotes a particular number.

Unlike number variables, string variables are guaranteed to be initialized even if you do not supply an initial value. By default, a string variable is set to an empty string: a string containing no characters. An empty string literal is written as "". The definition

```
string response;
```

has the same effect as

```
string response = "";
```

2.5.2 Concatenation

Use the + operator to *concatenate* strings; that is, to put them together to yield a longer string.

Given two strings, such as "Harry" and "Morgan", you can **concatenate** them to one long string. The result consists of all characters in the first string, followed by all characters in the second string. In C++, you use the + operator to concatenate two strings. For example,

```
string fname = "Harry";
string lname = "Morgan";
string name = fname + lname;
```

results in the string

```
"HarryMorgan"
```

What if you'd like the first and last name separated by a space? No problem:

```
string name = fname + " " + lname;
```

This statement concatenates three strings: fname, the string literal " ", and lname. The result is

```
"Harry Morgan"
```

2.5.3 String Input

You can read a string from the console:

```
cout << "Please enter your name: ";
string name;
cin >> name;
```

When a string is read with the >> operator, only one word is placed into the string variable. For example, suppose the user types

```
Harry Morgan
```

as the response to the prompt. This input consists of two words. After the call `cin >> name`, the string `"Harry"` is placed into the variable `name`. Use another input statement to read the second word.

2.5.4 String Functions

> The `length` member function yields the number of characters in a string.

The number of characters in a string is called the *length* of the string. For example, the length of `"Harry"` is 5. You can compute the length of a string with the `length` function. Unlike the `sqrt` or `pow` function, the `length` function is invoked with the **dot notation**. That is, you write the string whose length you want, then a period, then the name of the function, followed by parentheses:

```
int n = name.length();
```

> A member function is invoked using the dot notation.

Many C++ functions require you to use this dot notation, and you must memorize (or look up) which do and which don't. These functions are called **member functions**. We say that the member function `length` is *invoked on* the variable `name`.

Once you have a string, you can extract substrings by using the `substr` member function. The member function call

```
s.substr(start, length)
```

returns a string that is made from the characters in the string `s`, starting at character `start`, and containing `length` characters. Here is an example:

```
string greeting = "Hello, World!";
string sub = greeting.substr(0, 5);
// sub is "Hello"
```

> Use the `substr` member function to extract a substring of a string.

The `substr` operation makes a string that consists of five characters taken from the string `greeting`. Indeed, `"Hello"` is a string of length 5 that occurs inside `greeting`. A curious aspect of the `substr` operation is the starting position. Starting position 0 means "start at the beginning of the string". The first position in a string is labeled 0, the second one 1, and so on. For example, here are the position numbers in the greeting string:

```
H  e  l  l  o  ,     W  o  r  l  d  !
0  1  2  3  4  5  6  7  8  9  10 11 12
```

The position number of the last character (12) is always one less than the length of the string.

Let's figure out how to extract the substring `"World"`. Count characters starting at 0, not 1. You find that `W`, the 8th character, has position number 7. The string you want is 5 characters long. Therefore, the appropriate substring command is

```
string w = greeting.substr(7, 5);
```

If you omit the length, you get all characters from the given position to the end of the string. For example,

```
greeting.substr(7)
```

is the string "World!" (including the exclamation mark).

Here is a simple program that puts these concepts to work. The program asks for your name and that of your significant other. It then prints out your initials.

The operation first.substr(0, 1) makes a string consisting of one character, taken from the start of first. The program does the same for the second. Then it concatenates the resulting one-character strings with the string literal "&" to get a string of length 3, the initials string. (See Figure 4.)

first = | R | o | d | o | l | f | o |
        0 1 2 3 4 5 6

second = | S | a | l | l | y |
        0 1 2 3 4

initials = | R | & | S |
        0 1 2

Figure 4 Building the initials String

Initials are formed from the first letter of each name.

ch02/initials.cpp

```cpp
1   #include <iostream>
2   #include <string>
3
4   using namespace std;
5
6   int main()
7   {
8      cout << "Enter your first name: ";
9      string first;
10     cin >> first;
11     cout << "Enter your significant other's first name: ";
12     string second;
13     cin >> second;
14     string initials = first.substr(0, 1)
15        + "&" + second.substr(0, 1);
16     cout << initials << endl;
17
18     return 0;
19  }
```

Program Run

```
Enter your first name: Rodolfo
Enter your significant other's first name: Sally
R&S
```

Table 8 String Operations

Statement	Result	Comment
`string str = "C";` `str = str + "++";`	str is set to "C++"	When applied to strings, + denotes concatenation.
🚫 `string str = "C" + "++";`	**Error**	**Error:** You cannot concatenate two string literals.

`cout << "Enter name: ";`
`cin >> name;`
(User input: Harry Morgan)
	name contains "Harry"	The >> operator places the next
		word into the string variable.

`cout << "Enter name: ";`
`cin >> name >> last_name;`
(User input: Harry Morgan)
	name contains
	"Harry", last_name
	contains "Morgan"
		Use multiple >> operators to
		read more than one word.

`string greeting = "H & S";` `int n = greeting.length();`	n is set to 5	Each space counts as one character.
`string str = "Sally";` `string str2 = str.substr(1, 3);`	str2 is set to "all"	Extracts the substring of length 3 starting at position 1. (The initial position is 0.)
`string str = "Sally";` `string str2 = str.substr(1);`	str2 is set to "ally"	If you omit the length, all characters from the position until the end are included.
`string a = str.substr(0, 1);`	a is set to the initial letter in str	Extracts the substring of length 1 starting at position 0.
`string b = str.substr(str.length() - 1);`	b is set to the last letter in str	The last letter has position str.length() - 1. We need not specify the length.

SELF CHECK

25. What is the length of the string `"C++ Program"`?

26. Consider this string variable.

    `string str = "C++ Program";`

    Give a call to the `substr` member function that returns the substring `"gram"`.

27. Use string concatenation to turn the string variable `str` from Self Check 26 to `"C++ Programming"`.

28. What does the following statement sequence print?

    `string str = "Harry";`
    `cout << str.substr(0, 1) + str.substr(str.length() - 1);`

29. Give an input statement to read a name of the form "John Q. Public".

Practice It   Now you can try these exercises at the end of the chapter: R2.6, R2.9, P2.12, P2.19.

Random Fact 2.2 International Alphabets and Unicode

The English alphabet is pretty simple: upper- and lowercase *a* to *z*. Other European languages have accent marks and special characters. For example, German has three so-called *umlaut* characters, ä, ö, ü, and a *double-s* character ß. These are not optional frills; you couldn't write a page of German text without using these characters a few times. German keyboards have keys for these characters.

Hebrew, Arabic, and English

The German Keyboard Layout

This poses a problem for computer users and designers. The American standard character encoding (called ASCII, for American Standard Code for Information Interchange) specifies 128 codes: 52 upper- and lowercase characters, 10 digits, 32 typographical symbols, and 34 control characters (such as space, newline, and 32 others for controlling printers and other devices). The umlaut and double-s are not among them. Some German data processing systems replace seldom-used ASCII characters with German letters: [\ ] { | } ~ are replaced with Ä Ö Ü ä ö ü ß. While most people can live without these characters, C++ programmers definitely cannot. Other encoding schemes take advantage of the fact that one byte can encode 256 different characters, of which only 128 are standardized by ASCII. Unfortunately, there are multiple incompatible standards for such encodings, resulting in a certain amount of aggravation among European computer users.

Many countries don't use the Roman script at all. Russian, Greek, Hebrew, Arabic, and Thai letters, to name just a few, have completely different shapes. To complicate matters, Hebrew and Arabic are typed from right to left. Each of these alphabets has between 30 and 100 letters, and the countries using them have established encoding standards for them.

The situation is much more dramatic in languages that use the Chinese script: the Chinese dialects, Japanese, and Korean. The Chinese script is not alphabetic but ideographic. A character represents an idea or thing. Most words are made up of one, two, or three of these ideographic characters. (Over 50,000 ideographs are known, of which about 20,000 are in active use.) Therefore, two bytes are needed to encode them. China, Taiwan, Japan, and Korea have incompatible encoding standards for them. (Japanese and Korean writing uses a mixture of native syllabic and Chinese ideographic characters.)

The inconsistencies among character encodings have been a major nuisance for international electronic communication and for software manufacturers vying for a global market. Starting in 1988, a consortium of hardware and software manufacturers developed a uniform 21-bit encoding scheme called **Unicode** that is capable of encoding text in essentially all written languages of the world. About 100,000 characters have been given codes, including more than 70,000 Chinese, Japanese, and Korean ideographs. There are even plans to add codes for extinct languages, such as Egyptian hieroglyphs.

The Chinese Script

CHAPTER SUMMARY

Write variable definitions in C++.

- A variable is a storage location with a name.
- When defining a variable, you usually specify an initial value.
- When defining a variable, you also specify the type of its values.
- Use the `int` type for numbers that cannot have a fractional part.
- Use the `double` type for floating-point numbers.
- An assignment statement stores a new value in a variable, replacing the previously stored value.
- The assignment operator `=` does *not* denote mathematical equality.
- You cannot change the value of a variable that is defined as `const`.
- Use comments to add explanations for humans who read your code. The compiler ignores comments.

Use the arithmetic operations in C++.

- Use `*` for multiplication and `/` for division.
- The `++` operator adds 1 to a variable; the `--` operator subtracts 1.
- If both arguments of `/` are integers, the remainder is discarded.
- The `%` operator computes the remainder of an integer division.
- Assigning a floating-point variable to an integer drops the fractional part.
- The C++ library defines many mathematical functions such as `sqrt` (square root) and `pow` (raising to a power).

Write programs that read user input and write formatted output.

- Use the `>>` operator to read a value and place it in a variable.
- You use manipulators to specify how values should be formatted.

Carry out hand calculations when developing an algorithm.

- Pick concrete values for a typical situation to use in a hand calculation.

Write programs that process strings.

- Strings are sequences of characters.
- Use the `+` operator to *concatenate* strings; that is, put them together to yield a longer string.
- The `length` member function yields the number of characters in a string.

- A member function is invoked using the dot notation.
- Use the substr member function to extract a substring of a string

REVIEW EXERCISES

R2.1 What is the value of mystery after this sequence of statements?

```
int mystery = 1;
mystery = 1 - 2 * mystery;
mystery = mystery + 1;
```

R2.2 What is wrong with the following sequence of statements?

```
int mystery = 1;
mystery = mystery + 1;
int mystery = 1 - 2 * mystery;
```

R2.3 Write the following mathematical expressions in C++.

$$s = s_0 + v_0 t + \frac{1}{2} g t^2$$

$$G = 4\pi^2 \frac{a^3}{p^2(m_1 + m_2)}$$

$$FV = PV \cdot \left(1 + \frac{INT}{100}\right)^{YRS}$$

$$c = \sqrt{a^2 + b^2 - 2ab \cos \gamma}$$

R2.4 Write the following C++ expressions in mathematical notation.

a. dm = m * (sqrt(1 + v / c) / sqrt(1 - v / c) - 1);
b. volume = PI * r * r * h;
c. volume = 4 * PI * pow(r, 3) / 3;
d. z = sqrt(x * x + y * y);

R2.5 What are the values of the following expressions? In each line, assume that

```
double x = 2.5;
double y = -1.5;
int m = 18;
int n = 4;
```

a. x + n * y - (x + n) * y
b. m / n + m % n
c. 5 * x - n / 5
d. 1 - (1 - (1 - (1 - (1 - n))))
e. sqrt(sqrt(n))

R2.6 What are the values of the following expressions? In each line, assume that

```
string s = "Hello";
string t = "World";
```

      a. `s.length() + t.length()`

      b. `s.substr(1, 2)`

      c. `s.substr(s.length() / 2, 1)`

      d. `s + t`

      e. `t + s`

R2.7 Find at least five *compile-time* errors in the following program.

```
#include iostream

int main();
{
   cout << "Please enter two numbers:"
   cin << x, y;
   cout << "The sum of << x << "and" << y
      << "is: " x + y << endl;
   return;
}
```

R2.8 Find at least four *run-time* errors in the following program.

```
#include <iostream>

using namespace std;

int main()
{
   int total;
   int x1;
   cout << "Please enter a number:";
   cin >> x1;
   total = total + x1;
   cout << "Please enter another number:";
   int x2;
   cin >> x2;
   total = total + x1;
   double average = total / 2;
   cout << "The average of the two numbers is "
      << average << "endl";
   return 0;
}
```

R2.9 Explain the differences between 2, 2.0, "2", and "2.0".

R2.10 Explain what each of the following program segments computes.

      a. `int x = 2;`
          `int y = x + x;`

      b. `string s = "2";`
          `string t = s + s;`

R2.11 Write pseudocode for a program that reads a word and then prints the first character, the last character, and the characters in the middle. For example, if the input is `Harry`, the program prints `H y arr`.

R2.12 Write pseudocode for a program that reads a name (such as `Harold James Morgan`) and then prints a monogram consisting of the initial letters of the first, middle, and last names (such as `HJM`).

R2.13 Write pseudocode for a program that computes the first and last digit of a number. For example, if the input is 23456, the program should print out 2 and 6. *Hint:* %, log10.

R2.14 Modify the pseudocode for the program in How To 2.1 so that the program gives change in quarters, dimes, and nickels. You can assume that the price is a multiple of 5 cents. To develop your pseudocode, first work with a couple of specific values.

R2.15 A cocktail shaker is composed of three cone sections.

Using realistic values for the radii and heights, compute the total volume, using the formula given in Self Check 24 for a cone section. Then develop an algorithm that works for arbitrary dimensions.

R2.16 You are cutting off a piece of pie like this, where *c* is the length of the straight part (called the chord length) and *h* is the height of the piece.

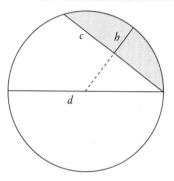

There is an approximate formula for the area: $A \approx \frac{2}{3}ch + \frac{h^3}{2c}$

However, *h* is not so easy to measure, whereas the diameter *d* of a pie is usually well-known. Calculate the area where the diameter of the pie is 12 inches and the chord length of the segment is 10 inches. Generalize to an algorithm that yields the area for any diameter and chord length.

R2.17 The following pseudocode describes how to obtain the name of a day, given the day number (0 = Sunday, 1 = Monday, and so on.)

> Define a string called names containing "SunMonTueWedThuFriSat".
> Compute the starting position as 3 x the day number.
> Extract the substring of names at the starting position with length 3.

Check this pseudocode, using the day number 4. Draw a diagram of the string that is being computed, similar to Figure 4 on page 59.

R2.18 The following pseudocode describes how to swap two letters in a word.

> We are given a string str and two positions i and j. (i comes before j)
> Set first to the substring from the start of the string to the last position before i.
> Set middle to the substring from positions i + 1 to j - 1.
> Set last to the substring from position j + 1 to the end of the string.
> Concatenate the following five strings: first, the string containing just the character at position j, middle, the string containing just the character at position i, and last.

Check this pseudocode, using the string "Gateway" and positions 2 and 4. Draw a diagram of the string that is being computed, similar to Figure 4 on page 59.

R2.19 Run the following program, and explain the output you get.

```cpp
#include <iostream>

using namespace std;

int main()
{
   int total;
   cout << "Please enter a number: ";
   double x1;
   cin >> x1;
   total = total + x1;
   cout << "total: " << total << endl;
   cout << "Please enter a number: ";
   double x2;
   cin >> x2;
   total = total + x2;
   cout << "total: " << total << endl;
   total = total / 2;
   cout << "total: " << total << endl;
   cout << "The average is " << total << endl;
   return 0;
}
```

Note the **trace messages** (in blue) that are inserted to show the current contents of the total variable. How do you fix the program? (The program has two separate errors.)

R2.20 Write a program that prints the values

```
3 * 1000 * 1000 * 1000
3.0 * 1000 * 1000 * 1000
```

Explain the results.

R2.21 This chapter contains a number of recommendations regarding variables and constants that make programs easier to read and maintain. Briefly summarize these recommendations.

PROGRAMMING EXERCISES

P2.1 Write a program that displays the dimensions of a letter-size (8.5 × 11 inches) sheet of paper in millimeters. There are 25.4 millimeters per inch. Use constants and comments in your program.

P2.2 Write a program that computes and displays the circumference of a letter-size (8.5 × 11 inches) sheet of paper and the length of its diagonal.

P2.3 Write a program that reads a number and displays the square, cube, and fourth power. Use the pow function only for the fourth power.

P2.4 Write a program that prompts the user for two integers and then prints

- The sum
- The difference

- The product
- The average

P2.5 Write a program that prompts the user for two integers and then prints
- The distance (absolute value of the difference)
- The maximum (the larger of the two)
- The minimum (the smaller of the two)

Hint: The max and min functions are defined in the <algorithm> header.

P2.6 Write a program that prompts the user for a measurement in meters and then converts it to miles, feet, and inches.

P2.7 Write a program that prompts the user for a radius and then prints
- The area and circumference of a circle with that radius
- The volume and surface area of a sphere with that radius

P2.8 Write a program that asks the user for the lengths of the sides of a rectangle and then prints
- The area and perimeter of the rectangle
- The length of the diagonal (use the Pythagorean theorem)

P2.9 Improve the program discussed in the How To 2.1 to allow input of quarters in addition to bills.

P2.10 Write a program that helps a person decide whether to buy a hybrid car. Your program's inputs should be:
- The cost of a new car
- The estimated miles driven per year
- The estimated gas price
- The estimated resale value after 5 years

Compute the total cost of owning the car for 5 years. (For simplicity, we will not take the cost of financing into account.) Obtain realistic prices for a new and used hybrid and a comparable car from the Web. Run your program twice, using today's gas price and 15,000 miles per year. Include pseudo-code and the program runs with your assignment.

P2.11 The following pseudocode describes how a bookstore computes the price of an order from the total price and the number of the books that were ordered.

> Read the total book price and the number of books.
> Compute the tax (7.5% of the total book price).
> Compute the shipping charge ($2 per book).
> The price of the order is the sum of the total book price, the tax, and the shipping charge.
> Print the price of the order.

Translate this pseudocode into a C++ program.

P2.12 The following pseudocode describes how to turn a string containing a ten-digit phone number (such as "4155551212") into a more readable string with parentheses and dashes, like this: "(415) 555-1212".

> Take the substring consisting of the first three characters and surround it with "(" and ")". This is the area code.
> Concatenate the area code, the substring consisting of the next three characters, a hyphen, and the substring consisting of the last four characters. This is the formatted number.

Translate this pseudocode into a C++ program that reads a telephone number into a string variable, computes the formatted number, and prints it.

P2.13 The following pseudocode describes how to extract the dollars and cents from a price given as a floating-point value. For example, a price 2.95 yields values 2 and 95 for the dollars and cents.

> Assign the price to an integer variable dollars.
> Multiply the difference price - dollars by 100 and add 0.5.
> Assign the result to an integer variable cents.

Translate this pseudocode into a C++ program. Read a price and print the dollars and cents. Test your program with inputs 2.95 and 4.35.

P2.14 *Giving change.* Implement a program that directs a cashier how to give change. The program has two inputs: the amount due and the amount received from the customer. Display the dollars, quarters, dimes, nickels, and pennies that the customer should receive in return.

P2.15 Write a program that asks the user to input
- The number of gallons of gas in the tank
- The fuel efficiency in miles per gallon
- The price of gas per gallon

Then print the cost per 100 miles and how far the car can go with the gas in the tank.

P2.16 *File names and extensions.* Write a program that prompts the user for the drive letter (C), the path (\Windows\System), the file name (Readme), and the extension (txt). Then print the complete file name C:\Windows\System\Readme.txt. (If you use UNIX or a Macintosh, skip the drive name and use / instead of \ to separate directories.)

P2.17 Write a program that reads a number between 1,000 and 999,999 from the user and prints it *with a comma separating the thousands*. Here is a sample dialog; the user input is in color:

```
Please enter an integer between 1000 and 999999: 23456
23,456
```

P2.18 Write a program that reads a number between 1,000 and 999,999 from the user, where the user enters a comma in the input. Then print the number without a comma. Here is a sample dialog; the user input is in color:

```
Please enter an integer between 1,000 and 999,999: 23,456
23456
```

Hint: Read the input as a string. Measure the length of the string. Suppose it contains n characters. Then extract substrings consisting of the first $n - 4$ characters and the last three characters.

P2.19 *Printing a grid.* Write a program that prints the following grid to play tic-tac-toe.

```
+--+--+--+
|  |  |  |
+--+--+--+
|  |  |  |
+--+--+--+
|  |  |  |
+--+--+--+
```

Of course, you could simply write seven statements of the form

```
cout << "+--+--+--+";
```

You should do it the smart way, though. Define string variables to hold two kinds of patterns: a comb-shaped pattern

```
+--+--+--+
|  |  |  |
```

and the bottom line. Print the comb three times and the bottom line once.

P2.20 Write a program that reads an integer and breaks it into a sequence of individual digits. For example, the input 16384 is displayed as

```
1 6 3 8 4
```

You may assume that the input has no more than five digits and is not negative.

P2.21 Write a program that reads two times in military format (0900, 1730) and prints the number of hours and minutes between the two times. Here is a sample run. User input is in color.

```
Please enter the first time: 0900
Please enter the second time: 1730
8 hours 30 minutes
```

Extra credit if you can deal with the case where the first time is later than the second:

```
Please enter the first time: 1730
Please enter the second time: 0900
15 hours 30 minutes
```

P2.22 *Writing large letters.* A large letter H can be produced like this:

```
*   *
*   *
*****
*   *
*   *
```

It can be defined as a string constant like this:

```
const string LETTER_H =
   "*   *\n*   *\n*****\n*   *\n*   *\n";
```

(The \n character is explained in Special Topic 1.1.) Do the same for the letters E, L, and O. Then write the message

```
H
E
L
L
O
```

in large letters.

P2.23 Write a program that transforms numbers 1, 2, 3, ..., 12 into the corresponding month names January, February, March, ..., December. *Hint:* Make a very long string "January February March ...", in which you add spaces such that each month name has *the same length*. Then use substr to extract the month you want.

Engineering P2.24 Consider the following circuit.

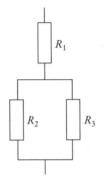

Write a program that reads the resistances of the three resistors and computes the total resistance, using Ohm's law.

Engineering P2.25 The dew point temperature T_d can be calculated (approximately) from the relative humidity RH and the actual temperature T by

$$T_d = \frac{b \cdot f(T, RH)}{a - f(T, RH)}$$

$$f(T, RH) = \frac{a \cdot T}{b + T} + \ln(RH)$$

where $a = 17.27$ and $b = 237.7°$ C.

Write a program that reads the relative humidity (between 0 and 1) and the temperature (in degrees C) and prints the dew point value. Use the C++ function log to compute the natural logarithm.

Engineering P2.26 The pipe clip temperature sensors shown here are robust sensors that can be clipped directly onto copper pipes to measure the temperature of the liquids in the pipes.

Each sensor contains a device called a *thermistor*. Thermistors are semiconductor devices that exhibit a temperature-dependent resistance described by:

$$R = R_0 \, e^{\beta\left(\frac{1}{T} - \frac{1}{T_0}\right)}$$

where R is the resistance (in Ω) at the temperature T (in $^\circ$K), and R_0 is the resistance (in Ω) at the temperature T_0 (in $^\circ$K). β is a constant that depends on the material used to make the thermistor. Thermistors are specified by providing values for R_0, T_0, and β.

The thermistors used to make the pipe clip temperature sensors have $R_0 = 1075$ Ω at $T_0 = 85$ $^\circ$C, and $\beta = 3969$ $^\circ$K. (Notice that β has units of $^\circ$K. Recall that the temperature in $^\circ$K is obtained by adding 273 to the temperature in $^\circ$C.) The liquid temperature, in $^\circ$C, is determined from the resistance R, in Ω, using

$$T = \frac{\beta T_0}{T_0 \ln\left(\dfrac{R}{R_0}\right) + \beta} - 273$$

Write a C++ program that prompts the user for the thermistor resistance R and prints a message giving the liquid temperature in $^\circ$C.

Engineering P2.27 The circuit shown below illustrates some important aspects of the connection between a power company and one of its customers. The customer is represented by three parameters, V_t, P, and pf. V_t is the voltage accessed by plugging into a wall outlet. Customers depend on having a dependable value of V_t in order for their appliances to work properly. Accordingly, the power company regulates the value of V_t carefully. P describes the amount of power used by the customer and is the primary factor

in determining the customer's electric bill. The power factor, pf, is less familiar. (The power factor is calculated as the cosine of an angle so that its value will always be between zero and one.) In this problem you will be asked to write a C++ program to investigate the significance of the power factor.

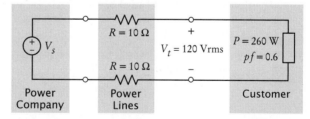

In the figure, the power lines are represented, somewhat simplistically, as resistances in Ohms. The power company is represented as an AC voltage source. The source voltage, V_s, required to provide the customer with power P at voltage V_t can be determined using the formula

$$V_s = \sqrt{\left(V_t + \frac{2RP}{V_t}\right)^2 + \left(\frac{2RP}{pf V_t}\right)^2 \left(1 - pf^2\right)}$$

(V_s has units of Vrms.) This formula indicates that the value of V_s depends on the value of pf. Write a C++ program that prompts the user for a power factor value and then prints a message giving the corresponding value of V_s, using the values for P, R, and V_t shown in the figure above.

Engineering P2.28   Consider the following tuning circuit connected to an antenna, where C is a variable capacitor whose capacitance ranges from C_{min} to C_{max}.

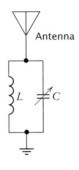

The tuning circuit selects the frequency $f = \dfrac{2\pi}{\sqrt{LC}}$. To design this circuit for a given frequency, take $C = \sqrt{C_{min} C_{max}}$ and calculate the required inductance L from f and C. Now the circuit can be tuned to any frequency in the range $f_{min} = \dfrac{2\pi}{\sqrt{LC_{max}}}$ to $f_{max} = \dfrac{2\pi}{\sqrt{LC_{min}}}$.

Write a C++ program to design a tuning circuit for a given frequency, using a variable capacitor with given values for C_{min} and C_{max}. (A typical input is $f = 16.7$ MHz, $C_{min} = 14$ pF, and $C_{max} = 365$ pF.) The program should read in f (in Hz), C_{min} and C_{max} (in F), and print the required inductance value and the range of frequencies to which the circuit can be tuned by varying the capacitance.

Engineering P2.29   According to the Coulomb force law, the electric force between two charged particles of charge Q_1 and Q_2 Coulombs, that are a distance r meters apart, is

$$F = \frac{Q_1 Q_2}{4\pi \varepsilon r^2}$$ Newtons, where $\varepsilon = 8.854 \times 10^{-12}$ Farads/meter. Write a program

that calculates the force on a pair of charged particles, based on the user input of Q_1 Coulombs, Q_2 Coulombs, and r meters, and then computes and displays the electric force.

ANSWERS TO SELF-CHECK QUESTIONS

1. One possible answer is

   ```
   int bottles_per_case = 8;
   ```

   You may choose a different variable name or a different initialization value, but your variable should have type `int`.

2. There are three errors:
   - You cannot have spaces in variable names.
   - The variable type should be `double` because it holds a fractional value.
   - There is a semicolon missing at the end of the statement.

3. ```
   double unit_price = 1.95;
   int quantity = 2;
   ```

4. ```
   cout << "Total price: " << unit_price * quantity << endl;
   ```

5. Change the definition of `cans_per_pack` to

   ```
   int cans_per_pack = 4;
   ```

6. You need to use a `*/` delimiter to close a comment that begins with a `/*`:

   ```
   double can_volume = 0.355; /* Liters in a 12-ounce can */
   ```

7. The program would compile, and it would display the same result. However, a person reading the program might find it confusing that fractional cans are being considered.

8. Its value is modified by the assignment statement.

9. Assignment would occur when one car is replaced by another in the parking space.

10. ```
    double interest = balance * p / 100;
    ```

11. ```
    double side_length = sqrt(area);
    ```

12. ```
    4 * PI * pow(radius, 3) / 3
    ```
    or `(4.0 / 3) * PI * pow(radius, 3)`,
    but not `(4 / 3) * PI * pow(radius, 3)`

13. 172 and 9

14. ```
    int leftover = 12 - amount % 12;
    ```

15. There is no prompt that alerts the program user to enter the quantity.

16. The `unit_price` variable is defined as an `int`. If the user were to enter a price such as 1.95, only the 1 would be placed into the variable.

17. The output is

    ```
    The total volume is20
    ```

    Note that there is no space between the `is` and `20`.

18. ```
    cout << "$" << fixed << setprecision(2) << total_price;
    ```

19. ```
    cout << "Bottles: " << setw(8) << bottles << endl
         << "Cans:    " << setw(8) << cans << endl;
    ```

    Note that the `setw` manipulator appears twice. Also note the added spaces in the string `"Cans:    "`.

20.
```
int pairs = (total_width - tile_width) / (2 * tile_width);
int tiles = 1 + 2 * pairs;
double gap = (total_width - tiles * tile_width) / 2;
```
Be sure that `pairs` is declared as an `int`.

21. Now there are groups of four tiles (gray/white/gray/black) following the initial black tile. Therefore, the algorithm is now

number of groups = integer part of (total width – tile width) / (4 x tile width)
number of tiles = 1 + 4 x number of groups

The formula for the gap is not changed.

22. Clearly, the answer depends only on whether the row and column numbers are even or odd, so let's first take the remainder after dividing by 2. Then we can enumerate all expected answers:

Row % 2	Column % 2	Color
0	0	0
0	1	1
1	0	1
1	1	0

In the first three entries of the table, the color is simply the sum of the remainders. In the fourth entry, the sum would be 2, but we want a zero. We can achieve that by taking another remainder operation:

color = ((row % 2) + (column % 2)) % 2

23. In nine years, the repair costs increased by $1,400. Therefore, the increase per year is $1,400 / 9 \approx $156. The repair cost in year 3 would be $100 + 2 \times $156 = $412. The repair cost in year n is $100 + n \times $156. To avoid accumulation of roundoff errors, it is actually a good idea to use the original expression that yielded $156, that is,

Repair cost in year n = 100 + n x 1400 / 9

24. The pseudocode follows easily from the equations.

bottom volume = π x r_1^2 x h_1
top volume = π x r_2^2 x h_2
middle volume = π x (r_1^2 + r_1 x r_2 + r_2^2) x h_3 / 3
total volume = bottom volume + top volume + middle volume

Measuring a typical wine bottle yields

$r_1 = 3.6, r_2 = 1.2, h_1 = 15, h_2 = 7, h_3 = 6$ (all in centimeters). Therefore,

bottom volume = 610.73

top volume = 31.67

middle volume = 135.72

total volume = 778.12

The actual volume is 750 ml, which is close enough to our computation to give confidence that it is correct.

25. The length is 11. The space counts as a character.

26. `str.substr(7, 4)`

27. `str = str + "ming";`

28. `Hy`

29. `cin >> first_name >> middle_initial >> last_name;`

CHAPTER 3

DECISIONS

To be able to implement decisions using if statements

To learn how to compare integers, floating-point numbers, and strings

To understand the Boolean data type

To develop strategies for validating user input

One of the essential features of computer programs is their ability to make decisions. Like a train that changes tracks depending on how the switches are set, a program can take different actions, depending on inputs and other circumstances.

In this chapter, you will learn how to program simple and complex decisions. You will apply what you learn to the task of checking user input.

3.1 The if Statement

The if statement allows a program to carry out different actions depending on the nature of the data to be processed.

The if statement is used to implement a decision. When a condition is fulfilled, one set of statements is executed. Otherwise, another set of statements is executed (see Syntax 3.1).

Here is an example using the if statement. In many countries, the number 13 is considered unlucky. Rather than offending superstitious tenants, building owners sometimes skip the thirteenth floor; floor 12 is immediately followed by floor 14. Of course, floor 13 is not usually left empty or, as some conspiracy theorists believe, filled with secret offices and research labs. It is simply called floor 14. The computer that controls the building elevators needs to compensate for this foible and adjust all floor numbers above 13.

Let's simulate this process in C++. We will ask the user to type in the desired floor number and then compute the actual floor. When the input is above 13, then we need to decrement the input to obtain the actual floor. For example, if the user provides an input of 20, the program determines the actual floor as 19. Otherwise, we simply use the supplied floor number.

This elevator panel "skips" the thirteenth floor. The floor is not actually missing—the computer that controls the elevator adjusts the floor numbers above 13.

```cpp
int actual_floor;

if (floor > 13)
{
   actual_floor = floor - 1;
}
else
{
   actual_floor = floor;
}
```

The flowchart in Figure 1 shows the branching behavior.

In our example, each branch of the if statement contains a single statement. You can include as many statements in each branch as you like. Sometimes, it happens that

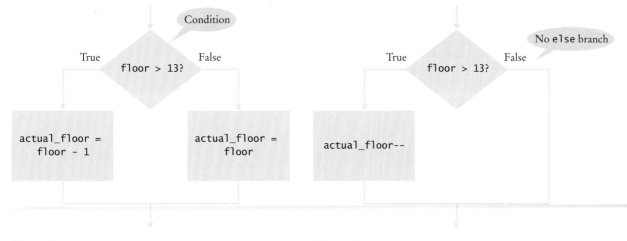

True   floor > 13?   False
Condition

actual_floor = floor - 1

actual_floor = floor

Figure 1
Flowchart for if Statement

True   floor > 13?   False
No else branch

actual_floor--

Figure 2
Flowchart for if Statement with No else Branch

there is nothing to do in the else branch of the statement. In that case, you can omit it entirely, such as in this example:

```
int actual_floor = floor;

if (floor > 13)
{
    actual_floor--;
} // No else needed
```

See Figure 2 for the flowchart.

The following program puts the if statement to work. This program asks for the desired floor and then prints out the actual floor.

An if statement is like a fork in the road. Depending upon a decision, different parts of the program are executed.

ch03/elevator1.cpp

```cpp
1   #include <iostream>
2
3   using namespace std;
4
5   int main()
6   {
7      int floor;
8      cout << "Floor: ";
9      cin >> floor;
10     int actual_floor;
11     if (floor > 13)
12     {
13        actual_floor = floor - 1;
14     }
15     else
16     {
17        actual_floor = floor;
18     }
19
20     cout << "The elevator will travel to the actual floor "
21        << actual_floor << endl;
22
23     return 0;
24  }
```

Program Run

```
Floor: 20
The elevator will travel to the actual floor 19
```

Syntax 3.1   if Statement

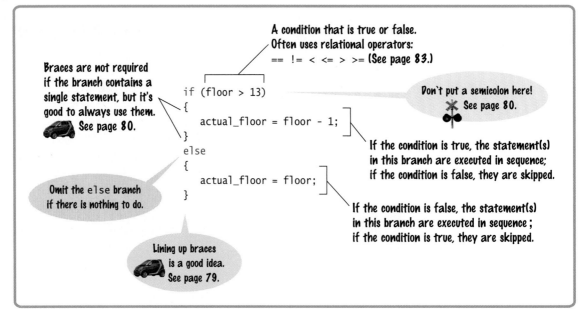

Braces are not required if the branch contains a single statement, but it's good to always use them. See page 80.

A condition that is true or false. Often uses relational operators:
== != < <= > >= (See page 83.)

```
if (floor > 13)
{
    actual_floor = floor - 1;
}
else
{
    actual_floor = floor;
}
```

Don't put a semicolon here! See page 80.

If the condition is true, the statement(s) in this branch are executed in sequence; if the condition is false, they are skipped.

Omit the else branch if there is nothing to do.

If the condition is false, the statement(s) in this branch are executed in sequence; if the condition is true, they are skipped.

Lining up braces is a good idea. See page 79.

SELF CHECK

1. In some Asian countries, the number 14 is considered unlucky. Some building owners play it safe and skip *both* the thirteenth and the fourteenth floor. How would you modify the sample program to handle such a building?

2. Consider the following if statement to compute a discounted price:

```
if (original_price > 100)
{
    discounted_price = original_price - 20;
}
else
{
    discounted_price = original_price - 10;
}
```

What is the discounted price if the original price is 95? 100? 105?

3. Compare this if statement with the one in Self Check 2:

```
if (original_price < 100)
{
    discounted_price = original_price - 10;
}
else
{
    discounted_price = original_price - 20;
}
```

Do the two statements always compute the same value? If not, when do the values differ?

4. Consider the following statements to compute a discounted price:

```
discounted_price = original_price;
if (original_price > 100)
{
    discounted_price = original_price - 10;
}
```

What is the discounted price if the original price is 95? 100? 105?

5. The variables fuel_amount and fuel_capacity hold the actual amount of fuel and the size of the fuel tank of a vehicle. If less than 10 percent is remaining in the tank, a status light should show a red color; otherwise it shows a green color. Simulate this process by printing out either "red" or "green".

Practice It Now you can try these exercises at the end of the chapter: R3.3, R3.4, P3.16.

Programming Tip 3.1

Brace Layout

Programmers vary in how they align braces in their code. In this book, we follow the simple rule of making { and } line up.

```
if (floor > 13)
{
    floor--;
}
```

This style makes it easy to spot matching braces.

Properly lining up your code makes your programs easier to read.

Some programmers put the opening brace on the same line as the `if`:

```
if (floor > 13) {
    floor--;
}
```

This style makes it harder to match the braces, but it saves a line of code, allowing you to view more code on the screen without scrolling. There are passionate advocates of both styles.

It is important that you pick a layout style and stick with it consistently within a given programming project. Which style you choose may depend on your personal preference or a coding style guide that you need to follow.

Programming Tip 3.2

Always Use Braces

When the body of an `if` statement consists of a single statement, you need not use braces. For example, the following is legal:

```
if (floor > 13)
    floor--;
```

However, it is a good idea to always include the braces:

```
if (floor > 13)
{
    floor--;
}
```

The braces makes your code easier to read, and you are less likely to make errors such as the one described in Common Error 3.1.

Common Error 3.1

A Semicolon After the `if` Condition

The following code fragment has an unfortunate error:

```
if (floor > 13) ; // ERROR
{
    floor--;
}
```

There should be no semicolon after the `if` condition. The compiler interprets this statement as follows: If `floor` is greater than 13, execute the statement that is denoted by a single semicolon, that is, the do-nothing statement. The statement enclosed in braces is no longer a part of the `if` statement. It is always executed. Even if the value of `floor` is not above 13, it is decremented.

Placing a semicolon after the `else` reserved word is also wrong:

```
if (floor > 13)
{
    actual_floor = floor - 1;
}
else ;
{
    actual_floor = floor;
}
```

In this case, the do-nothing statement is executed if `floor > 13` is not fulfilled. This is the end of the `if` statement. The next statement, enclosed in braces, is executed in both cases; that is, `actual_floor` is always set to `floor`.

Tabs

Block-structured code has the property that nested statements are indented by one or more levels:

```cpp
int main()
{
|  int floor;
|  ...
|  if (floor > 13)
|  {
|  |  floor--;
|  }  |
|  ...
|  return 0;
}  |  |
0  1  2     Indentation level
```

How do you move the cursor from the leftmost column to the appropriate indentation level? A perfectly reasonable strategy is to hit the space bar a sufficient number of times. However, many programmers use the Tab key instead. A tab moves the cursor to the next indentation level.

You use the Tab key to move the cursor to the next indentation level.

While the Tab *key* is nice, some editors use *tab characters* for alignment, which is not so nice. Tab characters can lead to problems when you send your file to another person or a printer. There is no universal agreement on the width of a tab character, and some software will ignore tabs altogether. It is therefore best to save your files with spaces instead of tabs. Most editors have a setting to automatically convert all tabs to spaces. Look at the documentation of your development environment to find out how to activate this useful setting.

The Selection Operator

C++ has a *selection operator* of the form

> *condition* ? *value*$_1$: *value*$_2$

The value of that expression is either *value*$_1$ if the test passes or *value*$_2$ if it fails. For example, we can compute the actual floor number as

```cpp
actual_floor = floor > 13 ? floor - 1 : floor;
```

which is equivalent to

```cpp
if (floor > 13)
{
   actual_floor =  floor - 1;
}
else
{
   actual_floor = floor;
}
```

You can use the selection operator anywhere that a value is expected, for example:

```cpp
cout << "Actual floor: " << (floor > 13 ? floor - 1 : floor);
```

We don't use the selection operator in this book, but it is a convenient construct that you will find in many C++ programs.

Avoid Duplication in Branches

Look to see whether you *duplicate code* in each branch. If so, move it out of the if statement. Here is an example of such duplication:

```
if (floor > 13)
{
    actual_floor = floor - 1;
    cout << "Actual floor: " << actual_floor << endl;
}
else
{
    actual_floor = floor;
    cout << "Actual floor: " << actual_floor << endl;
}
```

The output statement is exactly the same in both branches. This is not an error—the program will run correctly. However, you can simplify the program by moving the duplicated statement, like this:

```
if (floor > 13)
{
    actual_floor = floor - 1;
}
else
{
    actual_floor = floor;
}
cout << "Actual floor: " << actual_floor << endl;
```

Removing duplication is particularly important when programs are maintained for a long time. When there are two sets of statements with the same effect, it can easily happen that a programmer modifies one set but not the other.

3.2 Comparing Numbers and Strings

Relational operators
(< <= > >= == !=)
are used to compare
numbers and strings.

Every if statement contains a condition. In many cases, the condition involves comparing two values. For example, in the previous examples we tested floor > 13. The comparison > is called a **relational operator**. C++ has six relational operators (see Table 1).

As you can see, only two C++ relational operators (> and <) look as you would expect from the mathematical notation. Computer keyboards do not have keys for ≥, ≤, or ≠, but the >=, <=, and != operators are easy to remember because they look similar. The == operator is initially confusing to most newcomers to C++. In C++, = already has a meaning, namely assignment.

In C++, you use a relational operator to check whether one value is greater than another.

Table 1 Relational Operators		
C++	Math Notation	Description
>	>	Greater than
>=	≥	Greater than or equal
<	<	Less than
<=	≤	Less than or equal
==	=	Equal
!=	≠	Not equal

The == operator denotes equality testing:

```
floor = 13; // Assign 13 to floor
if (floor == 13)  // Test whether floor equals 13
```

You must remember to use == inside tests and to use = outside tests. (See Common Error 3.2 on page 85 for more information.)

You can compare strings as well:

```
if (input == "Quit") ...
```

Use != to check whether two strings are different. In C++, letter case matters. For example, "Quit" and "quit" are not the same string.

Syntax 3.2 Comparisons

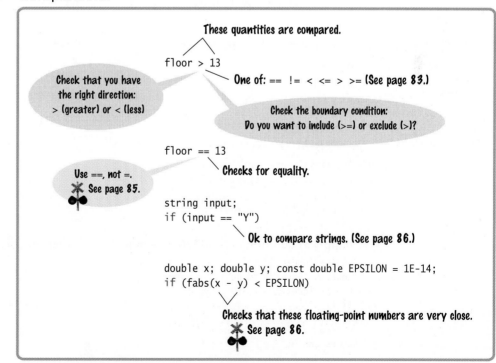

```
floor > 13
```
These quantities are compared.

Check that you have the right direction: > (greater) or < (less)

One of: == != < <= > >= (See page 83.)

Check the boundary condition: Do you want to include (>=) or exclude (>)?

```
floor == 13
```
Checks for equality.

Use ==, not =.
See page 85.

```
string input;
if (input == "Y")
```
Ok to compare strings. (See page 86.)

```
double x; double y; const double EPSILON = 1E-14;
if (fabs(x - y) < EPSILON)
```
Checks that these floating-point numbers are very close.
See page 86.

| Table 2 Relational Operator Examples |||
Expression	Value	Comment
3 <= 4	true	3 is less than 4; <= tests for "less than or equal".
🚫 3 =< 4	**Error**	The "less than or equal" operator is <=, not =<. The "less than" symbol comes first.
3 > 4	false	> is the opposite of <=.
4 < 4	false	The left-hand side must be strictly smaller than the right-hand side.
4 <= 4	true	Both sides are equal; <= tests for "less than or equal".
3 == 5 - 2	true	== tests for equality.
3 != 5 - 1	true	!= tests for inequality. It is true that 3 is not 5 – 1.
🚫 3 = 6 / 2	**Error**	Use == to test for equality.
1.0 / 3.0 == 0.333333333	false	Although the values are very close to one another, they are not exactly equal. See Common Error 3.3 on page 86.
🚫 "10" > 5	**Error**	You cannot compare a string to a number.

Table 2 summarizes how to use relational operators in C++.

SELF CHECK

6. Which of the following conditions are true, provided a is 3 and b is 4?

   a. a + 1 <= b

   b. a + 1 >= b

   c. a + 1 != b

7. Give the opposite of the condition

```
floor > 13
```

8. What is the error in this statement?

```
if (score_a = score_b)
{
    cout << "Tie" << endl;
}
```

9. Supply a condition in this if statement to test whether the user entered a Y:

```
string input;
cout << "Enter Y to quit." << endl;
cin >> input;
if (...)
{
    cout << "Goodbye." << endl;
    return 0;
}
```

10. How do you test that a string str is not the empty string?

Practice It   Now you can try these exercises at the end of the chapter: R3.2, R3.5, P3.14.

Confusing = and ==

The rule for the correct usage of = and == is very simple: In tests, always use == and never use =. If it is so simple, why can't the compiler be helpful and flag any errors?

Actually, the C++ language allows the use of = inside tests. To understand this, we have to go back in time. The creators of C, the predecessor to C++, were very frugal. They did not want to have special values true and false. Instead, they allowed any numeric value inside a condition, with the convention that 0 denotes false and any non-0 value denotes true. Furthermore, in C and C++ assignments have values. For example, the value of the assignment expression floor = 13 is 13.

These two features—namely that numbers can be used as truth values and that assignments are expressions with values—conspire to make a horrible pitfall. The test

```
if (floor = 13) // ERROR
```

is legal C++, but it does not test whether floor and 13 are equal. Instead, the code sets floor to 13, and since that value is not zero, the condition of the if statement is always fulfilled.

Fortunately, most compilers issue a warning when they encounter such a statement. You should take such warnings seriously. (See Programming Tip 3.5 for more advice about compiler warnings.)

Some shell-shocked programmers are so nervous about using = that they use == even when they want to make an assignment:

```
floor == floor - 1; // ERROR
```

This statement tests whether floor equals floor - 1. It doesn't do anything with the outcome of the test, but that is not an error. Some compilers will warn that "the code has no effect", but others will quietly accept the code.

Compile with Zero Warnings

There are two kinds of messages that the compiler gives you: *errors* and *warnings*. Error messages are fatal; the compiler will not translate a program with one or more errors. Warning messages are advisory; the compiler will translate the program, but there is a good chance that the program will not do what you expect it to do.

It is a good idea to learn how to activate warnings with your compiler, and to write code that emits no warnings at all. For example, consider the test

```
if (floor = 13)
```

One C++ compiler emits a curious warning message: "Suggest parentheses around assignment used as truth value". Sadly, the message is misleading because it was not written for students. Nevertheless, such a warning gives you another chance to look at the offending statement and fix it, in this case, by replacing the = with an ==.

In order to make warnings more visible, many compilers require you to take some special action. This might involve clicking a checkbox in an integrated environment or supplying a special option on the command line. Ask your instructor or lab assistant how to turn on warnings for your compiler.

Exact Comparison of Floating-Point Numbers

Floating-point numbers have only a limited precision, and calculations can introduce roundoff errors. You must take these inevitable roundoffs into account when comparing floating-point numbers. For example, the following code multiplies the square root of 2 by itself. Ideally, we expect to get the answer 2:

```
double r = sqrt(2.0);
if (r * r == 2)
{
    cout << "sqrt(2) squared is 2" << endl;
}
else
{
    cout << "sqrt(2) squared is not 2 but "
        << setprecision(18) << r * r << endl;
}
```

Take limited precision into account when comparing floating-point numbers.

This program displays

```
sqrt(2) squared is not 2 but 2.00000000000000044
```

It does not make sense in most circumstances to compare floating-point numbers exactly. Instead, we should test whether they are *close enough*. That is, the magnitude of their difference should be less than some threshold. Mathematically, we would write that x and y are close enough if

$$\left| x - y \right| < \varepsilon$$

for a very small number, ε. ε is the Greek letter epsilon, a letter used to denote a very small quantity. It is common to set ε to 10^{-14} when comparing double numbers:

```
const double EPSILON = 1E-14;
double r = sqrt(2.0);
if (fabs(r * r - 2) < EPSILON)
{
    cout << "sqrt(2) squared is approximately 2";
}
```

Include the <cmath> header to use the fabs function.

Lexicographic Ordering of Strings

If you compare strings using < <= > >=, they are compared in "lexicographic" order. This ordering is very similar to the way in which words are sorted in a dictionary.

For example, consider this code fragment.

```
string name = "Tom";
if (name < "Dick") ...
```

The condition is not fulfilled, because in the dictionary Dick comes before Tom. There are a few differences between the ordering in a dictionary and in C++. In C++:

- All uppercase letters come before the lowercase letters. For example, "Z" comes before "a".

To see which of two terms comes first in the dictionary, consider the first letter in which they differ.

- The space character comes before all printable characters.
- Numbers come before letters.
- For the ordering of punctuation marks, see Appendix D.

When comparing two strings, you compare the first letters of each word, then the second letters, and so on, until one of the strings ends or you find the first letter pair that doesn't match.

If one of the strings ends, the longer string is considered the "larger" one. For example, compare "car" with "cart". The first three letters match, and we reach the end of the first string. Therefore "car" comes before "cart" in lexicographic ordering.

When you reach a mismatch, the string containing the "larger" character is considered "larger". For example, let's compare "cat" with "cart". The first two letters match. Since t comes after r, the string "cat" comes after "cart" in the lexicographic ordering.

Lexicographic order is used to compare strings.

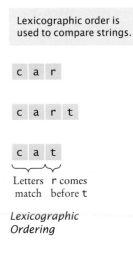

| c | a | r |

| c | a | r | t |

| c | a | t |

Letters   r comes
match   before t

Lexicographic Ordering

HOW TO 3.1   Implementing an if Statement

This How To walks you through the process of implementing an if statement. We will illustrate the steps with the following example problem:

The university bookstore has a Kilobyte Day sale every October 24, giving an 8 percent discount on all computer accessory purchases if the price is less than $128, and a 16 percent discount if the price is at least $128. Write a program that asks the cashier for the original price and then prints the discounted price.

Step 1   Decide upon the branching condition.

In our sample problem, the obvious choice for the condition is:

original price < 128?

That is just fine, and we will use that condition in our solution.

But you could equally well come up with a correct solution if you choose the opposite condition: Is the original price at least (≥) $128? You might choose this condition if you put yourself into the position of a shopper who wants to know when the bigger discount applies.

Sales discounts are often higher for expensive products. Use the if statement to implement such a decision.

Step 2   Give pseudocode for the work that needs to be done when the condition is true.

In this step, you list the action or actions that are taken in the "positive" branch. The details depend on your problem. You may want to print a message, compute values, or even exit the program.

In our example, we need to apply an 8 percent discount:

discounted price = 0.92 x original price

Step 3   Give pseudocode for the work (if any) that needs to be done when the condition is *not* true.

What do you want to do in the case that the condition of Step 1 is not fulfilled? Sometimes, you want to do nothing at all. In that case, use an if statement without an else branch.

In our example, the condition tested whether the price was less than $128. If that condition is *not* true, the price is at least $128, so the higher discount of 16 percent applies to the sale:

discounted price = 0.84 x original price

Step 4   Double-check relational operators.

First, be sure that the test goes in the right *direction*. It is a common error to confuse > and <. Next, consider whether you should use the < operator or its close cousin, the <= operator.

What should happen if the original price is exactly $128? Reading the problem carefully, we find that the lower discount applies if the original price is *less than* $128, and the higher discount applies when it is *at least* $128. A price of $128 should therefore *not* fulfill our condition, and we must use <, not <=.

Step 5   Remove duplication.

Check which actions are common to both branches, and move them outside. (See Programming Tip 3.4 on page 82.)

In our example, we have two statements of the form

discounted price = ___ x original price

They only differ in the discount rate. It is best to just set the rate in the branches, and to do the computation afterwards:

```
If original price < 128
    discount rate = 0.92
Else
    discount rate = 0.84
discounted price = discount rate x original price
```

Step 6   Test both branches.

Formulate two test cases, one that fulfills the condition of the if statement, and one that does not. Ask yourself what should happen in each case. Then follow the pseudocode and act each of them out.

In our example, let us consider two scenarios for the original price: $100 and $200. We expect that the first price is discounted by $8, the second by $32.

When the original price is 100, then the condition 100 < 128 is true, and we get

```
discount rate = 0.92
discounted price = 0.92 x 100 = 92
```

When the original price is 200, then the condition 200 < 128 is false, and

```
discount rate = 0.84
discounted price = 0.84 x 200 = 168
```

In both cases, we get the expected answer.

Step 7   Assemble the if statement in C++.

Type the skeleton

```
if ()
{
}
else
{
}
```

and fill it in, as shown in Syntax 3.1 on page 78. Omit the else branch if it is not needed. In our example, the completed statement is

```
if (original_price < 128)
{
   discount_rate = 0.92;
}
else
{
   discount_rate = 0.84;
}

discounted_price = discount_rate * original_price;
```

WORKED EXAMPLE 3.1   **Extracting the Middle**

This Worked Example shows how to extract the middle character from a string, or the two middle characters if the length of the string is even.

c	r	a	t	e
0	1	2	3	4

Random Fact 3.1 The Denver Airport Luggage Handling System

Making decisions is an essential part of any computer program. Nowhere is this more obvious than in a computer system that helps sort luggage at an airport. After scanning the luggage identification codes, the system sorts the items and routes them to different conveyor belts. Human operators then place the items onto trucks. When the city of Denver built a huge airport to replace an outdated and congested facility, the luggage system contractor went a step further. The new system was designed to replace the human operators with robotic carts. Unfortunately, the system plainly did not work. It was plagued by mechanical problems, such as luggage falling onto the tracks and jamming carts. Equally frustrating were the software glitches. Carts would uselessly accumulate at some locations when they were needed elsewhere.

The airport had been scheduled to open in 1993, but without a functioning luggage system, the opening was delayed for over a year while the contractor tried to fix the problems. The contractor never succeeded, and ultimately a manual system was installed. The delay cost the city and airlines close to a billion dollars, and the contractor, once the leading luggage systems vendor in the United States, went bankrupt.

Clearly, it is very risky to build a large system based on a technology that has never been tried on a smaller scale. As robots and the software that controls them get better over time, they will take on a larger share of luggage handling in the future. But it is likely that this will happen in an incremental fashion.

The Denver airport originally had a fully automatic system for moving luggage, replacing human operators with robotic carts. Unfortunately, the system never worked and was dismantled before the airport was opened.

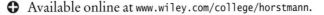

3.3 Multiple Alternatives

Multiple alternatives are required for decisions that have more than two cases.

In Section 3.1, you saw how to program a two-way branch with an `if` statement. In many situations, there are more than two cases. In this section, you will see how to implement a decision with multiple alternatives. For example, consider a program that displays the effect of an earthquake, as measured by the Richter scale (see Table 3).

The 1989 Loma Prieta earthquake that damaged the Bay Bridge in San Francisco and destroyed many buildings measured 7.1 on the Richter scale.

Table 3	Richter Scale
Value	Effect
8	Most structures fall
7	Many buildings destroyed
6	Many buildings considerably damaged, some collapse
4.5	Damage to poorly constructed buildings

The Richter scale is a measurement of the strength of an earthquake. Every step in the scale, for example from 6.0 to 7.0, signifies a tenfold increase in the strength of the quake.

In this case, there are five branches: one each for the four descriptions of damage, and one for no destruction. Figure 3 shows the flowchart for this multiple-branch statement.

You use multiple `if` statements to implement multiple alternatives, like this:

```cpp
if (richter >= 8.0)
{
   cout << "Most structures fall";
}
else if (richter >= 7.0)
{
   cout << "Many buildings destroyed";
}
else if (richter >= 6.0)
{
   cout << "Many buildings considerably damaged, some collapse";
}
else if (richter >= 4.5)
{
   cout << "Damage to poorly constructed buildings";
}
else
{
   cout << "No destruction of buildings";
}
```

As soon as one of the four tests succeeds, the effect is displayed, and no further tests are attempted. If none of the four cases applies, the final `else` clause applies, and a default message is printed. (See the `ch03/richter.cpp` file for the full program.)

Figure 3
Multiple Alternatives

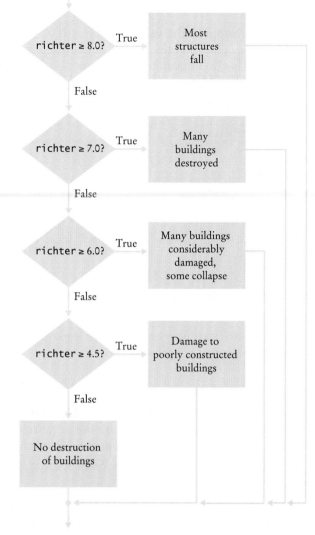

Here you must sort the conditions and test against the largest cutoff first. Suppose we reverse the order of tests:

```
if (richter >= 4.5) // Tests in wrong order
{
   cout << "Damage to poorly constructed buildings";
}
else if (richter >= 6.0)
{
   cout << "Many buildings considerably damaged, some collapse";
}
else if (richter >= 7.0)
{
   cout << "Many buildings destroyed";
}
else if (richter >= 8.0)
{
```

```
        cout << "Most structures fall";
    }
```

When using multiple if statements, pay attention to the order of the conditions.

This does not work. Suppose the value of `richter` is 7.1. That value is at least 4.5, matching the first case. The other tests will never be attempted.

In this example, it is also important that we use a sequence of `else if` clauses, not just multiple independent `if` statements. Consider this sequence of independent tests:

```
if (richter >= 8.0) // Didn't use else
{
    cout << "Most structures fall";
}
if (richter >= 7.0)
{
    cout << "Many buildings destroyed";
}
if (richter >= 6.0)
{
    cout << "Many buildings considerably damaged, some collapse";
}
if (richter >= 4.5)
{
    cout << "Damage to poorly constructed buildings";
}
```

Now the alternatives are no longer exclusive. If `richter` is 7.1, then the last *three* tests all match, and three messages are printed.

SELF CHECK

11. In a game program, the scores of players A and B are stored in variables `score_a` and `score_b`. Assuming that the player with the larger score wins, write a sequence of conditional statements that prints out `"A won"`, `"B won"`, or `"Game tied"`.

12. Write a conditional statement with three branches that sets s to 1 if x is positive, to −1 if x is negative, and to 0 if x is zero.

13. How could you achieve the task of Self Check 12 with only two branches?

14. Beginners sometimes write statements such as the following:
```
if (price > 100)
{
    discounted_price = price - 20;
}
else if (price <= 100)
{
    discounted_price = price - 10;
}
```
Explain how this code can be improved.

15. Suppose the user enters -1 into the `richter.cpp` program. What is printed?

16. Suppose we want to have the `richter.cpp` program check whether the user entered a negative number. What branch would you add to the `if` statement, and where?

Practice It   Now you can try these exercises at the end of the chapter: R3.20, P3.1, P3.9, P3.10.

The switch Statement

A sequence of if statements that compares a *single integer value* against several *constant* alternatives can be implemented as a switch statement. For example,

```
int digit;
...
switch (digit)
{
   case 1: digit_name = "one"; break;
   case 2: digit_name = "two"; break;
   case 3: digit_name = "three"; break;
   case 4: digit_name = "four"; break;
   case 5: digit_name = "five"; break;
   case 6: digit_name = "six"; break;
   case 7: digit_name = "seven"; break;
   case 8: digit_name = "eight"; break;
   case 9: digit_name = "nine"; break;
   default: digit_name = ""; break;
}
```

This is a shortcut for

```
int digit;
if (digit == 1) { digit_name = "one"; }
else if (digit == 2) { digit_name = "two"; }
else if (digit == 3) { digit_name = "three"; }
else if (digit == 4) { digit_name = "four"; }
else if (digit == 5) { digit_name = "five"; }
else if (digit == 6) { digit_name = "six"; }
else if (digit == 7) { digit_name = "seven"; }
else if (digit == 8) { digit_name = "eight"; }
else if (digit == 9) { digit_name = "nine"; }
else { digit_name = ""; }
```

Well, it isn't much of a shortcut, but it has one advantage—it is obvious that all branches test the *same* value, namely digit.

It is possible to have multiple case clauses for a branch, such as

```
case 1: case 3: case 5: case 7: case 9:
   odd = true; break;
```

The default branch is chosen if none of the case clauses match.

The switch statement lets you choose from a fixed set of alternatives.

Every branch of the switch must be terminated by a break instruction. If the break is missing, execution *falls through* to the next branch, and so on, until finally a break or the end of the switch is reached. In practice, this fall-through behavior is rarely useful, but it is a common cause of errors. If you accidentally forget the break statement, your program compiles but executes unwanted code. Many programmers consider the switch statement somewhat dangerous and prefer the if statement.

We leave it to you to use the switch statement for your own code or not. At any rate, you need to have a reading knowledge of switch in case you find it in other programmers' code.

3.4 Nested Branches

When a decision statement is contained inside the branch of another decision statement, the statements are *nested*.

It is often necessary to include an if statement inside another. Such an arrangement is called a *nested* set of statements. Here is a typical example.

In the United States, different tax rates are used depending on the taxpayer's marital status. There are different tax schedules for single and for married taxpayers. Married taxpayers add their income together and pay taxes on the total. Table 4 gives the tax rate computations, using a simplification of the schedules in effect for the 2008 tax year. A different tax rate applies to each "bracket". In this schedule, the income at the first bracket is taxed at 10 percent, and the income at the second bracket is taxed at 25 percent. The income limits for each bracket depend on the marital status.

Nested decisions are required for problems that have two levels of decision making.

Now compute the taxes due, given a filing status and an income figure. The key point is that there are two *levels* of decision making. First, you must branch on the marital status. Then, for each filing status, you must have another branch on income level.

Table 4 Federal Tax Rate Schedule		
If your status is Single and if the taxable income is	the tax is	of the amount over
at most $32,000	10%	$0
over $32,000	$3,200 + 25%	$32,000
If your status is Married and if the taxable income is	the tax is	of the amount over
at most $64,000	10%	$0
over $64,000	$6,400 + 25%	$64,000

The two-level decision process is reflected in two levels of if statements in the program at the end of this section. (See Figure 4 for a flowchart.)

Computing income taxes requires multiple levels of decisions.

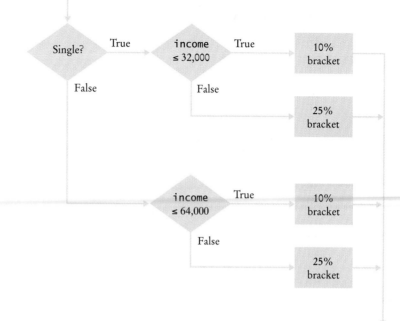

Figure 4   Income Tax Computation

In theory, nesting can go deeper than two levels. A three-level decision process (first by state, then by filing status, then by income level) requires three nesting levels.

ch03/tax.cpp

```cpp
1  #include <iostream>
2  #include <string>
3
4  using namespace std;
5
6  int main()
7  {
8     const double RATE1 = 0.10;
9     const double RATE2 = 0.25;
10    const double RATE1_SINGLE_LIMIT = 32000;
11    const double RATE1_MARRIED_LIMIT = 64000;
12
13    double tax1 = 0;
14    double tax2 = 0;
15
16    double income;
17    cout << "Please enter your income: ";
18    cin >> income;
19
20    cout << "Please enter s for single, m for married: ";
21    string marital_status;
22    cin >> marital_status;
23
```

```
24      if (marital_status == "s")
25      {
26         if (income <= RATE1_SINGLE_LIMIT)
27         {
28            tax1 = RATE1 * income;
29         }
30         else
31         {
32            tax1 = RATE1 * RATE1_SINGLE_LIMIT;
33            tax2 = RATE2 * (income - RATE1_SINGLE_LIMIT);
34         }
35      }
36      else
37      {
38         if (income <= RATE1_MARRIED_LIMIT)
39         {
40            tax1 = RATE1 * income;
41         }
42         else
43         {
44            tax1 = RATE1 * RATE1_MARRIED_LIMIT;
45            tax2 = RATE2 * (income - RATE1_MARRIED_LIMIT);
46         }
47      }
48
49      double total_tax = tax1 + tax2;
50
51      cout << "The tax is $" << total_tax << endl;
52      return 0;
53   }
```

Program Run

```
Please enter your income: 80000
Please enter s for single, m for married: m
The tax is $10400
```

SELF CHECK

17. What is the amount of tax that a single taxpayer pays on an income of $32,000?

18. Would that amount change if the first nested if statement changed from

    `if (income <= RATE1_SINGLE_LIMIT)`

    to

    `if (income < RATE1_SINGLE_LIMIT)`

19. Suppose Harry and Sally each make $40,000 per year. Would they save taxes if they married?

20. How would you modify the tax.cpp program in order to check that the user entered a correct value for the marital status (i.e., s or m)?

21. Some people object to higher tax rates for higher incomes, claiming that you might end up with less money after taxes when you get a raise for working hard. What is the flaw in this argument?

Practice It   Now you can try these exercises at the end of the chapter: R3.7, R3.19, P3.13, P3.19.

Hand-Tracing

A very useful technique for understanding whether a program works correctly is called *hand-tracing*. You simulate the program's activity on a sheet of paper. You can use this method with pseudocode or C++ code.

Get an index card, a cocktail napkin, or whatever sheet of paper is within reach. Make a column for each variable. Have the program code ready. Use a marker, such as a paper clip, to mark the current statement. In your mind, execute statements one at a time. Every time the value of a variable changes, cross out the old value and write the new value below the old one.

For example, let's trace the tax program with the data from the program run on page 95. In lines 13 and 14, tax1 and tax2 are initialized to 0.

Hand-tracing helps you understand whether a program works correctly.

```
6  int main()
7  {
8     const double RATE1 = 0.10;
9     const double RATE2 = 0.25;
10    const double RATE1_SINGLE_LIMIT = 32000;
11    const double RATE1_MARRIED_LIMIT = 64000;
12
13    double tax1 = 0;
14    double tax2 = 0;
15
```

tax1	tax2	income	marital status
0	0		

In lines 18 and 22, income and marital_status are initialized by input statements.

```
16    double income;
17    cout << "Please enter your income: ";
18    cin >> income;
19
20    cout << "Please enter s for single, m for married: ";
21    string marital_status;
22    cin >> marital_status;
23
```

tax1	tax2	income	marital status
0	0	80000	m

Because marital_status is not "s", we move to the else branch of the outer if statement (line 36).

```
24    if (marital_status == "s")
25    {
26       if (income <= RATE1_SINGLE_LIMIT)
27       {
28          tax1 = RATE1 * income;
29       }
30       else
31       {
32          tax1 = RATE1 * RATE1_SINGLE_LIMIT;
33          tax2 = RATE2 * (income - RATE1_SINGLE_LIMIT);
34       }
35    }
36    else
37    {
```

Since income is not <= 64000, we move to the else branch of the inner if statement (line 42).

```
38       if (income <= RATE1_MARRIED_LIMIT)
39       {
40          tax1 = RATE1 * income;
41       }
42       else
43       {
44          tax1 = RATE1 * RATE1_MARRIED_LIMIT;
45          tax2 = RATE2 * (income - RATE1_MARRIED_LIMIT);
46       }
```

The values of tax1 and tax2 are updated.

```
43      {
44          tax1 = RATE1 * RATE1_MARRIED_LIMIT;
45          tax2 = RATE2 * (income - RATE1_MARRIED_LIMIT);
46      }
47   }
```

tax1	tax2	income	marital status
~~0~~	~~0~~	80000	m
6400	4000		

Their sum total_tax is computed and printed. Then the program ends.

```
48
49      double total_tax = tax1 + tax2;
50
51      cout << "The tax is $" << total_tax << endl;
52      return 0;
53   }
```

tax1	tax2	income	marital status	total tax
~~0~~	~~0~~	80000	m	
6400	4000			10400

Because the program trace shows the expected output ($10,400), it successfully demonstrated that this test case works correctly.

Common Error 3.4

The Dangling else Problem

When an if statement is nested inside another if statement, the following error may occur.

```
double shipping_charge = 5.00; // $5 inside continental U.S.
if (country == "USA")
    if (state == "HI")
        shipping_charge = 10.00; // Hawaii is more expensive
else // Pitfall!
    shipping_charge = 20.00; // As are foreign shipments
```

The indentation level seems to suggest that the else is grouped with the test country == "USA". Unfortunately, that is not the case. The compiler ignores all indentation and matches the else with the preceding if. That is, the code is actually

```
double shipping_charge = 5.00; // $5 inside continental U.S.
if (country == "USA")
    if (state == "HI")
        shipping_charge = 10.00; // Hawaii is more expensive
    else // Pitfall!
        shipping_charge = 20.00; // As are foreign shipments
```

That isn't what you want. You want to group the else with the first if.

The ambiguous else is called a *dangling* else. You can avoid this pitfall if you *always use braces*, as recommended in Programming Tip 3.2 on page 80:

```
double shipping_charge = 5.00; // $5 inside continental U.S.
if (country == "USA")
{
    if (state == "HI")
    {
        shipping_charge = 10.00; // Hawaii is more expensive
    }
}
else
{
    shipping_charge = 20.00; // As are foreign shipments
}
```

3.5 Problem Solving: Flowcharts

Flow charts are made up of elements for tasks, input/outputs, and decisions.

You have seen examples of flowcharts earlier in this chapter. A flowchart shows the structure of decisions and tasks that are required to solve a problem. When you have to solve a complex problem, it is a good idea to draw a flowchart to visualize the flow of control.

The basic flowchart elements are shown in Figure 5.

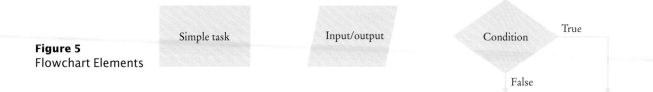

Figure 5
Flowchart Elements

Each branch of a decision can contain tasks and further decisions.

The basic idea is simple enough. Link tasks and input/output boxes in the sequence in which they should be executed. Whenever you need to make a decision, draw a diamond with two outcomes (see Figure 6).

Each branch can contain a sequence of tasks and even additional decisions. If there are multiple choices for a value, lay them out as in Figure 7.

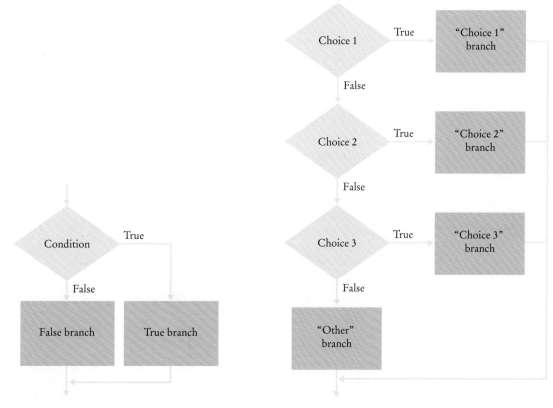

Figure 6 Flowchart with Two Outcomes

Figure 7 Flowchart with Multiple Choices

There is one issue that you need to be aware of when drawing flowcharts. Unconstrained branching and merging can lead to "spaghetti code", a messy network of possible pathways through a program.

There is a simple rule for avoiding spaghetti code: Never point an arrow *inside another branch*.

To understand the rule, consider this example: Shipping costs are $5 inside the United States, except that to Hawaii and Alaska they are $10. International shipping costs are also $10. You might start out with a flowchart like the following:

Spaghetti code has so many pathways that it becomes impossible to understand.

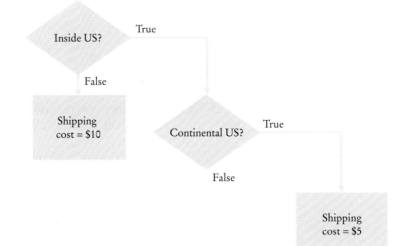

Now you may be tempted to reuse the "shipping cost = $10" task:

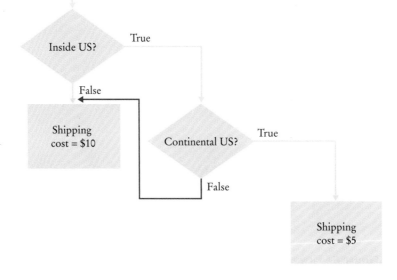

Don't do that! The red arrow points inside a different branch. Instead, add another task that sets the shipping cost to $10, like this:

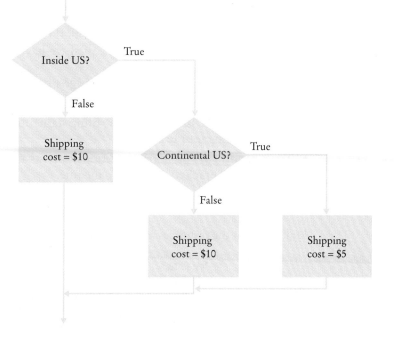

Not only do you avoid spaghetti code, but it is also a better design. In the future it may well happen that the cost for international shipments is different from that to Alaska and Hawaii.

Flowcharts can be very useful for getting an intuitive understanding of the flow of an algorithm. However, they get large rather quickly when you add more details. At that point, it makes sense to switch from flowcharts to pseudocode.

SELF CHECK

22. Draw a flowchart for a program that reads a value temp and prints "Frozen" if it is less than zero.

23. What is wrong with the flowchart at right?

24. How do you fix the flowchart of Self Check 23?

25. Draw a flowchart for a program that reads a value x. If it is less than zero, print "Error". Otherwise, print its square root.

26. Draw a flowchart for a program that reads a value temp. If it is less than zero, print "Ice". If it is greater than 100, print "Steam". Otherwise, print "Liquid".

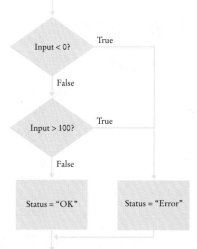

Practice It   Now you can try these exercises at the end of the chapter: R3.10, R3.11, R3.12.

3.6 Problem Solving: Test Cases

Consider how to test the tax computation program from Section 3.4. Of course, you cannot try out all possible inputs of filing status and income level. Even if you could, there would be no point in trying them all. If the program correctly computes one or two tax amounts in a given bracket, then we have a good reason to believe that all amounts will be correct.

Each branch of your program should be covered by a test case.

You want to aim for complete *coverage* of all decision points. Here is a plan for obtaining a comprehensive set of test cases:

- There are two possibilities for the filing status and two tax brackets for each status, yielding four test cases.
- Test a handful of *boundary* conditions, such as an income that is at the boundary between two brackets, and a zero income.
- If you are responsible for error checking (which is discussed in Section 3.8), also test an invalid input, such as a negative income.

Make a list of the test cases and the expected outputs:

Test Case	Expected Output	Comment
30,000 s	3,000	10% bracket
72,000 s	13,200	3,200 + 25% of 40,000
50,000 m	5,000	10% bracket
104,000 m	16,400	6,400 + 25% of 40,000
32,000 s	3,200	boundary case
0	0	boundary case

It is a good idea to design test cases before implementing a program.

When you develop a set of test cases, it is helpful to have a flowchart of your program (see Section 3.5). Check off each branch that has a test case. Include test cases for the boundary cases of each decision. For example, if a decision checks whether an input is less than 100, test with an input of 100.

It is always a good idea to design test cases *before* starting to code. Working through the test cases gives you a better understanding of the algorithm that you are about to implement.

SELF CHECK

27. Using Figure 1 on page 77 as a guide, follow the process described in Section 3.6 to design a set of test cases for the elevator.cpp program in Section 3.1.

28. What is a boundary test case for the algorithm in How To 3.1 on page 87? What is the expected output?

29. Using Figure 3 on page 91 as a guide, follow the process described in Section 3.6 to design a set of test cases for the richter.cpp program in Section 3.3.

30. Suppose you are designing a part of a program for a medical robot that has a sensor returning an *x* and *y* location (measured in cm). You need to check whether the sensor location is inside the circle, outside the circle, on the boundary (specifically, having a distance of less than 1 mm from the boundary). Assume the circle has center (0, 0) and radius 2 cm. Give a set of test cases.

Practice It   Now you can try these exercises at the end of the chapter: R3.13, R3.14.

Make a Schedule and Make Time for Unexpected Problems

Commercial software is notorious for being delivered later than promised. For example, Microsoft originally promised that its Windows Vista operating system would be available late in 2003, then in 2005, then in March 2006; it finally was released in January 2007. Some of the early promises might not have been realistic. It was in Microsoft's interest to let prospective customers expect the imminent availability of the product. Had customers known the actual delivery date, they might have switched to a different product in the meantime. Undeniably, though, Microsoft had not anticipated the full complexity of the tasks it had set itself to solve.

Microsoft can delay the delivery of its product, but it is likely that you cannot. As a student or a programmer, you are expected to manage your time wisely and to finish your assignments on time. You can probably do simple programming exercises the night before the due date, but an assignment that looks twice as hard may well take four times as long, because more things can go wrong. You should therefore make a schedule whenever you start a programming project.

First, estimate realistically how much time it will take you to:

- Design the program logic.
- Develop test cases.
- Type in the program and fix syntax errors.
- Test and debug the program.

For example, for the income tax program I might estimate an hour for the design; 30 minutes for developing test cases; an hour for data entry and fixing syntax errors; and an hour for testing and debugging. That is a total of 3.5 hours. If I work two hours a day on this project, it will take me almost two days.

Then think of things that can go wrong. Your computer might break down. You might be stumped by a problem with the computer system. (That is a particularly important concern for

Make a schedule for your programming work and build in time for problems.

beginners. It is *very* common to lose a day over a trivial problem just because it takes time to track down a person who knows the magic command to overcome it.) As a rule of thumb, *double* the time of your estimate. That is, you should start four days, not two days, before the due date. If nothing went wrong, great; you have the program done two days early. When the inevitable problem occurs, you have a cushion of time that protects you from embarrassment and failure.

3.7 Boolean Variables and Operators

Sometimes, you need to evaluate a logical condition in one part of a program and use it elsewhere. To store a condition that can be true or false, you use a *Boolean variable*. Boolean variables are named after the mathematician George Boole (1815–1864), a pioneer in the study of logic.

> The Boolean type bool has two values, false and true.

In C++, the bool data type represents the Boolean type. Variables of type bool can hold exactly two values, denoted false and true. These values are not strings or integers; they are special values, just for Boolean variables.

A Boolean variable is also called a flag because it can be either up (true) or down (false).

Here is a definition of a Boolean variable:

```
bool failed = true;
```

You can use the value later in your program to make a decision:

```
if (failed) // Only executed if failed has been set to true
{
    ...
}
```

When you make complex decisions, you often need to combine Boolean values. An operator that combines Boolean conditions is called a **Boolean operator**. In C++, the && operator (called *and*) yields true only when both conditions are true. The || operator (called *or*) yields the result true if at least one of the conditions is true.

Suppose you write a program that processes temperature values, and you want to test whether a given temperature corresponds to liquid water. (At sea level, water freezes at 0 degrees Celsius and boils at 100 degrees.) Water is liquid if the temperature is greater than zero *and* less than 100:

```
if (temp > 0 && temp < 100) { cout << "Liquid"; }
```

C++ has two Boolean operators that combine conditions: && (*and*) and || (*or*).

The condition of the test has two parts, joined by the && operator. (As shown in Table 5 and Appendix C, the > and < operators have higher precedence than the && operator.)

Each part is a Boolean value that can be true or false. The combined expression is true if both individual expressions are true. If either one of the expressions is false, then the result is also false (see Figure 8).

A	B	A && B
true	true	true
true	false	false
false	true	false
false	false	false

A	B	A || B
true	true	true
true	false	true
false	true	true
false	false	false

A	!A
true	false
false	true

Figure 8 Boolean Truth Tables

At this geyser in Iceland, you can see ice, liquid water, and steam.

Table 5 Selected Operators and Their Precedence

Operator	Description
++ -- + (unary) - (unary) !	Increment, decrement, positive, negative, Boolean *not*
* / %	Multiplication, division, remainder
+ -	Addition, subtraction
< <= > >=	Comparisons
== !=	Equal, not equal
&&	Boolean *and*
||	Boolean *or*

Conversely, let's test whether water is *not* liquid at a given temperature. That is the case when the temperature is at most 0 *or* at least 100. Use the || (*or*) operator to combine the expressions:

```
if (temp <= 0 || temp >= 100) { cout << "Not liquid"; }
```

Figure 9 shows flowcharts for these examples.

Sometimes you need to *invert* a condition with the *not* logical operator. The ! operator takes a single condition and evaluates to true if that condition is false and to false if the condition is true. In this example, output occurs if the value of the Boolean variable frozen is false:

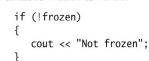
To invert a condition, use the ! (*not*) operator.

```
if (!frozen)
{
    cout << "Not frozen";
}
```

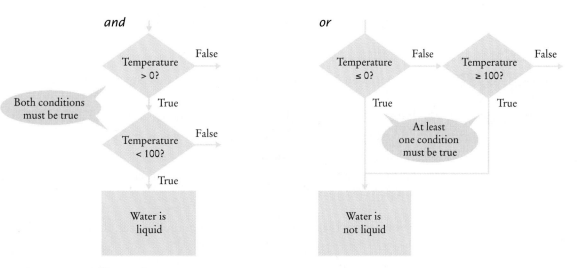

Figure 9 Flowcharts for *and* and *or* Combinations

Table 6 Boolean Operators

Expression	Value	Comment
0 < 200 && 200 < 100	false	Only the first condition is true. Note that the < operator has a higher precedence than the && operator.
0 < 200 || 200 < 100	true	The first condition is true.
0 < 200 || 100 < 200	true	The || is not a test for "either-or". If both conditions are true, the result is true.
🚫 0 < 200 < 100	true	**Error:** The expression 0 < 200 is true, which is converted to 1. The expression 1 < 100 is true. You never want to write such an expression; see Common Error 3.5 on page 107.
🚫 -10 && 10 > 0	true	**Error:** –10 is not zero. It is converted to true. You never want to write such an expression; see Common Error 3.5 on page 107.
0 < x && x < 100 || x == -1	(0 < x && x < 100) || x == -1	The && operator has a higher precedence than the || operator.
!(0 < 200)	false	0 < 200 is true, therefore its negation is false.
frozen == true	frozen	There is no need to compare a Boolean variable with true.
frozen == false	!frozen	It is clearer to use ! than to compare with false.

Table 6 illustrates additional examples of evaluating Boolean operators.

SELF CHECK

31. Suppose x and y are two integers. How do you test whether both of them are zero?

32. How do you test whether at least one of them is zero?

33. How do you test whether *exactly one of them* is zero?

34. What is the value of !!frozen?

35. What is the advantage of using the type bool rather than strings "false"/"true" or integers 0/1?

Practice It   Now you can try these exercises at the end of the chapter: R3.27, P3.22, P3.24.

Common Error 3.5

Combining Multiple Relational Operators

Consider the expression

```
if (0 <= temp <= 100) // Error
```

This looks just like the mathematical test $0 \leq \text{temp} \leq 100$. Unfortunately, it is not.

Let us dissect the expression `0 <= temp <= 100`. The first half, `0 <= temp`, is a test with outcome `true` or `false`, depending on the value of `temp`. The outcome of that test (`true` or `false`) is then compared against 100. Can one compare truth values and floating-point numbers? Is `true` larger than 100 or not? Unfortunately, to stay compatible with the C language, C++ converts `false` to 0 and `true` to 1. Therefore, the expression will always evaluate to `true`.

You must be careful not to mix logical and arithmetic expressions in your programs. Instead, use *and* to combine two separate tests:

```
if (0 <= temp && temp <= 100) ...
```

Another common error, along the same lines, is to write

```
if (x && y > 0) ... // Error
```

instead of

```
if (x > 0 && y > 0) ...
```

Unfortunately, the compiler will not issue an error message. Instead, it converts `x` to `true` or `false`. Zero is converted to `false`, and any nonzero value is converted to `true`. If `x` is not zero, then it tests whether `y` is greater than 0, and finally it computes the *and* of these two truth values. Naturally, that computation makes no sense.

Common Error 3.6

Confusing && and || Conditions

It is a surprisingly common error to confuse *and* and *or* conditions. A value lies between 0 and 100 if it is at least 0 *and* at most 100. It lies outside that range if it is less than 0 *or* greater than 100. There is no golden rule; you just have to think carefully.

Often the *and* or *or* is clearly stated, and then it isn't too hard to implement it. But sometimes the wording isn't as explicit. It is quite common that the individual conditions are nicely set apart in a bulleted list, but with little indication of how they should be combined. Consider these instructions for filing a tax return. You can claim single filing status if any one of the following is true:

• You were never married.

• You were legally separated or divorced on the last day of the tax year.

• You were widowed, and did not remarry.

Since the test passes if *any one* of the conditions is true, you must combine the conditions with *or*. Elsewhere, the same instructions state that you may use the more advantageous status of married filing jointly if all five of the following conditions are true:

• Your spouse died less than two years ago and you did not remarry.

• You have a child whom you can claim as dependent.

• That child lived in your home for all of the tax year.

• You paid over half the cost of keeping up your home for this child.

• You filed a joint return with your spouse the year he or she died.

Because *all* of the conditions must be true for the test to pass, you must combine them with an *and*.

Special Topic 3.4

Short-Circuit Evaluation of Boolean Operators

When the && and || operators are computed, evaluation stops as soon as the truth value is determined. When an && is evaluated and the first condition is false, the second condition is not evaluated, because it does not matter what the outcome of the second test is.

> The && and || operators are computed using *short-circuit evaluation:* As soon as the truth value is determined, no further conditions are evaluated.

For example, consider the expression

```
quantity > 0 && price / quantity < 10
```

Suppose the value of quantity is zero. Then the test quantity > 0 fails, and the second test is not attempted. That is just as well, because it is illegal to divide by zero.

Similarly, when the first condition of an || expression is true, then the remainder is not evaluated since the result must be true.

This process is called *short-circuit evaluation*.

In a short circuit, electricity travels along the path of least resistance. Similarly, short-circuit evaluation takes the fastest path for computing the result of a Boolean expression.

Special Topic 3.5

De Morgan's Law

Humans generally have a hard time comprehending logical conditions with *not* operators applied to *and*/*or* expressions. De Morgan's Law, named after the logician Augustus De Morgan (1806–1871), can be used to simplify these Boolean expressions.

Suppose we want to charge a higher shipping rate if we don't ship within the continental United States.

```
if (!(country == "USA"
        && state != "AK"
        && state != "HI"))
    shipping_charge = 20.00;
```

This test is a little bit complicated, and you have to think carefully through the logic. When it is *not* true that the country is USA *and* the state is not Alaska *and* the state is not Hawaii, then charge $20.00. Huh? It is not true that some people won't be confused by this code.

The computer doesn't care, but it takes human programmers to write and maintain the code. Therefore, it is useful to know how to simplify such a condition.

De Morgan's Law has two forms: one for the negation of an *and* expression and one for the negation of an *or* expression:

> De Morgan's law tells you how to negate && and || conditions.

```
!(A && B)    is the same as    !A || !B
!(A || B)    is the same as    !A && !B
```

Pay particular attention to the fact that the *and* and *or* operators are *reversed* by moving the *not* inward. For example, the negation of "the state is Alaska *or* it is Hawaii",

```
!(state == "AK" || state == "HI")
```

is "the state is not Alaska *and* it is not Hawaii":

```
!(state == "AK") && !(state == "HI")
```

That is, of course, the same as

```
state != "AK" && state != "HI"
```

Now apply the law to our shipping charge computation:

```
!(country == "USA"
    && state != "AK"
    && state != "HI")
```

is equivalent to

```
!(country == "USA")
    || !(state != "AK")
    || !(state != "HI")
```

That yields the simpler test

```
country != "USA"
    || state == "AK"
    || state == "HI"
```

To simplify conditions with negations of *and* or *or* expressions, it is usually a good idea to apply De Morgan's Law to move the negations to the innermost level.

3.8 Application: Input Validation

Like a quality control worker, you want to make sure that user input is correct before processing it.

An important application for the `if` statement is *input validation*. Whenever your program accepts user input, you need to make sure that the user-supplied values are valid before you use them in your computations.

Consider our elevator program. Assume that the elevator panel has buttons labeled 1 through 20 (but not 13). The following are illegal inputs:

- The number 13
- Zero or a negative number
- A number larger than 20
- An input that is not a sequence of digits, such as `five`

In each of these cases, we will want to give an error message and exit the program.

It is simple to guard against an input of 13:

```
if (floor == 13)
{
    cout << "Error: There is no thirteenth floor." << endl;
    return 1;
}
```

The statement

```
return 1;
```

immediately exits the `main` function and therefore terminates the program. It is a convention to return with the value 0 if the program completed normally, and with a non-zero value when an error was encountered.

When reading a
value, check that
it is within the
required range.

Here is how you ensure that the user doesn't enter a number outside the valid range:

```
if (floor <= 0 || floor > 20)
{
   cout << "Error: The floor must be between 1 and 20." << endl;
   return 1;
}
```

However, dealing with an input that is not a valid integer is a more serious problem. When the statement

```
cin >> floor;
```

is executed, and the user types in an input that is not an integer (such as five), then the integer variable floor is not set. Instead, the input stream cin is set to a failed state. You call the fail member function to test for that failed state.

```
if (cin.fail())
{
   cout << "Error: Not an integer." << endl;
   return 1;
}
```

Use the fail function
to test whether
the input stream
has failed.

The order of the if statements is important. You must *first* test for cin.fail(). After all, if the input failed, no value has been assigned to floor, and it makes no sense to compare it against other values.

Input failure is quite serious in C++. Once input has failed, all subsequent attempts at input will fail as well. You will learn in Chapter 8 how to write programs that are more tolerant of bad input. For now, our goal is simply to detect bad input and to exit the program when it occurs.

Here is the complete elevator program with input validation.

ch03/elevator2.cpp

```
1   #include <iostream>
2
3   using namespace std;
4
5   int main()
6   {
7      int floor;
8      cout << "Floor: ";
9      cin >> floor;
10
11     // The following statements check various input errors
12     if (cin.fail())
13     {
14        cout << "Error: Not an integer." << endl;
15        return 1;
16     }
17     if (floor == 13)
18     {
19        cout << "Error: There is no thirteenth floor." << endl;
20        return 1;
21     }
22     if (floor <= 0 || floor > 20)
23     {
24        cout << "Error: The floor must be between 1 and 20." << endl;
25        return 1;
```

```
26        }
27
28        // Now we know that the input is valid
29        int actual_floor;
30        if (floor > 13)
31        {
32            actual_floor = floor - 1;
33        }
34        else
35        {
36            actual_floor = floor;
37        }
38
39        cout << "The elevator will travel to the actual floor "
40            << actual_floor << endl;
41
42        return 0;
43    }
```

Program Run

```
Floor: 13
Error: There is no thirteenth floor.
```

36. Consider the `elevator2.cpp` program. What output do you get when the input is

  a. 100?

  b. −1?

  c. 20?

  d. thirteen?

37. Your task is to rewrite the `elevator2.cpp` program so that there is a single `if` statement with a complex condition:

```
if (...)
{
    cout << "Error: Bad input" << endl;
    return 1;
}
```

  What is the condition?

38. In the Sherlock Holmes story "The Adventure of the Sussex Vampire", the inimitable detective uttered these words: "Matilda Briggs was not the name of a young woman, Watson, ... It was a ship which is associated with the giant rat of Sumatra, a story for which the world is not yet prepared." Over a hundred years later, researchers found giant rats in Western New Guinea, another part of Indonesia.

  Suppose you are charged with writing a program that processes rat weights. It contains the statements

```
double weight;
cout << "Enter weight in kg: ";
cin >> weight;
```

  What input checks should you supply?

When processing inputs, you want to reject values that are too large. But how large is too large? These giant rats, found in Western New Guinea, are about five times the size of a city rat.

39. Consider the following test program:

```
int main()
{
   int m = 1;
   cout << "Enter an integer: ";
   cin >> m;
   int n = 2;
   cout << "Enter another integer: ";
   cin >> n;
   cout << m << " " << n << endl;
   return 0;
}
```

Run this program and enter three at the first prompt. What happens? Why?

Practice It   Now you can try these exercises at the end of the chapter: R3.1, R3.30, P3.26.

Random Fact 3.2 Artificial Intelligence

When one uses a sophisticated computer program such as a tax preparation package, one is bound to attribute some intelligence to the computer. The computer asks sensible questions and makes computations that we find a mental challenge. After all, if doing one's taxes were easy, we wouldn't need a computer to do it for us.

As programmers, however, we know that all this apparent intelligence is an illusion. Human programmers have carefully "coached" the software in all possible scenarios, and it simply replays the actions and decisions that were programmed into it.

Would it be possible to write computer programs that are genuinely intelligent in some sense? From the earliest days of computing, there was a sense that the human brain might be nothing but an immense computer, and that it might well be feasible to program computers to imitate some processes of human thought. Seri-

ous research into *artificial intelligence* began in the mid-1950s, and the first twenty years brought some impressive successes. Programs that play chess—surely an activity that appears to require remarkable intellectual powers—have become so good that they now routinely beat all but the best human players. As far back as 1975, an *expert-system* program called Mycin gained fame for being better in diagnosing meningitis in patients than the average physician.

However, there were serious setbacks as well. From 1982 to 1992, the Japanese government embarked on a massive research project, funded at over 40 billion Japanese yen. It was known as the *Fifth-Generation Project*. Its goal was to develop new hardware and software to greatly improve the performance of expert system software. At its outset, the project created fear in other countries that the Japanese computer industry was about to become the undisputed leader in the

field. However, the end results were disappointing and did little to bring artificial intelligence applications to market.

From the very outset, one of the stated goals of the AI community was to produce software that could translate text from one language to another, for example from English to Russian. That undertaking proved to be enormously complicated. Human language appears to be much more subtle and interwoven with the human experience than had originally been thought. Even the grammar-checking tools that come with word-processing programs today are more of a gimmick than a useful tool, and analyzing grammar is just the first step in translating sentences.

The CYC (from en*cyc*lopedia) project, started by Douglas Lenat in 1984, tries to codify the implicit assumptions that underlie human speech and writing. The team members started out analyzing news articles and asked themselves what unmentioned facts

CHAPTER SUMMARY

Use the if statement to implement a decision.

- The if statement allows a program to carry out different actions depending on the nature of the data to be processed.

Implement comparisons of numbers and objects.

- Relational operators (< <= > >= == !=) are used to compare numbers and strings.
- Lexicographic order is used to compare strings.

Implement complex decisions that require multiple if statements.

- Multiple alternatives are required for decisions that have more than two cases.
- When using multiple if statements, pay attention to the order of the conditions.

---

are necessary to actually understand the sentences. For example, consider the sentence "Last fall she enrolled in Michigan State". The reader automatically realizes that "fall" is not related to falling down in this context, but refers to the season. While there is a state of Michigan, here Michigan State denotes the university. A priori, a computer program has none of this knowledge. The goal of the CYC project is to extract and store the requisite facts—that is, (1) people enroll in universities; (2) Michigan is a state; (3) many states have universities named X State University, often abbreviated as X State; (4) most people enroll in a university in the fall. By 1995, the project had codified about 100,000 common-sense concepts and about a million facts of knowledge relating them. Even this massive amount of data has not proven sufficient for useful applications.

In recent years, artificial intelligence technology has seen substantial advances. One of the most astound-ing examples is the outcome of a series of "grand challenges" for autonomous vehicles posed by the Defense Advanced Research Projects Agency (DARPA). Competitors were invited to submit a computer-controlled vehicle that had to complete an obstacle course without a human driver or remote control. The first event, in 2004, was a disappointment, with none of the entrants finishing the route. In 2005, five vehicles completed a grueling 212 km course in the Mojave desert. Stanford's Stanley came in first, with an average speed of 30 km/h. In 2007, DARPA moved the competition to an "urban" environment, an abandoned air force base. Vehicles had to be able to interact with each other, following California traffic laws. As Stanford's Sebastian Thrun explained:

Winner of the 2007 DARPA Urban Challenge

"In the last Grand Challenge, it didn't really matter whether an obstacle was a rock or a bush, because either way you'd just drive around it. The current challenge is to move from just sensing the environment to understanding the environment."

Implement decisions whose branches require further decisions.

- When a decision statement is contained inside the branch of another decision statement, the statements are *nested*.
- Nested decisions are required for problems that have two levels of decision making.

Draw flowcharts for visualizing the control flow of a program.

- Flow charts are made up of elements for tasks, input/outputs, and decisions.
- Each branch of a decision can contain tasks and further decisions.
- Never point an arrow inside another branch.

Design test cases for your programs.

- Each branch of your program should be covered by a test case.
- It is a good idea to design test cases before implementing a program.

Use the Boolean data type to store and combine conditions that can be true or false.

- The Boolean type `bool` has two values, `false` and `true`.
- C++ has two Boolean operators that combine conditions: `&&` (*and*) and `||` (*or*).
- To invert a condition, use the `!` (*not*) operator.
- The `&&` and `||` operators are computed using *short-circuit evaluation*: As soon as the truth value is determined, no further conditions are evaluated.
- De Morgan's law tells you how to negate `&&` and `||` conditions.

Apply `if` statements to detect whether user input is valid.

- When reading a value, check that it is within the required range.
- Use the `fail` function to test whether the input stream has failed.

REVIEW EXERCISES

R3.1 Find the errors in the following `if` statements.

```
a. if x > 0 then cout << x;
b. if (x > 0) ; { y = 1; } else ; { y = -1; }
c. if (1 + x > pow(x, sqrt(2)) { y = y + x; }
d. if (x = 1) { y++; }
e. cin >> x; if (cin.fail()) { y = y + x; }
```

R3.2 What do these code fragments print?

```
a. int n = 1; int m = -1;
   if (n < -m) { cout << n; } else { cout << m; }
b. int n = 1; int m = -1;
   if (-n >= m) { cout << n; } else { cout << m; }
```

    c. `double x = 0; double y = 1;`
      `if (fabs(x - y) < 1) { cout << x; } else { cout << y; }`
    d. `double x = sqrt(2); double y = 2;`
      `if (x * x == y) { cout << x; } else { cout << y; }`

R3.3 Suppose x and y are variables of type `double`. Write a code fragment that sets y to x if x is positive and to 0 otherwise.

R3.4 Suppose x and y are variables of type `double`. Write a code fragment that sets y to the absolute value of x without calling the `fabs` function. Use an `if` statement.

R3.5 Explain why it is more difficult to compare floating-point numbers than integers. Write C++ code to test whether an integer n equals 10 and whether a floating-point number x equals 10.

R3.6 Common Error 3.2 on page 85 explains that a C++ compiler will not report an error when you use an assignment operator instead of a test for equality, but it may issue a warning. Write a test program containing a statement

    `if (floor = 13)`

What does your compiler do when you compile the program?

R3.7 Each square on a chess board can be described by a letter and number, such as g5 in this example:

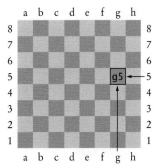

The following pseudocode describes an algorithm that determines whether a square with a given letter and number is dark (black) or light (white).

    If the letter is an a, c, e, or g
        If the number is odd
            color = "black"
        Else
            color = "white"
    Else
        If the number is even
            color = "black"
        Else
            color = "white"

Using the procedure in Programming Tip 3.6 on page 97, trace this pseudocode with input g5.

R3.8 Give a set of four test cases for the algorithm of Exercise R3.7 that covers all branches.

R3.9 In a scheduling program, we want to check whether two appointments overlap. For simplicity, appointments start at a full hour, and we use military time (with hours 0–23). The following pseudocode describes an algorithm that determines whether the appointment with start time **start1** and end time **end1** overlaps with the appointment with start time **start2** and end time **end2**.

```
If start1 > start2
    s = start1
Else
    s = start2
If end1 < end2
    e = end1
Else
    e = end2
If s < e
    The appointments overlap.
Else
    The appointments don't overlap.
```

Trace this algorithm with an appointment from 10–12 and one from 11–13, then with an appointment from 10–11 and one from 12–13.

R3.10 Draw a flow chart for the algorithm in Exercise R3.9.

R3.11 Draw a flow chart for the algorithm in Exercise P3.12.

R3.12 Draw a flow chart for the algorithm in Exercise P3.13.

R3.13 Develop a set of test cases for the algorithm in Exercise R3.9.

R3.14 Develop a set of test cases for the algorithm in Exercise P3.13.

R3.15 Write pseudocode for a program that prompts the user for a month and day and prints out whether it is one of the following four holidays:

- New Year's Day (January 1)
- Independence Day (July 4)
- Veterans Day (November 11)
- Christmas Day (December 25)

R3.16 Write pseudocode for a program that assigns letter grades for a quiz, according to the following table:

Score	Grade
90–100	A
80–89	B
70–79	C
60–69	D
< 60	F

R3.17 Explain how the lexicographic ordering of strings in C++ differs from the ordering of words in a dictionary or telephone book. *Hint:* Consider strings such as IBM, wiley.com, Century 21, and While-U-Wait.

R3.18 Of the following pairs of strings, which comes first in lexicographic order?

a. "Tom", "Dick"

b. "Tom", "Tomato"

c. "church", "Churchill"

    d. "car manufacturer", "carburetor"

    e. "Harry", "hairy"

    f. "C++", " Car"

    g. "Tom", "Tom"

    h. "Car", "Carl"

    i. "car", "bar"

R3.19 Explain the difference between a sequence of else if clauses and nested if statements. Give an example for each.

R3.20 Give an example of a sequence of else if clauses where the order of the tests does not matter. Give an example where the order of the tests matters.

R3.21 Rewrite the condition in Section 3.3 to use < operators instead of >= operators. What is the impact on the order of the comparisons?

R3.22 Give a set of test cases for the tax program in Exercise P3.18. Manually compute the expected results.

R3.23 Make up another C++ code example that shows the dangling else problem, using the following statement. A student with a GPA of at least 1.5, but less than 2, is on probation. With less than 1.5, the student is failing.

R3.24 Complete the following truth table by finding the truth values of the Boolean expressions for all combinations of the Boolean inputs p, q, and r.

p	q	r	(p && q) || !r	!(p && (q || !r))
false	false	false		
false	false	true		
false	true	false		
	...			
	5 more combinations			
	...			

R3.25 True or false? *A* && *B* is the same as *B* && *A* for any Boolean conditions *A* and *B*.

R3.26 The "advanced search" feature of many search engines allows you to use Boolean operators for complex queries, such as "(cats OR dogs) AND NOT pets". Contrast these search operators with the Boolean operators in C++.

R3.27 Suppose the value of b is false and the value of x is 0. What is the value of each of the following expressions?

    a. b && x == 0   **e.** b && x != 0

    b. b \|\| x == 0   **f.** b \|\| x != 0

    c. !b && x == 0   **g.** !b && x != 0

    d. !b \|\| x == 0   **h.** !b \|\| x != 0

R3.28 Simplify the following expressions. Here, b is a variable of type bool.

    a. b == true

    b. b == false

    c. b != true

    d. b != false

R3.29 Simplify the following statements. Here, b is a variable of type bool and n is a variable of type int.

    a. if (n == 0) { b = true; } else { b = false; }
        (*Hint:* What is the value of n == 0?)

    b. if (n == 0) { b = false; } else { b = true; }

    c. b = false; if (n > 1) { if (n < 2) { b = true; } }

    d. if (n < 1) { b = true; } else { b = n > 2; }

R3.30 What is wrong with the following program?

```
cout << "Enter the number of quarters: ";
cin >> quarters;
total = total + quarters * 0.25;
cout << "Total: " << total << endl;
if (cin.fail()) { cout << "Input error."; }
```

R3.31 Reading numbers is surprisingly difficult because a C++ input stream looks at the input one character at a time. First, white space is skipped. Then the stream consumes those input characters that can be a part of a number. Once the stream has recognized a number, it stops reading if it finds a character that cannot be a part of a number. However, if the first non-white space character is not a digit or a sign, or if the first character is a sign and the second one is not a digit, then the stream fails.

Consider a program reading an integer:

```
cout << "Enter the number of quarters: ";
int quarters;
cin >> quarters;
```

For each of the following user inputs, circle how many characters have been read and whether the stream is in the failed state or not.

    a. 15.9

    b. 15 9

    c. +159

    d. -15A9

    e. Fifteen

    f. -Fifteen

    g. + 15

    h. 1.5E3

    i. +1+5

PROGRAMMING EXERCISES

P3.1 Write a program that reads a temperature value and the letter C for Celsius or F for Fahrenheit. Print whether water is liquid, solid, or gaseous at the given temperature at sea level.

P3.2 The boiling point of water drops by about one degree centigrade for every 300 meters (or 1,000 feet) of altitude. Improve the program of Exercise P3.1 to allow the user to supply the altitude in meters or feet.

P3.3 Write a program that reads in three floating-point numbers and prints the largest of the three inputs. For example:

```
Please enter three numbers: 4 9 2.5
The largest number is 9.
```

P3.4 Write a program that reads in three strings and sorts them lexicographically.

```
Enter three strings: Charlie Able Baker
Able
Baker
Charlie
```

P3.5 Write a program that reads an integer and prints how many digits the number has, by checking whether the number is ≥ 10, ≥ 100, and so on. (Assume that all integers are less than ten billion.) If the number is negative, first multiply it with –1.

P3.6 Write a program that reads three numbers and prints "all the same" if they are all the same, "all different" if they are all different, and "neither" otherwise.

P3.7 Write a program that reads three numbers and prints "increasing" if they are in increasing order, "decreasing" if they are in decreasing order, and "neither" otherwise. Here, "increasing" means "strictly increasing", with each value larger than its predecessor. The sequence 3 4 4 would not be considered increasing.

P3.8 Repeat Exercise P3.7, but before reading the numbers, ask the user whether increasing/decreasing should be "strict" or "lenient". In lenient mode, the sequence 3 4 4 is increasing and the sequence 4 4 4 is both increasing and decreasing.

P3.9 Write a program that translates a letter grade into a number grade. Letter grades are A, B, C, D, and F, possibly followed by + or –. Their numeric values are 4, 3, 2, 1, and 0. There is no F+ or F–. A + increases the numeric value by 0.3, a – decreases it by 0.3. However, an A+ has value 4.0.

```
Enter a letter grade: B-
The numeric value is 2.7.
```

P3.10 Write a program that translates a number between 0 and 4 into the closest letter grade. For example, the number 2.8 (which might have been the average of several grades) would be converted to B–. Break ties in favor of the better grade; for example 2.85 should be a B.

P3.11 Write a program that takes user input describing a playing card in the following shorthand notation:

A	Ace
2 ... 10	Card values
J	Jack
Q	Queen
K	King
D	Diamonds
H	Hearts
S	Spades
C	Clubs

Your program should print the full description of the card. For example,

```
Enter the card notation: QS
Queen of Spades
```

P3.12 When two points in time are compared, each given as hours (in military time, ranging from 0 and 23) and minutes, the following pseudocode determines which comes first.

> If hour1 < hour2
>   time1 comes first.
> Else if hour1 and hour2 are the same
>   If minute1 < minute2
>   time1 comes first.
>   Else if minute1 and minute2 are the same
>   time1 and time2 are the same.
>   Else
>   time2 comes first.
> Else
>   time2 comes first.

Write a program that prompts the user for two points in time and prints the time that comes first, then the other time.

P3.13 The following algorithm yields the season (Spring, Summer, Fall, or Winter) for a given month and day.

> If month is 1, 2, or 3, season = "Winter"
> Else if month is 4, 5, or 6, season = "Spring"
> Else if month is 7, 8, or 9, season = "Summer"
> Else if month is 10, 11, or 12, season = "Fall"
> If month is divisible by 3 and day >= 21
>   If season is "Winter", season = "Spring"
>   Else if season is "Spring", season = "Summer"
>   Else if season is "Summer", season = "Fall"
>   Else season = "Winter"

Write a program that prompts the user for a month and day and then prints the season, as determined by this algorithm.

P3.14 Write a program that reads in two floating-point numbers and tests whether they are the same up to two decimal places. Here are two sample runs.

```
Enter two floating-point numbers: 2.0 1.99998
They are the same up to two decimal places.
Enter two floating-point numbers: 2.0 1.98999
They are different.
```

P3.15 Write a program to simulate a bank transaction. There are two bank accounts: checking and savings. First, ask for the initial balances of the bank accounts; reject negative balances. Then ask for the transactions; options are deposit, withdrawal, and transfer. Then ask for the account; options are checking and savings. Then ask for the amount; reject transactions that overdraw an account. At the end, print the balances of both accounts.

P3.16 Write a program that reads in the name and salary of an employee. Here the salary will denote an *hourly* wage, such as $9.25. Then ask how many hours the employee worked in the past week. Be sure to accept fractional hours. Any overtime work (over 40 hours per week) is paid at 150 percent of the regular wage. Compute the pay. Print a paycheck for the employee.

P3.17 Write a program that prompts for the day and month of the user's birthday and then prints a horoscope. Make up fortunes for programmers, like this:

```
Please enter your birthday (month and day): 6 16
Gemini are experts at figuring out the behavior of complicated programs.
You feel where bugs are coming from and then stay one step ahead. Tonight,
your style wins approval from a tough critic.
```

Each fortune should contain the name of the astrological sign. (You will find the names and date ranges of the signs at a distressingly large number of sites on the Internet.)

P3.18 Write a program that computes taxes for the following schedule:

If your status is Single and if the taxable income is over	but not over	the tax is	of the amount over
$0	$8,000	10%	$0
$8,000	$32,000	$800 + 15%	$8,000
$32,000		$4,400 + 25%	$32,000
If your status is Married and if the taxable income is over	but not over	the tax is	of the amount over
$0	$16,000	10%	$0
$16,000	$64,000	$1,600 + 15%	$16,000
$64,000		$8,800 + 25%	$64,000

P3.19 The original U.S. income tax of 1913 was quite simple. The tax was

- 1 percent on the first $50,000.
- 2 percent on the amount over $50,000 up to $75,000.
- 3 percent on the amount over $75,000 up to $100,000.
- 4 percent on the amount over $100,000 up to $250,000.
- 5 percent on the amount over $250,000 up to $500,000.
- 6 percent on the amount over $500,000.

There was no separate schedule for single or married taxpayers. Write a program that computes the income tax according to this schedule.

P3.20 The tax.cpp program uses a simplified version of the 2008 U.S. income tax schedule. Look up the tax brackets and rates for the current year, for both single and married filers, and implement a program that computes the actual income tax.

P3.21 *Unit conversion.* Write a unit conversion program that asks the users from which unit they want to convert (fl. oz, gal, oz, lb, in, ft, mi) and to which unit they want to convert (ml, l, g, kg, mm, cm, m, km). Reject incompatible conversions (such as gal → km). Ask for the value to be converted, then display the result:

```
Convert from? gal
Convert to? ml
Value? 2.5
2.5 gal = 9462.5 ml
```

P3.22 Write a program that prompts the user to provide a single character from the alphabet. Print Vowel or Consonant, depending on the user input. If the user input is not a letter (between a and z or A and Z), or is a string of length > 1, print an error message.

P3.23 *Roman numbers.* Write a program that converts a positive integer into the Roman number system. The Roman number system has digits

I	1
V	5
X	10
L	50
C	100
D	500
M	1,000

Numbers are formed according to the following rules. (1) Only numbers up to 3,999 are represented. (2) As in the decimal system, the thousands, hundreds, tens, and ones are expressed separately. (3) The numbers 1 to 9 are expressed as

I	1
II	2
III	3
IV	4
V	5
VI	6
VII	7
VIII	8
IX	9

As you can see, an I preceding a V or X is subtracted from the value, and you can never have more than three I's in a row. (4) Tens and hundreds are done the same way, except that the letters X, L, C and C, D, M are used instead of I, V, X, respectively.

Your program should take an input, such as 1978, and convert it to Roman numerals, MCMLXXVIII.

P3.24 Write a program that asks the user to enter a month (1 for January, 2 for February, and so on) and then prints the number of days in the month. For February, print "28 or 29 days".

```
Enter a month: 5
30 days
```

Do not use a separate if/else branch for each month. Use Boolean operators.

P3.25 A year with 366 days is called a leap year. A year is a leap year if it is divisible by four (for example, 1980), except that it is not a leap year if it is divisible by 100 (for example, 1900); however, it is a leap year if it is divisible by 400 (for example, 2000). There were no exceptions before the introduction of the Gregorian calendar on October 15, 1582 (1500 was a leap year). Write a program that asks the user for a year and computes whether that year is a leap year.

P3.26 Add error handling to Exercise P3.2. If the user does not enter a number when expected, or provides an invalid unit for the altitude, print an error message and end the program.

Engineering P3.27 Write a program that prompts the user for a wavelength value and prints a description of the corresponding part of the electromagnetic spectrum, as given in Table 7.

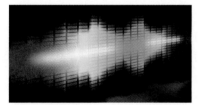

Table 7 Electromagnetic Spectrum		
Type	Wavelength (m)	Frequency (Hz)
Radio Waves	$> 10^{-1}$	$< 3 \times 10^9$
Microwaves	10^{-3} to 10^{-1}	3×10^9 to 3×10^{11}
Infrared	7×10^{-7} to 10^{-3}	3×10^{11} to 4×10^{14}
Visible light	4×10^{-7} to 7×10^{-7}	4×10^{14} to 7.5×10^{14}
Ultraviolet	10^{-8} to 4×10^{-7}	7.5×10^{14} to 3×10^{16}
X-rays	10^{-11} to 10^{-8}	3×10^{16} to 3×10^{19}
Gamma rays	$< 10^{-11}$	$> 3 \times 10^{19}$

Engineering P3.28 Repeat Exercise P3.27, modifying the program so that it prompts for the frequency instead.

Engineering P3.29 Repeat Exercise P3.27, modifying the program so that it first asks the user whether the input will be a wavelength or a frequency.

Engineering P3.30 A minivan has two sliding doors. Each door can be opened by either a dashboard switch, its inside handle, or its outside handle. However, the inside handles do not work if a child lock switch is activated. In order for the sliding doors to open, the gear shift must be in park, *and* the master unlock switch must be activated. (This book's author is the long-suffering owner of just such a vehicle.)

Your task is to simulate a portion of the control software for the vehicle. The input is a sequence of values for the switches and the gear shift, in the following order:

- Dashboard switches for left and right sliding door, child lock, and master unlock (0 for off or 1 for activated)
- Inside and outside handles on the left and right sliding doors (0 or 1)
- The gear shift setting (one of P N D 1 2 3 R).

A typical input would be 0 0 0 1 0 1 0 0 0 P.

Print "left door opens" and/or "right door opens" as appropriate. If neither door opens, print "both doors stay closed".

Engineering P3.31 Sound level L in units of decibel (dB) is determined by

$$L = 20 \log_{10}(p/p_0)$$

where p is the sound pressure of the sound (in Pascals, abbreviated Pa), and p_0 is a reference sound pressure equal to 20×10^{-6} Pa (where L is 0 dB). The following table gives descriptions for certain sound levels.

Threshold of pain	130 dB
Possible hearing damage	120 dB
Jack hammer at 1 m	100 dB
Traffic on a busy roadway at 10 m	90 dB
Normal conversation	60 dB
Calm library	30 dB
Light leaf rustling	0 dB

Write a program that reads a value and a unit, either dB or Pa, and then prints the closest description from the list above.

Engineering P3.32 The electric circuit shown below is designed to measure the temperature of the gas in a chamber.

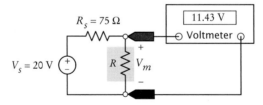

The resistor R represents a temperature sensor enclosed in the chamber. The resistance R, in Ω, is related to the temperature T, in °C, by the equation

$$R = R_0 + kT$$

In this device, assume $R_0 = 100\ \Omega$ and $k = 0.5$. The voltmeter displays the value of the voltage, V_m, across the sensor. This voltage V_m indicates the temperature, T, of the gas according to the equation

$$T = \frac{R}{k} - \frac{R_0}{k} = \frac{R_s}{k}\frac{V_m}{V_s - V_m} - \frac{R_0}{k}$$

Suppose the voltmeter voltage is constrained to the range $V_{min} = 12$ volts $\leq V_m \leq V_{max} = 18$ volts. Write a program that accepts a value of V_m and checks that it's between 12 and 18. The program should return the gas temperature in degrees Celsius when V_m is between 12 and 18 and an error message when it isn't.

Engineering P3.33

Crop damage due to frost is one of the many risks confronting farmers. The figure below shows a simple alarm circuit designed to warn of frost. The alarm circuit uses a device called a thermistor to sound a buzzer when the temperature drops below freezing. Thermistors are semiconductor devices that exhibit a temperature dependent resistance described by the equation

$$R = R_0 e^{\beta\left(\frac{1}{T} - \frac{1}{T_0}\right)}$$

where R is the resistance, in Ω, at the temperature T, in $^\circ$K, and R_0 is the resistance, in Ω, at the temperature T_0, in $^\circ$K. β is a constant that depends on the material used to make the thermistor.

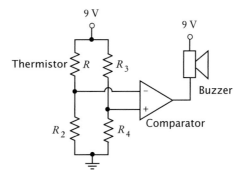

The circuit is designed so that the alarm will sound when

$$\frac{R_2}{R + R_2} < \frac{R_4}{R_3 + R_4}$$

The thermistor used in the alarm circuit has $R_0 = 33{,}192\ \Omega$ at $T_0 = 40\ ^\circ$C, and $\beta = 3{,}310\ ^\circ$K. (Notice that β has units of $^\circ$K. Recall that the temperature in $^\circ$K is obtained by adding 273° to the temperature in $^\circ$C.) The resistors R_2, R_3, and R_4 have a resistance of $156.3\ k\Omega = 156{,}300\ \Omega$.

Write a C++ program that prompts the user for a temperature in $^\circ$F and prints a message indicating whether or not the alarm will sound at that temperature.

Engineering P3.34 A mass $m = 2$ kilograms is attached to the end of a rope of length $r = 3$ meters. The mass is whirled around at high speed. The rope can withstand a maximum tension of $T = 60$ Newtons. Write a program that accepts a rotation speed v and determines if such a speed will cause the rope to break. *Hint:* $T = mv^2/r$.

Engineering P3.35 A mass m is attached to the end of a rope of length $r = 3$ meters. The rope can only be whirled around at speeds of 1, 10, 20, or 40 meters per second. The rope can withstand a maximum tension of $T = 60$ Newtons. Write a program where the user enters the value of the mass m, and the program determines the greatest speed at which it can be whirled without breaking the rope. *Hint:* $T = mv^2/r$.

Engineering P3.36 The average person can jump off the ground with a velocity of 7 mph without fear of leaving the planet. However, if an astronaut jumps with this velocity while standing on Halley's Comet, will the astronaut ever come back down? Create a program that allows the user to input a launch velocity (in mph) from the surface of Halley's Comet and determine whether a jumper will return to the surface. If not, the program should calculate how much more massive the comet must be in order to return the jumper to the surface.

Hint: Escape velocity is $v_{escape} = \sqrt{2\dfrac{GM}{R}}$, where $G = 6.67 \times 10^{-11} N\,m^2/kg^2$ is the gravitational constant, $M = 1.3 \times 10^{22} kg$ is the mass of Halley's comet, and $R = 1.153 \times 10^6 m$ is its radius.

ANSWERS TO SELF-CHECK QUESTIONS

1. Change the if statement to
   ```
   if (floor > 14)
   {
       actual_floor = floor - 2;
   }
   ```

2. 85. 90. 85.

3. The only difference is if original_price is 100. The statement in Self Check 2 sets discounted_price to 90; this one sets it to 80.

4. 95. 100. 95.

5. ```
   if (fuel_amount < 0.10 * fuel_capacity)
   {
       cout << "red" << endl;
   }
   else
   {
       cout << "green" << endl;
   }
   ```

6. (a) and (b) are both true, (c) is false.

7. `floor <= 13`

8. The values should be compared with ==, not =.

9. `input == "Y"`

10. `str != "" or str.length() > 0`

11. ```
    if (score_a > score_b)
    {
        cout << "A won";
    }
    else if (score_a < score_b)
    {
        cout << "B won";
    ```

```
      }
      else
      {
         cout << "Game tied";
      }
```

12.
```
   if (x > 0)
   {
      s = 1;
   }
   else if (x < 0)
   {
      s = -1;
   }
   else
   {
      s = 0;
   }
```

13. You could first set s to one of the three values:

```
   s = 0;
   if (x > 0) { s = 1; }
   else if (x < 0) { s = -1; }
```

14. The if (price <= 100) can be omitted, making it clear that the else branch is the sole alternative.

15. No destruction of buildings

16. Add a branch before the final else:

```
   else if (richter < 0) { cout << "Error: Negative input" << endl; }
```

17. $3,200

18. No. Then the computation is 0.10 × 32000 + 0.25 (32000 – 32000).

19. No. Their individual tax is $5,200 each, and if they married, they would pay $10,400. Actually, taxpayers in higher tax brackets (which our program does not model) may pay higher taxes when they marry, a phenomenon known as the *marriage penalty*.

20. Change else in line 36 to else if (marital_status == "m"), and add another branch after line 47:

```
   else { cout << "Error: marital status should be s or m." << endl; }
```

21. The higher tax rate is only applied on the income in the higher bracket. Suppose you are single and make $31,900. Should you try to get a $200 raise? Absolutely: you get to keep 90 percent of the first $100 and 75 percent of the next $100.

22.

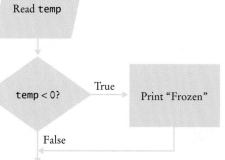

23. The "True" arrow from the first decision points into the "True" branch of the second decision, creating spaghetti code.

24. Here is one solution. In Section 3.7, you will see how you can combine the conditions for a more elegant solution.

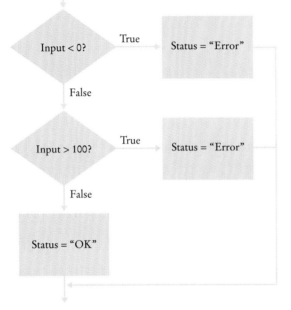

25.

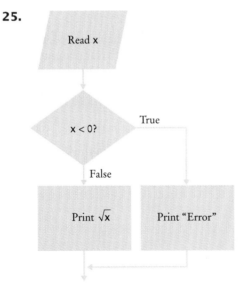

26.

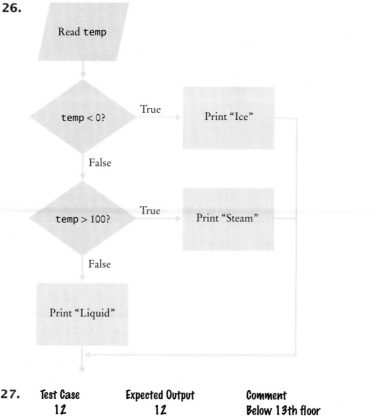

27.

Test Case	Expected Output	Comment
12	12	Below 13th floor
14	13	Above 13th floor
13	?	The specification is not clear— See Section 3.8 for a version of this program with error handling

28. A boundary test case is a price of $128. A 16 percent discount should apply because the problem statement states that the larger discount applies if the price is *at least* $128. Thus, the expected output is $107.52.

29.

Test Case	Expected Output	Comment
9	Most structures fall	
7.5	Many buildings destroyed	
6.5	Many buildings considerably...	
5	Damage to poorly...	
3	No destruction...	
8.0	Most structures fall	Boundary case. In this program, boundary cases are not as significant since the behavior of an earthquake changes gradually.
-1		The specification is not clear—see Self Check 16 for a version of this program with error handling.

30.

Test Case	Expected Output	Comment
(0.5, 0.5)	inside	
(4, 2)	outside	
(0, 2)	on the boundary	Exactly on the boundary
(1.414, 1.414)	on the boundary	Close to the boundary
(0, 1.9)	inside	Not less than 1 mm from the boundary
(0, 2.1)	outside	Not less than 1 mm from the boundary

31. `x == 0 && y == 0`

32. `x == 0 || y == 0`

33. `(x == 0 && y != 0) || (y == 0 && x != 0)`

34. The same as the value of `frozen`.

35. You are guaranteed that there are no other values. With strings or integers, you would need to check that no values such as `"maybe"` or −1 enter your calculations.

36. (a) `Error: The floor must be between 1 and 20.` (b) `Error: The floor must be between 1 and 20.` (c) `The elevator will travel to the actual floor 19` (d) `Error: Not an integer.`

37. `cin.fail() || floor == 13 || floor <= 0 || floor > 20`

38. Check for `cin.fail()`, to make sure a researcher didn't supply an input such as `oh my`. Check for `weight <= 0`, since any rat must surely have a positive weight. We don't know how giant a rat could be, but the New Guinea rats weighed no more than 2 kg. A regular house rat (*rattus rattus*) weighs up to 0.2 kg, so we'll say that any weight > 10 kg was surely an input error, perhaps confusing grams and kilograms. Thus, the checks are

```
if (cin.fail())
{
    cout << "Error: Not a number" << endl;
    return 1;
}

if (weight < 0)
{
    cout << "Error: Weight cannot be negative." << endl;
    return 1;
}

if (weight > 10)
{
    cout << "Error: Weight > 10 kg." << endl;
    return 1;
}
```

39. The first input fails. The value of `m` is unchanged. Because a previous input failed, the next input doesn't even try to get additional keystrokes. It also fails, and `n` is unchanged. The program prints `1 2`.

CHAPTER 4

LOOPS

CHAPTER GOALS

To implement while, for, and do loops

To avoid infinite loops and off-by-one errors

To understand nested loops

To implement programs that read and process data sets

To use a computer for simulations

CHAPTER CONTENTS

In a loop, a part of a program is repeated over and over, until a specific goal is reached. Loops are important for calculations that require repeated steps and for processing input consisting of many data items. In this chapter you will learn about loop statements in C++, as well as techniques for writing programs that process input and simulate activities in the real world.

4.1 The while Loop

In this section, you will learn how to repeatedly execute statements until a goal has been reached.

Recall the investment problem from Chapter 1. You put $10,000 into a bank account that earns 5 percent interest per year. How many years does it take for the account balance to be double the original investment?

In Chapter 1 we developed the following algorithm for this problem:

Because the interest earned also earns interest, a bank balance grows exponentially.

Start with a year value of 0, a column for the interest, and a balance of $10,000.

year	interest	balance
0		$10,000

Repeat the following steps while the balance is less than $20,000
  Add 1 to the year value.
  Compute the interest as balance x 0.05 (i.e., 5 percent interest).
  Add the interest to the balance.
Report the final year value as the answer.

You now know how to define and update the variables in C++. What you don't yet know is how to carry out "Repeat steps while the balance is less than $20,000".

In a particle accelerator, subatomic particles traverse a loop-shaped tunnel multiple times, gaining the speed required for physical experiments. Similarly, in computer science, statements in a loop are executed while a condition is true.

Figure 1 Flowchart of a while Loop

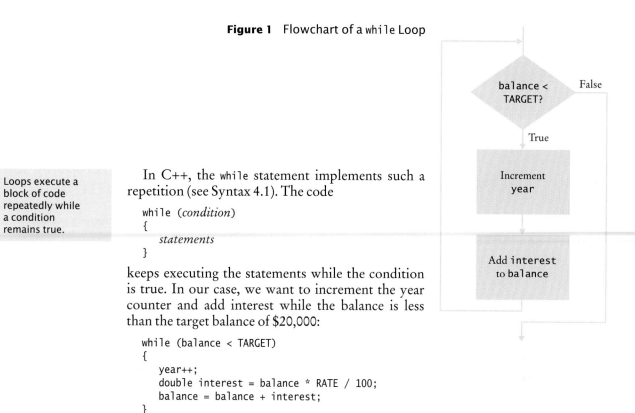

Loops execute a block of code repeatedly while a condition remains true.

In C++, the while statement implements such a repetition (see Syntax 4.1). The code

```
while (condition)
{
    statements
}
```

keeps executing the statements while the condition is true. In our case, we want to increment the year counter and add interest while the balance is less than the target balance of $20,000:

```
while (balance < TARGET)
{
    year++;
    double interest = balance * RATE / 100;
    balance = balance + interest;
}
```

A while statement is an example of a **loop**. If you draw a flowchart, the flow of execution loops again to the point where the condition is tested (see Figure 1).

Syntax 4.1 while Statement

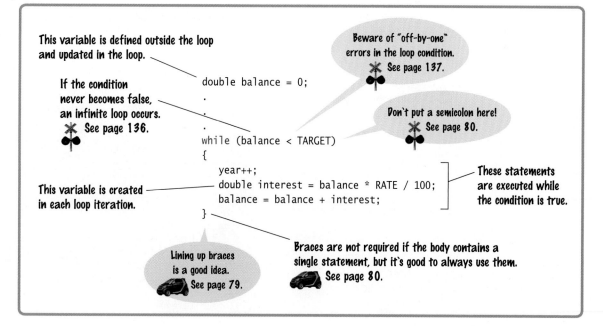

When you define a variable *inside* the loop body, the variable is created for each iteration of the loop and removed after the end of each iteration. For example, consider the interest variable in this loop:

```
while (balance < TARGET)
{
    year++;
    double interest = balance * RATE / 100;
    balance = balance + interest;
} // interest no longer defined here
```

> A new interest **variable** is created in each iteration.

In contrast, the balance and years variables were defined *outside* the loop body. That way, the same variable is used for all iterations of the loop.

Figure 2
Execution of the doublinv Loop

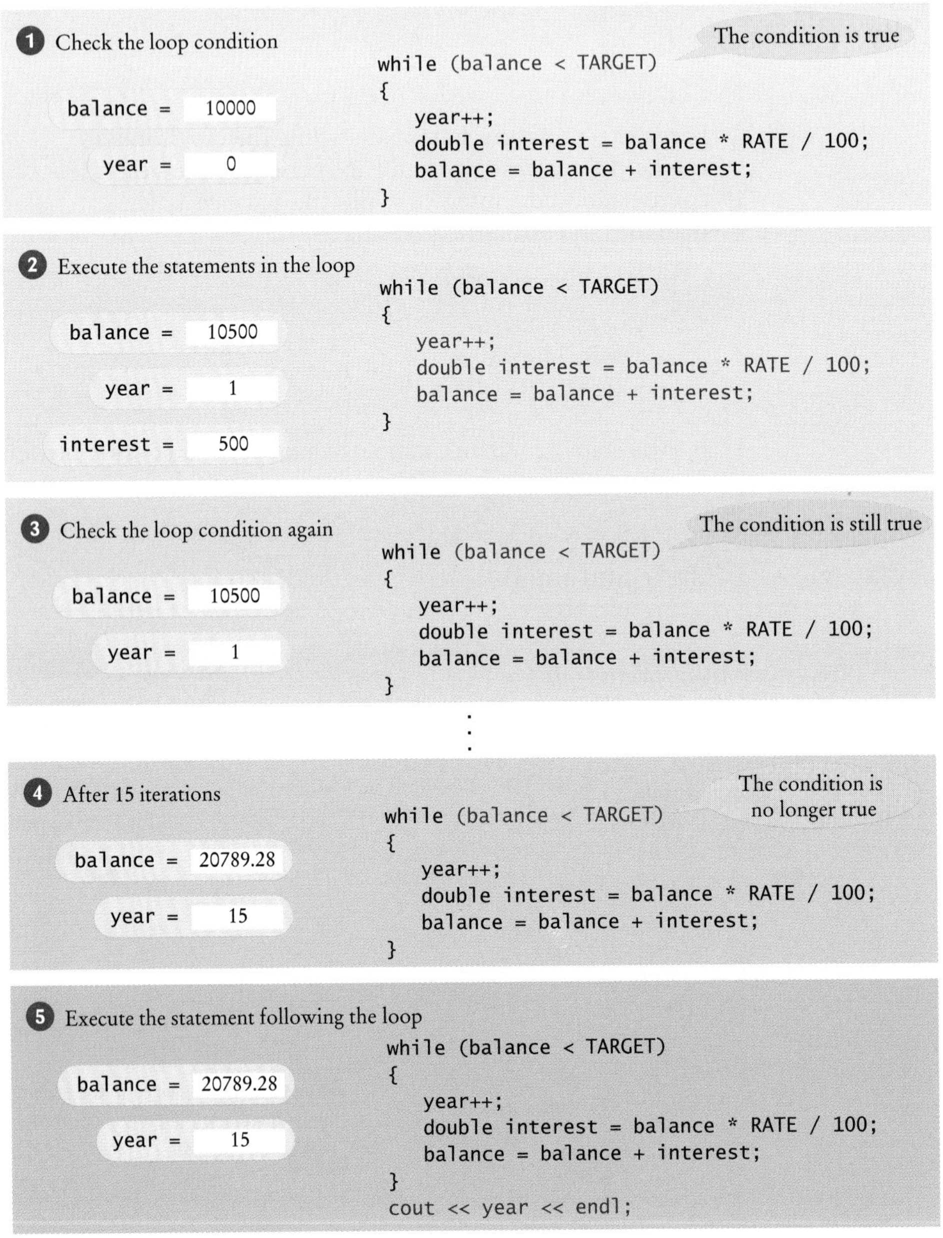

1 Check the loop condition

The condition is true

```
balance = 10000

year = 0
```

```
while (balance < TARGET)
{
    year++;
    double interest = balance * RATE / 100;
    balance = balance + interest;
}
```

2 Execute the statements in the loop

```
balance = 10500

year = 1

interest = 500
```

```
while (balance < TARGET)
{
    year++;
    double interest = balance * RATE / 100;
    balance = balance + interest;
}
```

3 Check the loop condition again

The condition is still true

```
balance = 10500

year = 1
```

```
while (balance < TARGET)
{
    year++;
    double interest = balance * RATE / 100;
    balance = balance + interest;
}
```

4 After 15 iterations

The condition is no longer true

```
balance = 20789.28

year = 15
```

```
while (balance < TARGET)
{
    year++;
    double interest = balance * RATE / 100;
    balance = balance + interest;
}
```

5 Execute the statement following the loop

```
balance = 20789.28

year = 15
```

```
while (balance < TARGET)
{
    year++;
    double interest = balance * RATE / 100;
    balance = balance + interest;
}
cout << year << endl;
```

Here is the program that solves the investment problem. Figure 2 illustrates the program's execution.

ch04/doublinv.cpp

```
 1   #include <iostream>
 2
 3   using namespace std;
 4
 5   int main()
 6   {
 7      const double RATE = 5;
 8      const double INITIAL_BALANCE = 10000;
 9      const double TARGET = 2 * INITIAL_BALANCE;
10
11      double balance = INITIAL_BALANCE;
12      int year = 0;
13
14      while (balance < TARGET)
15      {
16         year++;
17         double interest = balance * RATE / 100;
18         balance = balance + interest;
19      }
20
21      cout << "The investment doubled after "
22         << year << " years." << endl;
23
24      return 0;
25   }
```

Program Run

```
The investment doubled after 15 years.
```

SELF CHECK

1. How many years does it take for the investment to triple? Modify the program and run it.

2. If the interest rate is 10 percent per year, how many years does it take for the investment to double? Modify the program and run it.

3. Modify the program so that the balance after each year is printed. How did you do that?

4. Suppose we change the program so that the condition of the while loop is

   ```
   while (balance <= TARGET)
   ```

   What is the effect on the program? Why?

5. What does the following loop print?

   ```
   int n = 1;
   while (n < 100)
   {
      n = 2 * n;
      cout << n << " ";
   }
   ```

Practice It   Now you can try these exercises at the end of the chapter: R4.3, P4.11, P4.16.

Table 1 while Loop Examples

Loop	Output	Explanation
| ```
i = 5;
while (i > 0)
{
   cout << i << " ";
   i--;
}
``` | 5 4 3 2 1 | When i is 0, the loop condition is false, and the loop ends. |
| ```
i = 5;
while (i > 0)
{
   cout << i << " ";
   i++;
}
``` | 5 6 7 8 9 10 11 ... | The i++ statement is an error causing an "infinite loop" (see Common Error 4.1 on page 136). |
| ```
i = 5;
while (i > 5)
{
   cout << i << " ";
   i--;
}
``` | (No output) | The statement i > 5 is false, and the loop is never executed. |
| ```
i = 5;
while (i < 0)
{
   cout << i << " ";
   i--;
}
``` | (No output) | The programmer probably thought, "Stop when i is less than 0". However, the loop condition controls when the loop is executed, not when it ends (see Common Error 4.2 on page 137). |
| ```
i = 5;
while (i > 0) ;
{
   cout << i << " ";
   i--;
}
``` | (No output, program does not terminate) | Note the semicolon before the {. This loop has an empty body. It runs forever, checking whether i > 0 and doing nothing in the body. |

Common Error 4.1

Infinite Loops

A very annoying loop error is an *infinite loop:* a loop that runs forever and can be stopped only by killing the program or restarting the computer. If there are output statements in the program, then line after line of output flashes by on the screen. Otherwise, the program just sits there and *hangs*, seeming to do nothing. On some systems, you can terminate a hanging program by hitting Ctrl + C. On others, you can close the window in which the program runs.

A common reason for infinite loops is forgetting to update the variable that controls the loop:

```
year = 1;
while (year <= 20)
{
```
```

```
    balance = balance * (1 + RATE / 100);
}
```

Here the programmer forgot to add a year++ command in the loop. As a result, the year always stays at 1, and the loop never comes to an end.

Another common reason for an infinite loop is accidentally incrementing a counter that should be decremented (or vice versa). Consider this example:

```
year = 20;
while (year > 0)
{
    balance = balance * (1 + RATE / 100);
    year++;
}
```

The year variable really should have been decremented, not incremented. This is a common error because incrementing counters is so much more common than decrementing that your fingers may type the ++ on autopilot. As a consequence, year is always larger than 0, and the loop never ends. (Actually, year may eventually exceed the largest representable positive integer and *wrap around* to a negative number. Then the loop ends — of course, with a completely wrong result.)

Like this hamster who can't stop running in the treadmill, an infinite loop never ends.

Common Error 4.2

Don't Think "Are We There Yet?"

When doing something repetitive, most of us want to know when we are done. For example, you may think, "I want to get at least $20,000," and set the loop condition to

```
balance >= TARGET
```

But the while loop thinks the opposite: How long am I allowed to keep going? The correct loop condition is

```
while (balance < TARGET)
```

In other words: "Keep at it while the balance is less than the target."

When writing a loop condition, don't ask, "Are we there yet?" The condition determines how long the loop will keep going.

Common Error 4.3

Off-by-One Errors

Consider our computation of the number of years that are required to double an investment:

```
int year = 0;
while (balance < TARGET)
{
    year++;
    double interest = balance * RATE / 100;
    balance = balance + interest;
}
cout << "The investment doubled after " << year << " years." << endl;
```

Should year start at 0 or at 1? Should you test for balance < TARGET or for balance <= TARGET? It is easy to be **off by one** in these expressions.

Some people try to solve off-by-one errors by randomly inserting +1 or -1 until the program seems to work—a terrible strategy. It can take a long time to compile and test all the various possibilities. Expending a small amount of mental effort is a real time saver.

Fortunately, off-by-one errors are easy to avoid, simply by working through a couple of test cases and using the information from the test cases to come up with a rationale for your decisions.

> An off-by-one error is a common error when programming loops. Think through simple test cases to avoid this type of error.

Should year start at 0 or at 1? Look at a scenario with simple values: an initial balance of $100 and an interest rate of 50 percent. After year 1, the balance is $150, and after year 2 it is $225, or over $200. So the investment doubled after 2 years. The loop executed two times, incrementing year each time. Hence year must start at 0, not at 1.

year	balance
0	$100
1	$150
2	$225

In other words, the balance variable denotes the balance after the end of the year. At the outset, the balance variable contains the balance after year 0 and not after year 1.

Next, should you use a < or <= comparison in the test? If you want to settle this question with an example, you need to find a scenario in which the final balance is exactly twice the initial balance. This happens when the interest is 100 percent. The loop executes once. Now year is 1, and balance is exactly equal to 2 * INITIAL_BALANCE. Has the investment doubled after one year? It has. Therefore, the loop should not execute again. If the test condition is balance < TARGET, the loop stops, as it should. If the test condition had been balance <= TARGET, the loop would have executed once more.

In other words, you keep adding interest while the balance *has not yet doubled*.

Random Fact 4.1 The First Bug

According to legend, the first bug was found in the Mark II, a huge electromechanical computer at Harvard University. It really was caused by a bug—a moth was trapped in a relay switch.

Actually, from the note that the operator left in the log book next to the moth (see the photo), it appears as if the term "bug" had already been in active use at the time.

The pioneering computer scientist Maurice Wilkes wrote, "Somehow, at the Moore School and afterwards, one had always assumed there would be no particular difficulty in getting programs right. I can remember the exact instant in time at which it dawned on me that a great part of my future life would be spent finding mistakes in my own programs."

The First Bug

4.2 Problem Solving: Hand-Tracing

In Programming Tip 3.6, you learned about the method of hand-tracing. When you hand-trace code or pseudocode, you write the names of the variables on a sheet of paper, mentally execute each step of the code and update the variables.

It is best to have the code written or printed on a sheet of paper. Use a marker, such as a paper clip, to mark the current line. Whenever a variable changes, cross out the old value and write the new value below. When a program produces output, also write down the output in another column.

Consider this example. What value is displayed?

```cpp
int n = 1729;
int sum = 0;
while (n > 0)
{
   int digit = n % 10;
   sum = sum + digit;
   n = n / 10;
}
cout << sum << endl;
```

There are three variables: n, sum, and digit.

n	sum	digit

The first two variables are initialized with 1729 and 0 before the loop is entered.

```cpp
    int n = 1729;
⊂⊃  int sum = 0;
    while (n > 0)
    {
       int digit = n % 10;
       sum = sum + digit;
       n = n / 10;
    }
    cout << sum << endl;
```

n	sum	digit
1729	0	

Because n is greater than zero, enter the loop. The variable digit is set to 9 (the remainder of dividing 1729 by 10). The variable sum is set to 0 + 9 = 9.

```cpp
    int n = 1729;
    int sum = 0;
    while (n > 0)
    {
       int digit = n % 10;
⊂⊃     sum = sum + digit;
       n = n / 10;
    }
    cout << sum << endl;
```

n	sum	digit
1729	~~0~~	
	9	9

Finally, n becomes 172. (Recall that the remainder in the division 1729 / 10 is discarded because both arguments are integers.)

Cross out the old values and write the new ones under the old ones.

```
int n = 1729;
int sum = 0;
while (n > 0)
{
    int digit = n % 10;
    sum = sum + digit;
    n = n / 10;
}
cout << sum << endl;
```

n	sum	digit
~~1729~~	~~0~~	
172	9	9

Now check the loop condition again.

```
int n = 1729;
int sum = 0;
while (n > 0)
{
    int digit = n % 10;
    sum = sum + digit;
    n = n / 10;
}
cout << sum << endl;
```

Because n is still greater than zero, repeat the loop. Now digit becomes 2, sum is set to 9 + 2 = 11, and n is set to 17.

n	sum	digit
~~1729~~	~~0~~	
~~172~~	~~9~~	~~9~~
17	11	2

Repeat the loop once again, setting digit to 7, sum to 11 + 7 = 18, and n to 1.

n	sum	digit
~~1729~~	~~0~~	
~~172~~	~~9~~	~~9~~
~~17~~	~~11~~	~~2~~
1	18	7

Enter the loop for one last time. Now digit is set to 1, sum to 19, and n becomes zero.

n	sum	digit
~~1729~~	~~0~~	
~~172~~	~~9~~	~~9~~
~~17~~	~~11~~	~~2~~
~~1~~	~~18~~	~~7~~
0	19	1

```
    int n = 1729;
    int sum = 0;
    while (n > 0)
    {
        int digit = n % 10;
        sum = sum + digit;
        n = n / 10;
    }
    cout << sum << endl;
```

> Because n equals zero, this condition is not true.

The condition n > 0 is now false. Continue with the statement after the loop.

```
    int n = 1729;
    int sum = 0;
    while (n > 0)
    {
        int digit = n % 10;
        sum = sum + digit;
        n = n / 10;
    }
    cout << sum << endl;
```

n	sum	digit	output
1729	0		
172	9	9	
17	11	2	
1	18	7	
0	19	1	19

This statement is an output statement. The value that is output is the value of sum, which is 19.

Of course, you can get the same answer by just running the code. However, hand-tracing can give you an *insight* that you would not get if you simply ran the code. Consider again what happens in each iteration:

- We extract the last digit of n.
- We add that digit to sum.
- We strip the digit off n.

Hand-tracing can help you understand how an unfamiliar algorithm works.

In other words, the loop forms the sum of the digits in n. You now know what the loop does for any value of n, not just the one in the example. (Why would anyone want to form the sum of the digits? Operations of this kind are useful for checking the validity of credit card numbers and other forms of ID numbers—see Exercise P4.5.)

Hand-tracing can show errors in code or pseudocode.

Hand-tracing does not just help you understand code that works correctly. It is a powerful technique for finding errors in your code. When a program behaves in a way that you don't expect, get out a sheet of paper and track the values of the variables as you mentally step through the code.

You don't need a working program to do hand-tracing. You can hand-trace pseudocode. In fact, it is an excellent idea to hand-trace your pseudocode before you go to the trouble of translating it into actual code, to confirm that it works correctly.

SELF CHECK

6. Hand-trace the following code, showing the value of n and the output.

```
int n = 5;
while (n >= 0)
{
    n--;
    cout << n << endl;
}
```

7. Hand-trace the following code, showing the value of n and the output. What potential error do you notice?

```
int n = 1;
while (n <= 3)
{
    cout << n << ", ";
    n++;
}
```

8. Hand-trace the following code, assuming that a is 2 and n is 4. Then explain what the code does for arbitrary values of a and n.

```
int r = 1;
int i = 1;
while (i <= n)
{
    r = r * a;
    i++;
}
```

9. Trace the following code. What error do you observe?

```
int n = 1;
while (n != 50)
{
    cout << n << endl;
    n = n + 10;
}
```

10. The following pseudocode is intended to count the number of digits in the number n:

```
count = 1
temp = n
while (temp > 10)
    Increment count.
    Divide temp by 10.
```

Trace the pseudocode for n = 123 and n = 100. What error do you find?

Practice It   Now you can try these exercises at the end of the chapter: R4.1, R4.5.

4.3 The for Loop

The for loop is used when a value runs from a starting point to an ending point with a constant increment or decrement.

It often happens that you want to execute a sequence of statements a given number of times. You can use a while loop that is controlled by a counter, as in the following example:

```
counter = 1; // Initialize the counter
while (counter <= 10) // Check the counter
{
    cout << counter << endl;
    counter++; // Update the counter
}
```

Because this loop type is so common, there is a special form for it, called the for loop (see Syntax 4.2).

```
for (counter = 1; counter <= 10; counter++)
{
    cout << counter << endl;
}
```

Some people call this loop *count-controlled*. In contrast, the while loop of the preceding section can be called an *event-controlled* loop because it executes until an event occurs (for example, when the balance reaches the target). Another commonly-used term for a count-controlled loop is *definite*. You know from the outset that the loop body will be executed a definite number of times—ten times in our example. In contrast, you do not know how many iterations it takes to accumulate a target balance. Such a loop is called *indefinite*.

You can visualize the for *loop as an orderly sequence of steps.*

The for loop neatly groups the initialization, condition, and update expressions together. However, it is important to realize that these expressions are *not* executed together (see Figure 3).

- The initialization is executed once, before the loop is entered. **1**
- The condition is checked before each iteration. **2** **5**
- The update is executed after each iteration. **4**

Figure 3
Execution of a
for Loop

1 Initialize counter

```
for (counter = 1; counter <= 10; counter++)
{
    cout << counter << endl;
}
```

counter =   1

2 Check condition

```
for (counter = 1; counter <= 10; counter++)
{
    cout << counter << endl;
}
```

counter =   1

3 Execute loop body

```
for (counter = 1; counter <= 10; counter++)
{
    cout << counter << endl;
}
```

counter =   1

4 Update counter

```
for (counter = 1; counter <= 10; counter++)
{
    cout << counter << endl;
}
```

counter =   2

5 Check condition again

```
for (counter = 1; counter <= 10; counter++)
{
    cout << counter << endl;
}
```

counter =   2

Syntax 4.2 for Statement

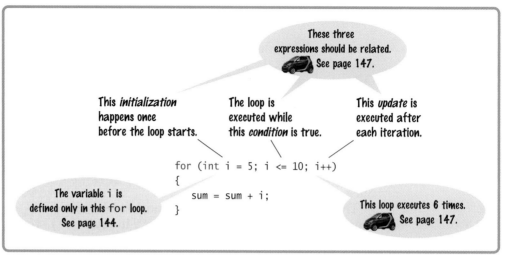

A for loop can count down instead of up:

```
for (counter = 10; counter >= 0; counter--) ...
```

The increment or decrement need not be in steps of 1:

```
for (counter = 0; counter <= 10; counter = counter + 2) ...
```

See Table 2 on page 146 for additional variations.

So far, we assumed that the counter variable had already been defined before the for loop. Alternatively, you can define a variable in the loop initialization. Such a variable is defined *only* in the loop:

```
for (int counter = 1; counter <= 10; counter++)
{
   ...
} // counter no longer defined here
```

Here is a typical use of the for loop. We want to print the balance of our savings account over a period of years, as shown in this table:

Year	Balance
1	10500.00
2	11025.00
3	11576.25
4	12155.06
5	12762.82

The for loop pattern applies because the variable year starts at 1 and then moves in constant increments until it reaches the target:

```
for (int year = 1; year <= nyears; year++)
{
   Update balance.
   Print year and balance.
}
```

Here is the complete program. Figure 4 shows the corresponding flowchart.

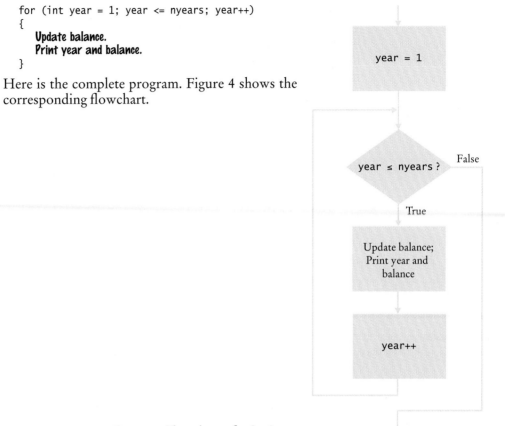

Figure 4 Flowchart of a for Loop

ch04/invtable.cpp

```cpp
1   #include <iostream>
2   #include <iomanip>
3
4   using namespace std;
5
6   int main()
7   {
8      const double RATE = 5;
9      const double INITIAL_BALANCE = 10000;
10     double balance = INITIAL_BALANCE;
11     int nyears;
12     cout << "Enter number of years: ";
13     cin >> nyears;
14
15     cout << fixed << setprecision(2);
16     for (int year = 1; year <= nyears; year++)
17     {
18        balance = balance * (1 + RATE / 100);
19        cout << setw(4) << year << setw(10) << balance << endl;
20     }
21
22     return 0;
23  }
```

Program Run

```
Enter number of years: 10
    1   10500.00
    2   11025.00
    3   11576.25
    4   12155.06
    5   12762.82
    6   13400.96
    7   14071.00
    8   14774.55
    9   15513.28
   10   16288.95
```

Table 2 for Loop Examples

Loop	Values of i	Comment
`for (i = 0; i <= 5; i++)`	0 1 2 3 4 5	Note that the loop is executed 6 times. (See Programming Tip 4.3 on page 147.)
`for (i = 5; i >= 0; i--)`	5 4 3 2 1 0	Use i-- for decreasing values.
`for (i = 0; i < 9; i = i + 2)`	0 2 4 6 8	Use i = i + 2 for a step size of 2.
`for (i = 0; i != 9; i = i + 2)`	0 2 4 6 8 10 12 14 ... (infinite loop)	You can use < or <= instead of != to avoid this problem.
`for (i = 1; i <= 20; i = i * 2)`	1 2 4 8 16	You can specify any rule for modifying i, such as doubling it in every step.
`for (i = 0; i < str.length(); i++)`	0 1 2 ... until the last valid index of the string str	In the loop body, use the expression str.substr(i, 1) to get a string containing the ith character.

SELF CHECK

11. Write the for loop of the invtable.cpp program as a while loop.

12. How many numbers does this loop print?
```
for (int n = 10; n >= 0; n--)
{
   cout << n << endl;
}
```

13. Write a for loop that prints all even numbers between 10 and 20 (inclusive).

14. Write a for loop that computes the sum of the integers from 1 to n.

15. How would you modify the for loop of the invtable.cpp program to print all balances until the investment has doubled?

Practice It Now you can try these exercises at the end of the chapter: R4.2, R4.7, P4.12.

Programming Tip 4.1

Use for Loops for Their Intended Purpose Only

A for loop is an *idiom* for a loop of a particular form. A value runs from the start to the end, with a constant increment or decrement.

The compiler won't check whether the initialization, condition, and update expressions are related. For example, the following loop is legal:

```cpp
// Confusing—unrelated expressions
for (cout << "Inputs: "; cin >> x; sum = sum + x)
{
    count++;
}
```

However, programmers reading such a for loop will be confused because it does not match their expectations. Use a while loop for iterations that do not follow the for idiom.

Programming Tip 4.2

Choose Loop Bounds That Match Your Task

Suppose you want to print line numbers that go from 1 to 10. Of course, you will want to use a loop

```cpp
for (int i = 1; i <= 10; i++)
```

The values for i are bounded by the relation $1 \leq i \leq 10$. Because there are $\leq$ on both bounds, the bounds are called *symmetric*.

When traversing the characters in a string, it is more natural to use the bounds

```cpp
for (int i = 0; i < str.length(); i++)
```

In this loop, i traverses all valid positions in the string. You can access the ith character as str.substr(i, 1). The values for i are bounded by $0 \leq i < \text{str.length()}$, with a $\leq$ to the left and a $<$ to the right. That is appropriate, because str.length() is not a valid position. Such bounds are called *asymmetric*.

In this case, it is not a good idea to use symmetric bounds:

```cpp
for (int i = 0; i <= str.length() - 1; i++) // Use < instead
```

The asymmetric form is easier to understand.

Programming Tip 4.3

Count Iterations

Finding the correct lower and upper bounds for an iteration can be confusing. Should you start at 0 or at 1? Should you use <= or < in the termination condition?

Counting the number of iterations is a very useful device for better understanding a loop. Counting is easier for loops with asymmetric bounds. The loop

```cpp
for (int i = a; i < b; i++)
```

is executed b - a times. For example, the loop

```cpp
for (int i = 0; i < 10; i++)
```

runs ten times, with values 0, 1, 2, 3, 4, 5, 6, 7, 8, and 9.

The loop with symmetric bounds,

```cpp
for (int i = a; i <= b; i++)
```

is executed b - a + 1 times. That "+1" is the source of many programming errors.

For example,

```
for (int i = 0; i <= 10; i++)
```

runs 11 times. Maybe that is what you want; if not, start at 1 or use < 10.

One way to visualize this "+1" error is by looking at a fence. Each section has one fence post to the left, and there is a final post on the right of the last section. Forgetting to count the last value is often called a "fence post error".

How many posts do you need for a fence with four sections? It is easy to be "off by one" with problems such as this one.

4.4 The do Loop

The do loop is appropriate when the loop body must be executed at least once.

Sometimes you want to execute the body of a loop at least once and perform the loop test after the body is executed. The do loop serves that purpose:

```
do
{
    statements
}
while (condition);
```

The body of the do loop is executed first, then the condition is tested.

Some people call such a loop a *post-test* loop because the condition is tested after completing the loop body. In contrast, while and for loops are *pre-test* loops. In those loop types, the condition is tested before entering the loop body.

A typical example for such a loop is input validation. Suppose you ask a user to enter a value < 100. If the user didn't pay attention and entered a larger value, you ask again, until the value is correct. Of course, you cannot test the value until the user has entered it. This is a perfect fit for the do loop (see Figure 5):

```
int value;
do
{
    cout << "Enter a value < 100: ";
    cin >> value;
}
while (value >= 100);
```

Figure 5 Flowchart of a do Loop

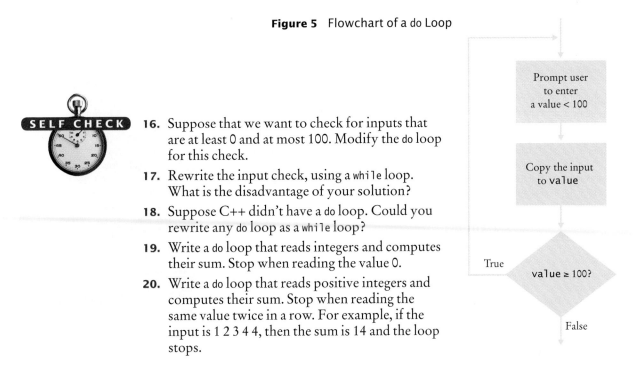

16. Suppose that we want to check for inputs that are at least 0 and at most 100. Modify the do loop for this check.

17. Rewrite the input check, using a while loop. What is the disadvantage of your solution?

18. Suppose C++ didn't have a do loop. Could you rewrite any do loop as a while loop?

19. Write a do loop that reads integers and computes their sum. Stop when reading the value 0.

20. Write a do loop that reads positive integers and computes their sum. Stop when reading the same value twice in a row. For example, if the input is 1 2 3 4 4, then the sum is 14 and the loop stops.

Practice It Now you can try these exercises at the end of the chapter: R4.8, R4.12, R4.13.

Programming Tip 4.4

Flowcharts for Loops

In Section 3.5, you learned how to use flowcharts to visualize the flow of control in a program. There are two types of loops that you can include in a flowchart; they correspond to a while loop and a do loop in C++. They differ in the placement of the condition—either before or after the loop body.

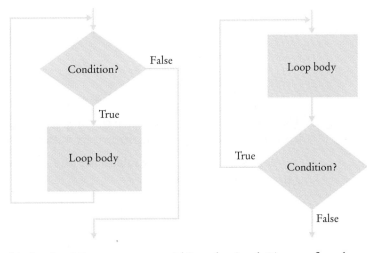

As described in Section 3.5, you want to avoid "spaghetti code" in your flowcharts. For loops, that means that you never want to have an arrow that points inside a loop body.

4.5 Processing Input

A sentinel value denotes the end of a data set, but it is not part of the data.

In this section, you will learn how to read and process a sequence of input values.

Whenever you read a sequence of inputs, you need to have some method of indicating the end of the sequence. Sometimes you are lucky and no input value can be zero. Then you can prompt the user to keep entering numbers, or 0 to finish the sequence. If zero is allowed but negative numbers are not, you can use –1 to indicate termination. A value that serves as a signal for termination is called a **sentinel**.

Let's put this technique to work in a program that computes the average of a set of salary values. In our sample program, we will use –1 as a sentinel. An employee would surely not work for a negative salary, but there may be volunteers who work for free.

Inside the loop, we read an input. If the input is not –1, we process it. In order to compute the average, we need the total sum of all salaries, and the number of inputs.

In the military, a sentinel guards a border or passage. In computer science, a sentinel value denotes the end of an input sequence or the border between input sequences.

```
while (...)
{
    cin >> salary;
    if (salary != -1)
    {
        sum = sum + salary;
        count++;
    }
}
```

We stay in the loop while the sentinel value is not detected.

```
while (salary != -1)
{
    ...
}
```

There is just one problem: When the loop is entered for the first time, no data value has been read. Be sure to initialize salary with some value other than the sentinel:

```
double salary = 0; // Any value other than -1 will do
```

Alternatively, use a do loop

```
do
{
    ...
}
while (salary != -1)
```

The following program reads inputs until the user enters the sentinel, and then computes and prints the average.

ch04/sentinel.cpp

```cpp
1   #include <iostream>
2
3   using namespace std;
4
5   int main()
6   {
7      double sum = 0;
8      int count = 0;
9      double salary = 0;
10     cout << "Enter salaries, -1 to finish: ";
11     while (salary != -1)
12     {
13        cin >> salary;
14        if (salary != -1)
15        {
16           sum = sum + salary;
17           count++;
18        }
19     }
20     if (count > 0)
21     {
22        double average = sum / count;
23        cout << "Average salary: " << average << endl;
24     }
25     else
26     {
27        cout << "No data" << endl;
28     }
29     return 0;
30  }
```

Program Run

```
Enter salaries, -1 to finish: 10 10 40 -1
Average salary: 20
```

Numeric sentinels only work if there is some restriction on the input. In many cases, though, there isn't. Suppose you want to compute the average of a data set that may contain 0 or negative values. Then you cannot use 0 or –1 to indicate the end of the input.

In such a situation, you can read input data until input fails. As you have seen in Section 3.8, the condition

```cpp
cin.fail()
```

is true if the preceding input has failed. For example, suppose that the input was read with these statements:

```cpp
double value;
cin >> value;
```

If the user enters a value that is not a number (such as Q), then the input fails.

We now encounter an additional complexity. You only know that input failed after you have entered the loop and attempted to read it. To remember the failure, use a Boolean variable:

```cpp
cout << "Enter values, Q to quit: ";
bool more = true;
while (more)
{
    cin >> value;
    if (cin.fail())
    {
        more = false;
    }
    else
    {
        Process value.
    }
}
```

You can use a Boolean variable to control a loop. Set the variable to true before entering the loop, then set it to false to leave the loop.

Some programmers dislike the introduction of a Boolean variable to control a loop. Special Topic 4.2 on page 153 shows an alternative mechanism for leaving a loop. However, when reading input, there is an easier way. The expression

```cpp
cin >> value
```

can be used in a condition. It evaluates to true if cin has *not* failed after reading value. Therefore, you can read and process a set of inputs with the following loop:

```cpp
cout << "Enter values, Q to quit: ";
while (cin >> value)
{
    Process value.
}
```

This loop is suitable for processing a single sequence of inputs. You will learn more about reading inputs in Chapter 8.

SELF CHECK

21. What does the sentinel.cpp program print when the user immediately types –1 when prompted for a value?

22. Why does the sentinel.cpp program have *two* checks of the form
    ```cpp
    salary != -1
    ```

23. What would happen if the definition of the salary variable in sentinel.cpp was changed to
    ```cpp
    double salary = -1;
    ```

24. We prompt the user "Enter values, Q to quit." What happens when the user enters a different letter?

25. What is wrong with the following loop for reading a sequence of values?
    ```cpp
    cout << "Enter values, Q to quit: ";
    while (!cin.fail())
    {
        double value;
        cin >> value;
        sum = sum + value;
        count++;
    }
    ```

Practice It Now you can try these exercises at the end of the chapter: R4.10, P4.6, P4.7.

Special Topic 4.1

Clearing the Failure State

When an input operation has failed, all further input operations also fail. If you want to read two number sequences and use a letter as a sentinel, you need to clear the failure state after reading the first sentinel. Call the `clear` function:

```
cout << "Enter values, Q to quit.\n";
while (cin >> values)
{
    Process input.
}
cin.clear();
```

Suppose the user has entered 30 10 5 Q. The input of Q has caused the failure. Because only successfully processed characters are removed from the input, the Q character is still present. Read it into a dummy variable:

```
string sentinel;
cin >> sentinel;
```

Now you can go on and read more inputs.

Special Topic 4.2

The Loop-and-a-Half Problem and the break Statement

Some programmers dislike loops that are controlled by a Boolean variable, such as:

```
bool more = true;
while (more)
{
    cin >> value;
    if (cin.fail())
    {
        more = false;
    }
    else
    {
        Process value.
    }
}
```

The actual test for loop termination is in the middle of the loop, not at the top. This is called a **loop and a half** because one must go halfway into the loop before knowing whether one needs to terminate.

As an alternative, you can use the break reserved word.

```
while (true)
{
    cin >> value;
    if (cin.fail()) { break; }
    Process value.
}
```

The break statement breaks out of the enclosing loop, independent of the loop condition.

In the loop-and-a-half case, break statements can be beneficial. But it is difficult to lay down clear rules as to when they are safe and when they should be avoided. We do not use the break statement in this book.

Redirection of Input and Output

Consider the `sentinel` program that computes the average value of an input sequence. If you use such a program, then it is quite likely that you already have the values in a file, and it seems a shame that you have to type them all in again. The command line interface of your operating system provides a way to link a file to the input of a program, as if all the characters in the file had actually been typed by a user. If you type

```
sentinel < numbers.txt
```

the program is executed. Its input instructions no longer expect input from the keyboard. All input commands get their input from the file `numbers.txt`. This process is called *input redirection*.

> Use input redirection to read input from a file. Use output redirection to capture program output in a file.

Input redirection is an excellent tool for testing programs. When you develop a program and fix its bugs, it is boring to keep entering the same input every time you run the program. Spend a few minutes putting the inputs into a file, and use redirection.

You can also redirect output. In this program, that is not terribly useful. If you run

```
sentinel < numbers.txt > output.txt
```

the file `output.txt` contains the input prompts and the output, such as

```
Enter a value, -1 to finish: Enter a value, -1 to finish:
Enter a value, -1 to finish: Enter a value, -1 to finish:
Average: 15
```

However, redirecting output is obviously useful for programs that produce lots of output. You can print the file containing the output or edit it before you turn it in for grading.

4.6 Problem Solving: Storyboards

When you design a program that interacts with a user, you need to make a plan for that interaction. What information does the user provide, and in which order? What information will your program display, and in which format? What should happen when there is an error? When does the program quit?

> A storyboard consists of annotated sketches for each step in an action sequence.

This planning is similar to the development of a movie or a computer game, where *storyboards* are used to plan action sequences. A storyboard is made up of panels that show a sketch of each step. Annotations explain what is happening and note any special situations. Storyboards are also used to develop software—see Figure 6.

Making a storyboard is very helpful when you begin designing a program. You need to ask yourself which information you need in order to compute the answers that the program user wants. You need to decide how to present those answers. These are important considerations that you want to settle before you design an algorithm for computing the answers.

> Developing a storyboard helps you understand the inputs and outputs that are required for a program.

Let's look at a simple example. We want to write a program that helps users with questions such as "How many tablespoons are in a pint?" or "How many inches are 30 centimeters?"

What information does the user provide?

- The quantity and unit to convert from
- The unit to convert to

Figure 6
Storyboard for the
Design of a Web
Application

What if there is more than one quantity? A user may have a whole table of centimeter values that should be converted into inches.

What if the user enters units that our program doesn't know how to handle, such as angstrom?

What if the user asks for impossible conversions, such as inches to gallons?

Let's get started with a storyboard panel. It is a good idea to write the user inputs in a different color. (Underline them if you don't have a color pen handy.)

Converting a Sequence of Values

What unit do you want to convert from? cm
What unit do you want to convert to? in
Enter values, terminated by zero ————— Allows conversion of multiple values
30
30 cm = 11.81 in ———
100   Format makes clear what got converted
100 cm = 39.37 in
0
What unit do you want to convert from?

The storyboard shows how we deal with a potential confusion. A user who wants to know how many inches are 30 centimeters may not read the first prompt carefully and specify inches. But then the output is "30 in = 76.2 cm", alerting the user to the problem.

The storyboard also raises an issue. How is the user supposed to know that "cm" and "in" are valid units? Would "centimeter" and "inches" also work? What happens when the user enters a wrong unit? Let's make another storyboard to demonstrate error handling.

Handling Unknown Units (needs improvement)

What unit do you want to convert from? cm
What unit do you want to convert to? inches
Sorry, unknown unit.
What unit do you want to convert to? inch
Sorry, unknown unit.
What unit do you want to convert to? grrr

To eliminate frustration, it is better to list the units that the user can supply.

From unit (in, ft, mi, mm, cm, m, km, oz, lb, g, kg, tsp, tbsp, pint, gall): cm
To unit: in ──────── No need to list the units again

We switched to a shorter prompt to make room for all the unit names. Exercise R4.17 explores a different alternative.

There is another issue that we haven't addressed yet. How does the user quit the program? The first storyboard gives the impression that the program will go on forever.

We can ask the user after seeing the sentinel that terminates an input sequence.

Exiting the Program

From unit (in, ft, mi, mm, cm, m, km, oz, lb, g, kg, tsp, tbsp, pint, gall): cm
To unit: in
Enter values, terminated by zero
30
30 cm = 11.81 in
0 ──────── Sentinel triggers the prompt to exit
More conversions (y, n)? n
(Program exits)

As you can see from this case study, a storyboard is essential for developing a working program. You need to know the flow of the user interaction in order to structure your program.

SELF CHECK   26.   Provide a storyboard panel for a program that reads a number of test scores and prints the average score. The program only needs to process one set of scores. Don't worry about error handling.

27. Google has a simple interface for converting units. You just type the question, and you get the answer.

Google [How many inches in 30 cm] [Search] Advanced Search

Web ⊞ Show options...   Results 1 - 10 of about **4,180,000** for **How many inches in 30 cm**. (0.24 seconds)

🖩 **30 centimeters = 11.8110236 inches**
More about calculator.

Make storyboards for an equivalent interface in a C++ program. Show the "happy day" scenario in which all goes well, and show the handling of two kinds of errors.

28. Consider a modification of the program in Self Check 26. Drop the lowest score before computing the average. Provide a storyboard for the situation in which a user only provides one score.

29. What is the problem with implementing the following storyboard in C++?

> **Computing Multiple Averages**
>
> Enter scores: 90 80 90 100 80
> The average is **88**
> Enter scores: 100 70 70 100 80
> The average is **88** ⎯⎯⎯ -1 is used as a sentinel to exit the program
> Enter scores: -1
> (Program exits)

30. Produce a storyboard for a program that compares the growth of a $10,000 investment for a given number of years under two interest rates.

Practice It   Now you can try these exercises at the end of the chapter: R4.17, R4.18, R4.19.

4.7 Common Loop Algorithms

In the following sections, we discuss some of the most common algorithms that are implemented as loops. You can use them as starting points for your loop designs.

4.7.1 Sum and Average Value

Computing the sum of a number of inputs is a very common task. Keep a *running total:* a variable to which you add each input value. Of course, the total should be initialized with 0.

```
double total = 0;
double input;
while (cin >> input)
{
   total = total + input;
}
```

To compute an average, keep a total and a count of all values.

To compute an average, count how many values you have, and divide by the count. Be sure to check that the count is not zero.

```
double total = 0;
int count = 0;
double input;
while (cin >> input)
{
    total = total + input;
    count++;
}
double average = 0;
if (count > 0) { average = total / count; }
```

4.7.2 Counting Matches

To count values that fulfill a condition, check all values and increment a counter for each match.

You often want to know how many values fulfill a particular condition. For example, you may want to count how many spaces are in a string. Keep a counter, a variable that is initialized with 0 and incremented whenever there is a match.

```
int spaces = 0;
for (int i = 0; i < str.length(); i++)
{
    string ch = str.substr(i, 1);
    if (ch == " ")
    {
        spaces++;
    }
}
```

For example, if str is the string "My Fair Lady", spaces is incremented twice (when i is 2 and 7).

Note that the spaces variable is declared outside the loop. We want the loop to update a single variable. The ch variable is declared inside the loop. A separate variable is created for each iteration and removed at the end of each loop iteration.

This loop can also be used for scanning inputs. The following loop reads text, a word at a time, and counts the number of words with at most three letters:

```
int short_words = 0;
string input;
while (cin >> input)
{
    if (input.length() <= 3)
    {
        short_words++;
    }
}
```

In a loop that counts matches, a counter is incremented whenever a match is found.

4.7.3 Finding the First Match

When you count the values that fulfill a condition, you need to look at all values. However, if your task is to find a match, then you can stop as soon as the condition is fulfilled.

Here is a loop that finds the first space in a string. Because we do not visit all elements in the string, a `while` loop is a better choice than a `for` loop:

When searching, you look at items until a match is found.

```
bool found = false;
int position = 0;
while (!found && position < str.length())
{
    string ch = str.substr(position, 1);
    if (ch == " ") { found = true; }
    else { position++; }
}
```

If a match was found, then `found` is `true` and `position` is the index of the first match. If the loop did not find a match, then `found` remains `false` after the end of the loop.

In the preceding example, we searched a string for a character that matches a condition. You can apply the same process for user input. Suppose you are asking a user to enter a positive value < 100. Keep asking until the user provides a correct input:

```
bool valid = false;
double input;
while (!valid)
{
    cout << "Please enter a positive value < 100: ";
    cin >> input;
    if (0 < input && input < 100) { valid = true; }
    else { cout << "Invalid input." << endl; }
}
```

Note that the variable `input` is declared *outside* the `while` loop because you will want to use the input after the loop has finished. If it had been declared inside the loop body, you would not be able to use it outside the loop.

4.7.4 Maximum and Minimum

To compute the largest value in a sequence, keep a variable that stores the largest element that you have encountered, and update it when you find a larger one:

```
double largest;
cin >> largest;
double input;
while (cin >> input)
{
    if (input > largest)
    {
        largest = input;
    }
}
```

This algorithm requires that there is at least one input.

To find the height of the tallest bus rider, remember the largest value so far, and update it whenever you see a taller one.

To compute the smallest value, simply reverse the comparison:

```
double smallest;
cin >> smallest;
double input;
while (cin >> input)
{
   if (input < smallest)
   {
      smallest = input;
   }
}
```

4.7.5 Comparing Adjacent Values

When processing a sequence of values in a loop, you sometimes need to compare a value with the value that just preceded it. For example, suppose you want to check whether a sequence of inputs contains adjacent duplicates such as 1 7 2 9 9 4 9.

Now you face a challenge. Consider the typical loop for reading a value:

```
double input;
while (cin >> input)
{
   // Now input contains the current input
   ...
}
```

To compare adjacent inputs, store the preceding input in a variable.

How can you compare the current input with the preceding one? At any time, input contains the current input, overwriting the previous one.

The answer is to store the previous input, like this:

```
double input;
double previous;
while (cin >> input)
{
   if (input == previous) { cout << "Duplicate input" << endl; }
   previous = input;
}
```

*When comparing adjacent values,
store the previous value in a variable.*

One problem remains. When the loop is entered for the first time, previous has not yet been set. You can solve this problem with an initial input operation outside the loop:

```
double input;
double previous;
cin >> previous;
while (cin >> input)
{
    if (input == previous) { cout << "Duplicate input" << endl; }
    previous = input;
}
```

SELF CHECK

31. What total is computed when no user input is provided in the algorithm in Section 4.7.1?

32. How do you compute the total of all positive inputs?

33. What is the value of position when no match is found in the algorithm in Section 4.7.3?

34. What is wrong with the following loop for finding the position of the first space in a string?

```
bool found = false;
for (int position = 0; !found && position < str.length(); position++)
{
    string ch = str.substr(position, 1);
    if (ch == " ") { found = true; }
}
```

35. How do you find the *last* space in a string?

36. What is wrong with the following loop for finding the smallest input value?

```
double smallest = 0;
double input;
while (cin >> input)
{
    if (input < smallest)
    {
        smallest = input;
    }
}
```

37. What happens with the algorithm in Section 4.7.5 when no input is provided at all?

Practice It Now you can try these exercises at the end of the chapter: P4.8, P4.13, P4.14.

<table>
<tr><td>HOW TO 4.1</td><td>**Writing a Loop**</td></tr>
</table>

This How To walks you through the process of implementing a loop statement. We will illustrate the steps with the following example problem:

Read twelve temperature values (one for each month), and display the number of the month with the highest temperature. For example, according to http://worldclimate.com, the average maximum temperatures for Death Valley are (in order by month):

18.2 22.6 26.4 31.1 36.6 42.2
45.7 44.5 40.2 33.1 24.2 17.6

In this case, the month with the highest temperature (45.7 degrees Celsius) is July, and the program should display 7.

Step 1   Decide what work must be done *inside* the loop.

Every loop needs to do some kind of repetitive work, such as

- Reading another item.
- Updating a value (such as a bank balance or total).
- Incrementing a counter.

If you can't figure out what needs to go inside the loop, start by writing down the steps that you would take if you solved the problem by hand. For example, with the temperature reading problem, you might write

> Read first value.
> Read second value.
> If second value is higher than the first, set highest temperature to that value, highest month to 2.
> Read next value.
> If value is higher than the first and second, set highest temperature to that value, highest month to 3.
> Read next value.
> If value is higher than the highest temperature seen so far, set highest temperature to that value,
>   highest month to 4.
> . . .

Now look at these steps and reduce them to a set of *uniform* actions that can be placed into the loop body. The first action is easy:

> Read next value.

The next action is trickier. In our description, we used tests "higher than the first", "higher than the first and second", "higher than the highest temperature seen so far". We need to settle on one test that works for all iterations. The last formulation is the most general.

Similarly, we must find a general way of setting the highest month. We need a variable that stores the current month, running from 1 to 12. Then we can formulate the second loop action:

> If value is higher than the highest temperature, set highest temperature to that value,
>   highest month to current month.

Altogether our loop is

```
Loop
    Read next value.
    If value is higher than the highest temperature, set highest temperature to that value,
        highest month to current month.
    Increment current month.
```

Step 2   Specify the loop condition.

What goal do you want to reach in your loop? Typical examples are:

- Has the counter reached the final value?
- Have you read the last input value?
- Has a value reached a given threshold?

In our example, we simply want the current month to reach 12.

Step 3   Determine the loop type.

We distinguish between two major loop types. A definite or count-controlled loop is executed a definite number of times. In an indefinite or event-controlled loop, the number of iterations is not known in advance—the loop is executed until some event happens. A typical example of the latter is a loop that reads data until a sentinel is encountered.

If you know in advance how many times a loop is repeated, use a for statement. For other loops, consider the loop condition. Do you need to complete one iteration of the loop body before you can tell when to terminate the loop? In that case, you should choose a do loop. Otherwise, use a while loop.

In our example, we read 12 temperature values. Therefore, we choose a for loop.

Step 4   Set up variables for entering the loop for the first time.

List all variables that are used and updated in the loop, and determine how to initialize them. Commonly, counters are initialized with 0 or 1, totals with 0.

In our example, the variables are

```
current month
highest value
highest month
```

We need to be careful how we set up the highest temperature value. We can't simply set it to 0. After all, our program needs to work with temperature values from Antarctica, all of which may be negative.

A good option is to set the highest temperature value to the first input value. Of course, then we need to remember to only read in another 11 values, with the current month starting at 2.

We also need to initialize the highest month with 1. After all, in an Australian city, we may never find a month that is warmer than January.

Step 5   Process the result after the loop has finished.

In many cases, the desired result is simply a variable that was updated in the loop body. For example, in our temperature program, the result is the highest month. Sometimes, the loop computes values that contribute to the final result. For example, suppose you are asked to average the temperatures. Then the loop should compute the sum, not the average. After the loop has completed, you are ready to compute the average: divide the sum by the number of inputs.

Here is our complete loop:

```
Read first value; store as highest value.
highest month = 1
for (current month = 2; current month <= 12; current month++)
    Read next value.
    If value is higher than the highest value, set highest value to that value,
        highest month to current month.
```

Step 6 Trace the loop with typical examples.

Hand-trace your loop code, as described in Section 4.2. Choose example values that are not too complex—executing the loop 3–5 times is enough to check for the most common errors. Pay special attention when entering the loop for the first and last time.

Sometimes, you want to make a slight modification to make tracing feasible. For example, when hand-tracing the investment doubling problem, use an interest rate of 20 percent rather than 5 percent. When hand-tracing the temperature loop, use 4 data values, not 12.

Let's say the data are 22.6 36.6 44.5 24.2. Here is the walkthrough:

current month	current value	highest month	highest value
		~~1~~	~~22.6~~
~~2~~	36.6	~~2~~	~~36.6~~
~~3~~	44.5	3	44.5
4	24.2		

The trace demonstrates that **highest month** and **highest value** are properly set.

Step 7 Implement the loop in C++.

Here's the loop for our example. Exercise P4.4 asks you to complete the program.

```cpp
double highest_value;
cin >> highest_value;
int highest_month = 1;
for (int current_month = 2; current_month <= 12; current_month++)
{
    double next_value;
    cin >> next_value;
    if (next_value > highest_value)
    {
        highest_value = next_value;
        highest_month = current_month;
    }
}
cout << highest_month << endl;
```

WORKED EXAMPLE 4.1   **Credit Card Processing**

This Worked Example uses a loop to remove spaces from a credit card number.

⊕ Available online at www.wiley.com/college/horstmann.

4.8 Nested Loops

When the body of a loop contains another loop, the loops are nested. A typical use of nested loops is printing a table with rows and columns.

In Section 3.4, you saw how to nest two `if` statements. Similarly, complex iterations sometimes require a **nested loop**: a loop inside another loop statement. When processing tables, nested loops occur naturally. An outer loop iterates over all rows of the table. An inner loop deals with the columns in the current row.

In this section you will see how to print a table. For simplicity, we will simply print powers x^n, as in the table at right.

Here is the pseudocode for printing the table:

Print table header.
For x from 1 to 10
    Print table row.
    Print endl.

How do you print a table row? You need to print a value for each exponent. This requires a second loop:

For n from 1 to 4
    Print x^n.

x^1	x^2	x^3	x^4
1	1	1	1
2	4	8	16
3	9	27	81
...	...	...	...
10	100	1000	10000

This loop must be placed inside the preceding loop. We say that the inner loop is *nested* inside the outer loop (see Figure 7).

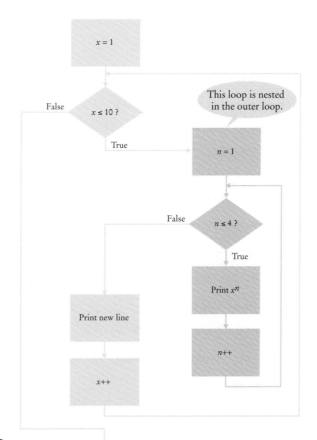

Figure 7
Flowchart of a Nested Loop

The hour and minute displays in a digital clock are an example of nested loops. The hours loop 12 times, and for each hour, the minutes loop 60 times.

There are 10 rows in the outer loop. For each *x*, the program prints four columns in the inner loop. Thus, a total of 10 × 4 = 40 values are printed.

Following is the complete program. Note that we also use loops to print the table header. However, those loops are not nested.

ch04/powtable.cpp

```
1   #include <iostream>
2   #include <iomanip>
3   #include <cmath>
4
5   using namespace std;
6
7   int main()
8   {
9      const int NMAX = 4;
10     const double XMAX = 10;
11
12     // Print table header
13
14     for (int n = 1; n <= NMAX; n++)
15     {
16        cout << setw(10) << n;
17     }
18     cout << endl;
19     for (int n = 1; n <= NMAX; n++)
20     {
21        cout << setw(10) << "x ";
22     }
23     cout << endl << endl;
24
25     // Print table body
26
27     for (double x = 1; x <= XMAX; x++)
28     {
29        // Print table row
30
31        for (int n = 1; n <= NMAX; n++)
32        {
33           cout << setw(10) << pow(x, n);
34        }
35        cout << endl;
36     }
37
38     return 0;
39  }
```

Program Run

```
    1         2         3         4
    x         x         x         x

    1         1         1         1
    2         4         8        16
    3         9        27        81
    4        16        64       256
    5        25       125       625
    6        36       216      1296
    7        49       343      2401
    8        64       512      4096
    9        81       729      6561
   10       100      1000     10000
```

Table 3 Nested Loop Examples		
Nested Loops	Output	Explanation

`for (i = 1; i <= 3; i++)`
`{`
`   for (j = 1; j <= 4; j++)  { cout << "*"; }`
`   cout << endl;`
`}`
	`****`
	`****`
	`****`
		Prints 3 rows of 4 asterisks each.

`for (i = 1; i <= 4; i++)`
`{`
`   for (j = 1; j <= 3; j++) { cout << "*"; }`
`   cout << endl;`
`}`
	`***`
	`***`
	`***`
	`***`
		Prints 4 rows of 3 asterisks each.

`for (i = 1; i <= 4; i++)`
`{`
`   for (j = 1; j <= i; j++) { cout << "*"; }`
`   cout << endl;`
`}`
	`*`
	`**`
	`***`
	`****`
		Prints 4 rows of lengths 1, 2, 3, and 4.

`for (i = 1; i <= 3; i++)`
`{`
`   for (j = 1; j <= 5; j++)`
`   {`
`      if (j % 2 == 0) { cout << "*"; }`
`      else { cout << "-"; }`
`   }`
`   cout << endl;`
`}`
	`-*-*-`
	`-*-*-`
	`-*-*-`
		Prints asterisks in even columns, dashes in odd columns.

`for (i = 1; i <= 3; i++)`
`{`
`   for (j = 1; j <= 5; j++)`
`   {`
`      if ((i + j) % 2 == 0) { cout << "*"; }`
`      else { cout << " "; }`
`   }`
`   cout << endl;`
`}`
	`* * *`
	` * * `
	`* * *`
		Prints a checkerboard pattern.

38. Why is there a statement cout << endl in the outer loop but not in the inner loop?

39. How would you change the program so that all powers from x^0 to x^5 are displayed?

40. If you make the change in Self Check 39, how many values are displayed?

41. What do the following nested loops display?

```
for (int i = 0; i < 3; i++)
{
   for (int j = 0; j < 4; j++)
   {
      cout << i + j;
   }
   cout << endl;
}
```

42. Write nested loops that make the following pattern of brackets:

```
[][][][]
[][][][]
[][][][]
```

Practice It   Now you can try these exercises at the end of the chapter: R4.23, P4.21, P4.22.

4.9 Random Numbers and Simulations

In a simulation, you use the computer to simulate an activity. You can introduce randomness by calling the random number generator.

A *simulation program* uses the computer to simulate an activity in the real world (or an imaginary one). Simulations are commonly used for predicting climate change, analyzing traffic, picking stocks, and many other applications in science and business. In the following sections, you will learn how to implement simulations that model phenomena with a degree of randomness.

4.9.1 Generating Random Numbers

Many events in the real world are difficult to predict with absolute precision, yet we can sometimes know the average behavior quite well. For example, a store may know from experience that a customer arrives every five minutes. Of course, that is an average—customers don't arrive in five minute intervals. To accurately model customer traffic, you want to take that random fluctuation into account. Now, how can you run such a simulation in the computer?

The C++ library has a *random number generator*, which produces numbers that appear to be completely random. Calling rand() yields a random integer between 0 and RAND_MAX (which is an implementation-dependent constant, typically, but not always, the largest valid int value). Call rand() again, and you get a different number. The rand function is declared in the <cstdlib> header.

The following program calls the rand function ten times.

ch04/random.cpp

```
1   #include <iostream>
2   #include <cstdlib>
3
4   using namespace std;
```

```
 5
 6  int main()
 7  {
 8     for (int i = 1; i <= 10; i++)
 9     {
10        int r = rand();
11        cout << r << endl;
12     }
13     return 0;
14  }
```

Program Run

```
1804289383
846930886
1681692777
1714636915
1957747793
424238335
719885386
1649760492
596516649
118964142
```

Actually, the numbers are not completely random. They are drawn from sequences of numbers that don't repeat for a long time. These sequences are actually computed from fairly simple formulas; they just behave like random numbers. For that reason, they are often called **pseudorandom numbers**.

Try running the program again. You will get the *exact same output*! This confirms that the random numbers are generated by formulas. However, when running simulations, you don't always want to get the same results. To overcome this problem, specify a *seed* for the random number sequence. Every time you use a new seed, the random number generator starts generating a new sequence. The seed is set with the srand function. A simple value to use as a seed is the current time:

```
srand(time(0));
```

Simply make this call once in your program, before generating any random numbers. Then the random numbers will be different in every program run. Also include the <ctime> header that declares the time function.

4.9.2 Simulating Die Tosses

In actual applications, you need to transform the output from the random number generator into different ranges. For example, to simulate the throw of a die, you need random numbers between 1 and 6.

Here is the general recipe for computing random integers between two bounds a and b. As you know from Programming Tip 4.3 on page 147, there are b - a + 1 values between a and b, including the bounds themselves. First compute rand() % (b - a + 1) to obtain a random value between 0 and b - a, then add a, yielding a random value between a and b:

```
int r = rand() % (b - a + 1) + a;
```

Here is a program that simulates the throw of a pair of dice.

ch04/dice.cpp

```cpp
1   #include <iostream>
2   #include <string>
3   #include <cstdlib>
4   #include <ctime>
5
6   using namespace std;
7
8   int main()
9   {
10     srand(time(0));
11
12     for (int i = 1; i <= 10; i++)
13     {
14        int d1 = rand() % 6 + 1;
15        int d2 = rand() % 6 + 1;
16        cout << d1 << " " << d2 << endl;
17     }
18     cout << endl;
19     return 0;
20  }
```

Program Run

```
5 1
2 1
1 2
5 1
1 2
6 4
4 4
6 1
6 3
5 2
```

4.9.3 The Monte Carlo Method

The Monte Carlo method is an ingenious method for finding approximate solutions to problems that cannot be precisely solved. (The method is named after the famous casino in Monte Carlo.) Here is a typical example: It is difficult to compute the number π, but you can approximate it quite well with the following simulation.

Simulate shooting a dart into a square surrounding a circle of radius 1. That is easy: generate random x and y coordinates between −1 and 1.

If the generated point lies inside the circle, we count it as a *hit*. That is the case when $x^2 + y^2 \leq 1$. Because our shots are entirely random, we expect that the ratio of *hits / tries* is approximately equal to the ratio of the areas of the circle and the square, that is, $\pi / 4$. Therefore, our estimate for π is $4 \times$ *hits / tries*. This method yields an estimate for π, using nothing but simple arithmetic.

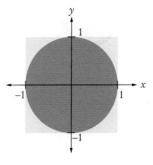

To run the Monte Carlo simulation, you have to work a little harder with random number generation. When you throw a die, it has to come up with one of six faces. When throwing a dart, however, there are many possible outcomes. You must generate a random floating-point number.

First, generate the following value:

```cpp
double r = rand() * 1.0 / RAND_MAX; // Between 0 and 1
```

The value r is a random floating-point value between 0 and 1. (You have to multiply by 1.0 to ensure that one of the operands of the / operator is a floating-point number. The division rand() / RAND_MAX would be an integer division — see Common Error 2.3.)

To generate a random value between –1 and 1, you compute:

```cpp
double x = -1 + 2 * r; // Between -1 and 1
```

As r ranges from 0 to 1, x ranges from $-1 + 2 \times 0 = -1$ to $-1 + 2 \times 1 = 1$.

Here is the program that carries out the simulation.

ch04/montecarlo.cpp

```cpp
1   #include <iostream>
2   #include <cstdlib>
3   #include <cmath>
4   #include <ctime>
5
6   using namespace std;
7
8   int main()
9   {
10     const int TRIES = 10000;
11
12     srand(time(0));
13
14     int hits = 0;
15     for (int i = 1; i <= TRIES; i++)
16     {
17        double r = rand() * 1.0 / RAND_MAX; // Between 0 and 1
18        double x = -1 + 2 * r; // Between -1 and 1
19        r = rand() * 1.0 / RAND_MAX;
20        double y = -1 + 2 * r;
21        if (x * x + y * y <= 1) { hits++; }
22     }
23     double pi_estimate = 4.0 * hits / TRIES;
24     cout << "Estimate for pi: " << pi_estimate << endl;
25     return 0;
26  }
```

Program Run

```
Estimate for pi: 3.1504
```

43. How do you simulate a coin toss with the `rand` function?

44. How do you simulate the picking of a random playing card?

45. Why does the `dice.cpp` file include the `<ctime>` header?

46. In many games, you throw a pair of dice to get a value between 2 and 12. What is wrong with this simulated throw of a pair of dice?

```
int sum = rand() % 11 + 2;
```

47. How do you generate a random floating-point number between 0 and 100?

Practice It   Now you can try these exercises at the end of the chapter: R4.24, P4.10, P4.25.

Random Fact 4.2 Software Piracy

As you read this, you have written a few computer programs, and you have experienced firsthand how much effort it takes to write even the humblest of programs. Writing a real software product, such as a financial application or a computer game, takes a lot of time and money. Few people, and fewer companies, are going to spend that kind of time and money if they don't have a reasonable chance to make more money from their effort. (Actually, some companies give away their software in the hope that users will upgrade to more elaborate paid versions or pay for consulting. Other companies give away the software that enables users to read and use files but sell the software needed to create those files. Finally, there are individuals who donate their time, out of enthusiasm, and produce programs that you can copy freely. See Random Fact 9.2 for more information.)

When selling software, a company must rely on the honesty of its customers. It is an easy matter for an unscrupulous person to make copies of computer programs without paying for them. In most countries that is illegal. Most governments provide legal protection, such as copyright laws and patents, to encourage the develop-

ment of new products. Countries that tolerate widespread piracy have found that they have an ample cheap supply of foreign software, but no local manufacturers willing to design good software for their own citizens, such as word processors in the local script or financial programs adapted to the local tax laws.

When a mass market for software first appeared, vendors were enraged by the money they lost through piracy. They tried to fight back by various schemes to ensure that only the legitimate owner could use the software, such as *dongles*—devices that must be attached to a printer port before the software will run. Legitimate users hated these measures. They paid for the software, but they had to suffer through inconveniences, such as having multiple dongles stick out from their computer. In the United States, market pressures forced most vendors to give up on these copy protection schemes, but they are still commonplace in other parts of the world.

Because it is so easy and inexpensive to pirate software, and the chance of being found out is minimal, you have to make a moral choice for yourself. If a package that you would really like to have is too expensive for your

budget, do you steal it, or do you stay honest and get by with a more affordable product?

Of course, piracy is not limited to software. The same issues arise for other digital products as well. You may have had the opportunity to obtain copies of songs or movies without payment. Or you may have been frustrated by a copy protection device on your music player that made it difficult for you to listen to songs that you paid for. Admittedly, it can be difficult to have a lot of sympathy for a musical ensemble whose publisher charges a lot of money for what seems to have been very little effort on their part, at least when compared to the effort that goes into designing and implementing a software package. Nevertheless, it seems only fair that artists and authors receive some compensation for their efforts. How to pay artists, authors, and programmers fairly, without burdening honest customers, is an unsolved problem at the time of this writing, and many computer scientists are engaged in research in this area.

CHAPTER SUMMARY

Explain the flow of execution in a loop.

- Loops execute a block of code repeatedly while a condition remains true.

- An off-by-one error is a common error when programming loops. Think through simple test cases to avoid this type of error.

Use the technique of hand-tracing to analyze the behavior of a program.

- Hand-tracing is a simulation of code execution in which you step through instructions and track the values of the variables.
- Hand-tracing can help you understand how an unfamiliar algorithm works.
- Hand-tracing can show errors in code or pseudocode.

Use for loops for implementing counting loops.

- The for loop is used when a value runs from a starting point to an ending point with a constant increment or decrement.

Choose between the while loop and the do loop.

- The do loop is appropriate when the loop body must be executed at least once.

Implement loops that read sequences of input data.

- A sentinel value denotes the end of a data set, but it is not part of the data.

- You can use a Boolean variable to control a loop. Set the variable to true before entering the loop, then set it to false to leave the loop.
- Use input redirection to read input from a file. Use output redirection to capture program output in a file.

Use the technique of storyboarding for planning user interactions.

- A storyboard consists of annotated sketches for each step in an action sequence.
- Developing a storyboard helps you understand the inputs and outputs that are required for a program.

Know the most common loop algorithms.

- To compute an average, keep a total and a count of all values.
- To count values that fulfill a condition, check all values and increment a counter for each match.
- If your goal is to find a match, exit the loop when the match is found.
- To find the largest value, update the largest value seen so far whenever you see a larger one.
- To compare adjacent inputs, store the preceding input in a variable.

Use nested loops to implement multiple levels of iteration.

- When the body of a loop contains another loop, the loops are nested. A typical use of nested loops is printing a table with rows and columns.

Apply loops to the implementation of simulations.

- In a simulation, you use the computer to simulate an activity. You can introduce randomness by calling the random number generator.

REVIEW EXERCISES

R4.1 Provide trace tables for these loops.

a.
```
int i = 0; int j = 10; int n = 0;
while (i < j) { i++; j--; n++; }
```
b.
```
int i = 0; int j = 0; int n = 0;
while (i < 10) { i++; n = n + i + j; j++; }
```
c.
```
int i = 10; int j = 0; int n = 0;
while (i > 0) { i--; j++; n = n + i - j; }
```
d.
```
int i = 0; int j = 10; int n = 0;
while (i != j) { i = i + 2; j = j - 2; n++; }
```

R4.2 What do these loops print?

a. `for (int i = 1; i < 10; i++) { cout << i << " "; }`
b. `for (int i = 1; i < 10; i += 2) { cout << i << " "; }`
c. `for (int i = 10; i > 1; i--) { cout << i << " "; }`
d. `for (int i = 0; i < 10; i++) { cout << i << " "; }`
e. `for (int i = 1; i < 10; i = i * 2) { cout << i << " "; }`
f. `for (int i = 1; i < 10; i++) { if (i % 2 == 0) { cout << i << " "; } }`

R4.3 What is an infinite loop? On your computer, how can you terminate a program that executes an infinite loop?

R4.4 What is an "off-by-one" error? Give an example from your own programming experience.

R4.5 Write a program trace for the pseudocode in Exercise P4.9, assuming the input values are 4 7 –2 –5 0.

R4.6 Is the following code legal?

```
for (int i = 0; i < 10; i++)
{
   for (int i = 0; i < 10; i++)
   {
      cout << i << " ";
   }
   cout << endl;
}
```

What does it print? Is it good coding style? If not, how would you improve it?

R4.7 How often do the following loops execute? Assume that i is not changed in the loop body.

a. for (int i = 1; i <= 10; i++) ...
b. for (int i = 0; i < 10; i++) ...
c. for (int i = 10; i > 0; i--) ...
d. for (int i = -10; i <= 10; i++) ...
e. for (int i = 10; i >= 0; i++) ...
f. for (int i = -10; i <= 10; i = i + 2) ...
g. for (int i = -10; i <= 10; i = i + 3) ...

R4.8 Write pseudocode for a program that prints a calendar such as the following:

```
Su  M  T  W Th  F Sa
          1  2  3  4
 5  6  7  8  9 10 11
12 13 14 15 16 17 18
19 20 21 22 23 24 25
26 27 28 29 30 31
```

R4.9 Write pseudocode for a program that prints a Celsius/Fahrenheit conversion table such as the following:

```
Celsius | Fahrenheit
--------+-----------
      0 |         32
     10 |         50
     20 |         68
    ...          ...
    100 |        212
```

R4.10 Write pseudocode for a program that reads a sequence of student records and prints the total score for each student. Each record has the student's first and last name, followed by a sequence of test scores and a sentinel of –1. The sequence is terminated by the word END. Here is a sample sequence:

```
Harry Morgan 94 71 86 95 -1
Sally Lin 99 98 100 95 90 -1
END
```

Provide a trace table for this sample input.

R4.11   Rewrite the following for loop into a while loop.

```
int s = 0;
for (int i = 1; i <= 10; i++)
{
   s = s + i;
}
```

R4.12   Rewrite the following do/while loop into a while loop.

```
int n;
cin >> n;
double x = 0;
double s;
do
{
   s = 1.0 / (1 + n * n);
   n++;
   x = x + s;
}
while (s > 0.01);
```

R4.13   Provide trace tables of the following loops.

a.
```
int s = 1;
int n = 1;
while (s < 10) { s = s + n; }
n++;
```

b.
```
int s = 1;
for (int n = 1; n < 5; n++) { s = s + n; }
```

c.
```
int s = 1;
int n = 1;
do
{
   s = s + n;
   n++;
}
while (s < 10 * n);
```

R4.14   What do the following loops print? Work out the answer by tracing the code, not by using the computer.

a.
```
int s = 1;
for (int n = 1; n <= 5; n++)
{
   s = s + n;
   cout << s << " ";
}
```

b.
```
int s = 1;
for (int n = 1; s <= 10; cout << s << " ")
{
   n = n + 2;
   s = s + n;
}
```

c.
```
int s = 1;
int n;
for (n = 1; n <= 5; n++)
{
   s = s + n;
   n++;
```

```
      }
      cout << s << " " << n;
```

R4.15 What do the following program segments print? Find the answers by tracing the code, not by using the computer.

    a.
```
int n = 1;
for (int i = 2; i < 5; i++) { n = n + i; }
cout << n;
```

    b.
```
int i;
double n = 1 / 2;
for (i = 2; i <= 5; i++) { n = n + 1.0 / i; }
cout << i;
```

    c.
```
double x = 1;
double y = 1;
int i = 0;
do
{
   y = y / 2;
   x = x + y;
   i++;
}
while (x < 1.8);
cout << i;
```

    d.
```
double x = 1;
double y = 1;
int i = 0;
while (y >= 1.5)
{
   x = x / 2;
   y = x + y;
   i++;
}
cout << i;
```

R4.16 Give an example of a for loop where symmetric bounds are more natural. Give an example of a for loop where asymmetric bounds are more natural.

R4.17 Add a storyboard panel for the conversion program in Section 4.6 on page 154 that shows a scenario where a user enters incompatible units.

R4.18 In Section 4.6, we decided to show users a list of all valid units in the prompt. If the program supports many more units, this approach is unworkable. Give a storyboard panel that illustrates an alternate approach: If the user enters an unknown unit, a list of all known units is shown.

R4.19 Change the storyboards in Section 4.6 to support a menu that asks users whether they want to convert units, see program help, or quit the program. The menu should be displayed at the beginning of the program, when a sequence of values has been converted, and when an error is displayed.

R4.20 Draw a flow chart for a program that carries out unit conversions as described in Section 4.6.

R4.21 In Section 4.7.4, the code for finding the largest and smallest input initializes the largest and smallest variables with an input value. Why can't you initialize them with zero?

R4.22 What are nested loops? Give an example where a nested loop is typically used.

R4.23 The nested loops

```
for (int i = 1; i <= height; i++)
{
    for (int j = 1; j <= width; j++) { cout << "*"; }
    cout << endl;
}
```

display a rectangle of a given width and height, such as

```
****
****
****
```

Write a *single* for loop that displays the same rectangle.

R4.24 Suppose you design an educational game to teach children how to read a clock. How do you generate random values for the hours and minutes?

R4.25 In a travel simulation, Harry will visit one of his friends that are located in three states. He has ten friends in California, three in Nevada, and two in Utah. How do you produce a random number between 1 and 3, denoting the destination state, with a probability that is proportional to the number of friends in each state?

PROGRAMMING EXERCISES

P4.1 Write programs with loops that compute

  a. The sum of all even numbers between 2 and 100 (inclusive).

  b. The sum of all squares between 1 and 100 (inclusive).

  c. All powers of 2 from 2^0 up to 2^{20}.

  d. The sum of all odd numbers between a and b (inclusive), where a and b are inputs.

  e. The sum of all odd digits of an input. (For example, if the input is 32677, the sum would be $3 + 7 + 7 = 17$.)

P4.2 Write programs that read a sequence of integer inputs and print

  a. The smallest and largest of the inputs.

  b. The number of even and odd inputs.

  c. Cumulative totals. For example, if the input is 1 7 2 9, the program should print 1 8 10 19.

  d. All adjacent duplicates. For example, if the input is 1 3 3 4 5 5 6 6 2, the program should print 3 5 6.

P4.3 Write programs that read a line of input as a string and print

  a. Only the uppercase letters in the string.

  b. Every second letter of the string.

  c. The string, with all vowels replaced by an underscore.

  d. The number of vowels in the string.

  e. The positions of all vowels in the string.

P4.4   Complete the program in How To 4.1 on page 162. Your program should read twelve temperature values and print the month with the highest temperature.

P4.5   *Credit Card Number Check.* The last digit of a credit card number is the *check digit*, which protects against transcription errors such as an error in a single digit or switching two digits. The following method is used to verify actual credit card numbers but, for simplicity, we will describe it for numbers with 8 digits instead of 16:

- Starting from the rightmost digit, form the sum of every other digit. For example, if the credit card number is 43589795, then you form the sum $5 + 7 + 8 + 3 = 23$.
- Double each of the digits that were not included in the preceding step. Add all digits of the resulting numbers. For example, with the number given above, doubling the digits, starting with the next-to-last one, yields 18 18 10 8. Adding all digits in these values yields $1 + 8 + 1 + 8 + 1 + 0 + 8 = 27$.
- Add the sums of the two preceding steps. If the last digit of the result is 0, the number is valid. In our case, $23 + 27 = 50$, so the number is valid.

Write a program that implements this algorithm. The user should supply an 8-digit number, and you should print out whether the number is valid or not. If it is not valid, you should print out the value of the check digit that would make the number valid.

P4.6   *Currency conversion.* Write a program that first asks the user to type today's exchange rate between U.S. dollars and Japanese yen, then reads U.S. dollar values and converts each to yen. Use 0 as a sentinel.

P4.7   Write a program that first asks the user to type in today's exchange rate between U.S. dollars and Japanese yen, then reads U.S. dollar values and converts each to Japanese yen. Use 0 as the sentinel value to denote the end of dollar inputs. Then the program reads a sequence of yen amounts and converts them to dollars. The second sequence is terminated by another zero value.

P4.8   Write a program that reads a set of floating-point values. Ask the user to enter the values, then print

- the average of the values.
- the smallest of the values.
- the largest of the values.
- the range, that is the difference between the smallest and largest.

Of course, you may only prompt for the values once.

P4.9 Translate the following pseudocode for finding the minimum value from a set of inputs into a C++ program.

> Set a Boolean variable "first" to true.
> While another value has been read successfully
>   If first is true
>   Set the minimum to the value.
>   Set first to false.
>   Else if the value is less than the minimum
>   Set the minimum to the value.
> Print the minimum.

P4.10 Translate the following pseudocode for randomly permuting the characters in a string into a C++ program.

> Read a word.
> Repeat word.length() times
>   Pick a random position i in the word.
>   Pick a random position j > i in the word.
>   Swap the letters at positions j and i.
> Print the word.

To swap the letters, construct substrings as follows:

first   i   middle   j   last

Then replace the string with

```
first + word.substr(j, 1) + middle + word.substr(i, 1) + last
```

P4.11 Write a program that reads a word and prints each character of the word on a separate line. For example, if the user provides the input "Harry", the program prints

```
H
a
r
r
y
```

P4.12 Write a program that reads a word and prints the word in reverse. For example, if the user provides the input "Harry", the program prints

```
yrraH
```

P4.13 Write a program that reads a word and prints the number of vowels in the word. For this exercise, assume that a e i o u y are vowels. For example, if the user provides the input "Harry", the program prints 2 vowels.

P4.14 Write a program that reads a word and prints the number of syllables in the word. For this exercise, assume that syllables are determined as follows: Each sequence of vowels a e i o u y, except for the last e in a word, is a vowel. However, if that algorithm yields a count of 0, change it to 1. For example,

Word	Syllables
Harry	2
hairy	2
hare	1
the	1

P4.15 Write a program that reads a word and prints all substrings, sorted by length. For example, if the user provides the input "rum", the program prints

```
r
u
m
ru
um
rum
```

P4.16 Write a program that reads a number and prints all of its *binary digits:* Print the remainder number % 2, then replace the number with number / 2. Keep going until the number is 0. For example, if the user provides the input 13, the output should be

```
1
0
1
1
```

P4.17 *Mean and standard deviation.* Write a program that reads a set of floating-point data values. Choose an appropriate mechanism for prompting for the end of the data set. When all values have been read, print out the count of the values, the average, and the standard deviation. The average of a data set $\{x_1, \ldots, x_n\}$ is $\bar{x} = \sum x_i / n$, where $\sum x_i = x_1 + \ldots + x_n$ is the sum of the input values. The standard deviation is

$$s = \sqrt{\frac{\sum (x_i - \bar{x})^2}{n - 1}}$$

However, this formula is not suitable for the task. By the time the program has computed $\bar{x}$, the individual x_i are long gone. Until you know how to save these values, use the numerically less stable formula

$$s = \sqrt{\frac{\sum x_i^2 - \frac{1}{n}\left(\sum x_i\right)^2}{n - 1}}$$

You can compute this quantity by keeping track of the count, the sum, and the sum of squares as you process the input values.

P4.18 The *Fibonacci numbers* are defined by the sequence

$$f_1 = 1$$
$$f_2 = 1$$
$$f_n = f_{n-1} + f_{n-2}$$

Reformulate that as

Fibonacci numbers describe the growth of a rabbit population.

```
fold1 = 1;
fold2 = 1;
fnew = fold1 + fold2;
```

After that, discard fold2, which is no longer needed, and set fold2 to fold1 and fold1 to fnew. Repeat fnew an appropriate number of times.

Implement a program that computes the Fibonacci numbers in that way.

P4.19 *Factoring of integers*. Write a program that asks the user for an integer and then prints out all its factors. For example, when the user enters 150, the program should print

```
2
3
5
5
```

P4.20 *Prime numbers*. Write a program that prompts the user for an integer and then prints out all prime numbers up to that integer. For example, when the user enters 20, the program should print

```
2
3
5
7
11
13
17
19
```

Recall that a number is a prime number if it is not divisible by any number except 1 and itself.

P4.21 Write a program that prints a multiplication table, like this:

```
 1    2    3    4    5    6    7    8    9   10
 2    4    6    8   10   12   14   16   18   20
 3    6    9   12   15   18   21   24   27   30
 . . .
10   20   30   40   50   60   70   80   90  100
```

P4.22 Write a program that reads an integer and displays, using asterisks, a filled and hollow square, placed next to each other. For example if the side length is 5, the program should display

```
***** *****
***** *   *
***** *   *
***** *   *
***** *****
```

P4.23 Write a program that reads an integer and displays, using asterisks, a filled diamond of the given side length. For example, if the side length is 4, the program should display

```
   *
  ***
 *****
*******
 *****
  ***
   *
```

P4.24 *The game of Nim*. This is a well-known game with a number of variants. The following variant has an interesting winning strategy. Two players alternately take marbles from a pile. In each move, a player chooses how many marbles to take. The player must take at least one but at most half of the marbles. Then the other player takes a turn. The player who takes the last marble loses.

You will write a program in which the computer plays against a human opponent. Generate a random integer between 10 and 100 to denote the initial size of the pile. Generate a random integer between 0 and 1 to decide whether the computer or the human takes the first turn. Generate a random integer between 0 and 1 to decide whether the computer plays *smart* or *stupid*. In stupid mode the computer simply takes a random legal value (between 1 and $n/2$) from the pile whenever it has a turn. In smart mode the computer takes off enough marbles to make the size of the pile a power of two minus 1—that is, 3, 7, 15, 31, or 63. That is always a legal move, except when the size of the pile is currently one less than a power of two. In that case, the computer makes a random legal move.

You will note that the computer cannot be beaten in smart mode when it has the first move, unless the pile size happens to be 15, 31, or 63. Of course, a human player who has the first turn and knows the winning strategy can win against the computer.

P4.25 *The Drunkard's Walk.* A drunkard in a grid of streets randomly picks one of four directions and stumbles to the next intersection, then again randomly picks one of four directions, and so on. You might think that on average the drunkard doesn't move very far because the choices cancel each other out, but that is actually not the case.

Represent locations as integer pairs (x, y). Implement the drunkard's walk over 100 intersections and print the beginning and ending location.

P4.26 *The Monty Hall Paradox.* Marilyn vos Savant described the following problem (loosely based on a game show hosted by Monty Hall) in a popular magazine: "Suppose you're on a game show, and you're given the choice of three doors: Behind one door is a car; behind the others, goats. You pick a door, say No. 1, and the host, who knows what's behind the doors, opens another door, say No. 3, which has a goat. He then says to you, "Do you want to pick door No. 2?" Is it to your advantage to switch your choice?"

Ms. vos Savant proved that it is to your advantage, but many of her readers, including some mathematics professors, disagreed, arguing that the probability would not change because another door was opened.

Your task is to simulate this game show. In each iteration, randomly pick a door number between 1 and 3 for placing the car. Randomly have the player pick a door. Randomly have the game show host pick one of the two doors having a goat. Now increment a counter for strategy 1 if the player wins by switching to the third door, and increment a counter for strategy 2 if the player wins by sticking with the original choice. Run 1,000 iterations and print both counters.

P4.27 *The Buffon Needle Experiment.* The following experiment was devised by Comte Georges-Louis Leclerc de Buffon (1707–1788), a French naturalist. A needle of length 1 inch is dropped onto paper that is ruled with lines 2 inches apart. If the needle drops onto a line, we count it as a *hit*. (See Figure 8.) Buffon conjectured that the quotient *tries*/*hits* approximates π.

Figure 8 The Buffon Needle Experiment

Figure 9
A Hit in the Buffon Needle Experiment

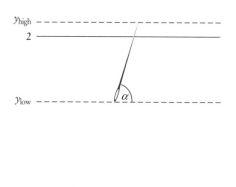

For the Buffon needle experiment, you must generate two random numbers: one to describe the starting position and one to describe the angle of the needle with the x-axis. Then you need to test whether the needle touches a grid line.

Generate the *lower* point of the needle. Its x-coordinate is irrelevant, and you may assume its y-coordinate y_{low} to be any random number between 0 and 2. The angle α between the needle and the x-axis can be any value between 0 degrees and 180 degrees (π radians). The upper end of the needle has y-coordinate

$$y_{high} = y_{low} + \sin\alpha$$

The needle is a hit if y_{high} is at least 2, as shown in Figure 9.

Stop after 10,000 tries and print the quotient tries/hits. (This program is not suitable for computing the value of π. You need π in the computation of the angle.)

Engineering P4.28 In a predator-prey simulation, you compute the populations of predators and prey, using the following equations:

$$prey_{n+1} = prey_n \times \left(1 + A - B \times pred_n\right)$$
$$pred_{n+1} = pred_n \times \left(1 - C + D \times prey_n\right)$$

Here, A is the rate at which prey birth exceeds natural death, B is the rate of predation, C is the rate at which predator deaths exceed births without food, and D represents predator increase in the presence of food.

Write a program that prompts users for these rates, the initial population sizes, and the number of periods. Then print the populations for the given number of periods. As inputs, try $A = 0.1$, $B = C = 0.01$, and $D = 0.00002$ with initial prey and predator populations of 1,000 and 20.

Engineering P4.29 *Projectile flight.* Suppose a cannonball is propelled straight into the air with a starting velocity v_0. Any calculus book will state that the position of the ball after t seconds is $s(t) = -\frac{1}{2}gt^2 + v_0 t$, where $g = 9.81$ m/sec^2 is the gravitational force of the earth. No calculus book ever mentions why someone would want to carry out such an obviously dangerous experiment, so we will do it in the safety of the computer.

In fact, we will confirm the theorem from calculus by a simulation. In our simulation, we will consider how the ball moves in very short time intervals Δt. In a short time interval the velocity v is nearly constant, and we can compute the distance the ball moves as $\Delta s = v\Delta t$. In our program, we will simply set

```
const double DELTA_T = 0.01;
```

and update the position by

```
s = s + v * DELTA_T;
```

The velocity changes constantly—in fact, it is reduced by the gravitational force of the earth. In a short time interval, $\Delta v = -g\Delta t$, we must keep the velocity updated as

```
v = v - g * DELTA_T;
```

In the next iteration the new velocity is used to update the distance.

Now run the simulation until the cannonball falls back to the earth. Get the initial velocity as an input (100 m/sec is a good value). Update the position and velocity 100 times per second, but print out the position only every full second. Also printout the values from the exact formula $s(t) = -\frac{1}{2}gt^2 + v_0t$ for comparison.

Note: You may wonder whether there is a benefit to this simulation when an exact formula is available. Well, the formula from the calculus book is *not* exact. Actually, the gravitational force diminishes the farther the cannonball is away from the surface of the earth. This complicates the algebra sufficiently that it is not possible to give an exact formula for the actual motion, but the computer simulation can simply be extended to apply a variable gravitational force. For cannonballs, the calculus-book formula is actually good enough, but computers are necessary to compute accurate trajectories for higher-flying objects such as ballistic missiles.

Engineering P4.30   A simple model for the hull of a ship is given by

$$|y| = \frac{B}{2}\left[1 - \left(\frac{2x}{L}\right)^2\right]\left[1 - \left(\frac{z}{T}\right)^2\right]$$

where B is the beam, L is the length, and T is the draft.

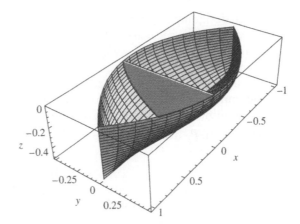

(*Note:* There are two values of y for each x and z because the hull is symmetric from starboard to port.)

The cross-sectional area at a point x is called the "section" in nautical parlance. To compute it, let z go from 0 to $-T$ in n increments, each of size T/n. For each value of z, compute the value for y. Then sum the areas of trapezoidal strips. At right are the strips where $n = 4$.

Write a program that reads in values for B, L, T, x, and n and then prints out the cross-sectional area at x.

Engineering P4.31   Radioactive decay of radioactive materials can be modeled by the equation $A = A_0 e^{-t(\log 2/h)}$, where A is the amount of the material at time t, A_0 is the amount at time 0, and h is the half-life.

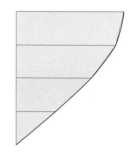

Technetium-99 is a radioisotope that is used in imaging of the brain. It has a half-life of 6 hours. Your program should display the relative amount A/A_0 in a patient body every hour for 24 hours after receiving a dose.

Engineering P4.32   The photo at left shows an electric device called a "transformer". Transformers are often constructed by wrapping coils of wire around a ferrite core. The figure below illustrates a situation that occurs in various audio devices such as cell phones and music players. In this circuit, a transformer is used to connect a speaker to the output of an audio amplifier.

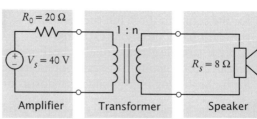

The symbol used to represent the transformer is intended to suggest two coils of wire. The parameter n of the transformer is called the "turns ratio" of the transformer. (The number of times that a wire is wrapped around the core to form a coil is called the number of turns in the coil. The turns ratio is literally the ratio of the number of turns in the two coils of wire.)

When designing the circuit, we are concerned primarily with the value of the power delivered to the speakers—that power causes the speakers to produce the sounds we want to hear. Suppose we were to connect the speakers directly to the amplifier without using the transformer. Some fraction of the power available from the amplifier would get to the speakers. The rest of the available power would be lost in the amplifier itself. The transformer is added to the circuit to increase the fraction of the amplifier power that is delivered to the speakers.

The power, P_s, delivered to the speakers is calculated using the formula

$$P_s = R_s \left(\frac{nV_s}{n^2 R_0 + R_s} \right)^2$$

Write a C++ program that models the circuit shown and varies the turns ratio from 0.01 to 2 in 0.01 increments, then determines the value of the turns ratio that maximizes the power delivered to the speakers.

ANSWERS TO SELF-CHECK QUESTIONS

1. 23 years.

2. 7 years.

3. Add a statement

   ```
   cout << balance << endl;
   ```

   as the last statement in the while loop.

4. The program prints the same output. This is because the balance after 14 years is slightly below $20,000, and after 15 years, it is slightly above $20,000.

5. 2 4 8 16 32 64 128

   Note that the value 128 is printed even though it is larger than 100.

6.
n	output
5	
4	4
3	3
2	2
1	1
0	0
-1	-1

7.
n	output
1	1,
2	1, 2,
3	1, 2, 3,
4	

   There is a comma after the last value. Usually, commas are between values only.

8.
a	n	r	i
2	4	1	1
		2	2
		4	3
		8	4
		16	5

   The code computes a^n.

9.
n	output
1	1
11	11
21	21
31	31
41	41
51	51
61	61
...	

   This is an infinite loop. n is never equal to 50.

10.
count	n
1	123
2	12.3
3	1.23

This yields the correct answer. The number 123 has 3 digits.

```
count  n
1      100
2      10
```

This yields the wrong answer. The number 100 also has 3 digits. The loop condition should have been

```
while (temp >= 10)
```

11.
```
int year = 1;
while (year <= nyears)
{
    balance = balance * (1 + RATE / 100);
    cout << setw(4) << year << setw(10) << balance << endl;
    year++;
}
```

12. 11 numbers: 10 9 8 7 6 5 4 3 2 1 0

13.
```
for (int i = 10; i <= 20; i = i + 2)
{
    cout << n << endl;
}
```

14.
```
int sum = 0;
for (int i = 1; i <= n; i++)
{
    sum = sum + i;
}
```

15.
```
for (int year = 1; balance <= 2 * INITIAL_BALANCE; year++)
```

However, it is best not to use a for loop in this case because the loop condition does not relate to the year variable. A while loop would be a better choice.

16.
```
do
{
    cout << "Enter a value between 0 and 100: ";
    cin >> value;
}
while (value < 0 || value > 100);
```

17.
```
int value = 100;
while (value >= 100)
{
    cout << "Enter a value < 100: ";
    cin >> value;
}
```

Here, the variable value had to be initialized with an artificial value to ensure that the loop is entered at least once.

18. Yes. The do loop

```
do { body } while (condition);
```

is equivalent to this while loop:

```
bool first = true;
while (first || condition) { body; first = false; }
```

19.
```
int x;
int sum = 0;
do
{
```

```
      cin >> x;
      sum = sum + x;
   }
   while (x != 0);
```

20.
```
int x = 0;
int previous;
do
{
   previous = x;
   cin >> x;
   sum = sum + x;
}
while (previous != x);
```

21. No data

22. The first check ends the loop after the sentinel has been read. The second check ensures that the sentinel is not processed as an input value.

23. The `while` loop would never be entered. The user would never be prompted for input. Since count stays 0, the program would then print "No data".

24. The stream also fails. A more accurate prompt would have been: "Enter values, a key other than a digit to quit." But that might be more confusing to the program user who would need now ponder which key to choose.

25. You don't know whether the input fails until after you try reading input.

26. *Computing the average*

> Enter scores, Q to quit: 90 80 90 100 80 Q
> The average is 88
> (Program exits)

27. *Simple conversion*

> Your conversion question: How many in are 30 cm   ⟋ Only one value can be converted.
> 30 cm = 11.81 in
> (Program exits) ————— Run program again for another question

Unknown unit

> Your conversion question: How many inches are 30 cm?
> Unknown unit: inches
> Known units are in, ft, mi, mm, cm, m, km, oz, lb, g, kg, tsp, tbsp, pint, gal
> (Program exits)

Program doesn't understand question syntax

> Your conversion question: What is an ångström?
> Please formulate your question as "How many (unit) are (value) (unit)?"
> (Program exits)

28. *One score is not enough*

> Enter scores, Q to quit: 90 Q
> Error: At least two scores are required.
> (Program exits)

29. It would not be possible to implement this interface using the C++ features we have covered up to this point. There is no way for the program to know when the first set of inputs ends. (When you read numbers with cin >> value, it is your choice whether to put them on a single line or multiple lines.)

30. *Comparing two interest rates*

> First interest rate in percent: 5
> Second interest rate in percent: 10
> Years: 5

Year	5%	10%
0	10000.00	10000.00
1	10500.00	11000.00
2	11025.00	12100.00
3	11576.25	13310.00
4	12155.06	14641.00
5	12762.82	16105.10

This row clarifies that 1 means the end of the first year

31. The total is zero.

32.
```
double total = 0;
double input;
while (cin >> input)
{
    if (input > 0) { total = total + input; }
}
```

33. position is str.length().

34. The loop will stop when a match is found, but you cannot access the match because position is not defined outside the loop.

35. Start the loop at the end of string:
```
bool found = false;
int position = str.length() - 1;
while (!found && position >= 0)
{
    string ch = str.substr(position, 1);
    if (ch == " ") { found = true; }
    else { position--; }
}
```

36. Unless the input contains zero or negative numbers, the smallest value is incorrectly computed as 0.

37. When executing cin >> previous, cin fails and previous is unchanged. The statement cin >> input also fails, and the while loop is never entered.

38. All values in the inner loop should be displayed on the same line.

39. Change lines 14, 19, and 31 to for (int n = 0; n <= NMAX; n++). Change NMAX to 5.

40. 60: The outer loop is executed 10 times, and the inner loop 6 times.

41. 0123
1234
2345

42.
```
for (int i = 1; i <= 3; i++)
{
   for (int j = 1; j <= 4; j++)
   {
      cout << "[]";
   }
   cout << endl;
}
```

43. Compute rand() % 2, and use 0 for heads, 1 for tails, or the other way around.

44. Compute rand() % 4 and associate the numbers 0 ... 3 with the four suits. Then compute rand() % 13 and associate the numbers 0 ... 12 with Jack, Ace, 2 ... 10, Queen, and King.

45. It is required for calling the time function.

46. The call will produce a value between 2 and 12, but all values have the same probability. When throwing a pair of dice, the number 7 is six times as likely as the number 2. The correct formula is

int sum = rand() % 6 + rand() % 6 + 2;

47. rand() * 100.0 / RAND_MAX

FUNCTIONS

Functions are a fundamental building block of C++ programs. A function packages a computation into a form that can be easily understood and reused. (The person in the image to the left is executing the function "make two cups of espresso".) In this chapter, you will learn how to design and implement your own functions. Using the process of stepwise refinement, you will be able to break up complex tasks into sets of cooperating functions.

5.1 Functions as Black Boxes

A function is a named sequence of instructions.

A **function** is a sequence of instructions with a name. You have already encountered several functions. For example, the function named pow, which was introduced in Chapter 2, contains instructions to compute a power x^y. Moreover, every C++ program has a function called main.

You *call* a function in order to execute its instructions. For example, consider the following program:

```
int main()
{
    double z = pow(2, 3);
    ...
}
```

By using the expression pow(2, 3), main *calls* the pow function, asking it to compute the power 2^3. The main function is temporarily suspended. The instructions of the pow function execute and compute the result. The pow function *returns* its result (that is, the value 8) back to main, and the main function resumes execution (see Figure 1).

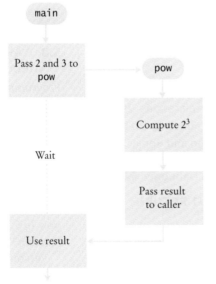

Figure 1 Execution Flow During a Function Call

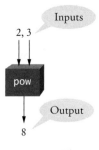

Figure 2   The pow Function as a Black Box

When another function calls the pow function, it provides "inputs", such as the expressions 2 and 3 in the call pow(2, 3). These expressions are called **arguments**. This terminology avoids confusion with other inputs, such as those provided by a human user. Similarly, the "output" that the pow function computes is called the **return value**.

> Arguments are supplied when a function is called. The return value is the result that the function computes.

Functions can have multiple arguments, but they have only one return value.

Note that the return value of a function is returned to the calling function, not displayed on the screen. For example, suppose your program contains a statement

```
double z = pow(2, 3);
```

When the pow function returns its result, the return value is stored in the variable z. If you want the value to be displayed, you need to add a statement such as cout << z.

At this point, you may wonder how the pow function performs its job. For example, how does pow(2, 3) compute that 2^3 is 8? By multiplying $2 \times 2 \times 2$? With logarithms? Fortunately, as a user of the function, you *don't need to know* how the function is implemented. You just need to know the *specification* of the function: If you provide arguments x and y, the function returns x^y. Engineers use the term **black box** for a device with a given specification but unknown implementation. You can think of pow as a black box, as shown in Figure 2.

When you design your own functions, you will want to make them appear as black boxes to other programmers. Those programmers want to use your functions without knowing what goes on inside. Even if you are the only person working on a program, making each function into a black box pays off: there are fewer details that you need to keep in mind.

Although a thermostat is usually white, you can think of it as a black box. The input is the desired temperature, and the output is a signal to the heater or air conditioner.

1. Consider the function call pow(3, 2). What are the arguments and return value?
2. What is the return value of the function call pow(pow(2, 2), 2)?
3. The ceil function in the C++ standard library takes a single argument *x* and returns the smallest integer ≥ *x*. What is the return value of ceil(2.3)?
4. It is possible to determine the answer to Self Check 3 without knowing how the ceil function is implemented. Use an engineering term to describe this aspect of the ceil function.

Practice It   Now you can try these exercises at the end of the chapter: R5.1, P5.1.

5.2 Implementing Functions

In this section, you will learn how to implement a function from a given specification. We will use a very simple example: a function to compute the volume of a cube with a given side length.

The cube_volume *function uses a given side length to compute the volume of a cube.*

When writing this function, you need to

> When defining a function, you provide a name for the function, a variable for each argument, and a type for the result.

- Pick a name for the function (cube_volume).
- Declare a variable for each argument (double side_length). These variables are called **parameter variables**.
- Specify the type of the return value (double).

Put all this information together to form the first line of the function's definition:

```
double cube_volume(double side_length)
```

Next, specify the *body* of the function: the statements that are executed when the function is called.

The volume of a cube of side length *s* is *s* × *s* × *s*. However, for greater clarity, our parameter variable has been called side_length, not *s*, so we need to compute side_length * side_length * side_length.

We will store this value in a variable called volume:

```
double volume = side_length * side_length * side_length;
```

In order to return the result of the function, use the return statement:

```
return volume;
```

The body of a function is enclosed in braces. Here is the complete function:

```
double cube_volume(double side_length)
{
   double volume = side_length * side_length * side_length;
   return volume;
}
```

The return *statement gives the function's result to the caller.*

Let's put this function to use. We'll supply a main function that calls the cube_volume function twice.

```cpp
int main()
{
    double result1 = cube_volume(2);
    double result2 = cube_volume(10);
    cout << "A cube with side length 2 has volume " << result1 << endl;
    cout << "A cube with side length 10 has volume " << result2 << endl;

    return 0;
}
```

When the function is called with different arguments, the function returns different results. Consider the call cube_volume(2). The argument 2 corresponds to the side_length parameter variable. Therefore, in this call, side_length is 2. The function computes side_length * side_length * side_length, or 2 * 2 * 2. When the function is called with a different argument, say 10, then the function computes 10 * 10 * 10.

Now we combine both functions into a test program. Because main calls cube_volume, the cube_volume function must be known before the main function is defined. This is easily achieved by placing cube_volume first and main last in the source file. (See Special Topic 5.1 on page 203 for an alternative.)

Syntax 5.1   Function Definition

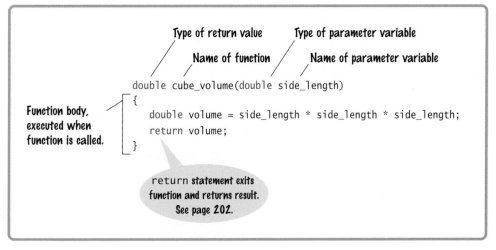

Here is the complete program. Note the comment that describes the behavior of the function. (Programming Tip 5.1 on page 199 describes the format of the comment.)

ch05/cube.cpp

```
1   #include <iostream>
2
3   using namespace std;
4
5   /**
6      Computes the volume of a cube.
7      @param side_length the side length of the cube
8      @return the volume
9   */
10  double cube_volume(double side_length)
11  {
12     double volume = side_length * side_length * side_length;
13     return volume;
14  }
15
16  int main()
17  {
18     double result1 = cube_volume(2);
19     double result2 = cube_volume(10);
20     cout << "A cube with side length 2 has volume " << result1 << endl;
21     cout << "A cube with side length 10 has volume " << result2 << endl;
22
23     return 0;
24  }
```

Program Run

```
A cube with side length 2 has volume 8
A cube with side length 10 has volume 1000
```

SELF CHECK

5. What is the value of cube_volume(3)?

6. What is the value of cube_volume(cube_volume(2))?

7. Provide an alternate implementation of the body of the cube_volume function by calling the pow function.

8. Define a function square_area that computes the area of a square of a given side length.

9. Consider this function:

```
int mystery(int x, int y)
{
   double result = (x + y) / (y - x);
   return result;
}
```

What is the result of the call mystery(2, 3)?

Practice It   Now you can try these exercises at the end of the chapter: R5.2, P5.2, P5.7.

Programming Tip 5.1

Function Comments

Whenever you write a function, you should *comment* its behavior. Comments are for human readers, not compilers, and there is no universal standard for the layout of a function comment. In this book, we will use the following layout:

```
/**
    Computes the volume of a cube.
    @param side_length the side length of the cube
    @return the volume
*/
double cube_volume(double side_length)
{
    double volume = side_length * side_length * side_length;
    return volume;
}
```

> Function comments explain the purpose of the function, the meaning of the parameter variables and return value, as well as any special requirements.

This particular documentation style is borrowed from the Java programming language. It is widely supported by C++ tools as well, for example by the Doxygen tool (www.doxygen.org).

The first line of the comment describes the purpose of the function. Each @param clause describes a parameter variable and the @return clause describes the return value.

Note that the function comment does not document the implementation (*how* the function does what it does) but rather the design (*what* the function does, its inputs, and its results). The comment allows other programmers to use the function as a "black box".

5.3 Parameter Passing

> Parameter variables hold the argument values supplied in the function call.

In this section, we examine the mechanism of passing arguments into functions. When a function is called, its *parameter variables* are created (Another commonly used term for a parameter variable is *formal parameter*.) In the function call, an expression is supplied for each parameter variable, called the *argument*. (Another commonly used term for this expression is *actual parameter*.) Each parameter variable is initialized with the value of the corresponding argument.

Consider the function call illustrated in Figure 3:

```
double result1 = cube_volume(2);
```

A recipe for a fruit pie may say to use any kind of fruit. Here, "fruit" is an example of a parameter variable. Apples and cherries are examples of arguments.

❶ Function call

```
double result1 = cube_volume(2);
```

result1 =

side_length =

❷ Initializing function parameter variable

```
double result1 = cube_volume(2);
```

result1 =

side_length = 2

❸ About to return to the caller

```
double volume = side_length * side_length * side_length;
return volume;
```

result1 =

side_length = 2

volume = 8

❹ After function call

```
double result1 = cube_volume(2);
```

result1 = 8

Figure 3 Parameter Passing

- The parameter variable side_length of the cube_volume function is created. **❶**
- The parameter variable is initialized with the value of the argument that was passed in the call. In our case, side_length is set to 2. **❷**
- The function computes the expression side_length * side_length * side_length, which has the value 8. That value is stored in the variable volume. **❸**
- The function returns. All of its variables are removed. The return value is transferred to the *caller*, that is, the function calling the cube_volume function. **❹**

Now consider what happens in a subsequent call cube_volume(10). A new parameter variable is created. (Recall that the previous parameter variable was removed when the first call to cube_volume returned.) It is initialized with the argument 10, and the process repeats. After the second function call is complete, its variables are again removed.

Like any other variables, parameter variables can only be set to values of compatible types. For example, the side_length parameter variable of the cube_volume function has type double. It is valid to call cube_volume(2.0) or cube_volume(2). In the latter call, the integer 2 is automatically converted to the double value 2.0. However, a call cube_volume("two") is not legal.

SELF CHECK

10. What does this program print? Use a diagram like Figure 3 to find the answer.

```
double mystery(int x, int y)
{
   double z = x + y;
   z = z / 2.0;
```

```
        return z;
    }
    int main()
    {
        int a = 4;
        int b = 7;
        cout << mystery(a, b) << endl;
    }
```

11. What does this program print? Use a diagram like Figure 3 to find the answer.

```
int mystery(int x)
{
    int y = x * x;
    return y;
}
int main()
{
    int a = 4;
    cout << mystery(a + 1) << endl;
}
```

12. What does the following program print? Use a diagram like Figure 3 to find the answer.

```
int mystery(int n)
{
    n++;
    n++;
    return n;
}
int main()
{
    int a = 5;
    cout << mystery(a) << endl;
}
```

Practice It   Now you can try these exercises at the end of the chapter: R5.5, P5.10.

Programming Tip 5.2

Do Not Modify Parameter Variables

In C++, a parameter variable is just like any other variable. You *can* modify the values of the parameter variables in the body of a function. For example,

```
int total_cents(int dollars, int cents)
{
    cents = dollars * 100 + cents; // Modifies parameter variable
    return cents;
}
```

However, many programmers find this practice confusing. It mixes the concept of a parameter (input to the function) with that of a variable (storage for a value). To avoid the confusion, simply introduce a separate variable:

```
int total_cents(int dollars, int cents)
{
    int result = dollars * 100 + cents;
    return result;
}
```

5.4 Return Values

The return statement terminates a function call and yields the function result.

You use the `return` statement to specify the result of a function. When the `return` statement is processed, the function exits *immediately*. This behavior is convenient for handling exceptional cases at the beginning:

```
double cube_volume(double side_length)
{
   if (side_length < 0) { return 0; }
   double volume = side_length * side_length * side_length;
   return volume;
}
```

If the function is called with a negative value for `side_length`, then the function returns 0 and the remainder of the function is not executed. (See Figure 4.)

In the preceding example, each `return` statement returned a constant or a variable. Actually, the `return` statement can return the value of any expression. Instead of saving the return value in a variable and returning the variable, it is often possible to eliminate the variable and return a more complex expression:

```
double cube_volume(double side_length)
{
   return side_length * side_length * side_length;
}
```

It is important that every branch of a function return a value. Consider the following incorrect function:

```
double cube_volume(double side_length)
{
   if (side_length >= 0)
   {
      return side_length * side_length * side_length;
   } // Error
}
```

Suppose you call `cube_volume` with a negative value for the side length. Of course, you aren't supposed to call that, but it might happen as the result of a coding error. Because the `if` condition is not true, the `return` statement is not executed. However, the function must return *something*. Depending on the circumstances, the compiler might

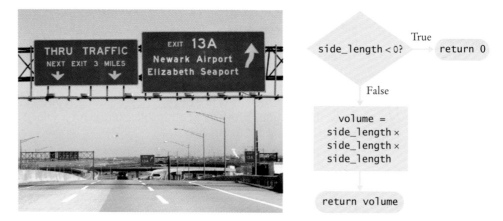

Figure 4 A return Statement Exits a Function Immediately

flag this as an error, or the function might return a random value. Protect against this problem by returning some safe value:

```
double cube_volume(double side_length)
{
   if (side_length >= 0)
   {
      return side_length * side_length * side_length;
   }
   return 0;
}
```

The last statement of every function ought to be a return statement. This ensures that *some* value gets returned when the function reaches the end.

Common Error 5.1

Missing Return Value

A function always needs to return something. If the code of the function contains several branches, make sure that each one of them returns a value:

```
int sign(double x)
{
   if (x < 0) { return -1; }
   if (x > 0) { return 1; }
   // Error: missing return value if x equals 0
}
```

This function computes the sign of a number: –1 for negative numbers and +1 for positive numbers. If the argument is zero, however, no value is returned. Most compilers will issue a warning in this situation, but if you ignore the warning and the function is ever called with an argument of 0, a random quantity will be returned.

Special Topic 5.1

Function Declarations

It is a compile-time error to call a function that the compiler does not know, just as it is an error to use an undefined variable. You can avoid this error if you define all functions before they are first used. First define lower-level helper functions, then the mid-level workhorse functions, and finally main in your program.

Some programmers prefer to list the main function first in their programs. If you share that preference, you need to learn how to **declare** the other functions at the top of the program. A declaration of a function lists the return type, function name, and parameter variables, but it contains no body:

```
double cube_volume(double side_length);
```

This is an advertisement that promises that the function is implemented elsewhere. It is easy to distinguish declarations from definitions: Declarations end in a semicolon, whereas definitions are followed by a {...} block. Declarations are also called **prototypes**.

In a function prototype, the names of the parameters are optional. You could also write

```
double cube_volume(double);
```

However, it is a good idea to include parameter names in order to document the purpose of each parameter.

The declarations of common functions such as pow are contained in header files. If you have a look inside <cmath>, you will find the declaration of pow and the other math functions.

Here is an alternate organization of the cube.cpp file:

```cpp
#include <iostream>

using namespace std;

// Declaration of cube_volume
double cube_volume(double side_length);

int main()
{
   double result1 = cube_volume(2); // Use of cube_volume
   double result2 = cube_volume(10);
   cout << "A cube with side length 2 has volume " << result1 << endl;
   cout << "A cube with side length 10 has volume " << result2 << endl;
   return 0;
}

// Definition of cube_volume
double cube_volume(double side_length)
{
   return side_length * side_length * side_length;
}
```

If you prefer this approach, go ahead and use it in your programs. You just need to be aware of one drawback. Whenever you change the name of a function or one of the parameter types, you need to fix it in both places: in the declaration and in the definition.

HOW TO 5.1

Implementing a Function

A function is a computation that can be used multiple times with different parameters, either in the same program or in different programs. Whenever a computation is needed more than once, turn it into a function.

To illustrate this process, suppose that you are helping archaeologists who research Egyptian pyramids. You have taken on the task of writing a function that determines the volume of a pyramid, given its height and base length.

Step 1   Describe what the function should do.

Provide a simple English description, such as "Compute the volume of a pyramid whose base is a square."

Step 2   Determine the function's "inputs".

Make a list of *all* the parameters that can vary. It is common for beginners to implement functions that are overly specific. For example, you may know that the great pyramid of Giza, the largest of the Egyptian pyramids, has a height of 146 meters and a base length of 230 meters. You should *not* use these numbers in your calculation, even if the original problem only asked about the great pyramid. It is just as easy—and far more useful—to write a function that computes the volume of *any* pyramid.

In our case, the parameters are the pyramid's height and base length. At this point, we have enough information to document the function:

```
/**
    Computes the volume of a pyramid whose base is a square.
    @param height  the height of the pyramid
    @param base_length  the length of one side of the pyramid's base
    @return  the volume of the pyramid
*/
```

Step 3 Determine the types of the parameter variables and the return value.

The height and base length can both be floating-point numbers. Therefore, we will choose the type `double` for both parameter variables. The computed volume is also a floating-point number, yielding a return type of `double`. Therefore, the function will be defined as

```
double pyramid_volume(double height, double base_length)
```

Step 4 Write pseudocode for obtaining the desired result.

In most cases, a function needs to carry out several steps to find the desired answer. You may need to use mathematical formulas, branches, or loops. Express your function in pseudocode.
An Internet search yields the fact that the volume of a pyramid is computed as

volume = 1/3 x height x base area

Since the base is a square, we have

base area = base length x base length

Using these two equations, we can compute the volume from the parameter variables.

Step 5 Implement the function body.

In our example, the function body is quite simple. Note the use of the `return` statement to return the result.

```
{
    double base_area = base_length * base_length;
    return height * base_area / 3;
}
```

Step 6 Test your function.

After implementing a function, you should test it in isolation. Such a test is called a **unit test**. Work out test cases by hand, and make sure that the function produces the correct results. For example, for a pyramid with height 9 and base length 10, we expect the area to be 1/3 × 9 × 100 = 300. If the height is 0, we expect an area of 0.

```
int main()
{
    cout << "Volume: " << pyramid_volume(9, 10) << endl;
    cout << "Expected: 300"
    cout << "Volume: " << pyramid_volume(0, 10) << endl;
    cout << "Expected: 0"
    return 0;
}
```

The output confirms that the function worked as expected:

```
Volume: 300
Expected: 300
Volume: 0
Expected: 0
```

WORKED EXAMPLE 5.1   **Matching and Replacing Parts of a String**

This Worked Example creates a function to find the first occurrence of one string in a given string and replace it with a second string.

WORKED EXAMPLE 5.2   **Using a Debugger**

In this Worked Example, you will learn how to use a debugger to find errors in a program.

5.5 Functions Without Return Values

> Use a return type of void to indicate that a function does not return a value.

Sometimes, you need to carry out a sequence of instructions that does not yield a value. If that instruction sequence occurs multiple times, you will want to package it into a function. In C++, you use the return type void to indicate the absence of a return value.

Here is a typical example. Your task is to print a string in a box, like this:

```
-------
!Hello!
-------
```

A void *function returns no value, but it can produce output.*

However, different strings can be substituted for Hello. A function for this task can be defined as follows:

```
void box_string(string str)
```

Now you develop the body of the function in the usual way, by formulating a general method for solving the task.

- Print a line that contains the - character n + 2 times, where n is the length of the string.
- Print a line containing the string, surrounded with a ! to the left and right.
- Print another line containing the - character n + 2 times.

Here is the function implementation:

```
/**
    Prints a string in a box.
    @param str the string to print
*/
void box_string(string str)
{
```

```cpp
      int n = str.length();
      for (int i = 0; i < n + 2; i++) { cout << "-"; }
      cout << endl;
      cout << "!" << str << "!" << endl;
      for (int i = 0; i < n + 2; i++) { cout << "-"; }
      cout << endl;
   }
```

Note that this function doesn't compute any value. It performs some actions and then returns to the caller. (See the sample program ch05/box.cpp.)

Because there is no return value, you cannot use box_string in an expression. You can call

```cpp
      box_string("Hello");
```

but not

```cpp
      result = box_string("Hello"); // Error: box_string doesn't return a result.
```

If you want to return from a void function before reaching the end, you use a return statement without a value. For example,

```cpp
      void box_string(string str)
      {
         int n = str.length();
         if (n == 0)
         {
            return; // Return immediately
         }
         ...
      }
```

SELF CHECK

13. How do you generate the following printout, using the box_string function?

    ```
    -------
    !Hello!
    -------
    -------
    !World!
    -------
    ```

14. What is wrong with the following statement?

    ```cpp
    cout << box_string("Hello");
    ```

15. Implement a function shout that prints a line consisting of a string followed by three exclamation marks. For example, shout("Hello") should print Hello!!!. The function should not return a value.

16. How would you modify the box_string function to leave a space around the string that is being boxed, like this:

    ```
    ---------
    ! Hello !
    ---------
    ```

17. The box_string function contains the code for printing a line of - characters twice. Place that code into a separate function print_line, and use that function to simplify box_string. What is the code of both functions?

Practice It   Now you can try these exercises at the end of the chapter: R5.4, P5.24.

5.6 Problem Solving: Reusable Functions

Eliminate replicated code or pseudocode by defining a function.

You have used many functions from the C++ standard library. These functions have been provided as a part of standard C++ so that programmers need not recreate them. Of course, the C++ library doesn't cover every conceivable need. You will often be able to save yourself time by designing your own functions that can be used for multiple problems.

When you write nearly identical code or pseudocode multiple times, either in the same program or in separate programs, consider introducing a function. Here is a typical example of code replication:

```cpp
int hours;
do
{
   cout << "Enter a value between 0 and 23: ";
   cin >> hours;
}
while (hours < 0 || hours > 23);

int minutes;
do
{
   cout << "Enter a value between 0 and 59: ";
   cin >> minutes;
}
while (minutes < 0 || minutes > 59);
```

This program segment reads two variables, making sure that each of them is within a certain range. It is easy to extract the common behavior into a function:

```cpp
/**
   Prompts a user to enter a value up to a given maximum until the user
   provides a valid input.
   @param high the largest allowable input
   @return the value provided by the user (between 0 and high, inclusive)
*/
int read_int_up_to(int high)
{
   int input;
   do
   {
      cout << "Enter a value between 0 and " << high << ": ";
      cin >> input;
   }
   while (input < 0 || input > high);
   return input;
}
```

Then use this function twice:

```cpp
int hours = read_int_up_to(23);
int minutes = read_int_up_to(59);
```

We have now removed the replication of the loop—it only occurs once, inside the function.

Note that the function can be reused in other programs that need to read integer values. However, we should consider the possibility that the smallest value need not always be zero.

When carrying out the same task multiple times, use a function.

Design your functions to be reusable. Supply parameter variables for the values that can vary when the function is reused.

Here is a better alternative:

```
/**
    Prompts a user to enter a value within a given range until the user
    provides a valid input.
    @param low the smallest allowable input
    @param high the largest allowable input
    @return the value provided by the user (between low and high, inclusive)
*/
int read_int_between(int low, int high)
{
    int input;
    do
    {
        cout << "Enter a value between " << low << " and " << high << ": ";
        cin >> input;
    }
    while (input < low || input > high);
    return input;
}
```

In our program, we call

```
int hours = read_int_between(0, 23);
```

Another program can call

```
int month = read_int_between(1, 12);
```

In general, you will want to provide parameter variables for the values that vary when a function is reused.

SELF CHECK

18. Consider the following statements:

```
int total_pennies = static_cast<int>(100 * total + 0.5);
int total_tax_pennies = static_cast<int>(100 * total * tax_rate + 0.5);
```

Introduce a function to reduce code duplication.

19. Consider this code that prints a page number on the left or right side of a page:

```
if (page % 2 == 0) { cout << page << endl; }
else { cout << setw(80) << page << endl; }
```

Introduce a function with return type `bool` to make the condition in the `if` statement easier to understand.

20. Consider the following function that computes compound interest for an account with an initial balance of $10,000 and an interest rate of 5 percent:

```
double balance(int years) { return 10000 * pow(1.05, years); }
```

How can you make this function more reusable?

21. The comment explains what the following loop does. Use a function instead.

```
// Counts the number of spaces
int spaces = 0;
for (int i = 0; i < input.length(); i++)
{
    if (input.substr(i, 1) == " ") { spaces++; }
}
```

22. In Self Check 21, you were asked to implement a function that counts spaces. How can you generalize it so that it can count any character? Why would you want to do this?

Practice It   Now you can try these exercises at the end of the chapter: R5.7, P5.23.

5.7 Problem Solving: Stepwise Refinement

Use the process of stepwise refinement to decompose complex tasks into simpler ones.

One of the most powerful strategies for problem solving is the process of **stepwise refinement**. To solve a difficult task, break it down into simpler tasks. Then keep breaking down the simpler tasks into even simpler ones, until you are left with tasks that you know how to solve.

Here is an application of this process to a problem of everyday life. You get up in the morning and simply must **get coffee**. How do you get coffee? You see whether you can get someone else, such as your mother or mate, to bring you some. If that fails, you must **make coffee**. How do you make coffee?

A production process is broken down into sequences of assembly steps.

If there is instant coffee available, you can **make instant coffee**. How do you make instant coffee? Simply **boil water** and mix the boiling water with the instant coffee. How do you boil water? If there is a microwave, then you fill a cup with water, place it in the microwave and heat it for three minutes. Otherwise, you fill a kettle with water and heat it on the stove until the water comes to a boil. On the other hand, if you don't have instant coffee, you must **brew coffee**. How do you brew coffee? You add water to the coffee maker, put in a filter, **grind coffee**, put the coffee in the filter, and turn the coffee maker on. How do you grind coffee? You add coffee beans to the coffee grinder and push the button for 60 seconds.

Figure 5 shows a flowchart view of the coffee-making solution. Refinements are shown as expanding boxes. In C++, you implement a refinement as a function. For example, a function brew_coffee would call grind_coffee, and it would be called from a function make_coffee.

Let us apply the process of stepwise refinement to a programming problem.

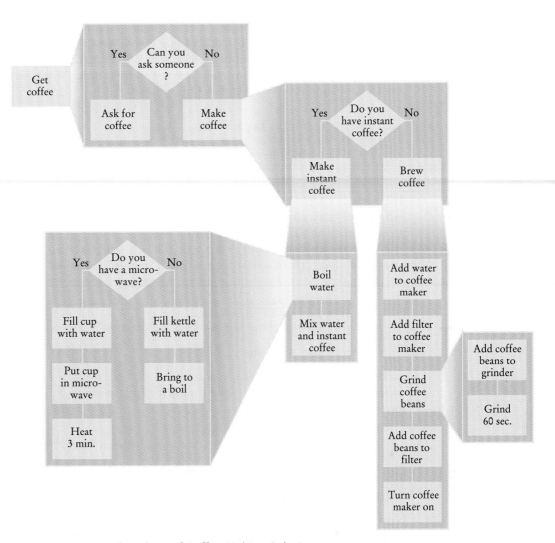

Figure 5 Flowchart of Coffee-Making Solution

When printing a check, it is customary to write the check amount both as a number ("$274.15") and as a text string ("two hundred seventy four dollars and 15 cents"). Doing so reduces the recipient's temptation to add a few digits in front of the amount.

For a human, this isn't particularly difficult, but how can a computer do this? There is no built-in function that turns 274 into "two hundred seventy four". We need to program this function. Here is the description of the function we want to write:

```
/**
    Turns a number into its English name.
    @param number a positive integer < 1,000
    @return the name of number (e.g., "two hundred seventy four")
*/
string int_name(int number)
```

When you discover that you need a function, write a description of the parameter variables and return values.

How can this function do its job? Let's look at a simple case first. If the number is between 1 and 9, we need to compute "one" ... "nine". In fact, we need the same computation *again* for the hundreds (two hundred). Using the stepwise decomposition process, we design another function for this simpler task. Again, rather than implementing the function, we first write the comment:

```
/**
    Turns a digit into its English name.
    @param digit an integer between 1 and 9
    @return the name of digit ("one" ... "nine")
*/
string digit_name(int digit)
```

A function may require simpler functions to carry out its work.

This sounds simple enough to implement, using an if statement with nine branches. No further functions should be required for completing the digit_name function, so we will worry about the implementation later.

Numbers between 10 and 19 are special cases. Let's have a separate function teen_name that converts them into strings "eleven", "twelve", "thirteen", and so on:

```
/**
    Turns a number between 10 and 19 into its English name.
    @param number an integer between 10 and 19
    @return the name of the number ("ten" ... "nineteen")
*/
string teen_name(int number)
```

Next, suppose that the number is between 20 and 99. Then we show the tens as "twenty", "thirty", ..., "ninety". For simplicity and consistency, put that computation into a separate function:

```
/**
    Gives the name of the tens part of a number between 20 and 99.
    @param number an integer between 20 and 99
    @return the name of the tens part of the number ("twenty" ... "ninety")
*/
string tens_name(int number)
```

Now suppose the number is at least 20 and at most 99. If the number is evenly divisible by 10, we use tens_name, and we are done. Otherwise, we print the tens with tens_name and the ones with digit_name. If the number is between 100 and 999, then we show a digit, the word "hundred", and the remainder as described previously.

Here is the pseudocode of the algorithm:

part = number (The part that still needs to be converted)
name = "" (The name of the number)

If part >= 100
    name = name of hundreds in part + " hundred"
    Remove hundreds from part.

If part >= 20
    Append tens_name(part) to name.
    Remove tens from part.
Else if part >= 10
    Append teen_name(part) to name.
    part = 0

If (part > 0)
    Append digit_name(part) to name.

This pseudocode has a number of important improvements over the verbal description. It shows how to arrange the tests, starting with the comparisons against the larger numbers, and it shows how the smaller number is subsequently processed in further if statements.

On the other hand, this pseudocode is vague about the actual conversion of the pieces, just referring to "name of hundreds" and the like. Furthermore, we were vague about spaces. As it stands, the code would produce strings with no spaces, twohundredseventyfour, for example. Compared to the complexity of the main problem, one would hope that spaces are a minor issue. It is best not to muddy the pseudocode with minor details.

Now turn the pseudocode into real code. The last three cases are easy, because helper functions are already developed for them:

```
if (part >= 20)
{
    name = name + " " + tens_name(part);
    part = part % 10;
}
else if (part >= 10)
{
    name = name + " " + teen_name(part);
    part = 0;
}

if (part > 0)
{
    name = name + " " + digit_name(part);
}
```

Finally, let us tackle the case of numbers between 100 and 999. Because part < 1000, part / 100 is a single digit, and we obtain its name by calling digit_name. Then we add the "hundred" suffix:

```
if (part >= 100)
{
    name = digit_name(part / 100) + " hundred";
    part = part % 100;
}
```

Now you have seen all the important building blocks for the int_name function. Here is the complete program:

ch05/intname.cpp

```
 1  #include <iostream>
 2  #include <string>
 3
 4  using namespace std;
 5
 6  /**
 7     Turns a digit into its English name.
 8     @param digit an integer between 1 and 9
 9     @return the name of digit ("one" ... "nine")
10  */
11  string digit_name(int digit)
12  {
```

```
13      if (digit == 1) return "one";
14      if (digit == 2) return "two";
15      if (digit == 3) return "three";
16      if (digit == 4) return "four";
17      if (digit == 5) return "five";
18      if (digit == 6) return "six";
19      if (digit == 7) return "seven";
20      if (digit == 8) return "eight";
21      if (digit == 9) return "nine";
22      return "";
23   }
24
25   /**
26      Turns a number between 10 and 19 into its English name.
27      @param number an integer between 10 and 19
28      @return the name of the given number ("ten" ... "nineteen")
29   */
30   string teen_name(int number)
31   {
32      if (number == 10) return "ten";
33      if (number == 11) return "eleven";
34      if (number == 12) return "twelve";
35      if (number == 13) return "thirteen";
36      if (number == 14) return "fourteen";
37      if (number == 15) return "fifteen";
38      if (number == 16) return "sixteen";
39      if (number == 17) return "seventeen";
40      if (number == 18) return "eighteen";
41      if (number == 19) return "nineteen";
42      return "";
43   }
44
45   /**
46      Gives the name of the tens part of a number between 20 and 99.
47      @param number an integer between 20 and 99
48      @return the name of the tens part of the number ("twenty" ... "ninety")
49   */
50   string tens_name(int number)
51   {
52      if (number >= 90) return "ninety";
53      if (number >= 80) return "eighty";
54      if (number >= 70) return "seventy";
55      if (number >= 60) return "sixty";
56      if (number >= 50) return "fifty";
57      if (number >= 40) return "forty";
58      if (number >= 30) return "thirty";
59      if (number >= 20) return "twenty";
60      return "";
61   }
62
63   /**
64      Turns a number into its English name.
65      @param number a positive integer < 1,000
66      @return the name of the number (e.g. "two hundred seventy four")
67   */
68   string int_name(int number)
69   {
70      int part = number; // The part that still needs to be converted
71      string name; // The return value
72
```

```
73      if (part >= 100)
74      {
75         name = digit_name(part / 100) + " hundred";
76         part = part % 100;
77      }
78
79      if (part >= 20)
80      {
81         name = name + " " + tens_name(part);
82         part = part % 10;
83      }
84      else if (part >= 10)
85      {
86         name = name + " " + teen_name(part);
87         part = 0;
88      }
89
90      if (part > 0)
91      {
92         name = name + " " + digit_name(part);
93      }
94
95      return name;
96   }
97
98   int main()
99   {
100      cout << "Please enter a positive integer: ";
101      int input;
102      cin >> input;
103      cout << int_name(input) << endl;
104      return 0;
105   }
```

Program Run

```
Please enter a positive integer: 729
seven hundred twenty nine
```

SELF CHECK

23. Explain how you can improve the int_name function so that it can handle arguments up to 9,999.

24. Why does line 87 set part = 0?

25. What happens when you call int_name(0)? How can you change the int_name function to handle this case correctly?

26. Trace the function call int_name(72), as described in Programming Tip 5.4.

27. Use the process of stepwise refinement to break down the task of printing the following table into simpler tasks.

```
+-----+-----------+
|   i | i * i * i |
+-----+-----------+
|   1 |         1 |
|   2 |         8 |
   ...
|  20 |      8000 |
+-----+-----------+
```

Practice It Now you can try these exercises at the end of the chapter: R5.12, P5.16, P5.19.

Programming Tip 5.3

Keep Functions Short

There is a certain cost for writing a function. You need to design, code, and test the function. The function needs to be documented. You need to spend some effort to make the function reusable rather than tied to a specific context. To avoid this cost, it is always tempting just to stuff more and more code in one place rather than going through the trouble of breaking up the code into separate functions. It is quite common to see inexperienced programmers produce functions that are several hundred lines long.

As a rule of thumb, a function that is so long that its code will not fit on a single screen in your development environment should probably be broken up.

Programming Tip 5.4

Tracing Functions

When you design a complex set of functions, it is a good idea to carry out a manual **walk-through** before entrusting your program to the computer.

Take an index card, or some other piece of paper, and write down the function call that you want to study. Write the name of the function and the names and values of the parameter variables, like this:

```
int_name(number = 416)
```

Then write the names and initial values of the function variables. Write them in a table, since you will update them as you walk through the code.

int_name(number = 416)	
part	name
416	""

We enter the test part >= 100. part / 100 is 4 and part % 100 is 16. digit_name(4) is easily seen to be "four". (Had digit_name been complicated, you would have started another sheet of paper to figure out that function call. It is quite common to accumulate several sheets in this way.)

Now name has changed to name + " " + digit_name(part / 100) + " hundred", that is "four hundred", and part has changed to part % 100, or 16.

int_name(number = 416)	
part	name
~~416~~	~~""~~
16	"four hundred"

Now you enter the branch part >= 10. teen_name(16) is sixteen, so the variables now have the values

int_name(number = 416)	
part	name
~~416~~	~~""~~
~~16~~	~~"four hundred"~~
0	"four hundred sixteen"

Now it becomes clear why you need to set part to 0 in line 87. Otherwise, you would enter the next branch and the result would be "four hundred sixteen six". Tracing the code is an effective way to understand the subtle aspects of a function.

Programming Tip 5.5

Stubs

When writing a larger program, it is not always feasible to implement and test all functions at once. You often need to test a function that calls another, but the other function hasn't yet been implemented. Then you can temporarily replace the missing function with a **stub**. A stub is a function that returns a simple value that is sufficient for testing another function. Here are examples of stub functions:

```
/**
    Turns a digit into its English name.
    @param digit an integer between 1 and 9
    @return the name of digit ("one" ... "nine")
*/
string digit_name(int digit)
{
    return "mumble";
}
```

Stubs are incomplete functions that can be used for testing.

```
/**
    Gives the name of the tens part of a number between 20 and 99.
    @param number an integer between 20 and 99
    @return the tens name of the number ("twenty" ... "ninety")
*/
string tens_name(int number)
{
    return "mumblety";
}
```

If you combine these stubs with the int_name function and test it with an argument of 274, you will get a result of "mumble hundred mumblety mumble", which indicates that the basic logic of the int_name function is working correctly.

5.8   Variable Scope and Global Variables

The scope of a variable is the part of the program in which it is visible.

It is possible to define the same variable name more than once in a program. When the variable name is used, you need to know to which definition it belongs. In this section, we discuss the rules for dealing with multiple definitions of the same name.

A variable that is defined within a function is visible from the point at which it is defined until the end of the block in which it was defined. This area is called the **scope** of the variable.

Consider the volume variables in the following example:

```
double cube_volume(double side_length)
{
   double volume = side_length * side_length * side_length;
   return volume;
}

int main()
{
   double volume = cube_volume(2);
   cout << volume << endl;

   return 0;
}
```

Each volume variable is defined in a separate function, and their scopes do not overlap.

*In the same way that there can be a street named "Main Street" in different cities,
a C++ program can have multiple variables with the same name.*

➕ Available online at www.wiley.com/college/horstmann.

It is not legal to define two variables with the same name in the same scope. For example, the following is *not* legal:

```cpp
int main()
{
    double volume = cube_volume(2);
    double volume = cube_volume(10);
        // ERROR: cannot define another volume variable in this scope
    ...
}
```

However, you can define another variable with the same name in a **nested block**. Here, we define two variables called amount.

```cpp
double withdraw(double balance, double amount)
{
    if (...)
    {
        double amount = 10; // Another variable named amount
        ...
    }
    ...
}
```

The scope of the parameter variable amount is the entire function, *except* inside the nested block. Inside the nested block, amount refers to the variable that was defined in that block. We say that the inner variable *shadows* the variable that is defined in the outer block. You should avoid this potentially confusing situation in the functions that you write, simply by renaming one of the variables.

Variables that are defined inside functions are called **local variables**. C++ also supports **global variables**: variables that are defined outside functions. A global variable is visible to all functions that are defined after it. For example, the <iostream> header defines global variables cin and cout.

Here is an example of a global variable:

```cpp
int balance = 10000; // A global variable

void withdraw(double amount)
{
    if (balance >= amount)
    {
        balance = balance - amount;
    }
}

int main()
{
    withdraw(1000);
    cout << balance << endl;
    return 0;
}
```

The scope of the variable balance extends over both the withdraw and the main functions.

Generally, global variables are not a good idea. When multiple functions update global variables, the result can be difficult to predict. Particularly in larger programs that are developed by multiple programmers, it is very important that the effect of each function be clear and easy to understand. You should avoid global variables in your programs.

A variable in a nested block shadows a variable with the same name in an outer block.

A local variable is defined inside a function. A global variable is defined outside a function.

Avoid global variables in your programs.

SELF CHECK

Consider this sample program:

```
 1  int x;
 2  int mystery(int x)
 3  {
 4     int s = 0;
 5     for (int i = 0; i < x; i++)
 6     {
 7        int x = i + 1;
 8        s = s + x;
 9     }
10     return x;
11  }
12  int main()
13  {
14     x = 4;
15     int s = mystery(x);
16     cout << s << endl;
17  }
```

28. Which line defines a global variable?

29. Which lines define local variables named x?

30. Which lines are in the scope of the definition of x in line 2?

31. Which variable is changed by the assignment in line 14?

32. This program defines two variables with the same name whose scopes don't overlap. What are they?

Practice It   Now you can try these exercises at the end of the chapter: R5.8, R5.9.

Programming Tip 5.6

Avoid Global Variables

There are a few cases where global variables are required (such as cin and cout), but they are quite rare. Programs with global variables are difficult to maintain and extend because you can no longer view each function as a "black box" that simply receives arguments and returns a result. When functions modify global variables, it becomes more difficult to understand the effect of function calls. As programs get larger, this difficulty mounts quickly. Instead of using global variables, use function parameters to transfer information from one part of a program to another.

5.9 Reference Parameters

If you want to write a function that changes the value of an argument, you must use a **reference parameter** in order to allow the change. We first explain why a different parameter type is necessary, then we show you the syntax for reference parameters.

Consider a function that simulates withdrawing a given amount of money from a bank account, provided that sufficient funds are available. If the amount of money is insufficient, a $10 penalty is deducted instead. The function would be used as follows:

```
double harrys_account = 1000;
withdraw(harrys_account, 100); // Now harrys_account is 900
withdraw(harrys_account, 1000); // Insufficient funds. Now harrys_account is 890
```

Here is a first attempt:

```
void withdraw(double balance, double amount) // Does not work
{
   const double PENALTY = 10;
   if (balance >= amount)
   {
      balance = balance - amount;
   }
   else
   {
      balance = balance - PENALTY;
   }
}
```

But this doesn't work.

Let's walk through the function call `withdraw(harrys_account, 100)` — see Figure 6. As the function starts, the parameter variable `balance` is created ❶ and set to the same value as `harrys_account`, and `amount` is set to 100 ❷. Then `balance` is modified ❸. Of course, that modification has no effect on `harrys_account`, because `balance` is a separate variable. When the function returns, `balance` is forgotten, and no money was withdrawn from `harrys_account` ❹.

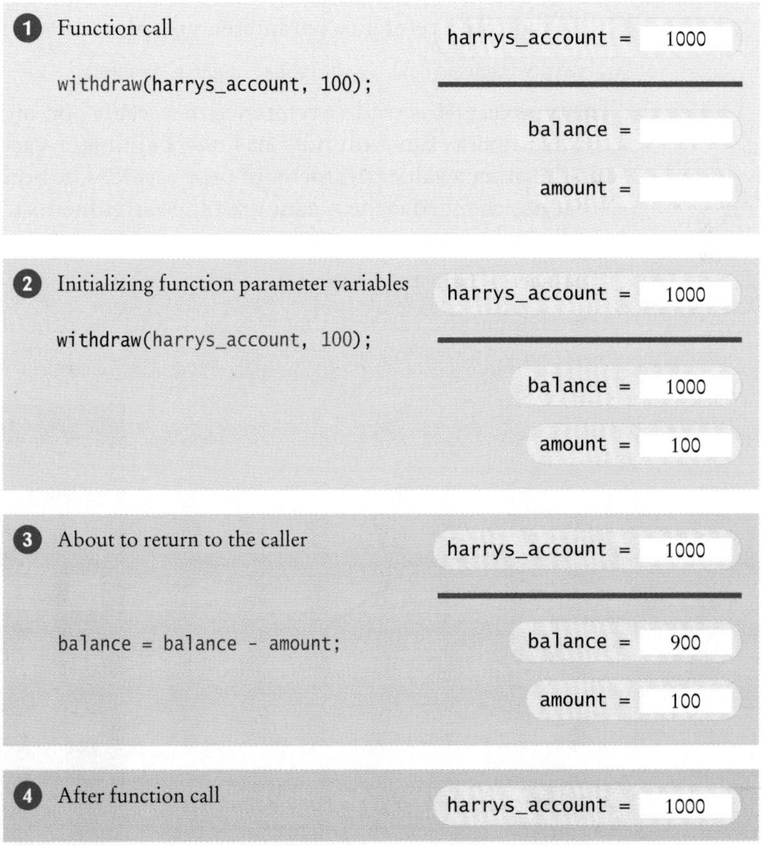

Figure 6   When `balance` and `account` are Value Parameters

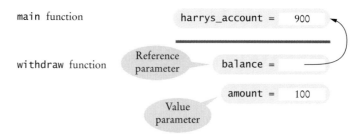

Figure 7   Reference and Value Parameters

Modifying a value
parameter has no
effect on the caller.

The parameter variable balance is called a **value parameter**, because it is initialized with the value of the supplied argument. All functions that we have written so far use value parameters. In this situation, though, we don't just want balance to have the same value as harrys_account. We want balance to refer to the actual variable harrys_account (or joes_account or whatever variable is supplied in the call). The contents of *that* variable should be updated.

A reference
parameter refers to
a variable that is
supplied in a
function call.

You use a reference parameter when you want to update a variable that was supplied in the function call. When we make balance into a reference parameter, then balance is not a new variable but a reference to an existing variable. Any change in balance is actually a change in the variable to which balance refers in that particular call.

Figure 7 shows the difference between value and reference parameters.

To indicate a reference parameter, you place an & after the type name.

```
void withdraw(double& balance, double amount)
```

The type double& is read "a reference to a double" or, more briefly, "double ref".

The withdraw function now has two parameter variables: one of type "double ref" and the other a value parameter of type double. The body of the function is unchanged. What has changed is the meaning of the assignments to the balance variable.

The assignment

```
balance = balance - amount;
```

now changes the variable that was passed to the function (see Figure 8).

A reference parameter for a bank balance is like an ATM card—it allows you to change the balance. In contrast, a value parameter can only tell you the balance.

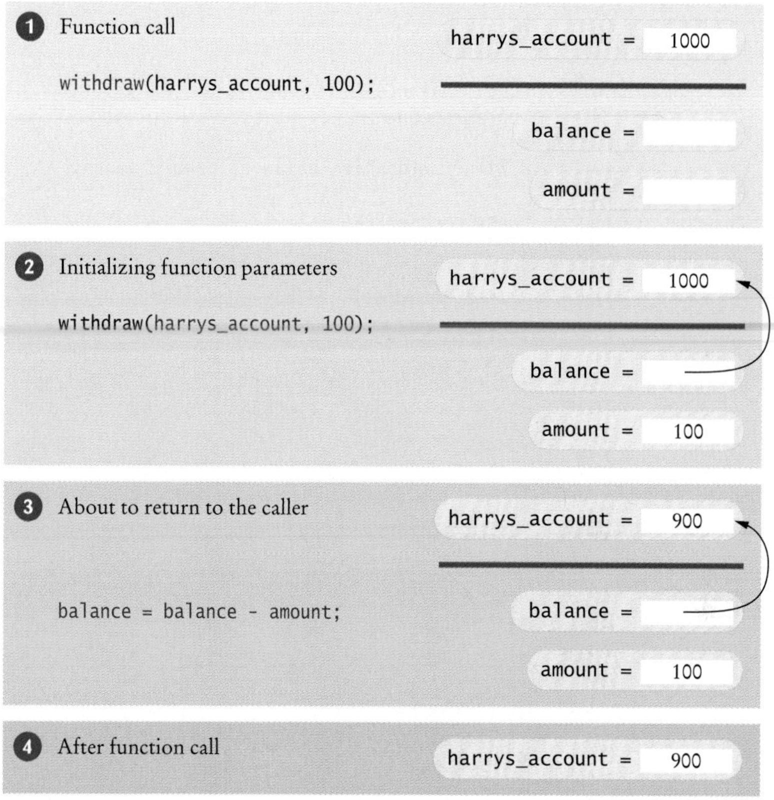

Figure 8   When balance is a Reference Parameter

For example, the call

    withdraw(harrys_account, 100);

modifies the variable harrys_account, and the call

    withdraw(sallys_account, 150);

modifies the variable sallys_account.

Modifying a reference parameter updates the variable that was supplied in the call.

The argument for a reference parameter must always be a *variable*. It would be an error to supply a number:

    withdraw(1000, 500); // Error: argument for reference parameter must be a variable

The reason is clear—the function modifies the reference parameter, but it is impossible to change the value of a number. For the same reason, you cannot supply an expression:

    withdraw(harrys_account + 150, 500);
        // Error: argument for reference parameter must be a variable

ch05/account.cpp

```
1   #include <iostream>
2
3   using namespace std;
4
```

```
5    /**
6        Withdraws the amount from the given balance, or withdraws
7        a penalty if the balance is insufficient.
8        @param balance the balance from which to make the withdrawal
9        @param amount the amount to withdraw
10   */
11   void withdraw(double& balance, double amount)
12   {
13       const double PENALTY = 10;
14       if (balance >= amount)
15       {
16           balance = balance - amount;
17       }
18       else
19       {
20           balance = balance - PENALTY;
21       }
22   }
23
24   int main()
25   {
26       double harrys_account = 1000;
27       double sallys_account = 500;
28       withdraw(harrys_account, 100);
29           // Now harrys_account is 900
30       withdraw(harrys_account, 1000); // Insufficient funds
31           // Now harrys_account is 890
32       withdraw(sallys_account, 150);
33       cout << "Harry's account: " << harrys_account << endl;
34       cout << "Sally's account: " << sallys_account << endl;
35
36       return 0;
37   }
```

Program Run

```
Harry's account: 890
Sally's account: 350
```

SELF CHECK

33. Would the withdraw function work correctly if the amount parameter was defined as double& instead of double?

34. The following function is intended to transfer the given amount of money from one account to another. Supply the function parameters.

```
void transfer(...)
{
   if (balance1 >= amount)
   {
      balance1 = balance1 - amount;
      balance2 = balance2 + amount;
   }
}
```

35. Change the withdraw function so that it returns a bool value indicating whether the withdrawal was successful. Do not charge a penalty if the balance was insufficient.

36. Write a function `minmax` so that the call `minmax(x, y, a, b)` sets a to the smaller of x and y and b to the larger of x and y.

37. What does this program print?

```cpp
void mystery(int& a, int& b)
{
    a = a - b;
    b = b + a;
    a = b - a;
}
int main()
{
    int x = 4;
    int y = 3;
    mystery(x, y);
    cout << x << " " << y << endl;
}
```

Practice It   Now you can try these exercises at the end of the chapter: R5.17, P5.14.

Programming Tip 5.7

Prefer Return Values to Reference Parameters

Some programmers use reference parameters as a mechanism for setting the result of a function. For example,

```cpp
void cube_volume(double side_length, double& volume)
{
    volume = side_length * side_length * side_length;
}
```

However, this function is less convenient than our previous `cube_volume` function. It cannot be used in expressions such as `cout << cube_volume(2)`.

Use a reference parameter only when a function needs to update a variable.

Special Topic 5.2

Constant References

It is not very efficient to have a value parameter that is a large object (such as a `string` value). Copying the object into a parameter variable is less efficient than using a reference parameter. With a reference parameter, only the location of the variable, not its value, needs to be transmitted to the function.

You can instruct the compiler to give you the efficiency of a reference parameter and the meaning of a value parameter, by using a **constant reference** as shown below. The function

```cpp
void shout(const string& str)
{
    cout << str << "!!!" << endl;
}
```

works exactly the same as the function

```cpp
void shout(string str)
{
    cout << str << "!!!" << endl;
}
```

There is just one difference: Calls to the first function execute a bit faster.

5.10 Recursive Functions (Optional)

Cleaning up a house can be solved recursively: Clean one room, then clean up the rest.

A recursive function is a function that calls itself. This is not as unusual as it sounds at first. Suppose you face the arduous task of cleaning up an entire house. You may well say to yourself, "I'll pick a room and clean it, and then I'll clean the other rooms." In other words, the cleanup task calls itself, but with a simpler input. Eventually, all the rooms will be cleaned.

In C++, a recursive function uses the same principle. Here is a typical example. We want to print triangle patterns like this:

```
[]
[][]
[][][]
[][][][]
```

Specifically, our task is to provide a function

```
void print_triangle(int side_length)
```

The triangle given above is printed by calling `print_triangle(4)`.

To see how recursion helps, consider how a triangle with side length 4 can be obtained from a triangle with side length 3.

```
[]
[][]
[][][]
[][][][]
```

Print the triangle with side length 3.
Print a line with four [].

More generally, for an arbitrary side length:

Print the triangle with side length – 1.
Print a line with side length [].

Here is the pseudocode translated to C++:

```
void print_triangle(int side_length)
{
    print_triangle(side_length - 1);
    for (int i = 0; i < side_length; i++)
    {
        cout << "[]";
    }
    cout << endl;
}
```

There is just one problem with this idea. When the side length is 1, we don't want to call `print_triangle(0)`, `print_triangle(-1)`, and so on. The solution is simply to treat this as a special case, and not to print anything when `side_length` is less than 1.

```
void print_triangle(int side_length)
{
    if (side_length < 1) { return; }
    print_triangle(side_length - 1);
    for (int i = 0; i < side_length; i++)
    {
        cout << "[]";
```

```
        }
      cout << endl;
   }
```

Look at the `print_triangle` function one more time and notice how utterly reasonable it is. If the side length is 0, nothing needs to be printed. The next part is just as reasonable. Print the smaller triangle *and don't think about why that works*. Then print a row of []. Clearly, the result is a triangle of the desired size.

There are two key requirements to make sure that the recursion is successful:

A recursive computation solves a problem by using the solution of the same problem with simpler inputs.

- Every recursive call must simplify the task in some way.
- There must be special cases to handle the simplest tasks directly.

For a recursion to terminate, there must be special cases for the simplest inputs.

The `print_triangle` function calls itself again with smaller and smaller side lengths. Eventually the side length must reach 0, and the function stops calling itself.

Here is what happens when we print a triangle with side length 4.

- The call `printTriangle(4)` calls `printTriangle(3)`.
  - The call `printTriangle(3)` calls `printTriangle(2)`.
    - The call `printTriangle(2)` calls `printTriangle(1)`.
      - The call `printTriangle(1)` calls `printTriangle(0)`.
        - The call `printTriangle(0)` returns, doing nothing.
      - The call `printTriangle(1)` prints [].
    - The call `printTriangle(2)` prints [][].
  - The call `printTriangle(3)` prints [][][].
- The call `print_triangle(4)` prints [][][][].

The call pattern of a recursive function looks complicated, and the key to the successful design of a recursive function is *not to think about it*.

This set of Russian dolls looks similar to the call pattern of a recursive function.

ch05/triangle.cpp

```
1   #include <iostream>
2
3   using namespace std;
4
5   /**
6      Prints a triangle with a given side length.
7      @param side_length the side length (number of [] along the base)
8   */
```

```
 9    void print_triangle(int side_length)
10    {
11       if (side_length < 1) { return; }
12       print_triangle(side_length - 1);
13       for (int i = 0; i < side_length; i++)
14       {
15          cout << "[]";
16       }
17       cout << endl;
18    }
19
20    int main()
21    {
22       cout << "Enter the side length: ";
23       int input;
24       cin >> input;
25       print_triangle(input);
26       return 0;
27    }
```

Program Run

```
Enter the side length: 10
[]
[][]
[][][]
[][][][]
[][][][][]
[][][][][][]
[][][][][][][]
[][][][][][][][]
[][][][][][][][][]
[][][][][][][][][][]
```

Recursion is not really necessary to print triangle shapes. You can use nested loops, like this:

```
for (int i = 0; i < side_length; i++)
{
   for (int j = 0; j < i; j++)
   {
      cout << "[]";
   }
   cout << endl;
}
```

However, this pair of loops is a bit tricky. Many people find the recursive solution simpler to understand.

38. Consider this slight modification of the print_triangle function:

```
void print_triangle(int side_length)
{
   if (side_length < 1) { return; }
   for (int i = 0; i < side_length; i++)
   {
      cout << "[]";
```

```
    }
    cout << endl;
    print_triangle(side_length - 1);
}
```

What is the result of print_triangle(4)?

39. Consider this recursive function:

```
int mystery(int n)
{
    if (n <= 0) { return 0; }
    return n + mystery(n - 1);
}
```

What is mystery(4)?

40. Consider this recursive function:

```
int mystery(int n)
{
    if (n <= 0) { return 0; }
    return mystery(n / 2) + 1;
}
```

What is mystery(20)?

41. Write a recursive function for printing n box shapes [] in a row.

42. The int_name function in Section 5.7 accepted arguments < 1,000. Using a recursive call, extend its range to 999,999. For example an input of 12,345 should return "twelve thousand three hundred forty five".

Practice It   Now you can try these exercises at the end of the chapter: R5.20, P5.28, P5.30.

HOW TO 5.2   **Thinking Recursively**

To solve a problem recursively requires a different mindset than to solve it by programming loops. In fact, it helps if you are, or pretend to be, a bit lazy and let others do most of the work for you. If you need to solve a complex problem, pretend that "someone else" will do most of the heavy lifting and solve the problem for all simpler inputs. Then you only need to figure out how you can turn the solutions with simpler inputs into a solution for the whole problem.

To illustrate the recursive thinking process, consider the problem of Section 4.2, computing the sum of the digits of a number. We want to design a function digit_sum that computes the sum of the digits of an integer n. For example, digit_sum(1729) = 1 + 7 + 2 + 9 = 19.

Step 1   Break the input into parts that can themselves be inputs to the problem.

In your mind, fix a particular input or set of inputs for the task that you want to solve, and think how you can simplify the inputs. Look for simplifications that can be solved by the same task, and whose solutions are related to the original task.

> The key to finding a recursive solution is reducing the input to a simpler input for the same problem.

In the digit sum problem, consider how we can simplify an input such as n = 1729. Would it help to subtract 1? After all, digit_sum(1729) = digit_sum(1728) + 1. But consider n = 1000. There seems to be no obvious relationship between digit_sum(1000) and digit_sum(999).

A much more promising idea is to remove the last digit, that is, compute n / 10 = 172. The digit sum of 172 is directly related to the digit sum of 1729.

Step 2   Combine solutions with simpler inputs into a solution of the original problem.

In your mind, consider the solutions for the simpler inputs that you have discovered in Step 1. Don't worry *how* those solutions are obtained. Simply have faith that the solutions are readily available. Just say to yourself: These are simpler inputs, so someone else will solve the problem for me.

In the case of the digit sum task, ask yourself how you can obtain `digit_sum(1729)` if you know `digit_sum(172)`. You simply add the last digit (9), and you are done. How do you get the last digit? As the remainder n % 10. The value `digit_sum(n)` can therefore be obtained as

> When designing a recursive solution, do not worry about multiple nested calls. Simply focus on reducing a problem to a slightly simpler one.

```
digit_sum(n / 10) + n % 10
```

Don't worry how `digit_sum(n / 10)` is computed. The input is smaller, and therefore it just works.

Step 3   Find solutions to the simplest inputs.

A recursive computation keeps simplifying its inputs. To make sure that the recursion comes to a stop, you must deal with the simplest inputs separately. Come up with special solutions for them. That is usually very easy.

Look at the simplest inputs for the `digit_sum` test:

- A number with a single digit
- 0

Random Fact 5.1 The Explosive Growth of Personal Computers

In 1971, Marcian E. "Ted" Hoff, an engineer at Intel Corporation, was working on a chip for a manufacturer of electronic calculators. He realized that it would be a better idea to develop a *general-purpose* chip that could be *programmed* to interface with the keys and display of a calculator, rather than to do yet another custom design. Thus, the *microprocessor* was born. At the time, its primary application was as a controller for calculators, washing machines, and the like. It took years for the computer industry to notice that a genuine central processing unit was now available as a single chip.

Hobbyists were the first to catch on. In 1974 the first computer *kit,* the Altair 8800, was available from MITS Electronics for about $350. The kit consisted of the microprocessor, a circuit board, a very small amount of memory, toggle switches, and a row of display lights. Purchasers had to solder and assemble it, then program it in machine language through the toggle switches. It was not a big hit.

The first big hit was the Apple II. It was a real computer with a keyboard, a monitor, and a floppy disk drive. When it was first released, users had a $3,000 machine that could play Space Invaders, run a primitive bookkeeping program, or let users program it in BASIC. The original Apple II did not even support lowercase letters, making it worthless for word processing. The breakthrough came in 1979 with a new spreadsheet program, VisiCalc. In a spreadsheet, you enter financial data and their relationships into a grid of rows and columns (see the figure at right). Then you modify some of the data and watch in real time how the others change. For example, you can see how changing the mix of widgets in a manufacturing plant might affect estimated costs and profits. Middle managers in companies, who understood computers and were fed up with having to wait for hours or days to get their data runs back from the computing center, snapped up VisiCalc and the computer that was needed to run it. For them, the computer was a spreadsheet machine.

The next big hit was the IBM Personal Computer, ever after known as the PC. It was the first widely available personal computer that used Intel's 16-bit processor, the 8086, whose successors are still being used in personal computers today. The success of the PC was based not on any engineering breakthroughs but on the fact that it was easy to *clone*. IBM published the computer's specifications in order to encourage third parties to develop plug-in cards. Perhaps IBM did not foresee that functionally equivalent versions of their computer could be recreated by others, but a variety of PC clone vendors emerged, and ultimately IBM stopped selling personal computers.

IBM never produced an *operating system* for its PCs—that is, the software that organizes the interaction between the user and the computer, starts application programs, and manages disk storage and other resources. Instead, IBM offered customers the option of three separate operating systems. Most customers couldn't care less about the operating system.

A number with a single digit is its own digit sum, so you can stop the recursion when n < 10, and return n in that case. Or, if you prefer, you can be even lazier. If n has a single digit, then digit_sum(n / 10) + n % 10 equals digit_sum(0) + n. You can simply terminate the recursion when n is zero.

Step 4   Implement the solution by combining the simple cases and the reduction step.

Now you are ready to implement the solution. Make separate cases for the simple inputs that you considered in Step 3. If the input isn't one of the simplest cases, then implement the logic you discovered in Step 2.

Here is the complete digit_sum function:

```
int digit_sum(int n)
{
   // Special case for terminating the recursion
   if (n == 0) { return 0; }
   // General case
   return digit_sum(n / 10) + n % 10;
}
```

They chose the system that was able to launch most of the few applications that existed at the time. It happened to be DOS (Disk Operating System) by Microsoft. Microsoft licensed the same operating system to other hardware vendors and encouraged software companies to write DOS applications. A huge number of useful application programs for PC-compatible machines was the result.

PC applications were certainly useful, but they were not easy to learn. Every vendor developed a different user interface: the collection of keystrokes, menu options, and settings that a user needed to master to use a software package effectively. Data exchange between applications was difficult, because each program used a different data format. The Apple Macintosh changed all that in 1984. The designers of the Macintosh had the vision to supply an intuitive user interface with the computer and to force software developers to adhere to it. It took Microsoft and PC-compatible manufacturers years to catch up.

Most personal computers are used for accessing information from online sources, entertainment, word processing, and home finance. Some analysts predict that the personal computer will merge with the television set and cable network into an entertainment and information appliance.

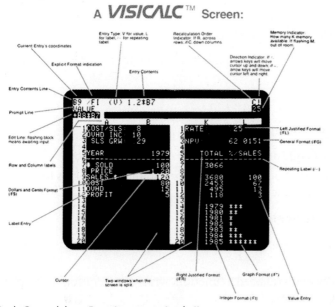

The Visicalc Spreadsheet Running on an Apple II

CHAPTER SUMMARY

Understand the concepts of functions, arguments, and return values.

- A function is a named sequence of instructions.
- Arguments are supplied when a function is called. The return value is the result that the function computes.

Be able to implement functions.

- When defining a function, you provide a name for the function, a variable for each argument, and a type for the result.
- Function comments explain the purpose of the function, the meaning of the parameter variables and return value, as well as any special requirements.

Describe the process of parameter passing.

- Parameter variables hold the argument values supplied in the function call.

Describe the process of returning a value from a function.

- The return statement terminates a function call and yields the function result.

Design and implement functions without return values.

- Use a return type of void to indicate that a function does not return a value.

Develop functions that can be reused for multiple problems.

- Eliminate replicated code or pseudocode by defining a function.
- Design your functions to be reusable. Supply parameter variables for the values that can vary when the function is reused.

Apply the design principle of stepwise refinement.

- Use the process of stepwise refinement to decompose complex tasks into simpler ones.
- When you discover that you need a function, write a description of the parameter variables and return values.
- A function may require simpler functions to carry out its work.

Determine the scope of variables in a program.

- The scope of a variable is the part of the program in which it is visible.
- A variable in a nested block shadows a variable with the same name in an outer block.
- A local variable is defined inside a function. A global variable is defined outside a function.
- Avoid global variables in your programs.

Describe how reference parameters work.

- Modifying a value parameter has no effect on the caller.
- A reference parameter refers to a variable that is supplied in a function call.
- Modifying a reference parameter updates the variable that was supplied in the call.

Understand recursive function calls and implement simple recursive functions.

- A recursive computation solves a problem by using the solution of the same problem with simpler inputs.
- For a recursion to terminate, there must be special cases for the simplest inputs.
- The key to finding a recursive solution is reducing the input to a simpler input for the same problem.
- When designing a recursive solution, do not worry about multiple nested calls. Simply focus on reducing a problem to a slightly simpler one.

REVIEW EXERCISES

R5.1 What is the difference between an argument and a return value? How many arguments can a function have? How many return values?

R5.2 In which sequence are the lines of the program cube.cpp on page 198 executed, starting with the first line of main?

R5.3 Give examples of the following, either from the C++ library or from the functions discussed in this chapter:

    a. A function with two double arguments and a double return value

    b. A function with a double argument and a double return value

    c. A function with two int arguments and an int return value

    d. A function with an int argument and a string return value

    e. A function with a string argument and no return value

    f. A function with a reference parameter and no return value

    g. A function with no arguments and an int return value

R5.4 True or false?

    a. A function has exactly one `return` statement.

    b. A function has at least one `return` statement.

    c. A function has at most one return value.

    d. A function with return value `void` never has a `return` statement.

    e. When executing a `return` statement, the function exits immediately.

    f. A function with return value `void` must print a result.

    g. A function without arguments always returns the same value.

R5.5 Consider these functions:

```
double f(double x) { return g(x) + sqrt(h(x)); }
double g(double x) { return 4 * h(x); }
double h(double x) { return x * x + k(x) - 1; }
double k(double x) { return 2 * (x + 1); }
```

Without actually compiling and running a program, determine the results of the following function calls:

    a. `double x1 = f(2);`

    b. `double x2 = g(h(2));`

    c. `double x3 = k(g(2) + h(2));`

    d. `double x4 = f(0) + f(1) + f(2);`

    e. `double x5 = f(-1) + g(-1) + h(-1) + k(-1);`

R5.6 Write pseudocode for a function that translates a telephone number with letters in it (such as 1-800-FLOWERS) into the actual phone number. Use the standard letters on a phone pad.

R5.7 Design a function that prints a floating-point number as a currency value (with a $ sign and two decimal digits).

    a. Indicate how the programs `ch02/volume2.cpp` and `ch04/invtable.cpp` should change to use your function.

    b. What change is required if the programs should show a different currency, such as euro?

R5.8 For each of the variables in the following program, indicate the scope. Then determine what the program prints, without actually running the program.

```
1   int a = 0;
2   int b = 0;
3   int f(int c)
4   {
```

```
 5      int n = 0;
 6      a = c;
 7      if (n < c)
 8      {
 9         n = a + b;
10      }
11      return n;
12  }
13
14  int g(int c)
15  {
16      int n = 0;
17      int a = c;
18      if (n < f(c))
19      {
20         n = a + b;
21      }
22      return n;
23  }
24
25  int main()
26  {
27      int i = 1;
28      int b = g(i);
29      cout << a + b + i << endl;
30      return 0;
31  }
```

R5.9 We have seen three kinds of variables in C++: global variables, parameter variables, and local variables. Classify the variables of Exercise R5.8 according to these categories.

R5.10 Use the process of stepwise refinement to describe the process of making scrambled eggs. Discuss what you do if you do not find eggs in the refrigerator.

R5.11 How many parameters does the following function have? How many return values does it have? *Hint:* The C++ notions of "parameter" and "return value" are not the same as the intuitive notions of "input" and "output".

```
void average(double& avg)
{
   cout << "Please enter two numbers: ";
   double x;
   double y;
   cin >> x >> y;
   avg = (x + y) / 2;
}
```

R5.12 Perform a walkthrough of the int_name function with the following arguments:

a. 5

b. 12

c. 21

d. 301

e. 324

f. 0

g. -2

R5.13 Consider the following function:

```
int f(int n)
{
   if (n <= 1) { return 1; }
   if (n % 2 == 0) // n is even
   {
      return f(n / 2);
   }
   else { return f(3 * n + 1); }
}
```

Perform traces of the computations f(1), f(2), f(3), f(4), f(5), f(6), f(7), f(8), f(9), and f(10).

R5.14 Eliminate the global variable in the code at the end of Section 5.8 by

a. passing the balance to the withdraw function and returning the updated balance.

b. passing the balance as a reference parameter to the withdraw function.

R5.15 Given the following functions, trace the function call print_roots(4).

```
int i;

int isqrt(int n)
{
   i = 1;
   while (i * i <= n) { i++; }
   return i - 1;
}

void print_roots(int n)
{
   for (i = 0; i <= n; i++) { cout << isqrt(i) << " "; }
}
```

How can you fix the code so that the output is as expected (that is, 0 1 1 1 2)?

R5.16 Consider the following function that is intended to swap the values of two integers:

```
void false_swap1(int& a, int& b)
{
   a = b;
   b = a;
}

int main()
{
   int x = 3;
   int y = 4;
   false_swap1(x, y);
   cout << x << " " << y << endl;
   return 0;
}
```

Why doesn't the function swap the contents of x and y? How can you rewrite the function to work correctly?

R5.17 Consider the following function that is intended to swap the values of two integers:

```
void false_swap2(int a, int b)
{
```

```
        int temp = a;
        a = b;
        b = temp;
    }

    int main()
    {
        int x = 3;
        int y = 4;
        false_swap2(x, y);
        cout << x << " " << y << endl;
        return 0;
    }
```

Why doesn't the function swap the contents of x and y? How can you rewrite the function to work correctly?

R5.18 The following function swaps two integers, without requiring a temporary variable:

```
    void tricky_swap(int& a, int& b)
    {
        a = a - b;
        b = a + b;
        a = b - a;
    }
```

However, it fails in one important case, namely when calling tricky_swap(x, x). Explain what should happen and what actually happens.

R5.19 Give pseudocode for a recursive function for printing all substrings of a given string. For example, the substrings of the string "rum" are "rum" itself, "ru", "um", "r", "u", "m", and the empty string. You may assume that all letters of the string are different.

R5.20 Give pseudocode for a recursive function that sorts all letters in a string. For example, the string "goodbye" would be sorted into "bdegooy".

PROGRAMMING EXERCISES

P5.1 The max function that is declared in the <algorithm> header returns the larger of its two arguments. Write a program that reads three floating-point numbers, uses the max function, and displays

  • the larger of the first two inputs.
  • the larger of the last two inputs.
  • the largest of all three inputs.

P5.2 Write a function that computes the balance of a bank account with a given initial balance and interest rate, after a given number of years. Assume interest is compounded yearly.

P5.3 Write the following functions and provide a program to test them.

  a. double smallest(double x, double y, double z), returning the smallest of the arguments

  b. double average(double x, double y, double z), returning the average of the arguments

P5.4 Write the following functions:

    a. `bool all_the_same(double x, double y, double z)`, returning true if the arguments are all the same

    b. `bool all_different(double x, double y, double z)`, returning true if the arguments are all different

    c. `bool sorted(double x, double y, double z)`, returning true if the arguments are sorted, with the smallest one coming first

Provide a program that tests your functions.

P5.5 Write the following functions:

    a. `int first_digit(int n)`, returning the first digit of the argument

    b. `int last_digit(int n)`, returning the last digit of the argument

    c. `int digits(int n)`, returning the number of digits of the argument

For example, `first_digit(1729)` is 1, `last_digit(1729)` is 9, and `digits(1729)` is 4. Provide a program that tests your functions.

P5.6 Write a function

```
string middle(string str)
```

that returns a string containing the middle character in `str` if the length of `str` is odd, or the two middle characters if the length is even. For example, `middle("middle")` returns `"dd"`.

P5.7 Write a function

```
string repeat(string str, int n)
```

that returns the string `str` repeated n times. For example, `repeat("ho", 3)` returns `"hohoho"`.

P5.8 Write a function

```
int count_vowels(string str)
```

that returns a count of all vowels in the string `str`. Vowels are the letters a, e, i, o, and u, and their uppercase variants.

P5.9 Write a function

```
int count_words(string str)
```

that returns a count of all words in the string `str`. Words are separated by spaces. For example, `count_words("Mary had a little lamb")` should return 5.

P5.10 It is a well-known phenomenon that most people are easily able to read a text whose words have two characters flipped, provided the first and last letter of each word are not changed. For example:

    I dn'ot gvie a dman for a man taht can olny sepll a wrod one way. (Mrak Taiwn)

Write a function `string scramble(string word)` that constructs a scrambled version of a given word, randomly flipping two characters other than the first and last one. Then write a program that reads words from `cin` and prints the scrambled words.

P5.11 Write functions

```
double sphere_volume(double r)
double sphere_surface(double r)
```

```
double cylinder_volume(double r, double h)
double cylinder_surface(double r, double h)
double cone_volume(double r, double h)
double cone_surface(double r, double h)
```

that compute the volume and surface area of a sphere with radius r, a cylinder with a circular base with radius r and height h, and a cone with a circular base with radius r and height h. Then write a program that prompts the user for the values of r and h, calls the six functions, and prints the results.

P5.12 Write functions

```
double distance(double x1, double x2, double y1, double y2)
void midpoint(double x1, double x2, double y1, double y2, double& xmid, double& ymid)
void slope(double x1, double x2, double y1, double y2, bool& vertical, double& s)
```

that compute the distance, midpoint, and slope of the line segment joining the points (x_1, y_1) and (x_2, y_2). The slope function should either set vertical to true and not set s, or set vertical to false and set s to the slope.

P5.13 Write a function

```
double read_double(string prompt)
```

that displays the prompt string, followed by a space, reads a floating-point number in, and returns it. Here is a typical usage:

```
salary = read_double("Please enter your salary:");
perc_raise = read_double("What percentage raise would you like?");
```

P5.14 Write a function void sort2(int& a, int& b) that swaps the values of a and b if a is greater than b and otherwise leaves a and b unchanged. For example,

```
int u = 2;
int v = 3;
int w = 4;
int x = 1;
sort2(u, v); // u is still 2, v is still 3
sort2(w, x); // w is now 1, x is now 4
```

P5.15 Write a function sort3(int& a, int& b, int& c) that swaps its three arguments to arrange them in sorted order. For example,

```
int v = 3;
int w = 4;
int x = 1;
sort3(v, w, x); // v is now 1, w is now 3, x is now 4
```

Hint: Use sort2 of Exercise P5.14.

P5.16 Enhance the int_name function so that it works correctly for values < 1,000,000,000.

P5.17 Enhance the int_name function so that it works correctly for negative values and zero. *Caution:* Make sure the improved function doesn't print 20 as "twenty zero".

P5.18 For some values (for example, 20), the int_name function returns a string with a leading space (" twenty"). Repair that blemish and ensure that spaces are inserted only when necessary. *Hint:* There are two ways of accomplishing this. Either ensure that leading spaces are never inserted, or remove leading spaces from the result before returning it.

P5.19 Write a program that prints a paycheck. Ask the program user for the name of the employee, the hourly rate, and the number of hours worked. If the number of hours exceeds 40, the employee is paid "time and a half", that is, 150 percent of the hourly rate on the hours exceeding 40. Your check should look similar to that in the figure below. Use fictitious names for the payer and the bank. Be sure to use stepwise refinement and break your solution into several functions. Use the `int_name` function to print the dollar amount of the check.

WILEY
John Wiley & Sons, Inc.
111 River Street
Hoboken, NJ 07030-5774

Publishers' Bank Minnesota
2000 Prince Blvd
Jonesville, MN 55400

CHECK
NUMBER **063331** $\frac{74\text{-}39}{311}$ 567390

Date	Amount
04/29/12	$\$*******274.15$

PAY   4659484

TWO HUNDRED SEVENTY FOUR AND 15 / 100 **************************************
TO THE ORDER OF:

        JOHN DOE
        1009 Franklin Blvd
        Sunnyvale, CA 95014

⑈478108240⑈ 200620375⑈ 1301

P5.20 Write a function that computes the weekday of a given date, using a formula known as *Zeller's congruence*. Let

d = the day of the month

mm = the modified month (3 = March, ..., 12 = December, 13 = January, 14 = February)

w = the weekday (0 = Monday, 1 = Tuesday, ..., 6 = Sunday)

Then

$$w = \left(d + 5 + \frac{(26 \times (mm + 1))}{10} + \frac{5 \times (year \,\%\, 100)}{4} + \frac{21 \times (year / 100)}{4} \right) \% \, 7$$

Here, all / denote integer division and % denotes the remainder operation.

P5.21 *Leap years.* Write a function

```
bool leap_year(int year)
```

that tests whether a year is a leap year: that is, a year with 366 days. Leap years are necessary to keep the calendar synchronized with the sun because the earth revolves around the sun once every 365.25 days. Actually, that figure is not entirely precise, and for all dates after 1582 the *Gregorian correction* applies. Usually years that are divisible by 4 are leap years, for example 1996. However, years that are divisible by 100 (for example, 1900) are not leap years, but years that are divisible by 400 are leap years (for example, 2000).

P5.22 Write a program that converts a Roman number such as MCMLXXVIII to its decimal number representation. *Hint:* First write a function that yields the numeric value of each of the letters. Then use the following algorithm:

```
total = 0
While the roman number string is not empty
    If the first character has a larger value than the second, or the string has length 1
        Add value(first character) to total.
        Remove the character.
    Else
        Add value(second character) - value(first character) to total.
        Remove both characters.
```

P5.23 In Exercise P3.23 you were asked to write a program to convert a number to its representation in Roman numerals. At the time, you did not know how to eliminate duplicate code, and as a consequence the resulting program was rather long. Rewrite that program by implementing and using the following function:

```
string roman_digit(int n, string one, string five, string ten)
```

That function translates one digit, using the strings specified for the one, five, and ten values. You would call the function as follows:

```
roman_ones = roman_digit(n % 10, "I", "V", "X");
n = n / 10;
roman_tens = roman_digit(n % 10, "X", "L", "C");
...
```

P5.24 *Postal bar codes.* For faster sorting of letters, the United States Postal Service encourages companies that send large volumes of mail to use a bar code denoting the zip code (see Figure 9).

```
**************** ECRLOT ** CO57

CODE  C671RTS2
JOHN DOE                                    CO57
1009 FRANKLIN BLVD
SUNNYVALE       CA  95014 – 5143
```

Ililllllllllllllllllllllllllllllllllllllllllllllll

Figure 9 A Postal Bar Code

The encoding scheme for a five-digit zip code is shown in Figure 10. There are full-height frame bars on each side. The five encoded digits are followed by a check digit, which is computed as follows: Add up all digits, and choose the check digit to make the sum a multiple of 10. For example, the zip code 95014 has a sum of 19, so the check digit is 1 to make the sum equal to 20.

Frame bars

Digit 1 Digit 2 Digit 3 Digit 4 Digit 5 Check Digit

Figure 10 Encoding for Five-Digit Bar Codes

Each digit of the zip code, and the check digit, is encoded according to the following table where 0 denotes a half bar and 1 a full bar.

Digit	Bar 1 (weight 7)	Bar 2 (weight 4)	Bar 3 (weight 2)	Bar 4 (weight 1)	Bar 5 (weight 0)
1	0	0	0	1	1
2	0	0	1	0	1
3	0	0	1	1	0
4	0	1	0	0	1
5	0	1	0	1	0
6	0	1	1	0	0
7	1	0	0	0	1
8	1	0	0	1	0
9	1	0	1	0	0
0	1	1	0	0	0

The digit can be easily computed from the bar code using the column weights 7, 4, 2, 1, 0. For example, 01100 is $0 \times 7 + 1 \times 4 + 1 \times 2 + 0 \times 1 \times 0 \times 0 = 6$. The only exception is 0, which would yield 11 according to the weight formula.

Write a program that asks the user for a zip code and prints the bar code. Use : for half bars, | for full bars. For example, 95014 becomes

    ||:|:::|:|:||::::::||:|::|:::|||

P5.25 Write a program that reads in a bar code (with : denoting half bars and | denoting full bars) and prints out the zip code it represents. Print an error message if the bar code is not correct.

P5.26 Write a program that prints instructions to get coffee, asking the user for input whenever a decision needs to be made. Decompose each task into a function, for example:

```
void brew_coffee()
{
   cout << "Add water to the coffee maker." << endl;
   cout << "Put a filter in the coffee maker." << endl;
   grind_coffee();
   cout << "Put the coffee in the filter." << endl;
   ...
}
```

P5.27 Write a recursive function

```
string reverse(string str)
```

that computes the reverse of a string. For example, reverse("flow") should return "wolf". *Hint:* Reverse the substring starting at the second character, then add the first character at the end. For example, to reverse "flow", first reverse "low" to "wol", then add the "f" at the end.

P5.28 Write a recursive function

```
bool is_palindrome(string str)
```

that returns true if str is a palindrome, that is, a word that is the same when reversed. Examples of palindrome are "deed", "rotor", or "aibohphobia". *Hint:* A word is a palindrome if the first and last letters match and the remainder is also a palindrome.

P5.29 Use recursion to implement a function bool find(string str, string match) that tests whether match is contained in str:

```
bool b = find("Mississippi", "sip"); // Sets b to true
```

Hint: If str starts with match, then you are done. If not, consider the string that you obtain by removing the first character.

P5.30 Use recursion to determine the number of digits in a number n. *Hint:* If n is < 10, it has one digit. Otherwise, it has one more digit than n / 10.

P5.31 Use recursion to compute a^n, where n is a positive integer. *Hint:* If n is 1, then $a^n = a$. Otherwise, $a^n = a \times a^{n-1}$.

Engineering P5.32 The effective focal length f of a lens of thickness d that has surfaces with radii of curvature R_1 and R_2 is given by

$$\frac{1}{f} = (n-1)\left[\frac{1}{R_1} - \frac{1}{R_2} + \frac{(n-1)d}{nR_1R_2}\right]$$

where n is the refractive index of the lens medium. Write a function that computes f in terms of the other parameters.

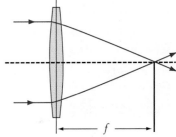

Engineering P5.33 A laboratory container is shaped like the frustum of a cone:

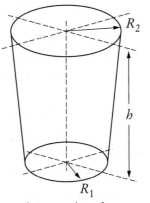

Write functions to compute the volume and surface area, using these equations:

$$V = \frac{1}{3}\pi h\left(R_1^2 + R_2^2 + R_1R_2\right)$$

$$S = \pi\left(R_1 + R_2\right)\sqrt{\left(R_2 - R_1\right)^2 + h^2} + \pi R_1^2$$

Engineering P5.34 In a movie theater, the angle θ at which a viewer sees the picture on the screen depends on the distance x of the viewer from the screen. For a movie theater with the dimensions shown in the picture below, write a function that computes the angle for a given distance.

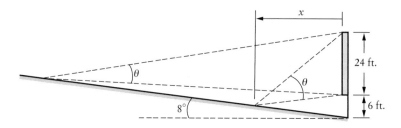

Next, provide a more general function that works for theaters with arbitrary dimensions.

Engineering P5.35 Electric wire, like that in the photo, is a cylindrical conductor covered by an insulating material. The resistance of a piece of wire is given by the formula

$$R = \frac{\rho L}{A} = \frac{4\rho L}{\pi d^2}$$

where ρ is the resistivity of the conductor, and L, A, and d are the length, cross-sectional area, and diameter of the wire. The resistivity of copper is 1.678×10^{-8} Ω m. The wire diameter, d, is commonly specified by the American wire gauge (AWG), which is an integer, n. The diameter of an AWG n wire is given by the formula

$$d = 0.127 \times 92^{\frac{36-n}{39}} \text{ mm}$$

Write a C++ function

```
double diameter(int wire_gauge)
```

that accepts the wire gauge and returns the corresponding wire diameter. Write another C++ function

```
double copper_wire_resistance(double length, int wire_gauge)
```

that accepts the length and gauge of a piece of copper wire and returns the resistance of that wire. The resistivity of aluminum is 2.82×10^{-8} Ω m. Write a third C++ function

```
double aluminum_wire_resistance(double length, int wire_gauge)
```

that accepts the length and gauge of a piece of aluminum wire and returns the resistance of that wire.

Write a C++ program to test these functions.

Engineering P5.36 The drag force on a car is given by

$$F_D = \frac{1}{2}\rho v^2 A C_D$$

where ρ is the density of air (1.23 kg/m^3), v is the velocity in units of m/s, A is the projected area of the car (2.5 m^2), and C_D is the drag coefficient (0.2).

The amount of power in watts required to overcome such drag force is $P = F_D v$, and the equivalent horsepower required is Hp = $P/746$. Write a program that accepts a car's velocity and computes the power in watts and in horsepower needed to overcome the resulting drag force. *Note:* 1 mph = 0.447 m/s.

ANSWERS TO SELF-CHECK QUESTIONS

1. The arguments are 3 and 2. The return value is 9.
2. The inner call to pow returns $2^2 = 4$. Therefore, the outer call returns $4^2 = 16$.
3. 3.
4. Users of the function can treat it as a *black box*.
5. 27.
6. $8 \times 8 \times 8 = 512$.
7. ```
double volume = pow(side_length, 3);
return volume;
```
8. ```
double square_area(double side_length)
{
    double area = side_length * side_length;
    return area;
}
```
9. (2 + 3) / (3 - 2) = 5
10. When the function is called, x is set to 4, y is set to 7, and z becomes 11. Then z is changed to 5.5, and that value is returned and printed.
11. When the function is called, x is set to 5. Then y is set to 25, and that value is returned and printed.
12. When the function is called, n is set to 5. Then n is incremented twice, setting it to 7. That value is returned and printed.
13. ```
box_string("Hello");
box_string("World");
```
14. The box_string function does not return a value. Therefore, you cannot use it in a << expression.
15. ```
void shout(string str)
{
    cout << str << "!!!" << endl;
}
```
16. ```
void box_string(string str)
{
    int n = str.length();
    for (int i = 0; i < n + 4; i++) { cout << "-"; }
    cout << endl;
    cout << "! " << str << " !" << endl;
    for (int i = 0; i < n + 4; i++) { cout << "-"; }
    cout << endl;
}
```
17. ```
void print_line(int count)
{
    for (int i = 0; i < count; i++)
    {
```

```
        cout << "-";
      }
      cout << endl;
   }
   void box_string(string str)
   {
      int n = str.length();
      print_line(n + 2);
      cout << "!" << str << "!" << endl;
      print_line(n + 2);
   }
```

18.
```
int total_pennies = round_to_pennies(total);
int total_tax_pennies = round_to_pennies(total * tax_rate);
```

where the function is defined as

```
/**
   @param amount an amount in dollars and cents
   @return the amount in pennies, rounded to the nearest penny
*/
int round_to_pennies(double amount)
{
   return static_cast<int>(100 * amount + 0.5);
}
```

19.
```
if (is_even(page)) ...
```

where the function is defined as follows:

```
bool is_even(int n)
{
   return n % 2 == 0;
}
```

20. Add parameter variables so you can pass the initial balance and interest rate to the function:

```
double balance(double initial_balance, double rate, int years)
{
   return initial_balance * pow(1 + rate / 100, years);
}
```

21.
```
int spaces = count_spaces(input);
```

where the function is defined as follows:

```
/**
   @param str any string
   @return the number spaces in str
*/
int count_spaces(string str)
{
   int count = 0;
   for (int i = 0; i < str.length(); i++)
   {
      if (str.substr(i, 1) == " ")
      {
         count++;
      }
   }
   return count;
}
```

22. It is very easy to replace the space with any character.

```
/**
   @param str any string
   @param ch a string of length 1
   @return the number of times that ch occurs in str
*/
int count(string str, string ch)
{
   int count = 0;
   for (int i = 0; i < str.length(); i++)
   {
      if (str.substr(i, 1) == ch) { count++; }
   }
   return count;
}
```

This is useful if you want to count other characters. For example, count(input, ",") counts how many commas are in the input.

23. Change line 75 to

```
name = name + digit_name(part / 100) + " hundred";
```

In line 72, add the statement

```
if (part >= 1000)
{
   name = digit_name(part / 1000) + "thousand ";
   part = part % 1000;
}
```

In line 65, change 1000 to 10000 in the comment.

24. In the case of "teens", we already have the last digit as part of the name.

25. Nothing is printed. One way of dealing with this case is to add the following statement before line 70.

```
if (number == 0) { return "zero"; }
```

26. Here is the approximate trace:

int_name(number = 72)	
part	name
~~72~~	~~" seventy"~~
2	" seventy two"

Note that the string starts with a blank space. Exercise P5.18 asks you to eliminate it.

27. Here is one possible solution. Break up the task **print table** into **print header** and **print body**. The **print header** task calls **print separator**, prints the header cells, and calls **print separator** again. The **print body** task repeatedly calls **print row** and then calls **print separator**.

28. 1.

29. 2, 7.

30. Lines 3, 4, 5, 6, 10, 11, but not 7 through 9.

31. The global variable defined in line 1.

32. The variables s defined in lines 4 and 15.

33. Yes, but since the function does not modify the `amount` parameter variable, there is no need to do so.

34. `void transfer(double& balance1, double& balance2, double amount)`

35.
```
bool withdraw(double& balance, double amount)
{
   if (balance >= amount)
   {
      balance = balance - amount;
      return true;
   }
   else
   {
      return false;
   }
}
```

36.
```
void minmax(double x, double y, double& a, double& b)
{
   if (x < y) { a = x; b = y; }
   else { a = y; b = x; }
}
```

37. The program sets x to 1, then y to 4, then x to 3. It prints 3 4.

38.
```
[][][][]
[][][]
[][]
[]
```

39. 4 + 3 + 2 + 1 + 0 = 10

40. mystery(10) + 1 = mystery(5) + 2 = mystery(2) + 3 = mystery(1) + 4 = mystery(0) + 5 = 5

41. The idea is to print one [], then print n - 1 of them.
```
void print_boxes(int n)
{
   if (n == 0) { return; }
   cout << "[]";
   print_boxes(n - 1);
}
```

42. Simply add the following to the beginning of the function:
```
if (part >= 1000)
{
   return int_name(part / 1000) + " thousand " + int_name(part % 1000);
}
```

ARRAYS AND VECTORS

To become familiar with using arrays and vectors to collect values

To learn about common algorithms for processing arrays and vectors

To write functions that receive and return arrays and vectors

To be able to use two-dimensional arrays

In many programs, you need to collect large numbers of values. In standard C++, you use arrays and vectors for this purpose. Arrays are a fundamental structure of the C++ language. The standard C++ library provides the vector construct as a more convenient alternative when working with collections whose size is not fixed. In this chapter, you will learn about arrays, vectors, and common algorithms for processing them.

6.1 Arrays

We start this chapter by introducing the array data type. Arrays are the fundamental mechanism in C++ for collecting multiple values. In the following sections, you will learn how to define arrays and how to access array elements.

6.1.1 Defining Arrays

Suppose you write a program that reads a sequence of values and prints out the sequence, marking the largest value, like this:

```
32
54
67.5
29
34.5
80
115 <= largest value
44.5
100
65
```

You do not know which value to mark as the largest one until you have seen them all. After all, the last value might be the largest one. Therefore, the program must first store all values before it can print them.

Could you simply store each value in a separate variable? If you know that there are ten inputs, then you can store the values in ten variables value1, value2, value3, ..., value10. However, such a sequence of variables is not very practical to use. You would have to write quite a bit of code ten times, once for each of the variables. To solve this problem, use an **array**: a structure for storing a sequence of values.

Figure 1
An Array of Size 10

Syntax 6.1 Defining an Array

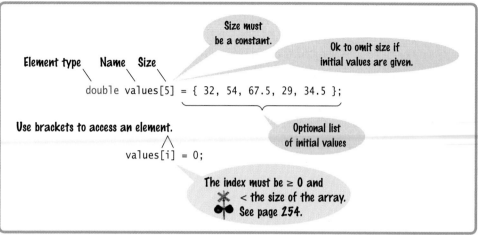

Here we define an array that can hold ten values:

```
double values[10];
```

This is the definition of a variable values whose type is "array of double". That is, values stores a sequence of floating-point numbers. The [10] indicates the *size* of the array. (See Figure 1.) The array size must be a constant that is known at compile time.

When you define an array, you can specify the initial values. For example,

```
double values[] = { 32, 54, 67.5, 29, 34.5, 80, 115, 44.5, 100, 65 };
```

When you supply initial values, you don't need to specify the array size. The compiler determines the size by counting the values.

Use an array to collect a sequence of values of the same type.

Table 1 Defining Arrays

`int numbers[10];`	An array of ten integers.
`const int SIZE = 10;` `int numbers[SIZE];`	It is a good idea to use a named constant for the size.
⚠ `int size = 10;` `int numbers[size];`	**Caution:** In standard C++, the size must be a constant. This array definition will not work with all compilers.
`int squares[5] = { 0, 1, 4, 9, 16 };`	An array of five integers, with initial values.
`int squares[] = { 0, 1, 4, 9, 16 };`	You can omit the array size if you supply initial values. The size is set to the number of initial values.
`int squares[5] = { 0, 1, 4 };`	If you supply fewer initial values than the size, the remaining values are set to 0. This array contains 0, 1, 4, 0, 0.
`string names[3];`	An array of three strings.

6.1.2 Accessing Array Elements

Individual elements in an array *values* are accessed by an integer index i, using the notation *values*[i].

The values stored in an array are called its **elements**. Each element has a position number, called an **index**. To access a value in the values array, you must specify which index you want to use. That is done with the [] operator:

```
values[4] = 34.5;
```

Now the element with index 4 is filled with 34.5. (See Figure 2).

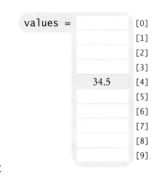

```
values =                    [0]
                            [1]
                            [2]
                            [3]
                  34.5      [4]
                            [5]
                            [6]
                            [7]
                            [8]
                            [9]
```

Figure 2
Filling an Array Element

You can display the contents of the element with index 4 with the following command:

```
cout << values[4] << endl;
```

As you can see, the element values[4] can be used like any variable of type double.

An array element can be used like any variable.

In C++, array positions are counted in a way that you may find surprising. If you look carefully at Figure 2, you will find that the *fifth* element was filled when we changed values[4]. In C++, the elements of arrays are numbered *starting at 0*. That is, the legal elements for the values array are

values[0], the first element

values[1], the second element

values[2], the third element

values[3], the fourth element

values[4], the fifth element

...

values[9], the tenth element

You will see in Chapter 7 why this numbering scheme was chosen in C++.

An array index must be at least zero and less than the size of the array.

You have to be careful about index values. Trying to access a element that does not exist in the array is a serious error. For example, if values has twenty elements, you are not allowed to access values[20].

Attempting to access an element whose index is not within the valid index range is called a **bounds error**. The compiler does not catch this type of error. Even the running program generates *no* error message. If you make a bounds error, you silently read or overwrite another memory location. As a consequence, your program may have random errors, and it can even crash.

Like a post office box that is identified by a box number, an array element is identified by an index.

The most common bounds error is the following:

```
double values[10];
cout << values[10];
```

There is no values[10] in an array with ten elements—the legal index values range from 0 to 9.

To visit all elements of an array, use a variable for the index. Suppose values has ten elements and the integer variable i takes values 0, 1, 2, and so on, up to 9. Then the expression values[i] yields each element in turn. For example, this loop displays all elements.

```
for (int i = 0; i < 10; i++)
{
    cout << values[i] << endl;
}
```

Note that in the loop condition the index is *less than* 10 because there is no element corresponding to values[10].

6.1.3 Partially Filled Arrays

With a partially filled array, you need to remember how many elements are filled.

An array cannot change size at run time. This is a problem when you don't know in advance how many elements you need. In that situation, you must come up with a good guess on the maximum number of elements that you need to store. We call this quantity the *capacity*. For example, we may decide that we sometimes want to store more than ten values, but never more than 100:

```
const int CAPACITY = 100;
double values[CAPACITY];
```

In a typical program run, only part of the array will be occupied by actual elements. We call such an array a *partially filled array*. You must keep a *companion variable* that counts how many elements are actually used. In Figure 3 we call the companion variable current_size.

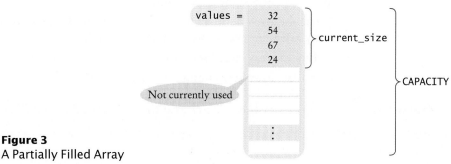

Figure 3
A Partially Filled Array

The following loop collects values and fills up the values array.

```
int current_size = 0;
double input;
while (cin >> input)
{
    if (current_size < CAPACITY)
    {
        values[current_size] = input;
        current_size++;
```

```
        }
    }
```

At the end of this loop, `current_size` contains the actual number of elements in the array. Note that you have to stop accepting inputs if the size of the array reaches the capacity.

To process the gathered array elements, you again use the companion variable, not the capacity. This loop prints the partially filled array:

```
for (int i = 0; i < current_size; i++)
{
    cout << values[i] << endl;
}
```

SELF CHECK

1. Define an array of integers containing the first five prime numbers.

2. Assume the array `primes` has been initialized as described in Self Check 1. What is its contents after executing the following loop?

```
for (int i = 0; i < 2; i++)
{
    primes[4 - i] = primes[i];
}
```

3. Assume the array `primes` has been initialized as described in Self Check 1. What is its contents after executing the following loop?

```
for (int i = 0; i < 5; i++)
{
    primes[i]++;
}
```

4. Given the definition

```
const int CAPACITY = 10;
double values[CAPACITY];
```

write statements to put a zero into the elements of the array `values` with the lowest and the highest valid index.

5. Given the array defined in Self Check 4, write a loop to print the elements of the array `values` in reverse order, starting with the last element.

6. Define an array called `words` that can hold ten values of type `string`.

7. Define an array containing two strings, `"Yes"`, and `"No"`.

Practice It   Now you can try these exercises at the end of the chapter: R6.1, R6.2, R6.6, P6.1.

Common Error 6.1

Bounds Errors

Perhaps the most common error in using arrays is accessing a nonexistent element.

```
double values[10];
values[10] = 5.4;
    // Error—values has 10 elements with subscripts 0 to 9
```

If your program accesses an array through an out-of-bounds subscript, there is no error message. Instead, the program will quietly (or not so quietly) corrupt some memory. Except for very short programs, in which the problem may go unnoticed, that corruption will make the program act unpredictably, and it can even cause the program to terminate. These are serious errors that can be difficult to detect.

Use Arrays for Sequences of Related Values

Arrays are intended for storing sequences of values with the same meaning. For example, an array of test scores makes perfect sense:

```
int scores[NUMBER_OF_SCORES];
```

But an array

```
double personal_data[3];
```

that holds a person's age, bank balance, and shoe size in positions 0, 1, and 2 is bad design. It would be tedious for the programmer to remember which of these data values is stored in which array location. In this situation, it is far better to use three separate variables.

Random Fact 6.1 An Early Internet Worm

In November 1988, Robert Morris, a student at Cornell University, launched a so-called virus program that infected about 6,000 computers connected to the Internet across the United States. Tens of thousands of computer users were unable to read their e-mail or otherwise use their computers. All major universities and many high-tech companies were affected. (The Internet was much smaller then than it is now.)

The particular kind of virus used in this attack is called a worm. The virus program crawled from one computer on the Internet to the next. The worm would attempt to connect to finger, a program in the UNIX operating system for finding information on a user who has an account on a particular computer on the network. Like many programs in UNIX, finger is written in the C language. In C, as in C++, arrays have a fixed size. To store the user name to be looked up (say, walters@cs.sjsu.edu), the finger program allocated an array of 512 characters, under the assumption that nobody would ever provide such a long input. Unfortunately, C, like C++, does not check that an array index is less than the length of the array. If you write into an array using an index that is too large, you simply overwrite memory locations that belong to some other objects. In some versions of the finger

program, the programmer had been lazy and had not checked whether the array holding the input characters was large enough to hold the input. So the worm program purposefully filled the 512-character array with 536 bytes. The excess 24 bytes would overwrite a return address, which the attacker knew was stored just after the line buffer. When that function was finished, it didn't return to its caller but to code supplied by the worm (see Figure 4). That code ran under the same superuser privileges as finger, allowing the worm to gain entry into the remote system. Had the programmer who wrote finger been more conscientious, this particular attack would not be possible. In C++, as in C, all programmers must be very careful not to overrun array boundaries.

One may well speculate what would possess the virus author to spend many weeks to plan the antisocial act of breaking into thousands of computers and disabling them. It appears that the break-in was fully intended by the author, but the disabling of the computers was a bug, caused by continuous reinfection. Morris was sentenced to 3 years probation, 400 hours of community service, and fined $10,000.

In recent years, computer attacks have intensified and the motives have become more sinister. Instead of disabling computers, viruses often steal

financial data or use the attacked computers for sending spam e-mail. Sadly, many of these attacks continue to be possible because of poorly written programs that are susceptible to buffer overrun errors.

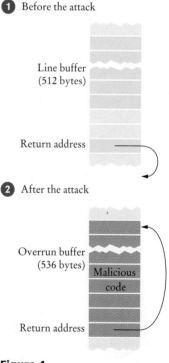

① Before the attack

Line buffer
(512 bytes)

Return address

② After the attack

Overrun buffer
(536 bytes)

Malicious code

Return address

Figure 4
A "Buffer Overrun" Attack

6.2 Common Array Algorithms

In the following sections, we discuss some of the most common algorithms for processing sequences of values. We present the algorithms so that you can use them with fully and partially filled arrays as well as vectors (which we will introduce in Section 6.7). When we use the expression **size of** values, you should replace it with a constant or variable that yields the number of elements in the array (or the expression values.size() if values is a vector.)

6.2.1 Filling

This loop fills an array with zeroes:

```
for (int i = 0; i < size of values; i++)
{
    values[i] = 0;
}
```

Next, let us fill an array squares with the numbers 0, 1, 4, 9, 16, and so on. Note that the element with index 0 contains 0^2, the element with index 1 contains 1^2, and so on.

```
for (int i = 0; i < size of squares; i++)
{
    squares[i] = i * i;
}
```

6.2.2 Copying

Consider two arrays:

```
int squares[5] = { 0, 1, 4, 9, 16 };
int lucky_numbers[5];
```

Now suppose you want to copy all values from the first array to the second. The following assignment is an error:

```
lucky_numbers = squares; // Error
```

In C++, you cannot assign one array to another. Instead, you must use a loop to copy all elements:

```
for (int i = 0; i < 5; i++)
{
    lucky_numbers[i] = squares[i];
}
```

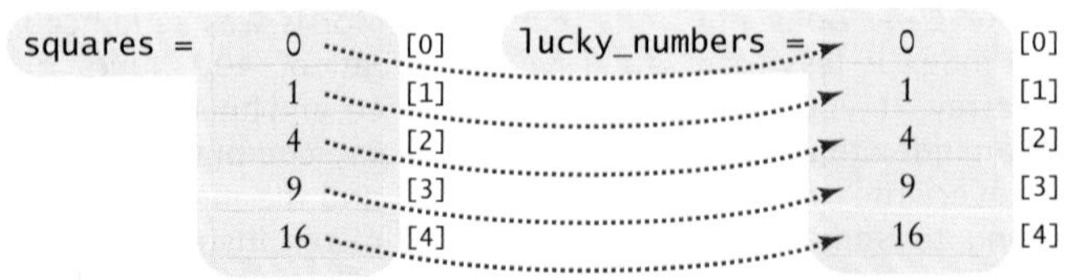

To copy an array, use a loop to copy its elements to a new array.

Figure 5   Copying Elements to Copy an Array

6.2.3 Sum and Average Value

You have already encountered this algorithm in Section 4.7.1. Here is the code for computing the sum of all elements in an array:

```
double total = 0;
for (int i = 0; i < size of values; i++)
{
   total = total + values[i];
}
```

To obtain the average, divide by the number of elements:

```
double average = total / size of values;
```

Be sure to check that the size is not zero.

6.2.4 Maximum and Minimum

Use the algorithm from Section 4.7.4 that keeps a variable for the largest element that you have encountered so far. Here is the implementation for arrays:

```
double largest = values[0];
for (int i = 1; i < size of values; i++)
{
   if (values[i] > largest)
   {
      largest = values[i];
   }
}
```

Note that the loop starts at 1 because we initialize largest with values[0].

To compute the smallest value, reverse the comparison.

These algorithms require that the array contain at least one element.

6.2.5 Element Separators

When separating elements, don't place a separator before the first element.

When you display the elements of a collection, you usually want to separate them, often with commas or vertical lines, like this:

```
1 | 4 | 9 | 16 | 25
```

Note that there is one fewer separator than there are numbers. Print the separator before each element *except the initial one* (with index 0):

```
for (int i = 0; i < size of values; i++)
{
   if (i > 0)
   {
      cout << " | ";
   }
   cout << values[i];
}
```

To print five elements, you need four separators.

6.2.6 Linear Search

A linear search inspects elements in sequence until a match is found.

To search for a specific element, visit the elements and stop when you encounter the match.

You often need to search for the position of an element so that you can replace or remove it. Visit all elements until you have found a match or you have come to the end of the array. Here we search for the position of the first element equal to 100.

```
int pos = 0;
bool found = false;
while (pos < size of values && !found)
{
   if (values[pos] == 100)
   {
      found = true;
   }
   else
   {
      pos++;
   }
}
```

If found is true, then pos is the position of the first match.

6.2.7 Removing an Element

Consider a partially filled array values whose current size is stored in the variable current_size. Suppose you want to remove the element with index pos from values. If the elements are not in any particular order, that task is easy to accomplish. Simply overwrite the element to be removed with the *last* element, then decrement the variable tracking the size. (See Figure 6.)

```
values[pos] = values[current_size - 1];
current_size--;
```

The situation is more complex if the order of the elements matters. Then you must move all elements following the element to be removed to a lower index, then decrement the variable holding the size of the array. (See Figure 7.)

```
for (int i = pos + 1; i < current_size; i++)
{
   values[i - 1] = values[i];
}
current_size--;
```

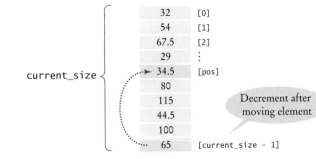

Figure 6
Removing an Element in an Unordered Array

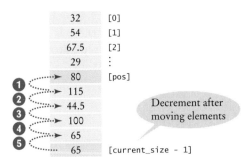

Figure 7
Removing an Element in an Ordered Array

6.2.8 Inserting an Element

If the order of the elements does not matter, you can simply insert new elements at the end, incrementing the variable tracking the size. (See Figure 8.) For a partially filled array:

```
if (current_size < CAPACITY)
{
   current_size++;
   values[current_size - 1] = new_element;
}
```

It is more work to insert an element at a particular position in the middle of a sequence. First, increase the variable holding the current size. Next, move all elements above the insertion location to a higher index. Finally, insert the new element. Here is the code for a partially filled array:

```
if (current_size < CAPACITY)
{
   current_size++;
   for (int i = current_size - 1; i > pos; i--)
   {
      values[i] = values[i - 1];
   }
   values[pos] = new_element;
}
```

> Before inserting an element, move elements to the end of the array *starting with the last one.*

Note the order of the movement: When you remove an element, you first move the next element down to a lower index, then the one after that, until you finally get to the end of the array. When you insert an element, you start at the end of the array, move that element to a higher index, then move the one before that, and so on until you finally get to the insertion location (see Figure 9).

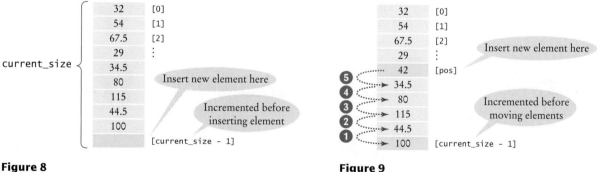

Figure 8
Inserting an Element in an Unordered Array

Figure 9
Inserting an Element in an Ordered Array

6.2.9 Swapping Elements

You often need to swap elements of an array. For example, the sorting algorithm in Special Topic 6.2 on page 263 sorts an array by repeatedly swapping elements.

Figure 10
Swapping Array Elements

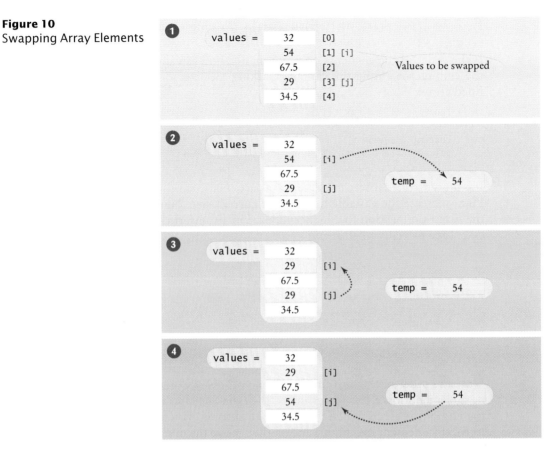

Consider the task of swapping the elements at positions i and j of an array values. We'd like to set values[i] to values[j]. But that overwrites the value that is currently stored in values[i], so we want to save that first:

Use a temporary variable when swapping two elements.

```
double temp = values[i];
values[i] = values[j];
```

Now we can set values[j] to the saved value.

```
values[j] = temp;
```

Figure 10 shows the process.

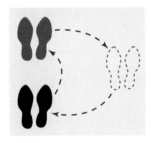

To swap two elements, you need a temporary variable.

6.2.10 Reading Input

If you know how many input values the user will supply, it is simple to place them into an array:

```
double values[NUMBER_OF_INPUTS];
for (i = 0; i < NUMBER_OF_INPUTS; i++)
{
   cin >> values[i];
}
```

However, this technique does not work if you need to read an arbitrary number of inputs. In that case, add the values to an array until the end of the input has been reached.

```
double values[CAPACITY];
int current_size = 0;
double input;
while (cin >> input)
{
    if (current_size < CAPACITY)
    {
        values[current_size] = input;
        current_size++;
    }
}
```

Now values is a partially filled array, and the companion variable current_size is set to the number of input values.

This loop discards any inputs that won't fit in the array. A better approach would be to copy values to a new larger array when the capacity is reached (see Section 6.2.2).

The following program solves the task that we set ourselves at the beginning of this chapter, to mark the largest value in an input sequence:

ch06/largest.cpp

```
1   #include <iostream>
2
3   using namespace std;
4
5   int main()
6   {
7       const int CAPACITY = 1000;
8       double values[CAPACITY];
9       int current_size = 0;
10
11      cout << "Please enter values, Q to quit:" << endl;
12      double input;
13      while (cin >> input)
14      {
15          if (current_size < CAPACITY)
16          {
17              values[current_size] = input;
18              current_size++;
19          }
20      }
21
22      double largest = values[0];
23      for (int i = 1; i < current_size; i++)
24      {
25          if (values[i] > largest)
26          {
27              largest = values[i];
28          }
29      }
30
31      for (int i = 0; i < current_size; i++)
32      {
33          cout << values[i];
34          if (values[i] == largest)
35          {
```

```
36              cout << " <== largest value";
37          }
38          cout << endl;
39      }
40
41      return 0;
42  }
```

Program Run

```
Please enter values, Q to quit:
34.5 80 115 44.5 Q
34.5
80
115 <== largest value
44.5
```

SELF CHECK

8. What is the output of the `largest.cpp` program with the following inputs?

    20 10 20 Q

9. Write a loop that counts how many elements in an array are equal to zero.

10. Consider the algorithm to find the largest element in an array. Why don't we initialize `largest` and `i` with zero, like this?

    ```
    double largest = 0;
    for (int i = 0; i < size of values; i++)
    {
        if (values[i] > largest)
        {
            largest = values[i];
        }
    }
    ```

11. When printing separators, we skipped the separator before the initial element. Rewrite the loop so that the separator is printed *after* each element, except for the last element.

12. What is wrong with these statements for printing an array with separators?

    ```
    cout << values[0];
    for (int i = 1; i < size of values; i++)
    {
        cout << ", " << values[i];
    }
    ```

13. When searching for a match, we used a `while` loop, not a `for` loop. What is wrong with using this loop instead?

    ```
    for (pos = 0; pos < size of values && !found; pos++)
    {
        if (values[pos] == 100)
        {
            found = true;
        }
    }
    ```

14. When inserting an element into an array, we moved the elements with larger index values, starting at the end. Why is it wrong to start at the insertion location, like this:

```
for (int i = pos; i < size of values - 1; i++)
{
    values[i + 1] = values[i];
}
```

Practice It   Now you can try these exercises at the end of the chapter: R6.10, R6.13, P6.6, P6.16.

Special Topic 6.1

Sorting with the C++ Library

You often want to sort the elements of an array or vector. Special Topic 6.2 shows you a sorting algorithm that is relatively simple but not very efficient. Efficient sorting algorithms are significantly more complex. Fortunately, the C++ library provides an efficient sort function. To sort an array a with size elements, call

```
sort(a, a + size);
```

To sort a vector values, make this call:

```
sort(values.begin(), values.end());
```

To fully understand the curious syntax of these calls, you will need to know advanced C++ that is beyond the scope of this book. But don't hesitate to call the sort function whenever you need to sort an array or vector.

To use the sort function, include the <algorithm> header in your program.

Special Topic 6.2

A Sorting Algorithm

A *sorting algorithm* rearranges the elements of a sequence so that they are stored in sorted order. Here is a simple sorting algorithm, called **selection sort**. Consider sorting the following array values:

```
[0] [1] [2] [3] [4]
11   9  17   5  12
```

An obvious first step is to find the smallest element. In this case the smallest element is 5, stored in values[3]. You should move the 5 to the beginning of the array. Of course, there is already an element stored in values[0], namely 11. Therefore you cannot simply move values[3] into values[0] without moving the 11 somewhere else. You don't yet know where the 11 should end up, but you know for certain that it should not be in values[0]. Simply get it out of the way by *swapping it* with values[3]:

```
5   9  17  11  12
```

Now the first element is in the correct place. In the foregoing figure, the darker color indicates the portion of the array that is already sorted.

Next take the minimum of the remaining entries values[1]...values[4]. That minimum value, 9, is already in the correct place. You don't need to do anything in this case, simply extend the sorted area by one to the right:

```
5   9  17  11  12
```

Repeat the process. The minimum value of the unsorted region is 11, which needs to be swapped with the first value of the unsorted region, 17:

```
5   9  11  17  12
```

Now the unsorted region is only two elements long; keep to the same successful strategy. The minimum element is 12. Swap it with the first value, 17:

| 5 | 9 | 11 | 12 | 17 |

That leaves you with an unprocessed region of length 1, but of course a region of length 1 is always sorted. You are done.

Here is the C++ code:

```cpp
for (int unsorted = 0; unsorted < size - 1; unsorted++)
{
    // Find the position of the minimum
    int min_pos = unsorted;
    for (int i = unsorted + 1; i < size; i++)
    {
        if (values[i] < values[min_pos]) { min_pos = i; }
    }
    // Swap the minimum into the sorted area
    if (min_pos != unsorted)
    {
        double temp = values[min_pos];
        values[min_pos] = values[unsorted];
        values[unsorted] = temp;
    }
}
```

This algorithm is simple to understand, but it is not very efficient. Computer scientists have studied sorting algorithms extensively and discovered significantly better algorithms. The sort function of the C++ library provides one such algorithm—see Special Topic 6.1 on page 263.

Special Topic 6.3

Binary Search

When an array is sorted, there is a much faster search algorithm than the linear search of Section 6.2.6.

Consider the following sorted array values:

	[0]	[1]	[2]	[3]	[4]	[5]	[6]	[7]
	1	5	8	9	12	17	20	32

We would like to see whether the value 15 is in the array. Let's narrow our search by finding whether the value is in the first or second half of the array. The last point in the first half of the data set, values[3], is 9, which is smaller than the value we are looking for. Hence, we should look in the second half of the array for a match, that is, in the sequence:

	[0]	[1]	[2]	[3]	[4]	[5]	[6]	[7]
	1	5	8	9	**12**	**17**	**20**	**32**

Now the last value of the first half of this sequence is 17; hence, the value must be located in the sequence:

	[0]	[1]	[2]	[3]	[4]	[5]	[6]	[7]
	1	5	8	9	**12**	**17**	20	32

The last value of the first half of this very short sequence is 12, which is smaller than the value that we are searching, so we must look in the second half:

	[0]	[1]	[2]	[3]	[4]	[5]	[6]	[7]
	1	5	8	9	12	**17**	20	32

We still don't have a match because 15 ≠ 17, and we cannot divide the subsequence further. If we wanted to insert 15 into the sequence, we would need to insert it just before values[5].

This search process is called a **binary search**, because we cut the size of the search in half in each step. That cutting in half works only because we know that the sequence of values is sorted. Here is an implementation in C++:

```cpp
bool found = false;
int low = 0;
int high = size - 1;
int pos = 0;
while (low <= high && !found)
{
    pos = (low + high) / 2; // Midpoint of the subsequence
    if (values[pos] == searched_value) { found = true; }
    else if (values[pos] < searched_value) { low = pos + 1; } // Look in second half
    else { high = pos - 1; } // Look in first half
}
if (found) { cout << "Found at position " << pos; }
else { cout << "Not found. Insert before position " << pos; }
```

6.3 Arrays and Functions

When passing an array to a function, also pass the size of the array.

In this section, we will explore how to write functions that process arrays.

A function that processes the values in an array needs to know the number of valid elements in the array. For example, here is a sum function that computes the sum of all elements in an array:

```cpp
double sum(double values[], int size)
{
    double total = 0;
    for (int i = 0; i < size; i++)
    {
        total = total + values[i];
    }
    return total;
}
```

Note the special syntax for array parameter variables. When writing an array parameter variable, you place an empty [] behind the parameter name. Do not specify the size of the array inside the brackets.

When you call the function, supply both the name of the array and the size. For example,

```cpp
double NUMBER_OF_SCORES = 10;
double scores[NUMBER_OF_SCORES]
    = { 32, 54, 67.5, 29, 34.5, 80, 115, 44.5, 100, 65 };
double total_score = sum(scores, NUMBER_OF_SCORES);
```

You can also pass a smaller size to the function:

```cpp
double partial_score = sum(scores, 5);
```

This call computes the sum of the first five elements of the scores array. Remember, the function has no way of knowing how many elements the array has. It simply relies on the size that the caller provides.

Array parameters are always reference parameters.

Array parameters are *always reference parameters*. (You will see the reason in Chapter 7.) Functions can modify array arguments, and those modifications affect the array that was passed into the function. For example, the following `multiply` function updates all elements in the array:

```cpp
void multiply(double values[], int size, double factor)
{
   for (int i = 0; i < size; i++)
   {
      values[i] = values[i] * factor;
   }
}
```

You do *not* use an & symbol to denote the reference parameter in this case.

A function's return type cannot be an array.

Although arrays can be function arguments, they cannot be function return types. If a function computes multiple values, the caller of the function must provide an array parameter variable to hold the result.

```cpp
void squares(int n, int result[])
{
   for (int i = 0; i < n; i++)
   {
      result[i] = i * i;
   }
}
```

When a function modifies the size of an array, it needs to tell its caller.

When a function changes the size of an array, it should indicate to the caller how many elements the array has after the call. The easiest way to do this is to return the new size. Here is an example—a function that adds input values to an array:

```cpp
int read_inputs(double inputs[], int capacity)
{
   int current_size = 0;
   double input;
   while (cin >> input)
   {
      if (current_size < capacity)
      {
         inputs[current_size] = input;
         current_size++;
      }
   }
   return current_size;
}
```

A function that adds elements to an array needs to know its capacity.

Note that this function also needs to know the capacity of the array. Generally, a function that adds elements to an array needs to know is capacity. You would call this function like this:

```cpp
const int MAXIMUM_NUMBER_OF_VALUES = 1000;
double values[MAXIMUM_NUMBER_OF_VALUES];
int current_size = read_inputs(values, MAXIMUM_NUMBER_OF_VALUES);
   // values is a partially filled array; the current_size variable specifies its size
```

Alternatively, you can pass the size as a reference parameter. This is more appropriate for functions that modify an existing array:

```cpp
void append_inputs(double inputs[], int capacity, int& current_size)
{
   double input;
   while (cin >> input)
   {
```

```
      if (current_size < capacity)
      {
         inputs[current_size] = input;
         current_size++;
      }
   }
}
```

This function is called as

```
append_inputs(values, MAXIMUM_NUMBER_OF_VALUES, current_size);
```

After the call, the current_size variable contains the new size.

The following example program reads values from standard input, doubles them, and prints the result. The program uses three functions:

- The read_inputs function fills an array with the input values. It returns the number of elements that were read.

- The multiply function modifies the contents of the array that it receives, demonstrating that arrays are passed by reference.

- The print function does not modify the contents of the array that it receives.

ch06/functions.cpp

```
 1  #include <iostream>
 2
 3  using namespace std;
 4
 5  /**
 6      Reads a sequence of floating-point numbers.
 7      @param inputs an array containing the numbers
 8      @param capacity the capacity of that array
 9      @return the number of inputs stored in the array
10  */
11  int read_inputs(double inputs[], int capacity)
12  {
13      int current_size = 0;
14      cout << "Please enter values, Q to quit:" << endl;
15      bool more = true;
16      while (more)
17      {
18         double input;
19         cin >> input;
20         if (cin.fail())
21         {
22            more = false;
23         }
24         else if (current_size < capacity)
25         {
26            inputs[current_size] = input;
27            current_size++;
28         }
29      }
30      return current_size;
31  }
32
33  /**
34      Multiplies all elements of an array by a factor.
35      @param values a partially filled array
36      @param size the number of elements in values
```

```
37      @param factor the value with which each element is multiplied
38  */
39  void multiply(double values[], int size, double factor)
40  {
41      for (int i = 0; i < size; i++)
42      {
43          values[i] = values[i] * factor;
44      }
45  }
46
47  /**
48      Prints the elements of a vector, separated by commas.
49      @param values a partially filled array
50      @param size the number of elements in values
51  */
52  void print(double values[], int size)
53  {
54      for (int i = 0; i < size; i++)
55      {
56          if (i > 0) { cout << ", "; }
57          cout << values[i];
58      }
59      cout << endl;
60  }
61
62  int main()
63  {
64      const int CAPACITY = 1000;
65      double values[CAPACITY];
66      int size = read_inputs(values, CAPACITY);
67      multiply(values, size, 2);
68      print(values, size);
69
70      return 0;
71  }
```

Program Run

```
Please enter values, Q to quit:
12 25 20 Q
24, 50, 40
```

SELF CHECK

15. What happens if you call the sum function and you lie about the size? For example, calling

    ```
    double result = sum(values, 1000);
    ```

    even though values has size 100.

16. How do you call the squares function to compute the first five squares and store the result in an array numbers?

17. Write a function that returns the first position of an element in an array, or −1 if the element is not present. Use the linear search algorithm of Section 6.2.6.

18. Rewrite the read_inputs function so that the array size is a reference parameter, not a return value.

19. Write the header for a function that appends two arrays into another array. Do not implement the function.

Practice It   Now you can try these exercises at the end of the chapter: R6.14, P6.8, P6.12.

Special Topic 6.4

Constant Array Parameters

When a function doesn't modify an array parameter, it is considered good style to add the const reserved word, like this:

```
double sum(const double values[], int size)
```

The const reserved word helps the reader of the code, making it clear that the function keeps the array elements unchanged. If the implementation of the function tries to modify the array, the compiler issues a warning.

6.4 Problem Solving: Adapting Algorithms

> By combining fundamental algorithms, you can solve complex programming tasks.

In Section 6.2, you were introduced to a number of fundamental array algorithms. These algorithms form the building blocks for many programs that process arrays. In general, it is a good problem-solving strategy to have a repertoire of fundamental algorithms that you can combine and adapt.

Consider this example problem: You are given the quiz scores of a student. You are to compute the final quiz score, which is the sum of all scores after dropping the lowest one. For example, if the scores are

```
8   7   8.5   9.5   7   4   10
```

then the final score is 50.

We do not have a ready-made algorithm for this situation. Instead, consider which algorithms may be related. These include:

- Calculating the sum (Section 6.2.3)
- Finding the minimum value (Section 6.2.4)
- Removing an element (Section 6.2.7)

Now we can formulate a plan of attack that combines these algorithms.

> Find the minimum.
> Remove it from the array.
> Calculate the sum.

Let's try it out with our example. The minimum of

	[0]	[1]	[2]	[3]	[4]	[5]	[6]
	8	7	8.5	9.5	7	4	10

is 4. How do we remove it?

Now we have a problem. The removal algorithm in Section 6.2.7 locates the element to be removed by using the *position* of the element, not the value.

But we have another algorithm for that:

- Linear search (Section 6.2.6)

We need to fix our plan of attack:

Find the minimum value.
Find its position.
Remove that position from the array.
Calculate the sum.

Will it work? Let's continue with our example.

We found a minimum value of 4. Linear search tells us that the value 4 occurs at position 5.

	[0]	[1]	[2]	[3]	[4]	[5]	[6]
	8	7	8.5	9.5	7	4	10

We remove it:

	[0]	[1]	[2]	[3]	[4]	[5]
	8	7	8.5	9.5	7	10

Finally, we compute the sum: $8 + 7 + 8.5 + 9.5 + 7 + 10 = 50$.

This walkthrough demonstrates that our strategy works.

Can we do better? It seems a bit inefficient to find the minimum and then make another pass through the array to obtain its position.

We can adapt the algorithm for finding the minimum to yield the position of the minimum. Here is the original algorithm:

```
double smallest = values[0];
for (int i = 1; i < size of values; i++)
{
   if (values[i] < smallest)
   {
      smallest = values[i];
   }
}
```

When we find the smallest value, we also want to update the position:

```
if (values[i] < smallest)
{
   smallest = values[i];
   smallest_position = i;
}
```

In fact, then there is no reason to keep track of the smallest value any longer. It is simply `values[smallest_position]`. With this insight, we can adapt the algorithm as follows:

```
int smallest_position = 0;
for (int i = 1; i < size of values; i++)
{
   if (values[i] < values[smallest_position])
   {
      smallest_position = i;
   }
}
```

With this adaptation, our problem is solved with the following strategy:

Find the position of the minimum.
Remove it from the array.
Calculate the sum.

In How To 6.1 on page 271, we develop a C++ program from this strategy.

The next section shows you a technique for discovering a new algorithm when none of the fundamental algorithms can be adapted to a task.

SELF CHECK

20. Section 6.2.7 has two algorithms for removing an element. Which of the two should be used to solve the task described in this section?
21. It isn't actually necessary to *remove* the minimum in order to compute the total score. Describe an alternative.
22. How can you print the number of positive and negative values in a given array, using one or more of the algorithms in Section 4.7?
23. How can you print all positive values in an array, separated by commas?
24. Consider the following algorithm for collecting all matches in an array:

```
int matches_size = 0;
for (int i = 0; i < size of values; i++)
{
    if (values[i] fulfills the condition)
    {
        matches[matches_size] = values[i];
        matches_size++;
    }
}
```

How can this algorithm help you with Self Check 23?

Practice It Now you can try these exercises at the end of the chapter: R6.15, R6.16.

HOW TO 6.1   Working with Arrays

When you process sequences of values, you usually need to use arrays. (In some very simple situations, you can process values as you read them in, without storing them.) This How To walks you through the necessary steps.

Consider the example problem from Section 6.4: You are given the quiz scores of a student. You are to compute the final quiz score, which is the sum of all scores after dropping the lowest one. For example, if the scores are

8 7 8.5 9.5 7 5 10

then the final score is 50.

Step 1   Decompose your task into steps.

You will usually want to break down your task into multiple steps, such as

• Reading the data into an array.
• Processing the data in one or more steps.
• Displaying the results.

In our sample problem, this yields the following pseudocode:

Read inputs.
Compute the final score.
Display the score.

When deciding how to process the data, you should be familiar with the array algorithms in Section 6.2. Many processing tasks can be solved by combining or adapting one or more of these algorithms.

The preceding section showed you how to decompose **Compute the final score** into fundamental algorithms:

Find the position of the minimum.
Remove it from the array.
Calculate the sum.

Step 2   Determine functions, arguments, and return values for each step.

Even though it may be possible to put all steps into the main function, this is rarely a good idea. The simplest and best approach is to make each nontrivial step into a separate function. In our example, we will implement four functions:

- read_inputs
- min_position
- remove
- sum
- final_score

For each function that processes an array, you will need to pass the array itself and the array size. For example,

```
double sum(double values[], int size)
```

If the function modifies the size, it needs to tell the caller what the new size is. The function can return the size, or it can use a reference parameter for the size. The second approach is a better choice for a function that modifies an existing array.

We use the first approach with the function that reads input values.

```
int read_inputs(double values[], int capacity) // Returns the size
```

The remove function modifies the current_size parameter:

```
void remove(double values[], int& current_size, int pos)
```

At this point, you should document each function, like this:

```
/**
    Removes an element from an array. The order of the elements is not preserved.
    @param values  a partially filled array
    @param current_size  the number of elements in values
    (will be reduced by 1 if the position is valid)
    @param pos  the position of the element to be removed
*/
void remove(double values[], int& current_size, int pos)
```

Step 3   Implement each function, using helper functions when needed.

We won't show the code for the read_inputs function because you have seen it already. Let us implement the final_score function. It calls three helper functions, min_position, remove, and sum:

```
/**
    Removes the smallest value of an array and returns the
    sum of the remaining values.
    @param values  a partially filled array
    @param current_size  the number of elements in values (will be reduced by 1)
    @return the sum of the values, excluding the minimum
*/
double final_score(double values[], int& current_size)
{
    int pos = min_position(values, current_size);
    remove(values, current_size, pos);
    return sum(values, current_size);
```

```
    }
```

We discussed the algorithm for `min_position` in the preceding section:

```
/**
    Gets the position of the minimum value from an array.
    @param values a partially filled array
    @param size the number of elements in values
    @return the position of the smallest element in values
*/
int min_position(double values[], int size)
{
    int smallest_position = 0;
    for (int i = 1; i < size; i++)
    {
        if (values[i] < values[smallest_position])
        {
            smallest_position = i;
        }
    }
    return smallest_position;
}
```

The remaining helper functions use the algorithms from Section 6.2. You will find the implementations in the book's companion code.

Step 4   Consider boundary conditions for the functions that you are implementing

Most functions that operate on arrays are a bit intricate, and you have to be careful that you handle both normal and exceptional situations. What happens with an empty array? An array that contains a single element? When no match is found? When there are multiple matches? Consider these boundary conditions and make sure that your functions work correctly.

Here is one example of such a consideration. How do we know that the `min_position` function will be called with an array of size at least 1? (Recall that you must have at least one element in order to find the minimum.) That function is called from the `final_score` function. However, the `final_score` function could conceivably be called with an empty array. We need to either include a test or add a restriction to the function comment. We will opt for the latter and change the comment for the `values` parameter variable of the `min_position` function to

   `@param values a partially filled array of size >= 1`

Consider another potential problem. What if there are multiple matches? That means that a student had more than one test with a low score. The `final_score` function removes only one of the occurrences of that low score, and that is the desired behavior.

Step 5   Assemble and test the complete program.

Now we are ready to combine the individual functions into a complete program. Before doing this, consider some test cases and their expected output:

Test Case	Expected Output	Comment
8 7 8.5 9.5 7 5 10	50	See Step 1.
8 7 7 9	24	Only one instance of the low score should be removed.
8	0	After removing the low score, no score remains.
(no inputs)	**Error**	That is not a legal input.

This `main` function completes the solution (see `ch06/scores.cpp`).

```cpp
int main()
{
   const int CAPACITY = 1000;
   double scores[CAPACITY];
   int current_size = read_inputs(scores, CAPACITY);
   if (current_size == 0)
   {
      cout << "At least one score is required." << endl;
   }
   else
   {
      double score = final_score(scores, current_size);
      cout << "Final score: " << score << endl;
   }
   return 0;
}
```

WORKED EXAMPLE 6.1   **Rolling the Dice**

This Worked Example shows how to analyze a set of die tosses to see whether the die is "fair".

6.5 Problem Solving: Discovering Algorithms by Manipulating Physical Objects

In Section 6.4, you saw how to solve a problem by combining and adapting known algorithms. But what do you do when none of the standard algorithms is sufficient for your task? In this section, you will learn a technique for discovering algorithms by manipulating physical objects.

Consider the following task. You are given an array whose size is an even number, and you are to switch the first and the second half. For example, if the array contains the eight numbers

| 9 | 13 | 21 | 4 | 11 | 7 | 1 | 3 |

then you should change it to

| 11 | 7 | 1 | 3 | 9 | 13 | 21 | 4 |

Many students find it quite challenging to come up with an algorithm. They may know that a loop is required, and they may realize that elements should be inserted (Section 6.2.8) or swapped (Section 6.2.9), but they do not have sufficient intuition to draw diagrams, describe an algorithm, or write down pseudocode.

One useful technique for discovering an algorithm is to manipulate physical objects. Start by lining up some objects to denote an array. Coins, playing cards, or small toys are good choices.

> Use a sequence of coins, playing cards, or toys to visualize an array of values.

➕ Available online at www.wiley.com/college/horstmann.

Manipulating physical objects can give you ideas for discovering algorithms.

Here we arrange eight coins.

Now let's step back and see what we can do to change the order of the coins. We can remove a coin (Section 6.2.7):

Visualizing the removal of an array element

We can insert a coin (Section 6.2.8):

Visualizing the insertion of an array element

Or we can swap two coins (Section 6.2.9).

Visualizing the swapping of two coins

Go ahead—line up some coins and try out these three operations right now so that you get a feel for them.

Now how does that help us with our problem, switching the first and the second half of the array?

Let's put the first coin into place, by swapping it with the fifth coin. However, as C++ programmers, we will say that we swap the coins in positions 0 and 4:

Next, we swap the coins in positions 1 and 5:

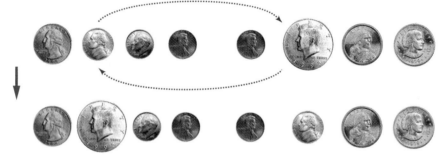

Two more swaps, and we are done:

Now an algorithm is becoming apparent:

```
i = 0
j = ... (we'll think about that in a minute)
while (don't know yet)
    swap elements at positions i and j
    i++
    j++
```

Where does the variable j start? When we have eight coins, the coin at position zero is moved to position 4. In general, it is moved to the middle of the array, or to position **size / 2.**

And how many iterations do we make? We need to swap all coins in the first half. That is, we need to swap **size / 2** coins. The pseudocode is

```
i = 0
j = size / 2
while (i < size / 2)
    swap elements at positions i and j
    i++
    j++
```

You can use paper clips as position markers or counters.

It is a good idea to make a walkthrough of the pseudocode (see Section 4.2). You can use paper clips to denote the positions of the variables i and j. If the walkthrough is successful, then we know that there was no "off-by-one" error in the pseudocode. Self Check 25 asks you to carry out the walkthrough, and Exercise P6.7 asks you to translate the pseudocode to C++. Exercise R6.17 suggests a different algorithm for switching the two halves of an array, by repeatedly removing and inserting coins.

Many people find that the manipulation of physical objects is less intimidating than drawing diagrams or mentally envisioning algorithms. Give it a try when you need to design a new algorithm!

SELF CHECK

25. Walk through the algorithm that we developed in this section, using two paper clips to indicate the positions for i and j. Explain why there are no bounds errors in the pseudocode.

26. Take out some coins and simulate the following pseudocode, using two paper clips to indicate the positions for i and j:

```
i = 0
j = size - 1
while (i < j)
    swap elements at positions i and j
    i++
    j--
```

What does the algorithm do?

27. Consider the task of rearranging all values in an array so that the even numbers come first. Otherwise, the order doesn't matter. For example, the array

1 4 14 2 1 3 5 6 23

could be rearranged to

4 2 14 6 1 5 3 23 1

Using coins and paperclips, discover an algorithm that solves this task by swapping elements, then describe it in pseudocode.

28. Discover an algorithm for the task of Self Check 27 that uses removal and insertion of elements instead of swapping.

29. Consider the algorithm in Section 4.7.4 that finds the largest element in a sequence of inputs—*not* the largest element in an array. Why is this algorithm better visualized by picking playing cards from a deck rather than arranging toy soldiers in a sequence?

Practice It   Now you can try these exercises at the end of the chapter: R6.17, R6.18, P6.7.

6.6 Two-Dimensional Arrays

It often happens that you want to store collections of values that have a two-dimensional layout. Such data sets commonly occur in financial and scientific applications. An arrangement consisting of rows and columns of values is called a *two-dimensional array*, or a *matrix*.

Let's explore how to store the example data shown in Figure 11: the medal counts of the figure skating competitions at the 2010 Winter Olympics.

	Gold	Silver	Bronze
Canada	1	0	1
China	1	1	0
Germany	0	0	1
Korea	1	0	0
Japan	0	1	1
Russia	0	1	1
United States	1	1	0

Figure 11 Figure Skating Medal Counts

6.6.1 Defining Two-Dimensional Arrays

C++ uses an array with two subscripts to store a two-dimensional array. For example, here is the definition of an array with 7 rows and 3 columns, suitable for storing our medal count data:

```
const int COUNTRIES = 7;
const int MEDALS = 3;
int counts[COUNTRIES][MEDALS];
```

You can initialize the array by grouping each row, as follows:

```
int counts[COUNTRIES][MEDALS] =
   {
      { 1, 0, 1 },
      { 1, 1, 0 },
      { 0, 0, 1 },
      { 1, 0, 0 },
      { 0, 1, 1 },
      { 0, 1, 1 },
      { 1, 1, 0 }
   };
```

Just as with one-dimensional arrays, you cannot change the size of a two-dimensional array once it has been defined.

Syntax 6.2   Two-Dimensional Array Definition

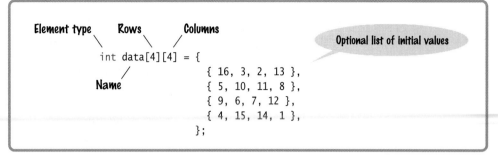

6.6.2 Accessing Elements

Individual elements in a two-dimensional array are accessed by using two subscripts, *array*[i][j].

To access a particular element in the two-dimensional array, you need to specify two subscripts in separate brackets to select the row and column, respectively (see Syntax 6.2 and Figure 12):

```
int value = counts[3][1];
```

To access all values in a two-dimensional array, you use two nested loops. For example, the following loop prints all elements of counts.

```
for (int i = 0; i < COUNTRIES; i++)
{
    // Process the ith row
    for (int j = 0; j < MEDALS; j++)
    {
        // Process the jth column in the ith row
        cout << setw(8) << counts[i][j];
    }
    cout << endl; // Start a new line at the end of the row
}
```

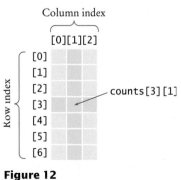

Figure 12
Accessing an Element in a
Two-Dimensional Array

6.6.3 Computing Row and Column Totals

A common task is to compute row or column totals. In our example, the row totals give us the total number of medals won by a particular country.

Finding the right index values is a bit tricky, and it is a good idea to make a quick sketch. To compute the total of row i, we need to visit the following elements:

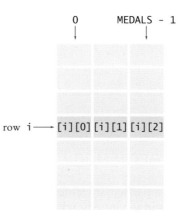

As you can see, we need to compute the sum of counts[i][j], where j ranges from 0 to MEDALS - 1. The following loop computes the total:

```
int total = 0;
for (int j = 0; j < MEDALS; j++)
{
   total = total + counts[i][j];
}
```

Computing column totals is similar. Form the sum of counts[i][j], where i ranges from 0 to COUNTRIES - 1.

```
int total = 0;
for (int i = 0; i < COUNTRIES; i++)
{
   total = total + counts[i][j];
}
```

6.6.4 Two-Dimensional Array Parameters

A two-dimensional array parameter must have a fixed number of columns.

When passing a two-dimensional array to a function, you must specify the number of columns *as a constant* with the parameter type. For example, this function computes the total of a given row:

```
const int COLUMNS = 3;

int row_total(int table[][COLUMNS], int row)
{
   int total = 0;
   for (int j = 0; j < COLUMNS; j++)
   {
      total = total + table[row][j];
   }
   return total;
}
```

This function can compute row totals of a two-dimensional array with an arbitrary number of rows, but the array must have 3 columns. You have to write a different function if you want to compute row totals of a two-dimensional array with 4 columns.

To understand this limitation, you need to know how the array elements are stored in memory. Although the array appears to be two-dimensional, the elements are still stored as a linear sequence. Figure 13 shows how the counts array is stored, row by row.

For example, to reach

```
counts[3][1]
```

the program must first skip past rows 0, 1, and 2 and then locate offset 1 in row 3. The offset from the start of the array is

$$3 \times number\ of\ columns + 1$$

Now consider the row_total function. The compiler generates code to find the element

```
table[i][j]
```

by computing the offset

```
i * COLUMNS + j
```

The compiler uses the value that you supplied in the second pair of brackets when declaring the parameter:

```
int row_total(int table[][COLUMNS], int row)
```

Note that the first pair of brackets should be empty, just as with one-dimensional arrays.

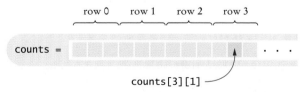

Figure 13 A Two-Dimensional Array is Stored as a Sequence of Rows

The `row_total` function did not need to know the number of rows of the array. If the number of rows is required, pass it as a variable, as in this example:

```
int column_total(int table[][COLUMNS], int rows, int column)
{
   int total = 0;
   for (int i = 0; i < rows; i++)
   {
      total = total + table[i][column];
   }
   return total;
}
```

Working with two-dimensional arrays is illustrated in the following program. The program prints out the medal counts and the row totals.

ch06/medals.cpp

```
1    #include <iostream>
2    #include <iomanip>
3    #include <string>
4
5    using namespace std;
6
7    const int COLUMNS = 3;
8
9    /**
10      Computes the total of a row in a table.
11      @param table a table with 3 columns
12      @param row the row that needs to be totaled
13      @return the sum of all elements in the given row
14   */
15   double row_total(int table[][COLUMNS], int row)
16   {
17      int total = 0;
18      for (int j = 0; j < COLUMNS; j++)
19      {
20         total = total + table[row][j];
21      }
22      return total;
23   }
24
25   int main()
26   {
27      const int COUNTRIES = 7;
28      const int MEDALS = 3;
29
30      string countries[] =
31         {
32            "Canada",
33            "China",
34            "Germany",
35            "Korea",
36            "Japan",
37            "Russia",
38            "United States"
39         };
40
41      int counts[COUNTRIES][MEDALS] =
42         {
```

```
43        { 1, 0, 1 },
44        { 1, 1, 0 },
45        { 0, 0, 1 },
46        { 1, 0, 0 },
47        { 0, 1, 1 },
48        { 0, 1, 1 },
49        { 1, 1, 0 }
50     };
51
52     cout << "          Country   Gold Silver Bronze   Total" << endl;
53
54     // Print countries, counts, and row totals
55     for (int i = 0; i < COUNTRIES; i++)
56     {
57        cout << setw(15) << countries[i];
58        // Process the ith row
59        for (int j = 0; j < MEDALS; j++)
60        {
61           cout << setw(8) << counts[i][j];
62        }
63        int total = row_total(counts, i);
64        cout << setw(8) << total << endl;
65     }
66
67     return 0;
68  }
```

Program Run

Country	Gold	Silver	Bronze	Total
Canada	1	0	1	2
China	1	1	0	2
Germany	0	0	1	1
Korea	1	0	0	1
Japan	0	1	1	2
Russia	0	1	1	2
United States	1	1	0	2

SELF CHECK

30. What results do you get if you total the columns in our sample data?

31. Consider an 8 × 8 array for a board game:

```
int board[8][8];
```

Using two nested loops, initialize the board so that zeroes and ones alternate, as on a checkerboard:

```
0 1 0 1 0 1 0 1
1 0 1 0 1 0 1 0
0 1 0 1 0 1 0 1
...
1 0 1 0 1 0 1 0
```

Hint: Check whether i + j is even.

32. Define a two-dimensional array for representing a tic-tac-toe board. The board has three rows and columns and contains strings "x", "o", and " ".

33. Write an assignment statement to place an "x" in the upper-right corner of the tic-tac-toe board.

34. Which elements are on the diagonal joining the upper-left and the lower-right corners of the tic-tac-toe board?

Practice It Now you can try these exercises at the end of the chapter: R6.23, P6.19, P6.20.

Common Error 6.2

Omitting the Column Size of a Two-Dimensional Array Parameter

When passing a one-dimensional array to a function, you specify the size of the array as a separate parameter variable:

```
void print(double values[], int size)
```

This function can print arrays of any size. However, for two-dimensional arrays you cannot simply pass the numbers of rows and columns as parameter variables:

```
void print(double table[][], int rows, int cols) // NO!
```

The function must know *at compile time* how many columns the two-dimensional array has. You must specify the number of columns with the array parameter variable. This number must be a constant:

```
const int COLUMNS = 3;
void print(const double table[][COLUMNS], int rows) // OK
```

This function can print tables with any number of rows, but the column size is fixed.

WORKED EXAMPLE 6.2   **A World Population Table**

This Worked Example shows how to print world population data in a table with row and column headers, and with totals for each of the data columns.

6.7 Vectors

A vector stores a sequence of values whose size can change.

When you write a program that collects values from user input, you don't always know how many values you will have. Unfortunately, the size of the array has to be known *when the program is compiled*.

In Section 6.1.3, you saw how you can address this problem with partially filled arrays. The vector construct, which we discuss in the following sections, offers a more convenient solution. A vector collects a sequence of values, just like an array does, but its size can change.

A vector expands to hold as many elements as needed.

➕ Available online at www.wiley.com/college/horstmann.

Syntax 6.3 Defining a Vector

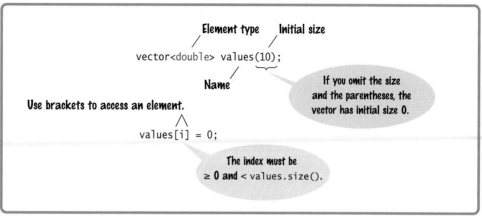

6.7.1 Defining Vectors

When you define a vector, you specify the type of the elements in angle brackets, like this:

```
vector<double> values;
```

You can optionally specify the initial size. For example, here is a definition of a vector whose initial size is 10:

```
vector<double> values(10);
```

If you define a vector without an initial size, it has size 0. While there would be no point in defining an array of size zero, it is often useful to have vectors with *initial* size zero, and then grow them as needed.

In order to use vectors in your program, you need to include the <vector> header.

Table 2 Defining Vectors

`vector<int> numbers(10);`	A vector of ten integers.
`vector<string> names(3);`	A vector of three strings.
`vector<double> values;`	A vector of size 0.
🚫 `vector<double> values();`	**Error:** Does not define a vector.

`vector<int> numbers;`
`for (int i = 1; i <= 10; i++)`
`{`
`    numbers.push_back(i);`
`}`
	A vector of ten integers, filled with 1, 2, 3, ..., 10.

`vector<int> numbers(10);`
`for (int i = 0; i < numbers.size(); i++)`
`{`
`    numbers[i] = i + 1;`
`}`
	Another way of defining a vector of ten integers and filling it with 1, 2, 3, ..., 10.

You access the vector elements as `values[i]`, just as you do with arrays.

The `size` member function returns the current size of a vector. In a loop that visits all vector elements, use the `size` member function like this:

> Use the `size` member function to obtain the current size of a vector.

```
for (int i = 0; i < values.size(); i++)
{
   cout << values[i] << endl;
}
```

6.7.2 Growing and Shrinking Vectors

> Use the `push_back` member function to add more elements to a vector.
> Use `pop_back` to reduce the size.

If you need additional elements, you use the `push_back` function to add an element to the end of the vector, thereby increasing its size by 1. The `push_back` function is a member function that you must call with the dot notation, like this:

```
values.push_back(37.5);
```

After this call, the vector `values` in Figure 14 has size 3, and `values[2]` contains the value 37.5.

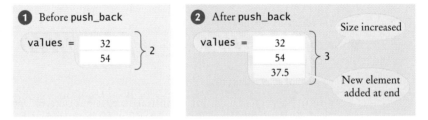

Figure 14   Adding an Element with `push_back`

It is very common to start with an empty vector and use the `push_back` function to fill it. For example,

```
vector<double> values; // Initially empty

values.push_back(32); // Now values has size 1 and element 32
values.push_back(54); // Now values has size 2 and elements 32, 54
values.push_back(37.5); // Now values has size 3 and elements 32, 54, 37.5
```

Another common use for the `push_back` member function is to fill a vector with input values.

```
vector<double> values;   // Initially empty

double input;
while (cin >> input)
{
   values.push_back(input);
}
```

Note how this input loop is *much* simpler than the one in Section 6.2.10.

Another member function, `pop_back`, removes the last element of a vector, shrinking its size by one (see Figure 15):

```
values.pop_back();
```

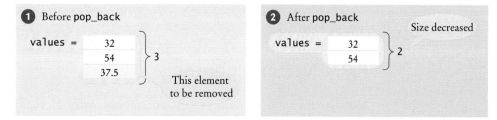

Figure 15   Removing an Element with pop_back

6.7.3 Vectors and Functions

Vectors can occur as function arguments and return values.

You can use vectors as function arguments in exactly the same way as any other values. For example, the following function computes the sum of a vector of floating-point numbers:

```cpp
double sum(vector<double> values)
{
   double total = 0;
   for (int i = 0; i < values.size(); i++)
   {
      total = total + values[i];
   }
   return total;
}
```

Use a reference parameter to modify the contents of a vector.

This function visits the vector elements, but it does not modify them. If your function modifies the elements, use a reference parameter. The following function multiplies all values of a vector with a given factor.

```cpp
void multiply(vector<double>& values, double factor) // Note the &
{
   for (int i = 0; i < values.size(); i++)
   {
      values[i] = values[i] * factor;
   }
}
```

Some programmers use a constant reference (see Special Topic 5.2) for vector parameters that are not modified, for example:

```cpp
double sum(const vector<double>& values) // const & added for efficiency
```

A function can return a vector.

A function can return a vector. Again, vectors are no different from any other values in this regard. Simply build up the result in the function and return it. In this example, the squares function returns a vector of squares from 0^2 up to $(n-1)^2$:

```cpp
vector<int> squares(int n)
{
   vector<int> result;
   for (int i = 0; i < n; i++)
   {
      result.push_back(i * i);
   }
   return result;
}
```

As you can see, it is easy to use vectors with functions—there are no special rules to keep in mind.

6.7.4 Vector Algorithms

Most of the algorithms in Section 6.2 apply without change to vectors—simply replace **size of** values with `values.size()`. In this section, we discuss which of the algorithms are different for vectors.

Copying

As discussed in Section 6.2.2, you need an explicit loop to make a copy of an array. It is much easier to make a copy of a vector. You simply assign it to another vector. Consider this example:

```
vector<int> squares;
for (int i = 0; i < 5; i++) { squares.push_back(i * i); }
vector<int> lucky_numbers; // Initially empty
lucky_numbers = squares; // Now lucky_numbers contains the same elements as squares
```

Finding Matches

Section 6.2.6 shows you how to find the first match, but sometimes you want to have all matches. This is tedious with arrays, but simple using a vector that collects the matches. Here we collect all elements that are greater than 100:

```
vector<double> matches;
for (int i = 0; i < values.size(); i++)
{
   if (values[i] > 100)
   {
      matches.push_back(values[i]);
   }
}
```

Removing an Element

When you remove an element from a vector, you want to adjust the size of the vector by calling the `pop_back` member function. Here is the code for removing an element at [pos] when the order doesn't matter.

```
int last_pos = values.size() - 1;
values[pos] = values[last_pos]; // Replace element at pos with last element
values.pop_back(); // Delete last element
```

When removing an element from an ordered vector, first move the elements, then reduce the size:

```
for (int i = pos + 1; i < values.size(); i++)
{
   values[i - 1] = values[i];
}
values.pop_back();
```

Inserting an Element

Inserting an element at the end of a vector requires no special code. Simply use the `push_back` member function.

When you insert an element in the middle, you still want to call push_back so that the size of the vector is increased. Use the following code:

```
int last_pos = values.size() - 1;
values.push_back(values[last_pos]);
for (int i = last_pos; i > pos; i--)
{
    values[i] = values[i - 1];
}
values[pos] = new_element;
```

SELF CHECK

35. Define a vector of integers that contains the first five prime numbers (2, 3, 5, 7, and 11). Use push_back to add the elements.

36. Answer Self Check 35 without using push_back.

37. What is the contents of the vector names after the following statements?

```
vector<string> names;
names.push_back("Ann");
names.push_back("Bob");
names.pop_back();
names.push_back("Cal");
```

38. Suppose you want to store a set of temperature measurements that is taken every five minutes. Should you use a vector or an array?

39. Suppose you want to store the names of the weekdays. Should you use a vector or an array of seven strings?

40. Write the header for a function that appends two vectors, yielding a third vector. Do not implement the function.

41. Consider this partially completed function that appends the elements of one vector to another.

```
void append(vector<double>__ target, vector<double>__ source)
{
    for (int i = 0; i < source.size(); i++)
    {
        target.push_back(source[i]);
    }
}
```

Specify whether the parameters should be value or reference parameters.

Practice It   Now you can try these exercises at the end of the chapter: R6.11, R6.25, P6.26, P6.27.

Programming Tip 6.2

Prefer Vectors over Arrays

For most programming tasks, vectors are easier to use than arrays. Vectors can grow and shrink. Even if a vector always stays the same size, it is convenient that a vector remembers its size. For a beginner, the sole advantage of an array is the initialization syntax. Advanced programmers sometimes prefer arrays because they are a bit more efficient. Moreover, you need to know how to use arrays if you work with older programs.

Random Fact 6.2 The First Programmer

Before pocket calculators and personal computers existed, navigators and engineers used mechanical adding machines, slide rules, and tables of logarithms and trigonometric functions to speed up computations. Unfortunately, the tables—for which values had to be computed by hand—were notoriously inaccurate. The mathematician Charles Babbage (1791–1871) had the insight that if a machine could be constructed that produced printed tables automatically, both calculation and typesetting errors could be avoided. Babbage set out to develop a machine for this purpose, which he called a *Difference Engine* because it used successive differences to compute polynomials. For example, consider the function $f(x) = x^3$. Write down the values for $f(1)$, $f(2)$, $f(3)$, and so on. Then take the *differences* between successive values:

```
1
        7
8
        19
27
        37
64
        61
125
        91
216
```

Repeat the process, taking the difference of successive values in the second column, and then repeat once again:

```
1
        7
8             12
        19            6
27            18
        37            6
64            24
        61            6
125           30
        91
216
```

Now the differences are all the same. You can retrieve the function values by a pattern of additions—you need to know the values at the fringe of the pattern and the constant difference. You can try it out yourself: Write the highlighted numbers on a sheet of paper, and fill in the others by adding the numbers that are in the north and northwest positions.

This method was very attractive, because mechanical addition machines had been known for some time. They consisted of cog wheels, with 10 cogs per wheel, to represent digits, and mechanisms to handle the carry from one digit to the next. Mechanical multiplication machines, on the other hand, were fragile and unreliable. Babbage built a successful prototype of the Difference Engine and, with his own money and government grants, proceeded to build the table-printing machine. However, because of funding problems and the difficulty of building the machine to the required precision, it was never completed.

While working on the Difference Engine, Babbage conceived of a much grander vision that he called the *Analytical Engine*. The Difference Engine was designed to carry out a limited set of computations—it was no smarter than a pocket calculator is today. But Babbage realized that such a machine could be made *programmable* by storing programs as well as data. The internal storage of the Analytical Engine was to consist of 1,000 registers of 50 decimal digits each. Programs and constants were to be stored on punched cards—a technique that was, at that time, commonly used on looms for weaving patterned fabrics.

Ada Augusta, Countess of Lovelace (1815–1852), the only child of Lord Byron, was a friend and sponsor of Charles Babbage. Ada Lovelace was one of the first people to realize the potential of such a machine, not just for computing mathematical tables but for processing data that were not numbers. She is considered by many to be the world's first programmer.

Replica of Babbage's Difference Engine

CHAPTER SUMMARY

Use arrays for collecting values.

- Use an array to collect a sequence of values of the same type.
- Individual elements in an array *values* are accessed by an integer index i, using the notation *values*[i].

- An array element can be used like any variable.
- An array index must be at least zero and less than the size of the array.
- A bounds error, which occurs if you supply an invalid array index, can corrupt data or cause your program to terminate.
- With a partially filled array, keep a companion variable for the current size.

Be able to use common array algorithms.

- To copy an array, use a loop to copy its elements to a new array.
- When separating elements, don't place a separator before the first element.
- A linear search inspects elements in sequence until a match is found.
- Before inserting an element, move elements to the end of the array *starting with the last one*.
- Use a temporary variable when swapping two elements.

Implement functions that process arrays.

- When passing an array to a function, also pass the size of the array.
- Array parameters are always reference parameters.
- A function's return type cannot be an array.
- When a function modifies the size of an array, it needs to tell its caller.
- A function that adds elements to an array needs to know its capacity.

Be able to combine and adapt algorithms for solving a programming problem.

- By combining fundamental algorithms, you can solve complex programming tasks.
- You should be familiar with the implementation of fundamental algorithms so that you can adapt them.

Discover algorithms by manipulating physical objects.

- Use a sequence of coins, playing cards, or toys to visualize an array of values.
- You can use paper clips as position markers or counters.

Use two-dimensional arrays for data that is arranged in rows and columns.

- Use a two-dimensional array to store tabular data.
- Individual elements in a two-dimensional array are accessed by using two subscripts, *array*[i][j].
- A two-dimensional array parameter must have a fixed number of columns.

Use vectors for managing collections whose size can change.

- A vector stores a sequence of values whose size can change.
- Use the size member function to obtain the current size of a vector.
- Use the push_back member function to add more elements to a vector. Use pop_back to reduce the size.
- Vectors can occur as function arguments and return values.
- Use a reference parameter to modify the contents of a vector.
- A function can return a vector.

REVIEW EXERCISES

R6.1 Write code that fills an array double values[10] with each set of values below.

a.	1	2	3	4	5	6	7	8	9	10
b.	0	2	4	6	8	10	12	14	16	18
c.	1	4	9	16	25	36	49	64	81	100
d.	0	0	0	0	0	0	0	0	0	0
e.	1	4	9	16	9	7	4	9	11	
f.	0	1	0	1	0	1	0	1	0	1
g.	0	1	2	3	4	0	1	2	3	4

R6.2 Consider the following array:

```
int a[] = { 1, 2, 3, 4, 5, 4, 3, 2, 1, 0 };
```

What is the value of total after the following loops complete?

```
a. int total = 0;
   for (int i = 0; i < 10; i++) { total = total + a[i]; }
b. int total = 0;
   for (int i = 0; i < 10; i = i + 2) { total = total + a[i]; }
c. int total = 0;
   for (int i = 1; i < 10; i = i + 2) { total = total + a[i]; }
d. int total = 0;
   for (int i = 2; i <= 10; i++) { total = total + a[i]; }
e. int total = 0;
   for (int i = 0; i < 10; i = 2 * i) { total = total + a[i]; }
f. int total = 0;
   for (int i = 9; i >= 0; i--) { total = total + a[i]; }
g. int total = 0;
   for (int i = 9; i >= 0; i = i - 2) { total = total + a[i]; }
h. int total = 0;
   for (int i = 0; i < 10; i++) { total = a[i] - total; }
```

R6.3 Consider the following array:

```
int a[] = { 1, 2, 3, 4, 5, 4, 3, 2, 1, 0 };
```

What are the contents of the array a after the following loops complete?

a. `for (int i = 1; i < 10; i++) { a[i] = a[i - 1]; }`
b. `for (int i = 9; i > 0; i--) { a[i] = a[i - 1]; }`
c. `for (int i = 0; i < 9; i++) { a[i] = a[i + 1]; }`
d. `for (int i = 8; i >= 0; i--) { a[i] = a[i + 1]; }`
e. `for (int i = 1; i < 10; i++) { a[i] = a[i] + a[i - 1]; }`
f. `for (int i = 1; i < 10; i = i + 2) { a[i] = 0; }`
g. `for (int i = 0; i < 5; i++) { a[i + 5] = a[i]; }`
h. `for (int i = 1; i < 5; i++) { a[i] = a[9 - i]; }`

R6.4 Write a loop that fills an array `int values[10]` with ten random numbers between 1 and 100. Write code for two nested loops that fill `values` with ten *different* random numbers between 1 and 100.

R6.5 Write C++ code for a loop that simultaneously computes both the maximum and minimum of an array.

R6.6 What is wrong with the following loop?

```
int values[10];
for (int i = 1; i <= 10; i++)
{
   values[i] = i * i;
}
```

Explain two ways of fixing the error.

R6.7 What is an index of an array? What are the legal index values? What is a bounds error?

R6.8 Write a program that contains a bounds error. Run the program. What happens on your computer?

R6.9 Write a loop that reads ten numbers and a second loop that displays them in the opposite order from which they were entered.

R6.10 Trace the flow of the element separator loop in Section 6.2.5 with the given example. Show two columns, one with the value of i and one with the output.

R6.11 Trace the flow of the finding matches loop in Section 6.7.4, where `values` contains the elements 110 90 100 120 80. Show two columns, for i and `matches`.

R6.12 Trace the flow of the linear search loop in Section 6.2.6, where `values` contains the elements 80 90 100 120 110. Show two columns, for `pos` and `found`. Repeat the trace when `values` contains 80 90 100 70.

R6.13 Trace both mechanisms for removing an element described in Section 6.2.7. Use an array `values` with elements 110 90 100 120 80, and remove the element at index 2.

R6.14 For the operations on partially filled arrays below, provide the header of a function.

  a. Sort the elements in decreasing order.
  b. Print all elements, separated by a given string.
  c. Count how many elements are less than a given value.
  d. Remove all elements that are less than a given value.
  e. Place all elements that are less than a given value in another array.

Do not implement the functions.

R6.15 You are given two arrays denoting x- and y-coordinates of a set of points in the plane. For plotting the point set, we need to know the x- and y-coordinates of the smallest rectangle containing the points.

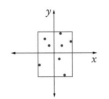

How can you obtain these values from the fundamental algorithms in Section 6.2?

R6.16 Solve the problem described in Section 6.4 by sorting the array first. How do you need to modify the algorithm for computing the total?

R6.17 Solve the task described in Section 6.5 using an algorithm that removes and inserts elements instead of switching them. Write the pseudocode for the algorithm, assuming that functions for removal and insertion exist. Act out the algorithm with a sequence of coins and explain why it is less efficient than the swapping algorithm developed in Section 6.5.

R6.18 Develop an algorithm for finding the most frequently occurring value in an array of numbers. Use a sequence of coins. Place paper clips below each coin that count how many other coins of the same value are in the sequence. Give the pseudocode for an algorithm that yields the correct answer, and describe how using the coins and paper clips helped you find the algorithm.

R6.19 Give pseudocode for a function that rotates the elements of an array by one position, moving the initial element to the end of the array, like this:

R6.20 Give pseudocode for a function that removes all negative values from a partially filled array, preserving the order of the remaining elements.

R6.21 Suppose values is a *sorted* partially filled array of integers. Give pseudocode that describes how a new value can be inserted in its proper position so that the resulting array stays sorted.

R6.22 A *run* is a sequence of adjacent repeated values. Give pseudocode for computing the length of the longest run in an array. For example, the longest run in the array with elements

    1 2 5 5 3 1 2 4 3 2 2 2 2 3 6 5 5 6 3 1

has length 4.

R6.23 Write pseudocode for an algorithm that fills the first and last column as well as the first and last row of a two-dimensional array of integers with –1.

R6.24 True or false?

  a. All elements of an array are of the same type.

  b. Arrays cannot contain strings as elements.

   c. Two-dimensional arrays always have the same number of rows and columns.

   d. Elements of different columns in a two-dimensional array can have different types.

   e. A function cannot return a two-dimensional array.

   f. All array parameters are reference parameters.

   g. A function cannot change the dimensions of a two-dimensional array that is passed as a parameter.

R6.25 How do you perform the following tasks with vectors in C++?

   a. Test that two vectors contain the same elements in the same order.

   b. Copy one vector to another.

   c. Fill a vector with zeroes, overwriting all elements in it.

   d. Remove all elements from a vector.

R6.26 True or false?

   a. All elements of a vector are of the same type.

   b. Vector subscripts must be integers.

   c. Vectors cannot contain strings as elements.

   d. Vectors cannot use strings as subscripts.

   e. All vector parameters are reference parameters.

   f. A function cannot return a vector.

   g. A function cannot change the length of a vector that is a reference parameter.

PROGRAMMING EXERCISES

P6.1 Write a program that initializes an array with ten random integers and then prints four lines of output, containing

   • Every element at an even index.

   • Every even element.

   • All elements in reverse order.

   • Only the first and last element.

P6.2 Write array functions that carry out the following tasks for an array of integers:

   a. Swap the first and last element in an array.

   b. Shift all elements by one to the right and move the last element into the first position. For example, 1 4 9 16 25 would be transformed into 25 1 4 9 16.

   c. Replace all even elements with 0.

   d. Replace each element except the first and last by the larger of its two neighbors.

   e. Remove the middle element if the array length is odd, or the middle two elements if the length is even.

   f. Move all even elements to the front, otherwise preserving the order of the elements.

   g. Return the second-largest element in the array.

h. Return true if the array is currently sorted in increasing order.

i. Return true if the array contains two adjacent duplicate values.

j. Return true if the array contains duplicate values (which need not be adjacent).

For each function, provide a test program.

P6.3 Modify the `largest.cpp` program to mark both the smallest and the largest element.

P6.4 Reimplement How To 6.1 without removing the minimum from the array of scores. Instead, compute the final score as the difference of the sum and the minimum of the scores.

P6.5 Write a function `void remove_min` that removes the minimum value from a partially filled array without calling other functions.

P6.6 Write a function that computes the *alternating sum* of all elements in an array. For example, if `alternating_sum` is called with an array containing

$$1 \quad 4 \quad 9 \quad 16 \quad 9 \quad 7 \quad 4 \quad 9 \quad 11$$

then it computes

$$1 - 4 + 9 - 16 + 9 - 7 + 4 - 9 + 11 = -2$$

P6.7 Write a function that implements the algorithm developed in Section 6.5.

P6.8 Write a function `reverse` that reverses the sequence of elements in an array. For example, if `reverse` is called with an array containing

$$1 \quad 4 \quad 9 \quad 16 \quad 9 \quad 7 \quad 4 \quad 9 \quad 11$$

then the array is changed to

$$11 \quad 9 \quad 4 \quad 7 \quad 9 \quad 16 \quad 9 \quad 4 \quad 1$$

P6.9 Write a function

```
bool equals(int a[], int a_size, int b[], int b_size)
```

that checks whether two arrays have the same elements in the same order.

P6.10 Write a function

```
bool same_set(int a[], int a_size, int b[], int b_size)
```

that checks whether two vectors have the same elements in some order, ignoring duplicates. For example, the two arrays

$$1 \quad 4 \quad 9 \quad 16 \quad 9 \quad 7 \quad 4 \quad 9 \quad 11$$

and

$$11 \quad 11 \quad 7 \quad 9 \quad 16 \quad 4 \quad 1$$

would be considered identical. You will probably need one or more helper functions.

P6.11 Write a function

```
bool same_elements(int a[], int b[], int size)
```

that checks whether two arrays have the same elements in some order, with the same multiplicities. For example,

$$1 \quad 4 \quad 9 \quad 16 \quad 9 \quad 7 \quad 4 \quad 9 \quad 11$$

and

$$11 \quad 1 \quad 4 \quad 9 \quad 16 \quad 9 \quad 7 \quad 4 \quad 9$$

would be considered identical, but

$$1 \quad 4 \quad 9 \quad 16 \quad 9 \quad 7 \quad 4 \quad 9 \quad 11$$

and

$$11 \quad 11 \quad 7 \quad 9 \quad 16 \quad 4 \quad 1 \quad 4 \quad 9$$

would not. You will probably need one or more helper functions.

P6.12 Write a function that removes duplicates from an array. For example, if `remove_duplicates` is called with an array containing

$$1 \quad 4 \quad 9 \quad 16 \quad 9 \quad 7 \quad 4 \quad 9 \quad 11$$

then the array is changed to

$$1 \quad 4 \quad 9 \quad 16 \quad 7 \quad 11$$

Your function should have a reference parameter for the array size that is updated when removing the duplicates.

P6.13 A *run* is a sequence of adjacent repeated values. Write a program that generates a sequence of 20 random die tosses and prints the die values, marking the runs by including them in parentheses, like this:

    1 2 (5 5) 3 1 2 4 3 (2 2 2 2) 3 6 (5 5) 6 3 1

Use the following pseudocode:

    Set a Boolean variable in_run to false.
    For each valid index i in the array
        If in_run
            If values[i] is different from the preceding value
            Print).
            in_run = false
        If not in_run
            If values[i] is the same as the following value
            Print (.
            in_run = true
        Print values[i].
    If in_run, print).

P6.14 Write a program that generates a sequence of 20 random die tosses and that prints the die values, marking only the longest run, like this:

    1 2 5 5 3 1 2 4 3 (2 2 2 2) 3 6 5 5 6 3 1

If there is more than one run of maximum length, mark the first one.

P6.15 Write a program that generates a sequence of 20 random values between 0 and 99, prints the sequence, sorts it, and prints the sorted sequence. Use the `sort` function from the standard C++ library.

P6.16 Write a program that produces ten random permutations of the numbers 1 to 10. To generate a random permutation, you need to fill an array with the numbers 1 to 10 so that no two elements have the same contents. You could do it by brute force, by generating random values until you have a value that is not yet in the array. But that is inefficient. Instead, follow this algorithm:

> **Make a second array and fill it with the numbers 1 to 10.**
> **Repeat 10 times**
>   **Pick a random element from the second array.**
>   **Remove it and append it to the permutation array.**

P6.17 It is a well-researched fact that men in a restroom generally prefer to maximize their distance from already occupied stalls, by occupying the middle of the longest sequence of unoccupied places.

For example, consider the situation where all ten stalls are empty.

```
_ _ _ _ _ _ _ _ _ _
```

The first visitor will occupy a middle position:

```
_ _ _ _ X _ _ _ _ _
```

The next visitor will be in the middle of the empty area at the right.

```
_ _ _ _ X _ _ X _ _
```

Given an array of `bool` values, where true indicates an occupied stall, find the position for the next visitor. Your computation should be placed in a function

```
next_visitor(bool occupied[], int stalls)
```

P6.18 In this assignment, you will model the game of *Bulgarian Solitaire*. The game starts with 45 cards. (They need not be playing cards. Unmarked index cards work just as well.) Randomly divide them into some number of piles of random size. For example, you might start with piles of size 20, 5, 1, 9, and 10. In each round, you take one card from each pile, forming a new pile with these cards. For example, the sample starting configuration would be transformed into piles of size 19, 4, 8, 9, and 5. The solitaire is over when the piles have size 1, 2, 3, 4, 5, 6, 7, 8, and 9, in some order. (It can be shown that you always end up with such a configuration.)

In your program, produce a random starting configuration and print it. Then keep applying the solitaire step and print the result. Stop when the solitaire final configuration is reached.

P6.19 *Magic squares.* An $n \times n$ matrix that is filled with the numbers 1, 2, 3, . . ., n^2 is a magic square if the sum of the elements in each row, in each column, and in the two diagonals is the same value.

16	3	2	13
5	10	11	8
9	6	7	12
4	15	14	1

Write a program that reads in 16 values from the keyboard and tests whether they form a magic square when put into a 4 × 4 array. You need to test two features:

    1. Does each of the numbers 1, 2, ..., 16 occur in the user input?

    2. When the numbers are put into a square, are the sums of the rows, columns, and diagonals equal to each other?

P6.20 Implement the following algorithm to construct magic $n \times n$ squares; it works only if n is odd.

```
Set row = n - 1, column = n / 2.
For k = 1 ... n
    Place k at [row][column].
    Increment row and column.
    If the row or column is n, replace it with 0.
    If the element at [row][column] has already been filled
        Set row and column to their previous value.
        Decrement row.
```

Here is the 5 × 5 square that you get if you follow this method:

11	18	25	2	9
10	12	19	21	3
4	6	13	20	22
23	5	7	14	16
17	24	1	8	15

Write a program whose input is the number n and whose output is the magic square of order n if n is odd.

P6.21 Write a function

```
void bar_chart(double values[], int size)
```

that displays a bar chart of the values in values, using asterisks, like this:

```
**********************
******************************************
*****************************
***************************
**************
```

You may assume that all values in values are positive. First figure out the maximum value in values. That value's bar should be drawn with 40 asterisks. Shorter bars should use proportionally fewer asterisks.

P6.22 Improve the bar_chart function of Exercise P6.21 to work correctly when values contains negative values.

P6.23 Improve the bar_chart function of Exercise P6.21 by adding an array of captions for each bar. The output should look like this:

```
      Egypt **********************
     France ******************************************
      Japan *****************************
    Uruguay ***************************
Switzerland **************
```

P6.24 A theater seating chart is implemented as a two-dimensional array of ticket prices, like this:

```
10 10 10 10 10 10 10 10 10 10
10 10 10 10 10 10 10 10 10 10
10 10 10 10 10 10 10 10 10 10
10 10 20 20 20 20 20 20 10 10
10 10 20 20 20 20 20 20 10 10
10 10 20 20 20 20 20 20 10 10
20 20 30 30 40 40 30 30 20 20
20 30 30 40 50 50 40 30 30 20
30 40 50 50 50 50 50 50 40 30
```

Write a program that prompts users to pick either a seat or a price. Mark sold seats by changing the price to 0. When a user specifies a seat, make sure it is available. When a user specifies a price, find any seat with that price.

P6.25 Write a program that plays tic-tac-toe. The tic-tac-toe game is played on a 3 × 3 grid as in

The game is played by two players, who take turns. The first player marks moves with a circle, the second with a cross. The player who has formed a horizontal, vertical, or diagonal sequence of three marks wins. Your program should draw the game board, ask the user for the coordinates of the next mark, change the players after every successful move, and pronounce the winner.

P6.26 Write a function

```
vector<int> append(vector<int> a, vector<int> b)
```

that appends one vector after another. For example, if a is

$$1 \quad 4 \quad 9 \quad 16$$

and b is

$$9 \quad 7 \quad 4 \quad 9 \quad 11$$

then append returns the vector

$$1 \quad 4 \quad 9 \quad 16 \quad 9 \quad 7 \quad 4 \quad 9 \quad 11$$

P6.27 Write a function

```
vector<int> merge(vector<int> a, vector<int> b)
```

that merges two vectors, alternating elements from both vectors. If one vector is shorter than the other, then alternate as long as you can and then append the remaining elements from the longer vector. For example, if a is

$$1 \quad 4 \quad 9 \quad 16$$

and b is

$$9 \quad 7 \quad 4 \quad 9 \quad 11$$

then merge returns the vector

$$1 \quad 9 \quad 4 \quad 7 \quad 9 \quad 4 \quad 16 \quad 9 \quad 11$$

P6.28 Write a function

```
vector<int> merge_sorted(vector<int> a, vector<int> b)
```

that merges two *sorted* vectors, producing a new sorted vector. Keep an index into each vector, indicating how much of it has been processed already. Each time, append the smallest unprocessed element from either vector, then advance the index. For example, if a is

$$1 \quad 4 \quad 9 \quad 16$$

and b is

$$4 \quad 7 \quad 9 \quad 9 \quad 11$$

then merge_sorted returns the vector

$$1 \quad 4 \quad 4 \quad 7 \quad 9 \quad 9 \quad 9 \quad 11 \quad 16$$

P6.29 Modify the ch06/image.cpp program in the book's companion code to generate the image of a checkerboard.

P6.30 Modify the ch06/animation.cpp program in the book's companion code to show a rectangle that travels from the left of the image to the right and then back to the left.

Engineering P6.31 Sample values from an experiment often need to be smoothed out. One simple approach is to replace each value in an array with the average of the value and its two neighboring values (or one neighboring value if it is at either end of the array). Implement a function

```
void smooth(double[] values, int size)
```

that carries out this operation. You should not create another array in your solution.

Engineering P6.32 Sounds can be represented by an array of "sample values" that describe the intensity of the sound at a point in time. The sound.cpp program in this book's companion code reads a sound file (in WAV format), calls a function process for processing the sample values, and saves the sound file. Your task is to implement the process function by introducing an echo. For each sound value, add the value from 0.2 seconds ago. Scale the result so that no value is larger than 32767.

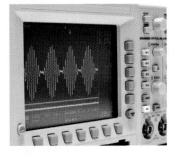

Engineering P6.33 You are given a two-dimensional array of values that give the height of a terrain at different points in a square. Write a function

```
void flood_map(double heights[10][10], double water_level)
```

that prints out a flood map, showing which of the points in the terrain would be flooded if the water level was the given value. In the flood map, print a * for each flooded point and a space for each point that is not flooded.

Here is a sample map:

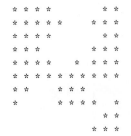

Then write a program that reads one hundred terrain height values and shows how the terrain gets flooded when the water level increases in ten steps from the lowest point in the terrain to the highest.

Engineering P6.34 Modify the ch06/image.cpp program in the book's companion code to generate the image of a sine wave.

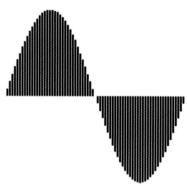

Draw a line of pixels for every five degrees.

Engineering P6.35 Modify the ch06/animation.cpp program to show an animated sine wave. In the ith frame, shift the sine wave by $5 \times i$ degrees.

Engineering P6.36 Write a program that models the movement of an object with mass m that is attached to an oscillating spring. When a spring is displaced from its equilibrium position by an amount x, Hooke's law states that the restoring force is

$$F = -kx$$

where k is a constant that depends on the spring. (Use 10 N/m for this simulation.)

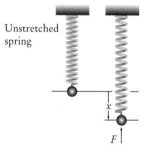

Start with a given displacement x (say, 0.5 meter). Set the initial velocity v to 0. Compute the acceleration a from Newton's law ($F = ma$) and Hooke's law, using a mass of 1 kg. Use a small time interval $\Delta t = 0.01$ second. Update the velocity—it changes by $a\Delta t$. Update the displacement—it changes by $v\Delta t$.

Every ten iterations, plot the spring displacement as a bar, where 1 pixel represents 1 cm. Modify the program ch06/image.cpp for creating an image.

ANSWERS TO SELF-CHECK QUESTIONS

1. `int primes[] = { 2, 3, 5, 7, 11 };`

2. `2, 3, 5, 3, 2`

3. `3, 4, 6, 8, 12`

4. ```
   values[0] = 0;
   values[CAPACITY - 1] = 0;
   ```

5. ```
   for (int i = SIZE - 1; i >= 0; i--)
   {
      cout << values[i] << endl;
   }
   ```

6. `string words[10];`

7. `string words[] = { "Yes", "No" };`

8. ```
   20 <== largest value
   10
   20 <== largest value
   ```

9. ```
   int count = 0;
   for (int i = 0; i < size; i++)
   {
      if (values[i] == 0)
      {
         count++;
      }
   }
   ```

10. If all elements of values are negative, then the result is incorrectly computed as 0.

11. ```
    for (int i = 0; i < size; i++)
    {
       cout << values[i];
       if (i < size - 1)
       {
          cout << " | ";
       }
    }
    ```
    Now you know why we set up the loop the other way.

12. If the sequence has no elements, then a random value is printed.

13. If there is a match, then pos is incremented before the loop exits.

14. This loop sets all elements to values[pos].

15. The sum function will add up all the numbers in the values array and the next 900 numbers, yielding a random result. (Actually, there is the chance that the program doesn't have the right to access all those numbers, in which case the operating system will terminate it.)

16. ```
    int numbers[5];
    squares(5, numbers);
    ```

17. ```
    int find_first(double values[], int size, double searched_value)
    {
       for (int pos = 0; pos < size; pos++)
       {
          if (values[pos] == searched_value)
          {
             return pos;
    ```
    ```

```
        }
    }
    return -1;
}
```

Note that the loop is simpler than that in Section 6.2.6 since we can simply return the position when a match is found.

18.
```
void read_inputs(double inputs[], int capacity, int& size)
{
    size = 0;
    double input;
    while (cin >> input)
    {
        if (size < capacity)
        {
            inputs[size] = input;
            size++;
        }
    }
}
```

19.
```
int append(double first[], int first_size,
        double second[], int second_size,
        double target[], int target_capacity)
```

Note the following:

- You must pass the sizes of the first and second arrays, so that the function knows how many elements to copy.
- You must pass the capacity of the target, so that the function won't write past the end.
- The target array is a parameter variable—functions cannot return arrays.
- The return type is int, so that the function can return the size of the target. (Alternatively, you could use a reference parameter int& target_size.)

20. Use the first algorithm. The order of elements does not matter when computing the sum.

21. **Find the minimum value.**
    Calculate the sum.
    Subtract the minimum value.

22. Use the algorithm for counting matches (Section 4.7.2) twice, once for counting the positive values and once for counting the negative values.

23. You need to modify the algorithm in Section 6.2.5.

```
bool first = true;
for (int i = 0; i < size of values; i++)
{
    if (values[i] > 0))
    {
        if (first) { first = false; }
        else { cout << ", "; }
    }
    cout << values[i];
}
```

Note that you can no longer use i > 0 as the criterion for printing a separator.

24. Use the algorithm to collect all positive values in an array, then use the algorithm in Section 6.2.5 to print the array of matches.

25. The paperclip for i assumes positions 0, 1, 2, 3. When i is incremented to 4, the condition i < **size / 2** becomes false, and the loop ends. Similarly, the paperclip for j assumes positions 4, 5, 6, 7, which are the valid positions for the second half of the array.

26. It reverses the elements in the array.

27. Here is one solution. The basic idea is to move all odd elements to the end. Put one paper clip at the beginning of the array and one at the end. If the element at the first paper clip is odd, swap it with the one at the other paper clip and move that paper clip to the left. Otherwise, move the first paper clip to the right. Stop when the two paper clips meet. Here is the pseudocode:

```
i = 0
j = size - 1
While (i < j)
    If (a[i] is odd)
        Swap elements at positions i and j.
        j--
    Else
        i++
```

28. Here is one solution. The idea is to remove all odd elements and move them to the end. The trick is to know when to stop. Nothing is gained by moving odd elements into the area that already contains moved elements, so we want to mark that area with another paper clip.

```
i = 0
moved = size
While (i < moved)
    If (a[i] is odd)
        Remove the element at position i and add it at the end.
        moved--
```

29. When you read inputs, you get to see values one at a time, and you can't peek ahead. Picking cards one at a time from a deck of cards simulates this process better than looking at a sequence of items, all of whom are revealed.

30. You get the total number of gold, silver, and bronze medals in the competition. In our example, there are four of each.

31.
```
for (int i = 0; i < 8; i++)
{
    for (j = 0; j < 8; j++)
    {
        board[i][j] = (i + j) % 2;
    }
}
```

32. `string board[3][3];`

33. `board[0][2] = "x";`

34. `board[0][0], board[1][1], board[2][2]`

35.
```
vector<int> primes;
primes.push_back(2);
primes.push_back(3);
primes.push_back(5);
primes.push_back(7);
primes.push_back(11);
```

36.
```
vector<int> primes(5);
primes[0] = 2; primes[1] = 3; primes[2] = 5; primes[3] = 7; primes[4] = 11;
```

37. `Ann, Cal`

38. The problem doesn't state how many measurements are taken. If the measurements go on for many months or years (which could well be the case in a scientific or industrial application), a vector is the better choice. If you know that the measurements are stored for a fixed period (say, one day), then an array will work equally well.

39. Because the numbers of weekdays doesn't change, there is no disadvantage to using an array.

40. `vector<double> append(vector<double> first, vector<double> second)`

Contrast this with the answer to Self Check 19.

41. target must be a reference parameter, source should be a value parameter.

CHAPTER 7

POINTERS

To be able to declare, initialize, and use pointers

To understand the relationship between arrays and pointers

To be able to convert between string objects and character pointers

To become familiar with dynamic memory allocation and deallocation

In the game on the left, the spinner's pointer moves to an item. A player follows the pointer and handles the item to which it points—by taking the ball or following the instructions written in the space. C++ also has pointers that can point to different values throughout a program run. Pointers let you work with data whose locations change or whose size is variable.

7.1 Defining and Using Pointers

With a variable, you can access a value at a fixed location. With a pointer, the location can vary. This capability has many useful applications. Pointers can be used to share values among different parts of a program. Pointers allow allocation of values on demand. Furthermore, as you will see in Chapter 10, pointers are necessary for implementing programs that manipulate objects of multiple related types. In this chapter, you will learn how to define pointers and access the values to which they point.

7.1.1 Defining Pointers

Consider a person who wants a program for making bank deposits and withdrawals, but who may not always use the same bank account. By using a pointer, it is possible to switch to a different account without modifying the code for deposits and withdrawals.

Let's start with a variable for storing an account balance:

```
double harrys_account = 0;
```

Now suppose that we want to write an algorithm that manipulates a bank account, but we anticipate that we may sometimes want to use harrys_account, sometimes another account. Using a pointer gives us that flexibility. A pointer tells you *where* a value is located, not what the value is.

A pointer denotes the location of a variable in memory.

Here is the definition of a pointer variable. The pointer variable is initialized with the location (also called the address) of the variable harrys_account (see Figure 1):

```
double* account_pointer = &harrys_account;
```

Like a pointer that points to different locations on a blackboard, a C++ pointer can point to different memory locations.

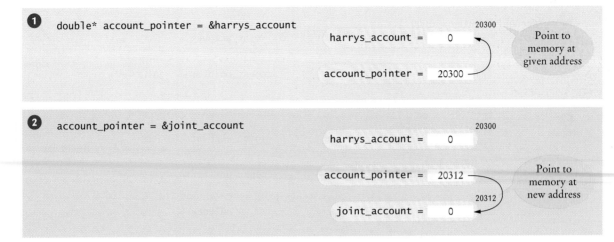

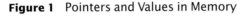

Figure 1   Pointers and Values in Memory

The type double*, or "pointer to double", denotes the location of a double variable. The & operator, also called the *address operator*, yields the location of a variable. Taking the address of a double variable yields a value of type double*.

Thinking about pointers can be rather abstract, but you can use a simple trick to make it more tangible. Every variable in a computer program is located in a specific memory location. You don't know where each variable is stored, but you can pretend you do. Let's pretend that we know that harrys_account is stored in location 20300. (That is just a made-up value.) As shown in Figure 1, the value of harrys_account is 0, but the value of &harrys_account is 20300. The value of account_pointer is also 20300. In our diagrams, we will draw an arrow from a pointer to the location, but of course the computer doesn't store arrows, just numbers.

By using a pointer, you can switch to a different account at any time. To access a different account, simply change the pointer value:

```
account_pointer = &joint_account;
```

7.1.2 Accessing Variables Through Pointers

When you have a pointer, you will want to access the variable to which it points. The * operator is used to read or update the variable to which a pointer points. When used with pointers, the * operator has no relationship with multiplication. In the C++ standard, this operator is called the *indirection operator*, but it is also commonly called the *dereferencing operator*.

This statement makes an initial deposit into the account to which account_pointer points (see Figure 2):

```
*account_pointer = 1000;
```

In other words, you can use *account_pointer in exactly the same way as harrys_account or joint_account. Which account is used depends on the value of the pointer. When the program executes this statement, it fetches the address stored in account_pointer. It then uses the variable at that address, as shown in Figure 2.

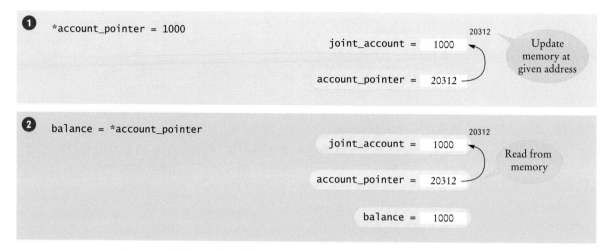

1 `*account_pointer = 1000`

```
                                    20312
              joint_account =    1000          Update
                                                memory at
              account_pointer =  20312         given address
```

2 `balance = *account_pointer`

```
                                    20312
              joint_account =    1000          Read from
                                                memory
              account_pointer =  20312

                   balance =    1000
```

Figure 2 Pointer Variables Can be on Either Side of an Assignment

An expression such as `*account_pointer` can be on the left or the right of an assignment. When it occurs on the left, then the value on the right is stored in the location to which the pointer refers. When it occurs on the right, then the value is fetched from the location and assigned to the variable on the left. For example, the following statement reads the variable to which `account_pointer` currently points, and places its contents into the `balance` variable:

`balance = *account_pointer;` **2**

You can have `*account_pointer` on both sides of an assignment. The following statement withdraws $100:

`*account_pointer = *account_pointer - 100;`

Table 1 contains additional pointer examples.

Syntax 7.1 Pointer Syntax

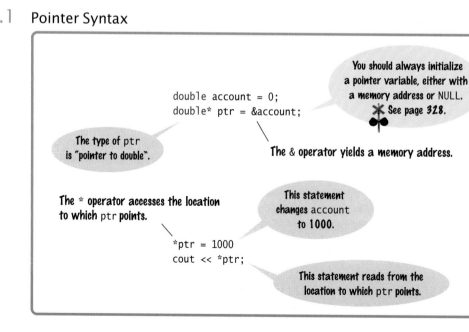

```
                        double account = 0;
                        double* ptr = &account;
```

You should always initialize a pointer variable, either with a memory address or NULL.
✳ See page 328.

The type of ptr is "pointer to double".

The & operator yields a memory address.

The * operator accesses the location to which ptr points.

This statement changes account to 1000.

```
                        *ptr = 1000
                        cout << *ptr;
```

This statement reads from the location to which ptr points.

Table 1 Pointer Syntax Examples

Assume the following declarations:
```
int m = 10; // Assumed to be at address 20300
int n = 20; // Assumed to be at address 20304
int* p = &m;
```

	Expression	Value	Comment
	p	20300	The address of m.
	*p	10	The value stored at that address.
	&n	20304	The address of n.
	p = &n;		Set p to the address of n.
	*p	20	The value stored at the changed address.
	m = *p;		Stores 20 into m.
🚫	m = p;	**Error**	m is an int value; p is an int* pointer. The types are not compatible.
🚫	&10	**Error**	You can only take the address of a variable.
	&p	The address of p, perhaps 20308	This is the location of a pointer variable, not the location of an integer.
🚫	double x = 0; p = &x;	**Error**	p has type int*, &x has type double*. These types are incompatible.

7.1.3 Initializing Pointers

With pointers, it is particularly important that you pay attention to proper initialization.

When you initialize a pointer, be sure that the pointer and the memory address have the same type. For example, the following initialization would be an error:

```
int balance = 1000;
double* account_pointer = &balance; // Error!
```

The address &balance is a pointer to an int value, that is, an expression of type int*. It is never legal to initialize a double* pointer with an int*.

If you define a pointer variable without providing an initial variable, the pointer contains a random address. Using that random address is an error. In practice, your program will likely crash or mysteriously misbehave if you use an uninitialized pointer:

> It is an error to use an uninitialized pointer.

```
double* account_pointer;
    // Forgot to initialize
*account_pointer = 1000;
    // NO! account_pointer contains an unpredictable value
```

The NULL pointer does not point to any object.

There is a special value, NULL, that you should use to indicate a pointer that doesn't point anywhere. If you define a pointer variable and are not ready to initialize it quite yet, set it to NULL.

```
double* account_pointer = NULL; // Will set later
```

You can later test whether the pointer is still NULL. If it is, don't use it.

```
if (account_pointer != NULL) { cout << *account_pointer; } // OK
```

Trying to access data through a NULL pointer is illegal, and it will cause your program to terminate.

The following program demonstrates the behavior of pointers. We execute the same withdrawal statement twice, but with different values for account_pointer. Each time, a different account is modified.

ch07/accounts.cpp

```
1   #include <iostream>
2
3   using namespace std;
4
5   int main()
6   {
7      double harrys_account = 0;
8      double joint_account = 2000;
9      double* account_pointer = &harrys_account;
10
11     *account_pointer = 1000; // Initial deposit
12
13     *account_pointer = *account_pointer - 100; // Withdraw $100
14     cout << "Balance: " << *account_pointer << endl; // Print balance
15
16     // Change the pointer value
17     account_pointer = &joint_account;
18
19     // The same statements affect a different account
20     *account_pointer = *account_pointer - 100; // Withdraw $100
21     cout << "Balance: " << *account_pointer << endl; // Print balance
22
23     return 0;
24  }
```

Program Run

```
Balance: 900
Balance: 1900
```

SELF CHECK

1. Consider this set of statements. What is printed?
   ```
   int a = 1;
   int b = 2;
   int* p = &a;
   cout << *p << endl;
   p = &b;
   cout << *p << endl;
   ```

2. Consider this set of statements. What is printed?
   ```
   int a = 1;
   int b = 2;
   ```

```
int* p = &a;
int* q = &b;
*p = *q;
cout << a << " " << b << endl;
```

3. Consider this set of statements. What is printed?

```
int a = 15;
int* p = &a;
int* q = &a;
cout << *p + *q << endl;
```

4. Consider this set of statements. What is printed?

```
int a = 15;
int* p = &a;
int* q = &a;
*p = *p + 10;
cout << *q << endl;
```

5. Consider this set of statements. What is printed?

```
int a = 15;
int* p = &a;
cout << *p << " " << p << endl;
```

Practice It   Now you can try these exercises at the end of the chapter: R7.1, R7.2, R7.4.

Common Error 7.1

Confusing Pointers with the Data to Which They Point

A pointer is a memory address—a number that tells where a value is located in memory. It is a common error to confuse the pointer with the variable to which it points:

```
double* account_pointer = &joint_account;
account_pointer = 1000; // Error
```

The assignment statement does not set the joint account balance to 1000. Instead, it sets the pointer to point to memory address 1000. The pointer account_pointer only describes *where* the joint account variable is, and it almost certainly is not located at address 1000. Most compilers will report an error for this assignment.

To actually access the variable, use *account_pointer:

```
*account_pointer = 1000; // OK
```

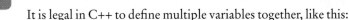

Programming Tip 7.1

Use a Separate Definition for Each Pointer Variable

It is legal in C++ to define multiple variables together, like this:

```
int i = 0, j = 1;
```

This style is confusing when used with pointers:

```
double* p, q;
```

The * associates only with the first variable. That is, p is a double* pointer, and q is a double value. To avoid any confusion, it is best to define each pointer variable separately:

```
double* p;
double* q;
```

Special Topic 7.1

Pointers and References

In Section 5.9, you saw how reference parameters enable a function to modify variables that are passed as arguments. Here is an example of a function with a reference parameter:

```cpp
void withdraw(double& balance, double amount)
{
   if (balance >= amount)
   {
      balance = balance - amount;
   }
}
```

If you call

```cpp
withdraw(harrys_checking, 1000);
```

then $1000 is withdrawn from `harrys_checking`, provided that sufficient funds are available.

You can use pointers to achieve the same effect:

```cpp
void withdraw(double* balance, double amount)
{
   if (*balance >= amount)
   {
      *balance = *balance - amount;
   }
}
```

However, then you need to call the function with the *address* of the account:

```cpp
withdraw(&harrys_checking, 1000);
```

These solutions are equivalent. Behind the scenes, the compiler translates reference parameters into pointers.

7.2 Arrays and Pointers

Pointers are particularly useful for understanding the peculiarities of arrays. In the following sections, we describe the relationship between arrays and pointers in C++.

7.2.1 Arrays as Pointers

Consider this declaration of an array:

```cpp
int a[10];
```

> The name of an array variable is a pointer to the starting element of the array.

As you know, `a[3]` denotes an array element. The array name *without* brackets denotes a pointer to the starting element (see Figure 3).

You can capture that pointer in a variable:

```cpp
int* p = a; // Now p points to a[0]
```

You can also use the array name as a pointer in expressions. The statement

```cpp
cout << *a;
```

has the same effect as the statement

```cpp
cout << a[0];
```

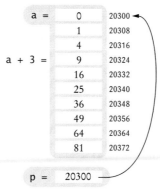

Figure 3   Pointers into an Array

7.2.2 Pointer Arithmetic

Pointers into arrays support *pointer arithmetic*. You can add an integer offset to the pointer to point to another array location. For example, suppose p points to the beginning of an array:

```
double a[10];
double* p = a;
```

Then the expression

```
p + 3
```

is a pointer to the array element with index 3, and

```
*(p + 3)
```

is that array element.

As you saw in the preceding section, we can use the array name as a pointer. That is, a + 3 is a pointer to the array element with index 3, and *(a + 3) has exactly the same meaning as a[3].

In fact, for any integer n, it is true that

```
a[n]  is the same as  *(a + n)
```

This relationship is called the *array/pointer duality law*.

This law explains why all C++ arrays start with an index of zero. The pointer a (or a + 0) points to the starting element of the array. That element must therefore be a[0].

To better understand pointer arithmetic, let's again pretend that we know actual memory addresses. Suppose the array a starts at address 20300. The array contains ten values of type double. A double value occupies 8 bytes of memory. Therefore, the array occupies 80 bytes, from 20300 to 20379. The starting value is located at address 20300, the next one at address 20308, and so on (see Figure 3). For example, the value of a + 3 is 20300 + 3 × 8 = 20324. (In general, if p is a pointer to a type T, then the address p + n is obtained by adding n × the size of a T value to the address p.)

Table 2 on page 317 shows pointer arithmetic and the array/pointer duality using this example.

7.2.3 Array Parameter Variables are Pointers

Once you understand the connection between arrays and pointers, it becomes clear why array parameter variables are different from other parameter types. As an example, consider this function that computes the sum of all values in an array:

```cpp
double sum(double a[], int size)
{
    double total = 0;
    for (int i = 0; i < size; i++)
    {
        total = total + a[i];
    }
    return total;
}
```

Here is a call to the function (see Figure 4):

```cpp
double data[10];
... // Initialize data
double s = sum(data, 10);
```

When passing an array to a function, only the starting address is passed.

The value `data` is passed to the `sum` function. It is actually a pointer of type `double*`, pointing to the starting element of the array. One would therefore expect that the function is declared as

```cpp
double sum(double* a, int size)
```

However, if you look closely at the function definition, you will see that the parameter variable is declared as an array with empty bounds:

```cpp
double sum(double a[], int size)
```

As viewed by the C++ compiler, these parameter declarations are completely equivalent. The `[]` notation is "syntactic sugar" for declaring a pointer. (Computer scientists use the term "syntactic sugar" to describe a notation that is easy to read for humans and that masks a complex implementation detail.) The array notation gives human

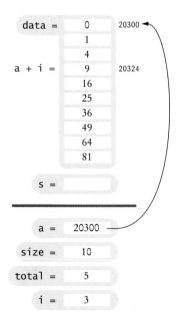

Figure 4
Passing an Array to a Function

Table 2 Arrays and Pointers		
Expression	Value	Comment
a	20300	The starting address of the array, here assumed to be 20300.
*a	0	The value stored at that address. (The array contains values 0, 1, 4, 9, ...)
a + 1	20308	The address of the next `double` value in the array. A `double` occupies 8 bytes.
a + 3	20324	The address of the element with index 3, obtained by skipping past 3 × 8 bytes.
*(a + 3)	9	The value stored at address 20324.
a[3]	9	The same as *(a + 3) by array/pointer duality.
*a + 3	3	The sum of *a and 3. Since there are no parentheses, the * refers only to a.
&a[3]	20324	The address of the element with index 3, the same as a + 3.

readers the illusion that an entire array is passed to the function, but in fact the function receives only the starting address for the array.

Now consider this statement in the body of the function:

```
total = total + a[i];
```

The C++ compiler considers a to be a *pointer*, not an array. The expression a[i] is syntactic sugar for *(a + i). That expression denotes the storage location that is i elements away from the address stored in the variable a. Figure 4 shows how a[i] is accessed when i is 3.

You can now understand why it is always necessary to pass the size of the array. The function receives a single memory address, which tells it where the array starts. That memory address enables the function to locate the values in the array. But the function also needs to know where to stop.

SELF CHECK

For Self Checks 6–9, draw the array and pointer as in Figure 3. Assume a starting address (20300 will work fine), and assume that each `int` value occupies 4 bytes.

6. What is the contents of the array a after these statements?

```
int a[] = { 2, 3, 5 };
int* p = a;
p++;
*p = 0;
```

7. What is the contents of the array a after these statements?

```
int a[] = { 2, 3, 5 };
int* p = a + 1;
*(p + 1) = 0;
```

8. What is the contents of the array a after these statements?

```
int a[] = { 2, 3, 5 };
int* p = a;
int* q = a + 2;
```

```
p++;
q--;
*p = *q;
```

9. What do the following statements print?

```
int a[] = { 2, 3, 5 };
cout << *a + 2 << " ";
cout << *(a + 2) << endl;
```

10. In Chapter 6, we defined a function

```
void squares(int n, int result[])
```

Declare the parameter variable using pointer notation.

Practice It   Now you can try these exercises at the end of the chapter: R7.7, R7.8, P7.4.

Special Topic 7.2

Using a Pointer to Step Through an Array

Consider again the sum function of Section 7.2.3. Now that you know that the first parameter variable of the sum function is a pointer, you can implement the function in a slightly different way. Rather than incrementing an integer index, you can increment a pointer variable to visit all array elements in turn:

```
double sum(double* a, int size)
{
    double total = 0;
    double* p = a; // p starts at the beginning of the array
    for (int i = 0; i < size; i++)
    {
        total = total + *p; // Add the value to which p points
        p++; // Advance p to the next array element
    }
    return total;
}
```

Initially, the pointer p points to the element a[0]. The increment

```
p++;
```

moves it to point to the next element (see Figure 5).

It is a tiny bit more efficient to use and increment a pointer than to access an array element as a[i]. For this reason, some programmers routinely use pointers instead of indexes to access array elements.

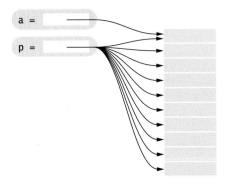

Figure 5   A Pointer Variable Traversing the Elements of an Array

Program Clearly, Not Cleverly

Some programmers take great pride in minimizing the number of instructions, even if the resulting code is hard to understand. For example, here is a legal implementation of the sum function:

```
double sum(double* a, int size)
{
   double total = 0;
   while (size-- > 0) // Loop size times
   {
      total = total + *a++; // Add the value to which a points; increment a
   }
   return total;
}
```

This implementation uses two tricks. First, the function parameter variables a and size are variables, and it is legal to modify them. Moreover, the expressions size-- and a++ mean "decrement or increment the variable and return the old value". In other words, the expression

```
size-- > 0
```

combines two tasks: to decrement size, and to test whether size was positive before the decrement. Similarly, the expression

```
*a++
```

increments the pointer to the next element, and it returns the element to which it pointed before the increment.

Please do not use this programming style. Your job as a programmer is not to dazzle other programmers with your cleverness, but to write code that is easy to understand and maintain.

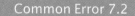

Returning a Pointer to a Local Variable

Consider this function that tries to return a pointer to an array containing two elements, the first and the last values of an array:

```
double* firstlast(double a[], int size)
{
   double result[2];
   result[0] = a[0];
   result[1] = a[size - 1];
   return result; // Error!
}
```

The function returns a pointer to the starting element of the result array. However, that array is a local variable of the firstlast function. The local variable no longer exists when the function exits. Its contents will soon be overwritten by other function calls.

You can solve this problem by passing an array to hold the answer:

```
void firstlast(const double a[], int size, double[] result)
{
   result[0] = a[0];
   result[1] = a[size - 1];
}
```

Then it is the responsibility of the caller to allocate an array to hold the result.

Constant Pointers

The following definition specifies a constant pointer:

```
const double* p = &balance;
```

You cannot modify the value to which p points. That is, the following statement is illegal:

```
*p = 0; // Error
```

Of course, you can read the value:

```
cout << *p; // OK
```

A constant array parameter variable is equivalent to a constant pointer. For example, consider the function

```
double sum(const double[] values, int size)
```

Recall from Section 7.2.3 that values is a pointer. The function could have been defined as

```
double sum(const double* values, int size)
```

The function can use the pointer values to read the array elements, but it cannot modify them.

7.3 C and C++ Strings

C++ has two mechanisms for manipulating strings. The string class supports character sequences of arbitrary length and provides convenient operations such as concatenation and string comparison. However, C++ also inherits a more primitive level of string handling from the C language, in which strings are represented as arrays of char values. In this sections, we will discuss the relationships between these types.

7.3.1 The char Type

A value of type char denotes an individual character. Character literals are enclosed in single quotes.

The char type denotes an individual character. Character literals are delimited by single quotes; for example,

```
char input = 'y';
```

Each character is actually encoded as an integer value. (See Appendix D for the encoding using the ASCII code, which is used on the majority of computers today.)

Note that 'y' is a single character, which is quite different from "y", a string containing the 'y' character.

Table 3 shows typical character literals.

7.3.2 C Strings

A literal string (enclosed in double quotes) is an array of char values with a zero terminator.

In the C programming language, strings are always represented as character arrays. C++ programmers often refer to arrays of char values as "C strings".

In particular, a literal string, such as "Harry", is *not* an object of type string. Instead, it is an array of char values. As with all arrays, a string literal can be assigned to a pointer variable that points to the initial character in the array:

```
const char* char_pointer = "Harry"; // Points to 'H'
```

Figure 6
A Character Array

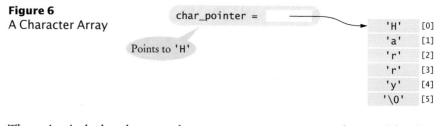

The string is declared as const because you are not supposed to modify a literal string. (See Special Topic 7.3 on page 320 for more information on constant pointers.)

A C string is terminated by a special character, called a *null terminator*, denoted '\0'. For example, the C string "Harry" contains *six* characters, namely 'H', 'a', 'r', 'r', 'y' and '\0' (See Figure 6.)

The terminator is a character that is encoded as the number zero—this is different from the character '0', the character denoting the zero digit. (Under the ASCII encoding scheme, the character denoting the zero digit is encoded as the number 48.)

Functions that operate on C strings rely on this terminator. Here is a typical example, the strlen function declared in the <cstring> header that computes the length of a character array. The function counts the number of characters until it reaches the terminator.

```
int strlen(const char s[])
{
   int i = 0;
   while (s[i] != '\0') { i++; } // Count characters before the null terminator
   return i;
}
```

The call strlen("Harry") returns 5.

7.3.3 Character Arrays

A literal string such as "Harry" is a constant. You are not allowed to modify its characters. If you want to modify the characters in a string, define a character array instead. For example:

```
char char_array[] = "Harry"; // An array of 6 characters
```

Table 3 **Character Literals**	
'y'	The character y
'0'	The character for the digit 0. In the ASCII code, '0' has the value 48.
' '	The space character
'\n'	The newline character
'\t'	The tab character
'\0'	The null terminator of a string
🚫 "y"	**Error:** Not a char value

The char_array variable is an array of 6 characters, initialized with 'H', 'a', 'r', 'r', 'y', and a null terminator. The compiler counts the characters in the string that is used for initializing the array, including the null terminator.

You can modify the characters in the array:

```
char_array[0] = 'L';
```

7.3.4 Converting Between C and C++ Strings

Before the C++ string class became widely available, direct manipulation of character arrays was common, but also quite challenging (see Special Topic 7.4 on page 323). If you use functions that receive or return C strings, you need to know how to convert between C strings and string objects.

Many library functions use pointers of type char*.

For example, the <cstdlib> header declares a useful function

```
int atoi(const char s[])
```

The atoi function converts a character array containing digits into its integer value:

```
char[] year = "2012";
int y = atoi(year); // Now y is the integer 2012
```

The c_str member function yields a char* pointer from a string object.

This functionality is inexplicably missing from the C++ string class. The c_str member function of the string class offers an "escape hatch". If s is a string, then s.c_str() yields a char* pointer to the characters in the string. Here is how you use that member function to call the atoi function:

```
string year = "2012";
int y = atoi(year.c_str());
```

You can initialize C++ string variables with C strings.

Conversely, converting from a C string to a C++ string is very easy. Simply initialize a string variable with any value of type char*, such as a string literal or character array. For example, the definition

```
string name = "Harry";
```

initializes the C++ string object name with the C string "Harry".

7.3.5 C++ Strings and the [] Operator

Up to this point, we have always used the substr member function to access individual characters in a C++ string. For example, if a string variable is defined as

```
string name = "Harry";
```

the expression

```
name.substr(3, 1)
```

yields a string of length 1 containing the character at index 3.

You can access individual characters with the [] operator:

```
name[0] = 'L';
```

You can access characters in a C++ string object with the [] operator.

Now the string is "Larry". The [] operator is more convenient than the substr function if you want to visit a string one character at a time.

Here is a useful example. The following function makes a copy of a string and changes all characters to uppercase:

```
/**
    Makes an uppercase version of a string.
    @param str a string
    @return a string with the characters in str converted to uppercase
*/
string uppercase(string str)
{
    string result = str; // Make a copy of str
    for (int i = 0; i < result.length(); i++)
    {
        result[i] = toupper(result[i]); // Convert each character to uppercase
    }
    return result;
}
```

For example, `uppercase("Harry")` returns a string with the characters `"HARRY"`.

The `toupper` function is defined in the `<cctype>` header. It converts lowercase characters to uppercase. (The `tolower` function does the opposite.)

SELF CHECK

11. How many `char` values are stored in the character array `"Hello, World!\n"`?

12. What is `strlen("Hello, World!\n")`?

13. Allocate a pointer variable that points to the string `"Hello"`.

14. Consider this statement:

    ```
    string title = "Agent" + 007;
    ```

    Does the statement compile? What is its effect?

15. Consider the following statements:

    ```
    cout << "Enter an integer, Q to quit";
    string input;
    cin >> input;
    if (input == "Q") { return; }
    ```

    If the input is not the letter Q, how do you extract the number stored in the string `input`?

Practice It Now you can try these exercises at the end of the chapter: R7.15, R7.16, P7.6.

Special Topic 7.4

Working with C Strings

Before the `string` class became widely available, it was common to work with character arrays directly.

Table 4 on page 324 shows several commonly used functions for manipulating C strings. All of these functions are declared in the `<cstring>` header.

Consider the task of concatenating a first name and a last name into a string. The `string` class makes this very easy:

```
string first = "Harry";
string last = "Smith";
string name = first + " " + last;
```

Let us implement this task with C strings. Allocate an array of characters for the result:

```
const int NAME_SIZE = 40;
char name[NAME_SIZE];
```

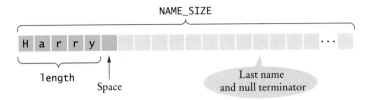

This array can hold strings with a length of at most 39, because one character is required for the null terminator.

Now copy the first name, using strncpy:

```
strncpy(name, first, NAME_SIZE - 1);
```

You must be careful not to overrun the target array. It is unlikely that a first name is longer than 39 characters, but a hacker could supply a longer input in order to overwrite memory.

Now, if there is still room, add a space and the last name, again being careful not to overrun the array boundaries.

```
int length = strlen(name);
if (length < NAME_SIZE - 1)
{
    strcat(name, " ");
    int n = NAME_SIZE - 2 - length; // Leave room for space, null terminator
    if (n > 0)
    {
        strncat(name, last, n);
    }
}
```

As you can see, the C string code is over three times as long as the code using C++ strings, and it is not as capable—if the target array is not long enough to hold the result, it is truncated.

Table 4 C String Functions

In this table, s and t are character arrays; n is an integer.

Function	Description
strlen(s)	Returns the length of s.
strcpy(t, s)	Copies the characters from s into t.
strncpy(t, s, n)	Copies at most n characters from s into t.
strcat(t, s)	Appends the characters from s after the end of the characters in t.
strncat(t, s, n)	Appends at most n characters from s after the end of the characters in t.
strcmp(s, t)	Returns 0 if s and t have the same contents, a negative integer if s comes before t in lexicographic order, a positive integer otherwise.

7.4 Dynamic Memory Allocation

> Use dynamic memory allocation if you do not know in advance how many values you need.

In many programming situations, you do not know beforehand how many values you need. To solve this problem, you can use *dynamic allocation* and ask the C++ run-time system to create new values whenever you need them. The run-time system keeps a large storage area, called the **heap**, that can allocate values and arrays of any type. When you ask for a

```
new double
```

> The new operator allocates memory from the heap.

then a storage location of type `double` is located on the heap, and a pointer to that location is returned. More usefully, the expression

```
new double[n]
```

allocates an array of size n, and yields a pointer to the starting element. (Here n need *not* be a constant.)

You will want to capture that pointer in a variable:

```
double* account_pointer = new double;
double* account_array = new double[n];
```

You now use the pointer as described previously in this chapter. If you allocated an array, the magic of array/pointer duality lets you use the array notation `account_array[i]` to access the ith element.

> You must reclaim dynamically allocated objects with the delete or delete[] operator.

When your program no longer needs memory that you previously allocated with the `new` operator, you must return it to the heap, using the `delete` operator:

```
delete account_pointer;
```

However, if you allocated an array, you must use the `delete[]` operator:

```
delete[] account_array;
```

This operator reminds the heap that the pointer points to an array, not a single value.

Syntax 7.2   Dynamic Memory Allocation

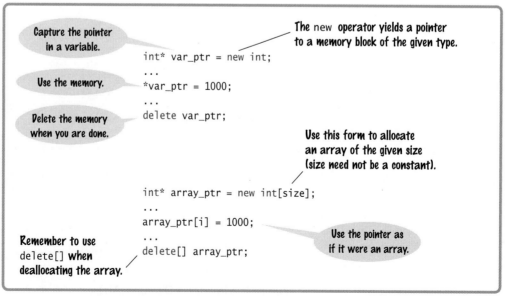

After you delete a memory block, you can no longer use it. The storage space may already be used elsewhere.

```
delete[] account_array;
account_array[0] = 1000; // NO! You no longer own the memory of account_array
```

Heap arrays have one significant advantage over array variables. If you declare an array variable, you must specify a fixed array size when you compile the program. But when you allocate an array on the heap, you can choose the size at run time.

Moreover, if you later need more elements, you are not stuck. You can allocate a bigger heap array, copy the elements from the smaller array into the bigger array, and delete the smaller array (see Figure 7):

```
double* bigger_array = new double[2 * n];
for (int i = 0; i < n; i++)
{
    bigger_array[i] = account_array[i];
}
delete[] account_array;
account_array = bigger_array;
n = 2 * n;
```

This is exactly what a vector does behind the scenes.

Heap allocation is a powerful feature, but you must be very careful to follow all rules precisely:

- Every call to new must be matched by exactly one call to delete.
- Use delete[] to delete arrays.
- Don't access a memory block after it has been deleted.

If you don't follow these rules, your program can crash or run unpredictably. Table 5 shows common errors.

Be sure to recycle any heap memory that your program no longer needs.

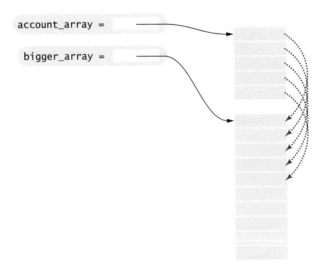

Figure 7 Growing a Dynamic Array

Table 5 Common Memory Allocation Errors	
Statements	Error

`int* p;`
`*p = 5;`
`delete p;`
	There is no call to `new int`.

`int* p = new int;`
`*p = 5;`
`p = new int;`
	The first allocated memory block was never deleted.

`int* p = new int[10];`
`*p = 5;`
`delete p;`
	The `delete[]` operator should have been used.

`int* p = new int[10];`
`int* q = p;`
`q[0] = 5;`
`delete p;`
`delete q;`
	The same memory block was deleted twice.

`int n = 4;`
`int* p = &n;`
`*p = 5;`
`delete p;`
	You can only delete memory blocks that you obtained from calling `new`.

SELF CHECK

16. What does this statement sequence print?

```
int* p = new int;
*p = 3;
cout << *p << endl;
delete p;
```

17. What does this statement sequence print?

```
int* p = new int[10];
for (int i = 0; i < 10; i++) { p[i] = i * i; }
cout << *p << " " << *(p + 1) << " " << p[2] << endl;
delete[] p;
```

18. What is wrong with this sequence of statements?

```
int* p = new int[10];
p[10] = 5;
delete[] p;
```

19. Consider this function

```
int* grow(int a[], int size)
{
   int* result = new int[2 * size];
   for (int i = 0; i < size; i++) { result[i] = a[i]; }
   for (int i = size; i < 2 * size; i++) { result[i] = 0; }
   return result;
}
```

What is the contents of the array to which p points after the following statements?

```
int primes[] = { 2, 3, 5, 7, 11 };
int* p = grow(primes, 5);
```

20. Consider the grow function of Self Check 19. What must its caller remember to do?

Practice It   Now you can try these exercises at the end of the chapter: R7.19, R7.21, P7.10.

Common Error 7.3

Dangling Pointers

A very common pointer error is to use a pointer that points to memory that has already been deleted. Such a pointer is called a **dangling pointer**. Because the freed memory will be reused for other purposes, you can create real damage by using a dangling pointer. Consider this example:

> Using a dangling pointer (a pointer that points to memory that has been deleted) is a serious programming error.

```
int* values = new int[n];
// Process values
delete[] values;
// Some other work
values[0] = 42;
```

This code will compile since the compiler does not track whether a pointer points to a valid memory location. However, the program may run with unpredictable results. If the program calls the new operator anywhere after deleting values, that call may allocate the same memory again. Now some other part of your program accesses the memory to which values points, and that program part will malfunction when you overwrite the memory. This can happen even if you don't see any call to new—such calls may occur in library functions.

Never use a pointer that has been deleted. Some programmers take the precaution of setting all deleted pointers to NULL:

```
delete[] values;
values = NULL;
```

This is not perfect protection—you might have saved values into another pointer variable—but it is a reasonable precaution.

Common Error 7.4

Memory Leaks

Another very common pointer error is to allocate memory on the heap and never deallocate it. A memory block that is never deallocated is called a **memory leak**.

If you allocate a few small blocks of memory and forget to deallocate them, this is not a huge problem. When the program exits, all allocated memory is returned to the operating system.

But if your program runs for a long time, or if it allocates lots of memory (perhaps in a loop), then it can run out of memory. Memory exhaustion will cause your program to crash. In extreme cases, the computer may freeze up if your program exhausted all available memory. Avoiding memory leaks is particularly important in programs that need to run for months or years, without restarting, and in programs that run on resource-constrained devices such as cell phones.

> Every call to new should have a matching call to delete.

Even if you write short-lived programs, you should make it a habit to avoid memory leaks. Make sure that every call to the new operator has a corresponding call to the delete operator.

7.5 Arrays and Vectors of Pointers

When you have a sequence of pointers, you can place them into an array or vector. An array and a vector of ten int* pointers are defined as

```
int* pointer_array[10];
vector<int*> pointer_vector(10);
```

The expression pointer_array[i] or pointer_vector[i] denotes the pointer with index i in the sequence.

One application of such pointer sequences are two-dimensional arrays in which each row has a different length, such as the triangular array shown in Figure 8.

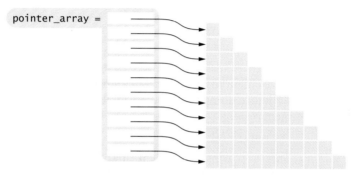

Figure 8   A Triangular Array

In this situation, it would not be very efficient to use a two-dimensional array, because almost half of the elements would be wasted.

We will develop a program that uses such an array for simulating a *Galton board* (Figure 9). A Galton board consists of a pyramidal arrangement of pegs, and a row of bins at the bottom. Balls are dropped onto the top peg and travel toward the bins. At each peg, there is a 50 percent chance of moving left or right. The balls in the bins approximate a bell-curve distribution.

The Galton board can only show the balls in the bins, but we can do better by keeping a counter for each peg, incrementing it as a ball travels past it.

We will simulate a board with ten rows of pegs. Each row requires an array of counters.

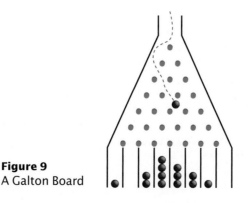

Figure 9
A Galton Board

Figure 10
Movement of a Ball in
the Galton Board Array

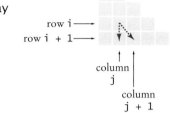

row i ⟶

row i + 1 ⟶

column
j

column
j + 1

The following statements initialize the triangular array:

```
int* counts[10];
for (int i = 0; i < 10; i++)
{
    counts[i] = new int[i + 1];
}
```

Note that the first element counts[0] contains a pointer to an array of length 1, and the last element counts[9] contains a pointer to an array of length 10.

Before doing the simulation, let us consider how to print out the values. The element counts[i] points to an array. The element of index j of that array is

```
counts[i][j]
```

This loop prints all elements in the ith row:

```
for (int j = 0; j <= i; j++)
{
    cout << setw(4) << counts[i][j];
}
cout << endl;
```

Now let's simulate a falling ball. The movements to the left and right in Figure 9 correspond to movements to the next row, either straight down or to the right, in Figure 10. More precisely, if the ball is currently at row i and column j, then it will go to row i + 1 and, with a 50 percent chance, either stay in column j or go to column j + 1.

The program below has the details. In the sample program run, notice how 1,000 balls have hit the top peg, and how the bottommost row of pegs approximates a bell-curve distribution.

ch07/galton.cpp

```
 1   #include <iostream>
 2   #include <iomanip>
 3   #include <cstdlib>
 4   #include <ctime>
 5
 6   using namespace std;
 7
 8   int main()
 9   {
10       srand(time(0));
11
12       int* counts[10];
13
14       // Allocate the rows
15       for (int i = 0; i < 10; i++)
16       {
```

```
17        counts[i] = new int[i + 1];
18        for (int j = 0; j <= i; j++)
19        {
20           counts[i][j] = 0;
21        }
22     }
23
24     const int RUNS = 1000;
25
26     // Simulate 1,000 balls
27     for (int run = 0; run < RUNS; run++)
28     {
29        // Add a ball to the top
30        counts[0][0]++;
31        // Have the ball run to the bottom
32        int j = 0;
33        for (int i = 1; i < 10; i++)
34        {
35           int r = rand() % 2;
36           // If r is even, move down, otherwise to the right
37           if (r == 1)
38           {
39              j++;
40           }
41           counts[i][j]++;
42        }
43     }
44
45     // Print all counts
46     for (int i = 0; i < 10; i++)
47     {
48        for (int j = 0; j <= i; j++)
49        {
50           cout << setw(4) << counts[i][j];
51        }
52        cout << endl;
53     }
54
55     // Deallocate the rows
56     for (int i = 0; i < 10; i++)
57     {
58        delete[] counts[i];
59     }
60
61     return 0;
62  }
```

Program Run

```
1000
 480 520
 241 500 259
 124 345 411 120
  68 232 365 271  64
  32 164 283 329 161  31
  16  88 229 303 254  88  22
   9  47 147 277 273 190  44  13
   5  24 103 203 288 228 113  33   3
   1  18  64 149 239 265 186  61  15   2
```

21. Why didn't we initialize the triangular array with the following loop?

```
for (int i = 0; i < 10; i++)
{
    counts[i] = new int[i];
}
```

22. Suppose a program initializes a triangular array as we did in this section, and then accesses a non-existent element with the statement

```
counts[1][2]++
```

Will the program compile? If so, what happens at run time?

23. Initialize a triangular 10 × 10 array where the first row has length 10 and the last row has length 1.

24. What changes would need to be made to the galton.cpp program so that counts is a vector<int*>?

25. What changes would need to be made to the galton.cpp program so that *each row* is a vector<int>?

Practice It Now you can try these exercises at the end of the chapter: R7.22, P7.11, P7.12.

7.6 Problem Solving: Draw a Picture

When designing programs that use pointers, you want to visualize how the pointers connect the data that you are working with. In most situations, it is essential that you draw a diagram that shows the connections.

Start with the data that will be accessed or modified through the pointers. These may be account balances, counters, character strings, or other items. Focus on what is being pointed at.

Then draw the variable or variables that contain the pointers. These will be the front-end to your system. Processing usually starts with a pointer, then locates the actual data.

Draw the data that is being processed, then draw the pointer variables. When drawing the pointer arrows, illustrate a typical situation.

Finally, draw the pointers as arrows. If the pointers will vary as the program executes, draw a typical arrangement. It can also be useful to draw several diagrams that show how the pointers change.

Consider the following problem: The media center of a university loans out equipment, such as microphones, cables, and so on, to faculty and students. We want to track the name of each item, and the name of the user who checked it out.

In this case, the data that are being accessed are item and user names. We will store all names in a long array of characters, adding new names to the end as needed. If a name is already present, we don't store it twice. This is an efficient way of storing strings, provided that few strings need to be removed. Here is a section of the character array:

> Microphone TX-10\0 Smith, Diane\0 Lee, Tim\0 Tape recorder\0 Mini DVI cable\0 ...

Next, let us draw the pointers to the item names. they are stored in an array of pointers called items. Some items may have the same name. In the example below, we have two microphones with the same name.

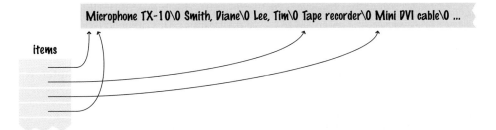

Finally, there is a parallel array `checked_out_to` of pointers to user names. Sometimes, items can be checked out to the same user. Other items aren't checked out at all—the user name pointer is `NULL`. When you draw a diagram, try to include examples of all scenarios.

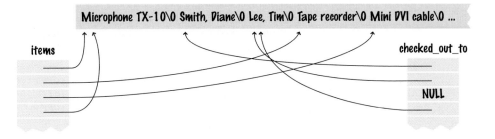

Now that you have a pointer diagram, you can use it to visualize operations on the data. Suppose we want to print a report of all items that are currently checked out. This can be achieved by visiting all pointers in both arrays. The pointer `items[i]` gives the name of the item, and `checked_out_to[i]` is either `NULL`, in which case we do not want to include this item, or it is the name of the user.

Because programming with pointers is complex, you should always draw diagrams whenever you use pointers.

SELF CHECK

26. Consider the `sum` function in Section 7.2.3. Draw a picture of its parameter variables when it is called as `sum(data + 3, 7)`, where `data` is an array of length 10.

27. One way to reverse all elements in an array is to have pointers to the first and last location, swap the elements that are being pointed to, and then increment the first pointer and decrement the second pointer. Repeat until both pointers reach the middle of the array. Draw a picture of the pointers in this algorithm after a couple of iterations.

28. One way to test whether two strings have the same contents is to have pointers to the strings and compare the characters that are being pointed to. If both are the `'\0'` terminator, stop—the strings are identical. If the characters are different, stop—the strings are different. Otherwise, increment both pointers. Draw a picture of the pointers in this algorithm after a couple of iterations. Be sure to pick strings that match the algorithm state.

29. Draw a picture showing the contents of the `counts` array in the `galton.cpp` program on page 330 after the fifth iteration of the loop in lines 56–59.

30. Suppose you want to sort the names of the items in the media center. There is no need to move the strings. All you need to do is rearrange the string pointers. Draw a picture that shows the result.

Practice It Now you can try these exercises at the end of the chapter: R7.25, R7.26, R7.27.

HOW TO 7.1   Working with Pointers

You use pointers because you want flexibility in your program: the ability to change the relationships between data. This How To walks you through the decision-making process for using pointers.

We will illustrate the steps with the task of simulating a part of the control logic for a departmental photocopier. A person making a copy enters a user number. There are 100 different users, with numbers 0 to 99. Each user is linked to a copy account, either the master account or one of ten project accounts. That linkage is maintained by the administrator, and it can change as users work on different projects. When copies are made, the appropriate account should be incremented.

Users identify themselves on the copier control panel. Using pointers, the relationships between users and copy accounts can be flexible.

Step 1 Draw a picture.

As described in Section 7.6, it is a good idea to draw a picture that shows the pointers in your program.

In our example, we need to track the copy accounts: a master account and ten project accounts. For each user, we need a pointer to the copy account:

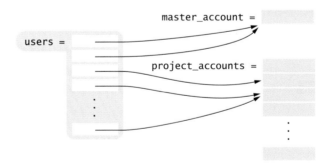

Step 2 Declare pointer variables.

This step is usually easy. With numerical data, you will have pointers of type `int*` or `double*`. If you manipulate character arrays, you use `char*` pointers. In Chapter 10, you will use pointers to objects.

How many pointer variables do you have? If you only have one or two, just declare variables such as

```
double* account_pointer;
```

If you have a sequence of pointers, use a vector or array, such as

```
vector<char*> lines;
```

In our example, the purpose is to manipulate copy counters. Therefore, our data are integers and the pointers have type int*. We know that we will have exactly 100 pointers, one for each user. Therefore, we can choose an array

```
int* users[100];
```

Step 3   Initialize the pointers with variable addresses or heap memory.

Will you allocate variables and then take their addresses with the & operator? That is fine if you have a fixed amount of data that you want to reach through the pointers. Otherwise, use the new operator to allocate memory dynamically. Be sure to deallocate the memory when you are done, using the delete or delete[] operator.

In our example, there is no need for dynamic allocation, so we will just take addresses of variables.

```
int master_account;
int project_accounts[10];
for (int i = 0; i < 100; i++)
{
    users[i] = &master_account;
}
// Here we reassign several users to project accounts.
// The following code is a simulation of the actions that would
// occur in an administration interface, which we do not implement.
users[2] = project_accounts + 1
users[3] = project_accounts + 2
users[99] = project_accounts + 2
```

Step 4   Use the * or [] operator to access your data.

When you access a single variable through a pointer, use the * operator to read or write the variable. For example,

```
*account_pointer = *account_pointer + 20;
```

When you have a pointer to an array, use the [] notation. Simply think of the pointer as the array:

```
account_array[i] = account_array[i] + 20;
```

If you have an array or vector of pointers, then you need brackets to get at an individual pointer. Then supply another * or [] to get at the value. You saw an example in the Galton board simulator where a count was accessed as

```
counts[i][j]
```

Implement your algorithm, keeping these access rules in mind.

In our example, we read the user ID and number of copies. Then we increment the copy account:

```
cin >> id >> copies;
*users[id] = *users[id] + copies;
```

Exercise P7.12 asks you to complete this simulation.

WORKED EXAMPLE 7.1   **Producing a Mass Mailing**

This Worked Example uses pointers to create a template for a mass mailing

⊕ Available online at www.wiley.com/college/horstmann.

Random Fact 7.1 Embedded Systems

An *embedded system* is a computer system that controls a device. The device contains a processor and other hardware and is controlled by a computer program. Unlike a personal computer, which has been designed to be flexible and run many different computer programs, the hardware and software of an embedded system are tailored to a specific device. Computer controlled devices are becoming increasingly common, ranging from washing machines to medical equipment, cell phones, automobile engines, and spacecraft.

Several challenges are specific to programming embedded systems. Most importantly, a much higher standard of quality control applies. Vendors are often unconcerned about bugs in personal computer software, because they can always make you install a patch or upgrade to the next version. But in an embedded system, that is not an option. Few consumers would feel comfortable upgrading the software in their washing machines or automobile engines. If you ever handed in a programming assignment that you believed to be correct, only to have the instructor or grader find bugs in it, then you know how hard it is to write software that can reliably do its task for many years without a chance of changing it. Quality standards are especially important in devices whose failure would destroy property or endanger human life. Many personal computer purchasers buy computers that are fast and have a lot of storage, because the investment is paid back over time when many programs are run on the same equipment. But the hardware for an embedded device is not shared––it is dedicated to one device. A separate processor, memory, and so on, are built for every copy of the device. If it is possible to shave a few pennies off the manufacturing cost of every unit, the savings can add up quickly for devices that are produced in large volumes. Thus, the programmer of an embedded-system has a much larger economic incentive to conserve resources than the desktop software programmer. Unfortunately, trying to conserve resources usually makes it harder to write programs that work correctly.

C and C++ are commonly used languages for developing embedded systems.

The Controller of an Embedded System

7.7 Structures and Pointers (Optional)

7.7.1 Structures

A structure combines member values into a single value.

In C++, you use a **structure** to aggregate items of arbitrary types into a single value. For example, a street address is composed of a house number and a street name. A structure named StreetAddress can be defined to combine these two values into a single entity. In C++, we define a structure with the struct reserved word:

```
struct StreetAddress
{
    int house_number;
    string street_name;
};
```

This definition yields a new type, StreetAddress, that you can use for declaring variables:

```
StreetAddress white_house;
```

You use the dot notation to access members of a structure.

The variable white_house has two named parts, called *members*, house_number and street_name. You use the "dot notation" to access each member, like this:

```
white_house.house_number = 1600;
white_house.street_name = "Pennsylvania Avenue";
```

7.7.2 Pointers to Structures

It is common to allocate structure values dynamically, using the new operator:

```
StreetAddress* address_pointer = new StreetAddress;
```

Suppose you want to set the house number of the structure to which address_pointer points:

```
*address_pointer.house_number = 1600; // Error
```

Unfortunately, that is a syntax error. The dot operator has a higher precedence than the * operator. That is, the compiler thinks that you mean

```
*(address_pointer.house_number) = 1600; // Error
```

However, address_pointer is a pointer, not a structure. You can't apply the dot (.) operator to a pointer, and the compiler reports an error. Instead, you must make it clear that you first want to apply the * operator, then the dot:

```
(*address_pointer).house_number = 1600; // OK
```

> Use the -> operator to access a structure member through a pointer.

Because this is such a common situation, the designers of C++ supply an operator to abbreviate the "follow pointer and access member" operation. That operator is written -> and usually pronounced "arrow".

```
address_pointer->house_number = 1600; // OK
```

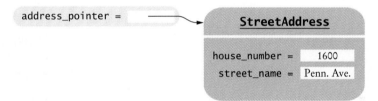

Figure 11 A Pointer to a Structure

7.7.3 Structures with Pointer Members

A member of a structure can be a pointer. This situation commonly arises when information is shared among structure values. Consider this example. In an organization with multiple offices, each employee has a name and an office location:

```
struct Employee
{
   string name;
   StreetAddress* office;
}
```

Here, we define two employees who both work for the accounting office:

```
StreetAddress accounting;
accounting.house_number = "1729";
accounting.street_name = "Park Avenue";

Employee harry;
harry.name = "Smith, Harry";
harry.office = &accounting;
```

```
Employee sally;
sally.name = "Lee, Sally";
sally.office = &accounting;
```

Figure 12 shows how these structures are related.

This sharing of information has an important benefit. Suppose the accounting office moves across the street:

```
accounting.house_number = 1720;
```

Now both Harry's and Sally's office addresses are automatically updated.

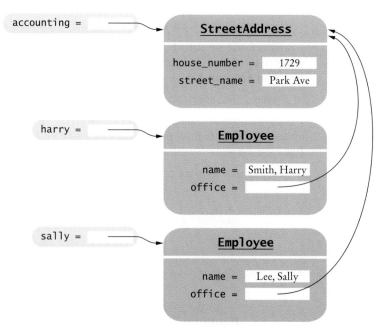

Figure 12 Two Pointers to a Shared Structure

SELF CHECK

31. Declare a variable of type StreetAddress and initialize it with the address of the State Department: 2201 C Street NW.

32. Declare a pointer variable of type StreetAddress* and initialize it with a structure containing the address of the State Department: 2201 C Street NW.

33. Define a structure type Date to describe dates such as "July 4" or "December 31".

34. Using the structure type that you defined in Self Check 33, define a variable independence_day and initialize it as July 4.

35. How do you print out Harry's office address?

Practice It Now you can try these exercises at the end of the chapter: R7.23, R7.24, P7.16.

CHAPTER SUMMARY

Define and use pointer variables.

- A pointer denotes the location of a variable in memory.
- The type T* denotes a pointer to a variable of type T.
- The & operator yields the location of a variable.
- The * operator accesses the variable to which a pointer points.
- It is an error to use an uninitialized pointer.
- The NULL pointer does not point to any object.

Understand the relationship between arrays and pointers in C++.

- The name of an array variable is a pointer to the starting element of the array.
- Pointer arithmetic means adding an integer offset to an array pointer, yielding a pointer that skips past the given number of elements.
- The array/pointer duality law states that a[n] is identical to *(a + n), where a is a pointer into an array and n is an integer offset.
- When passing an array to a function, only the starting address is passed.

Use C++ string objects with functions that process character arrays.

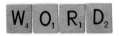

- A value of type char denotes an individual character. Character literals are enclosed in single quotes.
- A literal string (enclosed in double quotes) is an array of char values with a zero terminator.
- Many library functions use pointers of type char*.
- The c_str member function yields a char* pointer from a string object.
- You can initialize C++ string variables with C strings.
- You can access characters in a C++ string object with the [] operator.

Allocate and deallocate memory in programs whose memory requirements aren't known until run time.

- Use dynamic memory allocation if you do not know in advance how many values you need.
- The new operator allocates memory from the heap.
- You must reclaim dynamically allocated objects with the delete or delete[] operator.
- Using a dangling pointer (a pointer that points to memory that has been deleted) is a serious programming error.
- Every call to new should have a matching call to delete.

Work with arrays and vectors of pointers.

Draw diagrams for visualizing pointers and the data to which they point.

- Draw the data that is being processed, then draw the pointer variables. When drawing the pointer arrows, illustrate a typical situation.

Use structures to aggregate data items and work with pointers to structures.

- A structure combines member values into a single value.
- You use the dot notation to access members of a structure.
- Use the -> operator to access a structure member through a pointer.

REVIEW EXERCISES

R7.1 Trace the following code. Assume that a and b are stored at 20300 and 20308. Your trace table should have entries for a, b, and p.

```
double a = 1000;
double b = 2000;
double* p = &a;
*p = 3000;
p = &b;
a = *p * 2;
```

R7.2 Trace the following code. Assume that a and b are stored at 20300 and 20308. Your trace table should have entries for a, b, p, and q.

```
double a = 1000;
double b = 2000;
double* p = &a;
double* q = &b;
*p = *q;
p = q;
*p = 3000;
```

R7.3 What does the following code print?

```
double a = 1000;
double b = 2000;
double* p = &a;
double* q = p;
b = *q;
p = &b;
a = *p + *q;
cout << a << " " << b << endl;
```

R7.4 Explain the mistakes in the following code. Not all lines contain mistakes. Each line depends on the lines preceding it.

```
1   double a = 1000;
2   double* p = a;
3   int* p = &a;
4   double* q;
5   *q = 2000;
```

```
6   int* r = NULL;
7   *r = 3000;
```

R7.5 Suppose that a system allows the use of any string as a password, even the empty string. However, when a user connects to the system for the first time, no password has been assigned. Describe how you can use a `string*` variable and the `NULL` pointer to distinguish unassigned passwords from empty ones.

R7.6 Given the definitions

```
double primes[] = { 2, 3, 5, 7, 11, 13 };
double* p = primes + 3;
```

draw a diagram that explains the meanings of the following expressions:

  a. `primes[1]`
  b. `primes + 1`
  c. `*(primes + 1)`
  d. `p[1]`
  e. `p + 1`

R7.7 Suppose the array `primes`, defined as

```
double primes[] = { 2, 3, 5, 7, 11, 13 };
```

starts at memory location 20300. What are the values of

  a. `primes`
  b. `*primes`
  c. `primes + 4`
  d. `*(primes + 4)`
  e. `primes[4]`
  f. `&primes[4]`

R7.8 Suppose the array `primes` is defined as

```
double primes[] = { 2, 3, 5, 7, 11, 13 };
```

Consider the `sum` function discussed in Section 7.2.3. What are the values of

  a. `sum(primes, 6);`
  b. `sum(primes, 4);`
  c. `sum(primes + 2, 4);`
  d. `sum(primes, 0);`
  e. `sum(NULL, 4);`

R7.9 Suppose the array `primes`, defined as

```
double primes[] = { 2, 3, 5, 7, 11, 13 };
```

starts at memory location 20300. Trace the function call `sum(primes, 4)`, using the definition of sum from Special Topic 7.2 on page 318. In your trace table, show the values for `a`, `size`, `total`, `p`, and `i`.

R7.10 Pointers are addresses and have a numerical value. You can print out the value of a pointer as `cout << (unsigned)(p)`. Write a program to compare `p`, `p + 1`, `q`, and `q + 1`, where `p` is an `int*` and `q` is a `double*`. Explain the results.

R7.11 A pointer variable can contain a pointer to a single variable, a pointer to an array, `NULL`, or a random value. Write code that creates and sets four pointer variables `a`, `b`, `c`, and `d` to show each of these possibilities.

R7.12 Implement a function firstlast that obtains the first and last values in an array of integers and stores the result in an array *argument*.

R7.13 Explain the meanings of the following expressions:

    a. "Harry" + 1

    b. *("Harry" + 2)

    c. "Harry"[3]

    d. [4]"Harry"

R7.14 What is the difference between the following two variable definitions?

    a. char a[6] = "Hello";

    b. char* b = "Hello";

R7.15 What is the difference between the following three variable definitions?

    a. char* p = NULL;

    b. char* q = "";

    c. char r[1] = { '\0' };

R7.16 Consider this program segment:

```
char a[] = "Mary had a little lamb";
char* p = a;
int count = 0;
while (*p != '\0')
{
   count++;
   while (*p != ' ' && *p != '\0') { p++; }
   while (*p == ' ') { p++; }
}
```

What is the value of count at the end of the outer while loop?

R7.17 Consider the following code that repeats a C++ string three times.

```
string a = "Hello";
string b = a + a + a;
```

Suppose s is a C string, and t is declared as

```
char t[100];
```

Write the equivalent code for C strings that stores the threefold repetition of s (or as much of it as will fit) into t.

R7.18 Which of the following assignments are legal in C++?

```
void f(int p[])
{
   int* q;
   const int* r;
   int s[10];
   p = q;   ①
   p = r;   ②
   p = s;   ③
   q = p;   ④
   q = r;   ⑤
   q = s;   ⑥
   r = p;   ⑦
```

```
           r = q;  ⑧
           r = s;  ⑨
           s = p;  ⑩
           s = q;  ⑪
           s = r;  ⑫
       }
```

R7.19 What happens if you forget to delete an object that you obtained from the heap? What happens if you delete it twice?

R7.20 Write a program that accesses a deleted pointer, an uninitialized pointer, and a NULL pointer. What happens when you run your program?

R7.21 Find the mistakes in the following code. Not all lines contain mistakes. Each line depends on the lines preceding it. Watch out for uninitialized pointers, NULL pointers, pointers to deleted objects, and confusing pointers with objects.

```
 1  int* p = new int;
 2  p = 5;
 3  *p = *p + 5;
 4  string s = "Harry";
 5  *s = "Sally";
 6  delete &s;
 7  int* a = new int[10];
 8  *a = 5;
 9  a[10] = 5;
10  delete a;
11  int* q;
12  *q = 5;
13  q = p;
14  delete q;
15  delete p;
```

R7.22 How do you define a triangular two-dimensional array using just vectors, not arrays or pointers?

R7.23 Rewrite the statements in Section 7.7.3 so that the street address and employee structures are allocated on the heap.

R7.24 Design a structure type Person that contains the name of a person and pointers to the person's father and mother. Write statements that define a structure value for yourself and your parents, correctly establishing the pointer links. (Use NULL for your parents' parents.)

R7.25 Draw a figure showing the result of a call to the maximum function in Exercise P7.4.

R7.26 Draw a figure showing the pointers in the lines array in Exercise P7.13 after reading a few lines.

R7.27 Section 7.6 described an arrangement where each item had a pointer to the user who had checked out the item. This makes it difficult to find out the items that a particular user checked out. To solve this problem, have an array of strings user_names and a parallel array loaned_items. loaned_items[i] points to an array of char* pointers, each of which is a name of an item that the ith user checked out. If the ith user didn't check out any items, then loaned_items[i] is NULL. Draw a picture of this arrangement.

PROGRAMMING EXERCISES

P7.1 Write a function

```
void sort2(double* p, double* p)
```

that receives two pointers and sorts the values to which they point. If you call

```
sort2(&x, &y)
```

then x <= y after the call.

P7.2 Write a function

```
double replace_if_greater(double* p, double x)
```

that replaces the value to which p points with x if x is greater. Return the old value to which p pointed.

P7.3 Write a function that computes the average value of an array of floating-point data:

```
double average(double* a, int size)
```

In the function, use a pointer variable, not an integer index, to traverse the array elements.

P7.4 Write a function that returns a pointer to the maximum value of an array of floating-point data:

```
double* maximum(double* a, int size)
```

If size is 0, return NULL.

P7.5 Write a function that reverses the values of an array of floating-point data:

```
void reverse(double* a, int size)
```

In the function, use two pointer variables, not integer indexes, to traverse the array elements.

P7.6 Implement the strncpy function of the standard library.

P7.7 Implement the standard library function

```
int strspn(const char s[], const char t[])
```

that returns the length of the initial portion of s consisting of the characters in t (in any order).

P7.8 Write a function

```
void reverse(char s[])
```

that reverses a character string. For example, "Harry" becomes "yrraH".

P7.9 Using the strncpy and strncat functions, implement a function

```
void safe_concat(const char a[], const char b[], char result[],
    int result_maxlength)
```

that concatenates the strings a and b to the buffer result. Be sure not to overrun the buffer. It can hold result_maxlength characters, not counting the '\0' terminator. (That is, the buffer has result_maxlength + 1 bytes available.)

P7.10 Write a function int* read_data(int& size) that reads data from cin until the user terminates input by entering Q. The function should set the size reference parameter to the number of numeric inputs. Return a pointer to an array on the heap. That array should have exactly size elements. Of course, you won't know at the outset how many elements the user will enter. Start with an array of 10 elements, and double the size whenever the array fills up. At the end, allocate an array of the correct size and copy all inputs into it. Be sure to delete any intermediate arrays.

P7.11 Enhance the Galton board simulation by printing a bar chart of the bottommost counters. Draw the bars vertically, below the last row of numbers.

```
 1  18  64 149 239 265 186  61  15   2
    *   *   *   *   *   *    *   *
        *   *   *   *   *    *
        *   *   *   *   *    *
            *   *   *   *
            *   *   *   *
            *   *   *   *
            *   *   *   *
                *   *   *
                *   *   *
                *   *
                *   *
                *   *
                    *
```

P7.12 Complete the copier simulation of How To 7.1 on page 334. Your program should first show the main menu:

```
U)ser A)dministrator Q)uit
```

For a user, prompt for the ID and the number of copies, increment the appropriate account, and return to the main menu.

For an administrator, show this menu:

```
B)alance M)aster P)roject
```

In the balance option, show the balances of the master account and the ten project accounts. In the master option, prompt for a user ID and link it to the master account. In the project option, prompt for user and project IDs. Afterward, return to the main menu.

P7.13 Write a program that reads lines of text and appends them to a char buffer[1000]. Stop after reading 1,000 characters. As you read in the text, replace all newline characters '\n' with '\0' terminators. Establish an array char* lines[100], so that the pointers in that array point to the beginnings of the lines in the text. Consider only 100 input lines if the input has more lines. Then display the lines in reverse order, starting with the last input line.

P7.14 The program in Exercise P7.13 is limited by the fact that it can only handle inputs of 1,000 characters or 100 lines. Remove this limitation as follows. Concatenate the input in one long string object. Use the c_str member function to obtain a char* into the string's character buffer. Store the beginnings of the lines as a vector<char*>.

P7.15 Exercise P7.14 demonstrated how to use the string and vector classes to implement resizable arrays. In this exercise, you should implement that capability manually. Allocate a buffer of 1,000 characters from the heap (new char[1000]). Whenever the buffer fills up, allocate a buffer of twice the size, copy the buffer contents, and delete the old buffer. Do the same for the array of char* pointers—start with a new char*[100] and keep doubling the size.

P7.16 Modify Exercise P7.13 so that you first print the lines in the order that they were entered, then print them in sorted order. When you sort the lines, only rearrange the pointers in the lines array.

P7.17 When you read a long document, there is a good chance that many words occur multiple times. Instead of storing each word, it may be beneficial to only store unique words, and to represent the document as a vector of pointers to the unique words. Write a program that implements this strategy. Read a word at a time from cin. Keep a vector<char*> of words. If the new word is not contained in this vector, allocate memory, copy the word into it, and append a pointer to the new memory. If the word is already present, then append a pointer to the existing word.

P7.18 Define a structure Student with a name and a vector<Course*> of courses. Define a structure Course with a name and a vector<Student*> of enrolled students.

Define a function void print_student(Student* s) that prints the name of a student and the names of all courses that the student takes. Define a function void print_course(Course* c) that prints the name of a course and the names of all students in that course.

Define a function void enroll(Student* s, Course* c) that enrolls the given student in the given course, updating both vectors.

In your main function, define several students and courses, and enroll students in the courses. Then call print_student for all students and print_course for all courses.

Engineering P7.19 Write a program that simulates a device that gathers measurements and processes them.

A gather function gathers data values (which you should simulate with random integers between 0 and 100) and places them in an array. When the array is full, the gather function calls a function new_array to request a new array to fill.

A process function processes a data value (for this exercise, it simply updates global variables for computing the maximum, minimum, and average). When it has reached the end of the array, it calls a function next_array to request a new array to process.

Because the gather function may fill arrays faster than the process function processes them, store the pointers to the filled arrays in another array. The new_array and next_array functions need to maintain that array of pointers.

In a real device, data gathering and processing happen in parallel. Simulate this by calling the gather and process functions randomly from main.

Engineering P7.20 Write a program that simulates the control software for a "people mover" system, a set of driverless trains that move in two concentric circular tracks. A set of switches allows trains to switch tracks.

In your program, the outer and inner tracks should each be divided into ten segments. Each track segment can contain a train that moves either clockwise or counterclockwise. A train moves to an adjacent segment in its track or, if that segment is occupied, to the adjacent segment in the other track.

Define a Segment structure. Each segment has a pointer to the next and previous segments in its track, a pointer to the next and previous segments in the other track, and a train indicator that is 0 (empty), +1 (train moving clockwise), or –1 (train moving counterclockwise). Populate the system with four trains at random segments, two in each direction. Display the tracks and trains in each step, like this:

```
+--------------->--+
|  x  x  x  x  x  |
|  ----------<----  |
|  |              |  |
|  ->--<----------  |
|  x  x  x  x  x  |
+-----------------+
```

The two rectangles indicate the tracks. Each switch that allows a train to switch between the outer and inner track is indicated by an x. Each train is drawn as a > or <, indicating its current direction. Your program should show fifty rounds. In each round, all trains move once.

ANSWERS TO SELF-CHECK QUESTIONS

1. 1
2

2. 2 2

3. 30

4. 25

5. 15 followed by the memory address of the variable a. The address can differ from one program run to the next.

6. 2 0 5

7. 2 3 0

8. 2 3 5

9. 4 5

10. `void squares(int n, int* result)`

11. 15: `'H''e''l''l''o'',' ' 'W''o''r''l''d''!''\n''\0'`

12. 14. The null terminator is not counted, and `'\n'` counts as a single character.

13. `char* p = "Hello";`

14. The statement compiles, but it has a disastrous effect. The type of `"Agent"` is a `char*`. It is legal to add an integer to a `char*`. The result is a pointer that is seven characters away from the start of the array. The array only contains 6 characters, so the result points to some other part of memory. The `title` string will be constructed with whatever characters are found there, until a zero is encountered. The result is unpredictable.

15. `int number = atoi(input.c_str());`

16. 3

17. 0 1 4

18. The access `p[10]` is illegal; the returned array has elements with index 0 … 9.

19. `p` points to an array of size 10 with elements 2, 3, 5, 7, 11, 0, 0, 0, 0, 0.

20. Call `delete[]` on the returned pointer after it is no longer needed.

21. Then the first row would have had 0 elements and the last row would have had 9 elements.

22. The program will compile. `counts[1]` is an `int*` pointer, and it is legal to apply `[2]`. `counts[1][2]` will access the memory address `counts[1] + 2`, which unfortunately points to some other memory. That memory will be overwritten, and it is not possible to predict the effect.

23.
```
int* triangular_array[10];
for (int i = 0; i < 10; i++)
{
    triangular_array[i] = new int[10 - i];
}
```

24. Include the `<vector>` header and replace the declaration of counts with `vector<int*> counts(10)`. The remainder of the program need not change.

25. Change the declaration of counts to `vector<int> counts[10]`. Change the row allocation loop body to

```
counts[i] = vector<int>(i + 1);
```

Drop the deallocation loop.

26.

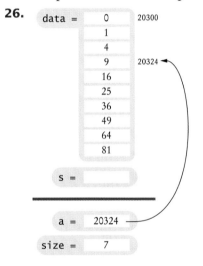

27.

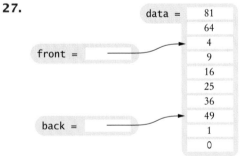

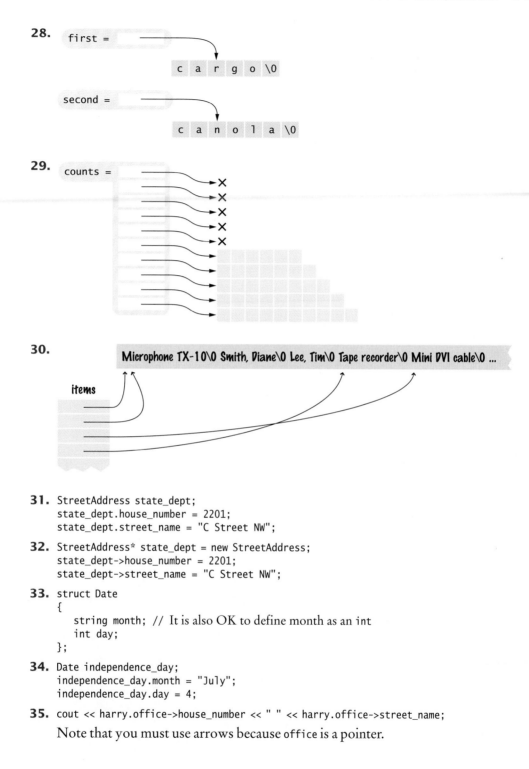

28.

first =

c a r g o \0

second =

c a n o l a \0

29.

counts =

30.

Microphone TX-10\0 Smith, Diane\0 Lee, Tim\0 Tape recorder\0 Mini DVI cable\0 ...

items

31.
```
StreetAddress state_dept;
state_dept.house_number = 2201;
state_dept.street_name = "C Street NW";
```

32.
```
StreetAddress* state_dept = new StreetAddress;
state_dept->house_number = 2201;
state_dept->street_name = "C Street NW";
```

33.
```
struct Date
{
    string month; // It is also OK to define month as an int
    int day;
};
```

34.
```
Date independence_day;
independence_day.month = "July";
independence_day.day = 4;
```

35.
```
cout << harry.office->house_number << " " << harry.office->street_name;
```
Note that you must use arrows because office is a pointer.

To be able to read and write files

To convert between strings and numbers
using string streams

To process command line arguments

To understand the concepts of sequential and random access

In this chapter, you will learn how to read and write files using the C++ stream library—a very useful skill for processing real world data. As an application, you will learn how to encrypt data. (The Enigma machine shown at left is an encryption device used by Germany in World War II. Pioneering British computer scientists broke the code and were able to intercept encoded messages, which was a significant help in winning the war.) Later in the chapter, you will learn to process binary files, such as those that store image data.

8.1 Reading and Writing Text Files

The C++ input/output library is based on the concept of **streams**. An *input stream* is a source of data, and an *output stream* is a destination for data. The most common sources and destinations for data are the files on your hard disk.

Data arrive in an input stream just like items on a conveyor belt, one at a time.

> To read or write files, you use variables of type fstream, ifstream, or ofstream.

To access a file, you use a file stream. There are three types of file streams: ifstream (for input), ofstream (for output), and fstream (for both input and output). Include the <fstream> header when you use any of these file streams.

In the following sections, you will learn how to process data from files. File processing is a very useful skill in many disciplines because it is exceedingly common to analyze large data sets stored in files.

8.1.1 Opening a Stream

To read anything from a file stream, you need to *open* it. When you open a stream, you give the name of the file stored on disk. Suppose you want to read data from a file named input.dat, located in the same directory as the program. Then you use the following function call to open the file:

```
in_file.open("input.dat");
```

This statement associates the variable in_file with the file named input.dat.

Note that all streams are objects, and you use the dot notation for calling functions that manipulate them.

> When opening a file stream, you supply the name of the file stored on disk.

To open a file for writing, you use an ofstream variable. To open the same file for both reading and writing, you use an fstream variable.

File names can contain directory path information, such as

```
~/homework/input.dat (UNIX)
c:\homework\input.dat (Windows)
```

When you specify the file name as a string literal, and the name contains backslash characters (as in a Windows filename), you must supply each backslash *twice*:

```
in_file.open("c:\\homework\\input.dat");
```

Recall that a single backslash inside a string literal is an **escape character** that is combined with another character to form a special meaning, such as \n for a newline character. The \\ combination denotes a single backslash.

If you want to pass a name that is stored in a string variable, use the c_str function to convert the C++ string to a C string:

```
cout << "Please enter the file name:";
string filename;
cin >> filename;
ifstream in_file;
in_file.open(filename.c_str());
```

When the program ends, all streams that you have opened will be automatically closed. You can also manually close a stream with the close member function:

```
in_file.close();
```

Manual closing is only necessary if you want to use the stream variable again to process another file.

8.1.2 Reading from a File

Read from a file stream with the same operations that you use with cin.

Reading data from a file stream is completely straightforward: You simply use the same functions that you have always used for reading from cin:

```
string name;
double value;
in_file >> name >> value;
```

The fail function tells you whether input has failed. You have already used this function with cin, to check for errors in console input. File streams behave in the same way. When you try to read a number from a file, and the next data item is not a properly formatted number, then the stream fails. After reading data, you should test for success before processing:

```
if (!in_file.fail())
{
    Process input.
}
```

Alternatively, you can use the fact that the >> operator returns a "not failed" condition, allowing you to combine an input statement and a test:

```
if (in_file >> name >> value)
{
    Process input.
}
```

When you read input from a file, number format errors are not the only reason for failure. Suppose you have consumed all of the data contained in a file and try to read more items. A file stream enters the failed state, whereas cin would just wait for more

Syntax 8.1   Working with File Streams

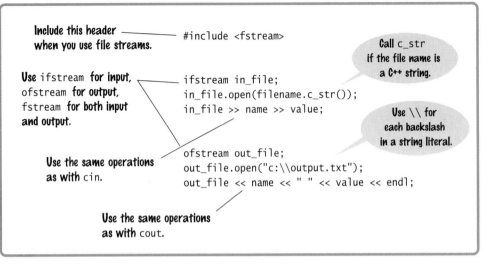

Include this header — #include <fstream>
when you use file streams.

Call c_str
if the file name is
a C++ string.

Use ifstream for input,
ofstream for output,
fstream for both input
and output.

```
ifstream in_file;
in_file.open(filename.c_str());
in_file >> name >> value;
```

Use \\ for
each backslash
in a string literal.

Use the same operations
as with cin.

```
ofstream out_file;
out_file.open("c:\\output.txt");
out_file << name << " " << value << endl;
```

Use the same operations
as with cout.

user input. Moreover, if you open a file and the name is invalid, or if there is no file of that name, then the file stream is also in a failed state. It is a good idea to test for failure immediately after calling open.

8.1.3 Writing to a File

Write to a file stream with the same operations that you use with cout.

In order to write to a file, you define an ofstream or fstream variable and open it. Then you send information to the output file, using the same operations that you used with cout:

```
ofstream out_file;
out_file.open("output.txt");
out_file << name << " " << value << endl;
```

8.1.4 A File Processing Example

Here is a typical example of processing data in a file. The Social Security Administration publishes lists of the most popular baby names on their web site, http://www.ssa.gov/OACT/babynames/. If you query the 1,000 most popular names for a given decade, the browser displays the result on the screen (see Figure 1).

To save the data as text, simply select it and paste the result into a file. This book's companion code contains a file called babynames.txt with the data for the 1990s.

Each line in the file contains seven entries:

- The rank (from 1 to 1,000)
- The name, frequency, and percentage of the male name of that rank
- The name, frequency, and percentage of the female name of that rank

For example, the line

```
10  Joseph  260365  1.2681  Megan  160312  0.8168
```

shows that the 10th most common boy's name was Joseph, with 260,365 births, or 1.2681 percent of all births during that period. The 10th most common girl's name was Megan. Why are there many more Josephs than Megans? Parents seem to use a wider set of girl's names, making each one of them less frequent.

Let us test that conjecture, by determining the names given to the top 50 percent of boys and girls in the list.

To process each line, we first read the rank:

```
int rank;
in_file >> rank;
```

We then read a set of three values for the boy's name:

```
string name;
int count;
double percent;
in_file >> name >> count >> percent;
```

Sellers of personalized items can find trends in popular names by processing data files from the Social Security Administration.

Then we repeat that step for girls. Because the actions are identical, we supply a helper function process_name for that purpose. To stop processing after reaching 50 percent, we can add up the frequencies and stop when they reach 50 percent. However, it turns out to be a bit simpler to initialize a total with 50 and subtract the frequencies. We need separate totals for boys and girls. When a total falls below 0, we stop printing. When both totals fall below 0, we stop reading.

Popular baby names of the 1990s - Mozilla Firefox 3 Beta 5

File Edit View History Bookmarks Tools Help

http://www.ssa.gov/OACT/babynames/decades/n

SocialSecurityOnline   **Popular Names**

www.socialsecurity.gov   Home   Questions?   Contact Us   Search   GO

Popular Baby Names   **Popular Baby Names By Decade**

Select another decade?
[Decade ▼] [Go]

Number of births

Most Popular 1000 Names of the 1990s

All names are from Social Security card applications for births that occurred in the United States. The data below were extracted from our records at the end of February 2000. See limitations of such data. The most popular 1000 names of the 1990s were taken from a universe that includes 20,531,547 male births and 19,627,269 female births.

Most Popular Names of the 1990s

	Male			Female		
Rank	Name	Number	Percent	Name	Number	Percent
1	Michael	462,085	2.2506	Jessica	302,962	1.5436
2	Christopher	361,250	1.7595	Ashley	301,702	1.5372
3	Matthew	351,477	1.7119	Emily	237,133	1.2082
4	Joshua	328,955	1.6022	Sarah	224,000	1.1413
5	Jacob	298,016	1.4515	Samantha	223,913	1.1408
6	Nicholas	275,222	1.3405	Amanda	190,901	0.9726
7	Andrew	272,600	1.3277	Brittany	190,779	0.9720
8	Daniel	271,734	1.3235	Elizabeth	172,383	0.8783
9	Tyler	262,218	1.2771	Taylor	168,977	0.8609
10	Joseph	260,365	1.2681	Megan	160,312	0.8168
11	Brandon	259,299	1.2629	Hannah	158,647	0.8083
12	David	253,193	1.2332	Kayla	155,844	0.7940

Done   Adblock

Figure 1   Querying Baby Names

Note that the `in_file` parameter variable of the `process_name` function in the code below is a reference parameter. Reading or writing modifies a stream variable. The stream variable monitors how many characters have been read or written so far. Any read or write operation changes that data. For that reason, you must always make stream parameter variables reference parameters.

The complete program is shown below. As you can see, reading from a file is just as easy as reading keyboard input.

Have a look at the program output. Remarkably, only 69 boy names and 153 girl names account for half of all births. That's good news for those who are in the business of producing personalized doodads. Exercise P8.10 asks you to study how this distribution has changed over the years.

ch08/babynames.cpp

```
1   #include <iostream>
2   #include <fstream>
3   #include <string>
4
5   using namespace std;
6
7   /**
8      Reads name information, prints the name if total >= 0, and adjusts the total.
9      @param in_file the input stream
10     @param total the total percentage that should still be processed
11  */
12  void process_name(ifstream& in_file, double& total)
13  {
14     string name;
15     int count;
16     double percent;
17     in_file >> name >> count >> percent;
18
19     if (in_file.fail()) { return; } // Check for failure after each input
20     if (total > 0) { cout << name << " "; }
21     total = total - percent;
22  }
23
24  int main()
25  {
26     ifstream in_file;
27     in_file.open("babynames.txt");
28     if (in_file.fail()) { return 0; } // Check for failure after opening
29
30     double boy_total = 50;
31     double girl_total = 50;
32
33     while (boy_total > 0 || girl_total > 0)
34     {
35        int rank;
36        in_file >> rank;
37        if (in_file.fail()) { return 0; }
38
39        cout << rank << " ";
40
41        process_name(in_file, boy_total);
42        process_name(in_file, girl_total);
43
```

```
44        cout << endl;
45     }
46
47     return 0;
48  }
```

Program Run

```
1 Michael Jessica
2 Christopher Ashley
3 Matthew Emily
4 Joshua Sarah
5 Jacob Samantha
6 Nicholas Amanda
7 Andrew Brittany
8 Daniel Elizabeth
9 Tyler Taylor
10 Joseph Megan
...
68 Dustin Gabrielle
69 Noah Katie
70 Caitlin
71 Lindsey
...
150 Hayley
151 Rebekah
152 Jocelyn
153 Cassidy
```

SELF CHECK

1. What happens if you call in_file.open("")?

2. What is wrong with the following code?
   ```
   ifstream out_file;
   out_file.open("output.txt");
   out_file << "Hello, World!" << endl;
   ```

3. What is wrong with the following function?
   ```
   double sum(ifstream in)
   {
      double total = 0;
      double input;
      while (in >> input) { total = total + input; }
      return total;
   }
   ```

4. How do you modify the babynames.cpp program so that you get the most common names that make up 10 percent of the population?

5. How do you modify the babynames.cpp program so that the program output is saved to a file 00?

Practice It   Now you can try these exercises at the end of the chapter: R8.3, R8.6, P8.1.

8.2 Reading Text Input

In the following sections, you will learn how to process text with complex contents such as that which often occurs in real-life situations.

8.2.1 Reading Words

When reading a string with the >> operator, the white space between words is consumed.

You already know how to read the next word from a stream, using the >> operator.

```
string word;
in_file >> word;
```

Here is precisely what happens when that operation is executed. First, any input characters that are white space are removed from the stream, but they are not added to the word. White space includes spaces, tab characters, and the newline characters that separate lines. The first character that is not white space becomes the first character in the string word. More characters are added until either another white space character occurs, or the end of the file has been reached. The white space after the word is not removed from the stream.

8.2.2 Reading Characters

You can get individual characters from a stream and unget the last one.

Instead of reading an entire word, you can read one character at a time by calling the get function:

```
char ch;
in_file.get(ch);
```

The get function returns the "not failed" condition. The following loop processes all characters in a file:

```
while (in_file.get(ch))
{
    Process the character ch.
}
```

The get function reads white space characters. This is useful if you need to process characters such as spaces, tabs, or newlines. On the other hand, if you are not interested in white space, use the >> operator instead.

```
in_file >> ch; // ch is set to the next non-white space character
```

If you read a character and you regretted it, you can *unget* it, so that the next input operation can read it again. However, you can unget only the last character. This is called *one-character lookahead.* You get a chance to look at the next character in the input stream, and you can make a decision whether you want to consume it or put it back.

A typical situation for lookahead is to look for numbers:

```
char ch;
in_file.get(ch);
if (isdigit(ch))
{
    in_file.unget(); // Put the digit back so that it is part of the number
    int n;
    data >> n; // Read integer starting with ch
}
```

If you read a character from a stream and you don't like what you get, you can unget it.

The isdigit function is one of several useful functions that categorize characters—see Table 1. All return true or false as to whether the argument passes the test. You must include the <cctype> header to use these functions.

8.2.3 Reading Lines

You can read a line of input with the getline function and then process it further.

When each line of a file is a data record, it is often best to read entire lines with the getline function:

```
string line;
getline(in_file, line);
```

The next input line (without the newline character) is placed into the string line.

The getline function returns the "not failed" condition. You can use the following loop to process each line in a file:

```
while (getline(in_file, line))
{
    Process line.
}
```

Note that getline is not a member function, but an ordinary function that is not called with the dot notation.

Table 1 Character Functions in <cctype>	
Function	Accepted Characters
isdigit	0 ... 9
isalpha	a ... z, A ... Z
islower	a ... z
isupper	A ... Z
isalnum	a ... z, A ... Z, 0 ... 9
isspace	White space (space, tab, newline, and the rarely used carriage return, form feed, and vertical tab)

Here is a typical example of processing lines in a file. A file with population data from the CIA World Factbook site (https://www.cia.gov/library/publications/the-world-factbook/index.html) contains lines such as the following:

```
China    1330044605
India    1147995898
United States 303824646
...
```

Because each line is a data record, it is natural to use the `getline` function for reading lines into a string variable. To extract the data from that string, you need to find out where the name ends and the number starts.

Locate the first digit:

```
int i = 0;
while (!isdigit(line[i])) { i++; }
```

Then go backward and skip white space:

```
int j = i - 1;
while (isspace(line[j])) { j--; }
```

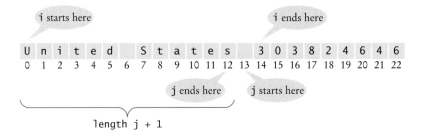

Finally, extract the country name and population:

```
string country_name = line.substr(0, j + 1);
string population = line.substr(i);
```

There is just one problem. The population is stored in a string, not a number. You will see in Section 8.4 how to extract the population number using streams.

SELF CHECK

6. Suppose the input stream contains the characters `6,995.0`. What is the value of `number` and `ch` after these statements?

```
int number;
char ch;
in_file >> number;
in_file.get(ch);
```

7. Suppose the input stream contains the characters `Hello, World!`. What is the value of `word` and `ch` after these statements?

```
string word;
char ch;
in_file >> word >> ch;
if (isupper(ch)) { in_file.unget(); in_file >> word; }
```

8. Your input file contains a sequence of numbers, but sometimes a value is not available and marked as `N/A`. How can you read the numbers and skip over the markers?

9. What is the effect of the following loop?

```
char ch;
while (in_file.get(ch) && isspace(ch)) { }
in_file.unget();
```

10. Why can't you simply read the population data file with the following loop?

```
while (in_file >> country_name >> population)
{
    Process country name and population.
}
```

Practice It   Now you can try these exercises at the end of the chapter: P8.6, P8.7, P8.9.

8.3 Writing Text Output

You use the >> operator to send strings and numbers to a stream. To write a single character to a stream, use

```
out_file.put(ch);
```

To control how the output is formatted, you use stream *manipulators*. A manipulator is a value that affects the behavior of the stream. It is sent to a stream using the << operator. The setw manipulator, which you have already used, is a typical example. The statement

```
out_file << setw(10);
```

> Use the setw manipulator to set the width of the next output.

does not cause any immediate output, but when the next item is written, it is padded with sufficient spaces so that the output spans ten characters. (If a value does not fit into the given width, it is not truncated.)

Occasionally, you need to pad numbers with leading zeroes, for example to print hours and minutes as 09:01. This is achieved with the setfill manipulator:

```
out_file << setfill('0') << setw(2) << hours
    << ":" << setw(2) << minutes << setfill(' ');
```

Now, a zero is used to pad the field. Afterward, the space is restored as the fill character.

By default, the fill characters appear before the item:

```
out_file << setw(10) << 123 << endl << setw(10) << 4567;
```

produces

```
       123
      4567
```

A manipulator is like a control button on a sound mixer. It doesn't produce an output, but it affects how the output looks.

The numbers line up to the right. That alignment works well for numbers, but not for strings. Usually, you want strings to line up at the left. You use the `left` and `right` manipulators to set the alignment. The following example uses left alignment for a string and then switches back to right alignment for a number:

```
out_file << left << setw(10) << word << right << setw(10) << number;
```

The default format for floating-point numbers is called *general* format. That format displays as many digits as are specified by the *precision* (6 by default), switching to scientific notation for large and small numbers. For example,

```
out_file << 12.3456789 << " " << 123456789.0;
```

yields

```
12.3457 1.23457e+08
```

The *fixed* format prints all values with the same number of digits after the decimal point. In the fixed format, the same numbers are displayed as

```
12.345679 123456789.000000
```

Use the `fixed` manipulator to select that format, and the `setprecision` manipulator to change the precision.

For example,

```
out_file << fixed << setprecision(2) << 1.2 << " " << 1.235
```

yields

```
1.20 1.24
```

Use the fixed and setprecision manipulators to format floating-point numbers with a fixed number of digits after the decimal point.

		Table 2 **Stream Manipulators**	
Manipulator	Purpose	Example	Output

setw	Sets the field width of the next item only.	`out_file << setw(6) << 123 << endl`
		`        << 123 << endl`
		`        << setw(6) << 12345678;`
			123
			123
			12345678

setfill	Sets the fill character for padding a field. (The default character is a space.)	`out_file << setfill('0') << setw(6)` `        << 123;`	000123
left	Selects left alignment.	`out_file << left << setw(6) << 123;`	123
right	Selects right alignment (default).	`out_file << right << setw(6) << 123;`	123
fixed	Selects fixed format for floating-point numbers.	`double x = 123.4567;` `out_file << x << endl << fixed << x;`	123.457 123.456700

setprecision	Sets the number of significant digits for general format, the number of digits after the decimal point for fixed format.	`double x = 123.4567;`
		`out_file << fixed << x << endl`
		`        << setprecision(2) << x;`
			123.456700
			123.46

Table 2 summarizes the stream manipulators. Note that all manipulators set the state of the stream object for all subsequent operations, with the exception of setw. After each output operation, the field width is reset to 0. To use any of these manipulators, include the <iomanip> header.

SELF CHECK

11. What is the output of the following statement?

```
cout << fixed << 123456.0;
```

12. How do you change the statement so that the result is 123456.00?

13. What is the output of the following statement?

```
cout << setw(8) << setfill('0') << 123456;
```

14. What is the output of the following statement?

```
cout << setw(2) << setfill('0') << 123456;
```

15. Why doesn't the following statement sequence line up the numbers?

```
cout << setw(10) << setprecision(2) << fixed << 1.234 << endl << 56.7;
```

Practice It   Now you can try these exercises at the end of the chapter: R8.7, R8.8, P8.18.

8.4 String Streams

In the preceding sections, you saw how file streams read characters from a file and write characters to a file. The istringstream class reads characters from a string, and the ostringstream class writes characters to a string. That doesn't sound so exciting—we already know how to access and change the characters of a string. However, the string stream classes have the same **interface** as the other stream classes. In particular, you can use the familiar >> and << operators to read and write numbers that are contained in strings. For that reason, the istringstream and ostringstream classes are called *adapters*—they adapt strings to the stream interface. Include the <sstream> header when you use string streams.

Here is a typical example. Suppose the string date contains a date such as "January 24, 1973", and we want to separate it into month, day, and year. First, construct an istringstream object. Then use the str function to set the stream to the string that you want to read:

```
istringstream strm;
strm.str("January 24, 1973");
```

Like an adapter that converts your power plugs to international outlets, the string stream adapters allow you to access strings as streams.

Use an istringstream to convert the numbers inside a string to integers or floating-point numbers.

Next, simply use the >> operator to read the month name, the day, the comma separator, and the year:

```
string month;
int day;
string comma;
int year;
strm >> month >> day >> comma >> year;
```

Now month is "January", day is 24, and year is 1973. Note that this input statement yields day and year as *integers*. Had we taken the string apart with substr, we would have obtained only strings, not numbers.

In fact, converting strings that contain digits to their integer values is such a common operation that it is useful to write a helper function for this purpose:

```
int string_to_int(string s)
{
   istringstream strm;
   strm.str(s);
   int n = 0;
   strm >> n;
   return n;
}
```

For example, string_to_int("1973") is the *integer* 1973.

Use an ostringstream to convert numeric values to strings.

By writing to a string stream, you can convert integers or floating-point numbers to strings. First construct an ostringstream object:

```
ostringstream strm;
```

Next, use the << operator to add a number to the stream. The number is converted into a sequence of characters:

```
strm << fixed << setprecision(5) << 10.0 / 3;
```

Now the stream contains the string "3.33333". To obtain that string from the stream, call the str member function:

```
string output = strm.str();
```

You can build up more complex strings in the same way. Here we build a data string of the month, day, and year:

```
string month = "January";
int day = 24;
int year = 1973;
ostringstream strm;
strm << month << " " << day << ", " << year;
string output = strm.str();
```

Now output is the string "January 24, 1973". Note that we converted the *integers* day and year into a string. Again, converting an integer into a string is such a common operation that is useful to have a helper function for it:

```
string int_to_string(int n)
{
   ostringstream strm;
   strm << n;
   return strm.str();
}
```

For example, int_to_string(1973) is the string "1973".

SELF CHECK

16. What is the value of n after these statements?

    ```
    istrstream strm;
    strm.str("123,456");
    int n;
    int m;
    char ch;
    strm >> n >> ch >> m;
    n = 1000 * n + m;
    ```

17. What does string_to_int("123,456") return?

18. What does string_to_int("$123") return?

19. What is the value of strm.str() after these statements?

    ```
    ostringstream strm;
    strm << setprecision(5) << 10.0 / 3;
    ```

20. Write a function that converts a floating-point number to a string. Provide a parameter variable for the number of digits after the decimal point.

Practice It Now you can try these exercises at the end of the chapter: R8.9, P8.10, P8.13.

8.5 Command Line Arguments

Depending on the operating system and C++ development environment used, there are different methods of starting a program—for example, by selecting "Run" in the compilation environment, by clicking on an icon, or by typing the name of the program at a prompt in a command shell window. The latter method is called "invoking the program from the command line". When you use this method, you must type the name of the program, of course, but you can also type in additional information that the program can use. These additional strings are called **command line arguments**. For example, if you start a program with the command line

    prog -v input.dat

then the program receives two command line arguments: the strings "-v" and "input. dat". It is entirely up to the program what to do with these strings. It is customary to interpret strings starting with a hyphen (-) as options and other strings as file names.

To receive command line arguments, you need to define the main function in a different way. You define two parameter variables: an integer and an array of string literals of type char*.

> Programs that start from the command line can receive the name of the program and the command line arguments in the main function.

    int main(int argc, char* argv[])
    {
        ...
    }

Here argc is the count of arguments, and argv contains the values of the arguments. In our example, argc is 3, and argv contains the three strings

    argv[0]:   "prog"
    argv[1]:   "-v"
    argv[2]:   "input.dat"

Note that argv[0] is always the name of the program and that argc is always at least 1.

Plain text	M	e	e	t		m	e		a	t		t	h	e	
Encrypted text	P	h	h	w	#	p	h	#	d	w	#	w	k	h	#

Figure 2 Caesar Cipher

Let's write a program that *encrypts* a file—that is, scrambles it so that it is unreadable except to those who know the decryption method. Ignoring 2,000 years of progress in the field of encryption, we will use a method familiar to Julius Caesar, replacing an A with a D, a B with an E, and so on. That is, each character *c* is replaced with $c + 3$ (see Figure 2).

The program takes the following command line arguments:

- An optional -d flag to indicate decryption instead of encryption
- The input file name
- The output file name

For example,

    caesar input.txt encrypt.txt

encrypts the file input.txt and places the result into encrypt.txt.

    caesar -d encrypt.txt output.txt

decrypts the file encrypt.txt and places the result into output.txt.

The emperor Julius Caesar used a simple scheme to encrypt messages.

ch08/caesar.cpp

```
1   #include <iostream>
2   #include <fstream>
3   #include <string>
4   #include <sstream>
5
6   using namespace std;
7
8   /**
9      Encrypts a stream using the Caesar cipher.
10     @param in the stream to read from
11     @param out the stream to write to
12     @param k the encryption key
13  */
14  void encrypt_file(ifstream& in, ofstream& out, int k)
15  {
16     char ch;
17     while (in.get(ch))
18     {
19        out.put(ch + k);
20     }
21  }
22
```

```
23   int main(int argc, char* argv[])
24   {
25      int key = 3;
26      int file_count = 0; // The number of files specified
27      ifstream in_file;
28      ofstream out_file;
29
30      for (int i = 1; i < argc; i++) // Process all command-line arguments
31      {
32         string arg = argv[i]; // The currently processed argument
33         if (arg == "-d") // The decryption option
34         {
35            key = -3;
36         }
37         else // It is a file name
38         {
39            file_count++;
40            if (file_count == 1) // The first file name
41            {
42               in_file.open(arg.c_str());
43               if (in_file.fail()) // Exit the program if opening failed
44               {
45                  cout << "Error opening input file " << arg << endl;
46                  return 1;
47               }
48            }
49            else if (file_count == 2) // The second file name
50            {
51               out_file.open(arg.c_str());
52               if (out_file.fail())
53               {
54                  cout << "Error opening output file " << arg << endl;
55                  return 1;
56               }
57            }
58         }
59      }
60
61      if (file_count != 2) // Exit if the user didn't specify two files
62      {
63         cout << "Usage: " << argv[0] << " [-d] infile outfile" << endl;
64         return 1;
65      }
66
67      encrypt_file(in_file, out_file, key);
68      return 0;
69   }
```

SELF CHECK

21. If the program is invoked with caesar -d encrypt.txt, what is argc, and what are the elements of argv?

22. Trace the program when it is invoked as described in Self Check 21.

23. Encrypt CAESAR using the Caesar cipher.

24. What does the program do with spaces?

Practice It   Now you can try these exercises at the end of the chapter: R8.11, P8.5, P8.17.

Random Fact 8.1 Encryption Algorithms

The exercises at the end of this chapter give a few algorithms to encrypt text. Don't actually use any of those methods to send secret messages to your lover. Any skilled cryptographer can *break* these schemes in a very short time—that is, reconstruct the original text without knowing the secret keyword.

In 1978 Ron Rivest, Adi Shamir, and Leonard Adleman introduced an encryption method that is much more powerful. The method is called *RSA encryption*, after the last names of its inventors. The exact scheme is too complicated to present here, but it is not actually difficult to follow. You can find the details in http://theory.lcs.mit.edu/~rivest/rsapaper.pdf.

RSA is a remarkable encryption method. There are two keys: a public key and a private key. (See the figure.) You can print the public key on your business card (or in your e-mail signature block) and give it to anyone. Then anyone can send you messages that only you can decrypt. Even though everyone else knows the public key, and even if they intercept all the messages coming to you, they cannot break the scheme and actually read the messages. In 1994, hundreds of researchers, collaborating over the Internet, cracked an RSA message encrypted with a 129-digit key. Messages encrypted with a key of 230 digits or more are expected to be secure.

The inventors of the algorithm obtained a *patent* for it. A patent is a deal that society makes with an inventor. For a period of 20 years, the inventor has an exclusive right for its commercialization, may collect royalties from others wishing to manufacture the invention, and may even stop competitors from using it altogether. In return, the inventor must publish the invention, so that others may learn from it, and must relinquish all claim to it after the monopoly period ends. The presumption is that in the absence of patent law, inventors would be reluctant to go through the trouble of inventing, or they would try to cloak their techniques to prevent others from copying their devices.

There has been some controversy about the RSA patent. Had there not been patent protection, would the inventors have published the method anyway, thereby giving the benefit to society without the cost of the 20-year monopoly? In this case, the answer is probably yes. The inventors were academic researchers, who live on salaries rather than sales receipts and are usually rewarded for their discoveries by a boost in their reputation and careers. Would their followers have been as active in discovering (and patenting) improvements? There is no way of knowing, of course. Is an algorithm even patentable, or is it a mathematical fact that belongs to nobody? The patent office did take the latter attitude for a long time. The RSA inventors and many others described their inventions in terms of imaginary electronic devices, rather than algorithms, to circumvent that restriction. Nowadays, the patent office will award software patents.

There is another interesting aspect to the RSA story. A programmer, Phil Zimmermann, developed a program called PGP (for *Pretty Good Privacy*) that is based on RSA. Anyone can use the program to encrypt messages, and decryption is not feasible even with the most powerful computers. You can get a copy of a free PGP implementation from the GNU project (http://www.gnupg.org). The existence of strong encryption methods bothers the United States government to no end. Criminals and foreign agents can send communications that the police and intelligence agencies cannot decipher. The government considered charging Zimmermann with breaching a law that forbids the unauthorized export of munitions, arguing that he should have known that his program would appear on the Internet. There have been serious proposals to make it illegal for private citizens to use these encryption methods, or to keep the keys secret from law enforcement.

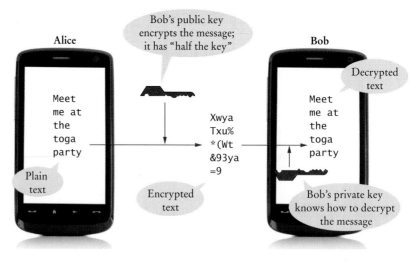

Public-Key Encryption

HOW TO 8.1

Processing Text Files

Processing text files that contain real data can be surprisingly challenging. This How To gives you step-by-step guidance.

As an example, we will consider this task: Read two country data files, worldpop.txt and worldarea.txt (supplied with the book's companion code). Both files contain the same countries in the same order. Write a file world_pop_density.txt that contains country names and population densities (people per square km), with the country names aligned left and the numbers aligned right:

```
Afghanistan            50.56
Akrotiri              127.64
Albania               125.91
Algeria                14.18
American Samoa        288.92
. . .
```

Singapore is one of the most densely populated countries in the world.

Step 1   Understand the processing task.

As always, you need to have a clear understanding of the task before designing a solution. Can you carry out the task by hand (perhaps with smaller input files)? If not, get more information about the problem.

The following pseudocode describes our processing task:

> While there are more lines to be read
>   Read a line from each file.
>   Extract the country name.
>   population = number following the country name in the first line
>   area = number following the country name in the second line
>   If area != 0
>   density = population / area
>   Print country name and density.

Step 2   Determine which files you need to read and write.

This should be clear from the problem. In our example, there are two input files, the population data and the area data, and one output file.

Step 3   Choose a method for obtaining the file names.

There are three options:

- Hard-coding the file names (such as "worldpop.txt")
- Asking the user:
  ```
  cout << "Enter filename: ";
  cin >> filename;
  in_file.open(filename.c_str());
  ```
- Using command-line arguments for the file names

In our example, we use hard-coded file names for simplicity.

Step 4   Choose between line, word, and character-based input.

As a rule of thumb, read lines if the input data is grouped by lines. That is the case with tabular data, as in our example, or when you need to report line numbers.

When gathering data that can be distributed over several lines, then it makes more sense to read words. Keep in mind that you lose all white space when you read words.

Reading characters is mostly useful for tasks that require access to individual characters. Examples include analyzing character frequencies, changing tabs to spaces, or encryption.

Step 5   With line-oriented input, extract the required data.

It is simple to read a line of input with the `getline` function. Then you need to get the data out of that line. You can extract substrings, as described in Section 8.2. Alternatively, you can turn the line into an `istringstream` and extract its components with the `>>` operator. The latter approach is easier when the number of items on each line is constant. In our example, that is not the case—country names can consist of more than one string. Therefore, we choose to extract substrings from each input line.

If you need any of the substrings as numbers, you must convert them (see Section 8.4).

Step 6   Place repeatedly occurring tasks into functions.

Processing input files usually has repetitive tasks, such as skipping over white space or extracting numbers from strings. It really pays off to develop a set of functions to handle these tedious operations.

In our example, we have a common task that calls for a helper function: extracting the country name and the value that follows. This task can be implemented in a helper function

```
void read_line(string line, string& country, double& value)
```

We also need a helper function `string_to_double` to convert the population and area values to floating-point numbers. This function is similar to `string_to_int` that was developed in Section 8.4.

Step 7   If required, use manipulators to format the output.

If you are asked to format your output, use manipulators, as described in Section 8.3. Usually, you want to switch to fixed format for the output and set the precision. Then use `setw` before every value, and use `left` for aligning strings and `right` for aligning numbers:

```
out << setw(40) << left << country << setw(15) << right << density << endl;
```

Here is the complete program:

ch08/popdensity.cpp

```
 1   #include <cctype>
 2   #include <fstream>
 3   #include <iostream>
 4   #include <iomanip>
 5   #include <sstream>
 6   #include <string>
 7
 8   using namespace std;
 9
10   /**
11       Converts a string to a floating-point number, e.g. "3.14" -> 3.14.
12       @param s a string representing a floating-point number
13       @return the equivalent floating-point number
14   */
15   double string_to_double(string s)
16   {
17       istringstream stream;
18       stream.str(s);
19       double x = 0;
```

```
20        stream >> x;
21        return x;
22    }
23
24    /**
25        Extracts the country and associated value from an input line.
26        @param line a line containing a country name, followed by a number
27        @param country the string for holding the country name
28        @param value the variable for holding the associated value
29        @return true if a line has been read, false at the end of the stream
30    */
31    void read_line(string line, string& country, double& value)
32    {
33        int i = 0; // Locate the start of the first digit
34        while (!isdigit(line[i])) { i++; }
35        int j = i - 1; // Locate the end of the preceding word
36        while (isspace(line[j])) { j--; }
37
38        country = line.substr(0, j + 1); // Extract the country name
39        value = string_to_double(line.substr(i)); // Extract the number value
40    }
41
42    int main()
43    {
44        ifstream in1;
45        ifstream in2;
46        in1.open("worldpop.txt"); // Open input files
47        in2.open("worldarea.txt");
48
49        ofstream out;
50        out.open("world_pop_density.txt"); // Open output file
51        out << fixed << setprecision(2);
52
53        string line1;
54        string line2;
55
56        // Read lines from each file
57        while (getline(in1, line1) && getline(in2, line2))
58        {
59            string country;
60            double population;
61            double area;
62
63            // Split the lines into country and associated value
64            read_line(line1, country, population);
65            read_line(line2, country, area);
66
67            // Compute and print the population density
68            double density = 0;
69            if (area != 0) // Protect against division by zero
70            {
71                density = population * 1.0 / area;
72            }
73            out << setw(40) << left << country
74                << setw(15) << right << density << endl;
75        }
76
77        return 0;
78    }
```

Looking for for Duplicates

This Worked Example processes a file to locate lines that contain repeated words.

8.6 Random Access and Binary Files

In the following sections, you will learn how to read and write data at arbitrary positions in a file, and how to edit image files.

8.6.1 Random Access

> You can access any position in a random access file by moving the *file pointer* prior to a read or write operation.

So far, you've read from a file an item at a time and written to a file an item at a time, without skipping forward or backward. That access pattern is called **sequential access**. In many applications, we would like to access specific items in a file without first having to read all preceding items. This access pattern is called **random access** (see Figure 3). There is nothing "random" about random access—the term means that you can read and modify any item stored at any location in the file.

Only file streams support random access; the cin and cout streams, which are attached to the keyboard and the terminal, do not. Each file stream has two special positions: the *get* position and the *put* position (see Figure 4). These positions determine where the next character is read or written.

The following function calls move the get and put positions to a given value, counted from the beginning of the stream.

```
strm.seekg(position);
strm.seekp(position);
```

To determine the current values of the get and put positions (counted from the beginning of the file), use

```
position = strm.tellg();
position = strm.tellp();
```

8.6.2 Binary Files

Many files, in particular those containing images and sounds, do not store information as text but as binary numbers. The numbers are represented as sequences of

Figure 3 Sequential and Random Access

Figure 4 Get and Put Positions

At a sit-down dinner, food is served sequentially. At a buffet, you have "random access" to all food items.

bytes, just as they are in the memory of the computer. (Each byte is a value between 0 and 255.) In binary format, a floating-point number always occupies 8 bytes. We will study random access with a binary file format for images.

We have to cover a few technical issues about binary files. To open a binary file for reading and writing, use the following command:

```
fstream strm;
strm.open(filename, ios::in | ios::out | ios::binary);
```

You read a byte with the call

```
int input = strm.get();
```

This call returns a value between 0 and 255. To read an integer, read four bytes b_0, b_1, b_2, b_3 and combine them to $b_0 + b_1 \cdot 256 + b_2 \cdot 256^2 + b_3 \cdot 256^3$. We will supply a helper function for this task.

The >> operator cannot be used to read numbers from a binary file.

8.6.3 Processing Image Files

In this section, you will learn how to write a program for editing image files in the BMP format. Unlike the more common GIF, PNG, and JPEG formats, the BMP format is quite simple because it does not use data compression. As a consequence, BMP files are huge and you will rarely find them in the wild. However, image editors can convert any image into BMP format.

There are different versions of the BMP format; we will only cover the simplest and most common one, sometimes called the 24-bit true color format. In this format, each pixel is represented as a sequence of three bytes, one each for the blue, green, and red value. For example, the color cyan (a mixture of blue and green) is 255 255 0, red is 0 0 255, and medium gray is 128 128 128.

A BMP file starts with a header that contains various pieces of information. We only need the following items:

Position	Item
2	The size of this file in bytes
10	The start of the image data
18	The width of the image in pixels
22	The height of the image in pixels

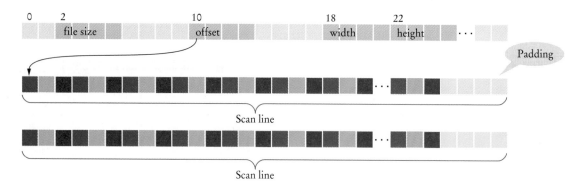

Figure 5 The BMP File Format for 24-bit True Color Images

The image is stored as a sequence of pixel rows, starting with the pixels of the bottommost row of the image. Each pixel row contains a sequence of blue/green/red triplets. The end of the row is padded with additional bytes so that the number of bytes in the row is divisible by 4. (See Figure 5.) For example, if a row consisted of merely three pixels, one cyan, one red, and one medium gray one, the row would be encoded as

255 255 0 0 0 255 128 128 128 x y z

where x y z are padding bytes to bring the row length up to 12, a multiple of 4. It is these little twists that make working with real-life file formats such a joyful experience.

The sample program at the end of this section reads every pixel of a BMP file and replaces it with its negative, turning white to black, cyan to red, and so on. The result is a negative image of the kind that old-fashioned film cameras used to produce (see Figure 6).

Figure 6 An Image and Its Negative

To try out this program, take one of your favorite images, use an image editor to convert to BMP format (or use queen-mary.bmp from the code files for this book), then run the program and view the transformed file in an image editor. Exercises P8.21 and P8.22 ask you to produce more interesting effects.

ch08/imagemod.cpp

```cpp
1   #include <iostream>
2   #include <fstream>
3   #include <cstdlib>
4
5   using namespace std;
6
7   /**
8       Processes a pixel by forming the negative.
9       @param blue  the blue value of the pixel
10      @param green  the green value of the pixel
11      @param red  the red value of the pixel
12  */
13  void process(int& blue, int& green, int& red)
14  {
15      blue = 255 - blue;
16      green = 255 - green;
17      red = 255 - red;
18  }
19
20  /**
21      Gets an integer from a binary stream.
22      @param stream  the stream
23      @param offset  the offset at which to read the integer
24      @return  the integer starting at the given offset
25  */
26  int get_int(fstream& stream, int offset)
27  {
28      stream.seekg(offset);
29      int result = 0;
30      int base = 1;
31      for (int i = 0; i < 4; i++)
32      {
33          result = result + stream.get() * base;
34          base = base * 256;
35      }
36      return result;
37  }
38
39  int main()
40  {
41      cout << "Please enter the file name: ";
42      string filename;
43      cin >> filename;
44
45      fstream stream;
46      // Open as a binary file
47      stream.open(filename.c_str(), ios::in | ios::out | ios::binary);
48
49      int file_size = get_int(stream, 2); // Get the image dimensions
50      int start = get_int(stream, 10);
51      int width = get_int(stream, 18);
52      int height = get_int(stream, 22);
```

```
53
54    // Scan lines must occupy multiples of four bytes
55    int scanline_size = width * 3;
56    int padding = 0;
57    if (scanline_size % 4 != 0)
58    {
59       padding = 4 - scanline_size % 4;
60    }
61
62    if (file_size != start + (scanline_size + padding) * height)
63    {
64       cout << "Not a 24-bit true color image file." << endl;
65       return 1;
66    }
67
68    stream.seekg(start); // Go to the start of the pixels
69
70    for (int i = 0; i < height; i++) // For each scan line
71    {
72       for (int j = 0; j < width; j++) // For each pixel
73       {
74          int pos = stream.tellg(); // Go to the start of the pixel
75
76          int blue = stream.get(); // Read the pixel
77          int green = stream.get();
78          int red = stream.get();
79
80          process(blue, green, red); // Process the pixel
81
82          stream.seekp(pos); // Go back to the start of the pixel
83
84          stream.put(blue); // Write the pixel
85          stream.put(green);
86          stream.put(red);
87       }
88
89       stream.seekg(padding, ios::cur); // Skip the padding
90    }
91
92    return 0;
93 }
```

SELF CHECK

25. In plain English, what does the following code segment do?
    ```
    strm.seekp(0);
    strm.put(0);
    ```

26. How would you modify the imagemod.cpp program to flip the green and blue values of each pixel for a psychedelic effect?

27. What happens if you run the imagemod.cpp program twice on the same image file?

28. Could we have implemented the image modification program with sequential access only? If not, why not?

29. Suppose a BMP file stores a 100 × 100 pixel image in BMP format, with the image data starting at offset 64. What is the total file size?

Practice It   Now you can try these exercises at the end of the chapter: R8.12, R8.13, P8.21.

Random Fact 8.2 Databases and Privacy

Most companies use computers to keep huge data files of customer records and other business information. Databases not only lower the cost of doing business; they improve the quality of service that companies can offer. Nowadays it is almost unimaginable how time-consuming it used to be to withdraw money from a bank branch or to make travel reservations.

Today most databases are organized according to the relational model. Suppose a company stores your orders and payments. They will probably not repeat your name and address on every order; that would take unnecessary space. Instead, they will keep one file of all their customer names and identify each customer by a unique customer number. Only that customer number, not the entire customer information, is kept with an order record.

To print an invoice, the database program must issue a query against both the customer and order files and pull the necessary information (name, address, articles ordered) from both. Frequently, queries involve more than two files. For example, the company may have a file of addresses of car owners and a file of people with good payment history and may want to find all of its customers who placed an order in the last month, drive an expensive car, and pay their bills, so they can send them another catalog. This kind of query is, of course, much faster if all customer files use the same key, which is why so many organizations in the United States try to collect the Social Security numbers of their customers.

The Social Security Act of 1935 provided that each contributor be assigned a Social Security number to track contributions into the Social Security Fund. These numbers have a distinctive format, such as 078-05-1120. (This particular number was printed on sample cards that were inserted in wallets. It actually was the Social Security number of the secretary of a vice president at the wallet manufacturer. When thousands of people used it as their own, the number was voided, and the secretary received a new number.) The figure at right shows a Social Security card. Although they had not originally been intended for use as a universal identification number, Social Security numbers have become just that.

Some people are very concerned about the fact that just about every organization wants to store their Social Security number and other personal information. There is the possibility that companies and the government can merge multiple databases and derive information about us that we may wish they did not have or that simply may be untrue. An insurance company may deny coverage, or charge a higher premium, if it finds that you have too many relatives with a certain disease. You may be denied a job because of an inaccurate credit or medical report, and you may not even know the reason. These are very disturbing developments that have had a very negative impact for a small but growing number of people.

In many industrialized countries (but not currently in the United States), citizens have a right to control what information about themselves should be communicated to others and under what circumstances.

Customers

Cust. #:	Name
11439	Doe, John

Orders

Order #:	Cust. #:	Item
59673	11439	DOS for Historians
59897	11439	Big C++
61013	11439	C++ for Everyone

Relational Database Files

SOCIAL SECURITY
078-05-1120
THIS NUMBER HAS BEEN ESTABLISHED FOR
JOHN DOE
SIGNATURE

Social Security Card

CHAPTER SUMMARY

Develop programs that read and write files.

- To read or write files, you use variables of type fstream, ifstream, or ofstream.
- When opening a file stream, you supply the name of the file stored on disk.
- Read from a file stream with the same operations that you use with cin.
- Write to a file stream with the same operations that you use with cout.
- Always use a reference parameter for a stream.

Be able to process text in files.

- When reading a string with the >> operator, the white space between words is consumed.
- You can get individual characters from a stream and unget the last one.
- You can read a line of input with the getline function and then process it further.

Write programs that neatly format their output.

- Use the setw manipulator to set the width of the next output.
- Use the fixed and setprecision manipulators to format floating-point numbers with a fixed number of digits after the decimal point.

Convert between strings and numbers.

- Use an istringstream to convert the numbers inside a string to integers or floating-point numbers.
- Use an ostringstream to convert numeric values to strings.

Process the command line arguments of a C++ program.

- Programs that start from the command line can receive the name of the program and the command line arguments in the main function.

Develop programs that read and write binary files.

- You can access any position in a random access file by moving the file pointer prior to a read or write operation.

REVIEW EXERCISES

R8.1 When do you open a file as an ifstream, as an ofstream, or as an fstream? Could you simply open all files as an fstream?

R8.2 What happens if you write to a file that you only opened for reading? Try it out if you don't know.

R8.3 What happens if you try to open a file for reading that doesn't exist? What happens if you try to open a file for writing that doesn't exist?

R8.4 What happens if you try to open a file for writing, but the file or device is write-protected (sometimes called read-only)? Try it out with a short test program.

R8.5 How do you open a file whose name contains a backslash, such as temp\output.dat or c:emp\output.dat?

R8.6 Why are the in and out parameter variables of the encrypt_file function in Section 8.5 reference parameters and not value parameters?

R8.7 Give an output statement to write a date and time in ISO 8601 format, such as

    2011-03-01 09:35

Assume that the date and time are given in five integer variables year, month, day, hour, minute.

R8.8 Give an output statement to write one line of a table containing a product description, quantity, unit price, and total price in dollars and cents. You want the columns to line up, like this:

Item	Qty	Price	Total
Toaster	3	$29.95	$89.85
Hair Dryer	1	$24.95	$24.95
Car Vacuum	2	$19.99	$39.98

R8.9 How can you convert the string "3.14" into the floating-point number 3.14? How can you convert the floating-point number 3.14 into the string "3.14"?

R8.10 What is a command line? How can a program read its command line?

R8.11 If a program woozle is started with the command

    woozle -DNAME=Piglet -I\eeyore -v heff.cpp a.cpp lump.cpp

what is the value of argc, and what are the values of argv[0], argv[1], and so on?

R8.12 What is the difference between sequential access and random access?

R8.13 What is the difference between a text file and a binary file?

R8.14 What are the get and put positions in a file? How do you move them? How do you tell their current positions?

R8.15 What happens if you try to move the get or put position past the end of a file? What happens if you try to move the get or put position of cin or cout? Try it out and report your results.

PROGRAMMING EXERCISES

P8.1 Write a program that carries out the following tasks:

> Open a file with the name hello.txt.
> Store the message "Hello, World!" in the file.
> Close the file.
> Open the same file again.
> Read the message into a string variable and print it.

P8.2 Write a program that reads a file containing floating-point numbers. Print the average of the numbers in the file. Prompt the user for the file name.

P8.3 Repeat Exercise P8.2, but allow the user to specify the file name on the command-line. If the user doesn't specify any file name, then prompt the user for the name.

P8.4 Write a program that reads a file containing two columns of floating-point numbers. Prompt the user for the file name. Print the average of each column.

P8.5 Write a program find that searches all files specified on the command line and prints out all lines containing a keyword. For example, if you call

```
find Tim report.txt address.txt homework.cpp
```

then the program might print

```
report.txt: discussed the results of my meeting with Tim T
address.txt: Torrey, Tim|11801 Trenton Court|Dallas|TX
address.txt: Walters, Winnie|59 Timothy Circle|Detroit|MI
homework.cpp: Time now;
```

The keyword is always the first command-line argument.

P8.6 Write a program that checks the spelling of all words in a file. It should read each word of a file and check whether it is contained in a word list. A word list is available on most UNIX systems (including Linux and Mac OS X) in the file /usr/share/dict/words. (If you don't have access to a UNIX system, you can find a copy of the file on the Internet by searching for /usr/share/dict/words.) The program should print out all words that it cannot find in the word list. Follow this pseudocode:

Open the dictionary file.
Define a vector of strings called words.
For each word in the dictionary file
    Append the word to the words vector.
Open the file to be checked.
For each word in that file
    If the word is not contained in the words vector
        Print the word.

P8.7 Write a program that reads each line in a file, reverses its characters, and writes the resulting line to another file. Suppose the user specifies input.txt and output.txt when prompted for the file names, and input.txt contains the lines

```
Mary had a little lamb
Its fleece was white as snow
And everywhere that Mary went
the lamb was sure to go.
```

After the program is finished, output.txt should contain

```
bmal elttil a dah yraM
wons sa etihw saw eceelf stI
tnew yraM taht erehwyreve dnA
.og ot erus saw bmal ehT
```

P8.8 Write a program that reads each line in a file, reverses its characters, and writes the resulting line to the same file. Use the following pseudocode:

While the end of the file has not been reached
    pos1 = current get position
    Read a line.

> If the line was successfully read
>   pos2 = current get position
>   Set put position to pos1.
>   Write the reversed line.
>   Set get position to pos2.

P8.9 Write a program that reads each line in a file, reverses its lines, and writes them to another file. Suppose the user specifies `input.txt` and `output.txt` when prompted for the file names, and `input.txt` contains the lines

```
Mary had a little lamb
Its fleece was white as snow
And everywhere that Mary went
The lamb was sure to go.
```

After the program is finished, `output.txt` should contain

```
The lamb was sure to go.
And everywhere that Mary went
Its fleece was white as snow
Mary had a little lamb
```

P8.10 Get the data for names in prior decades from the Social Security Administration. Paste the table data in files named `babynames80s.txt`, etc. Modify the `babynames.cpp` program so that it prompts the user for a file name. The numbers in the files have comma separators, so modify the program to handle them. Can you spot a trend in the frequencies?

P8.11 Write a program that reads in `babynames.txt` and produces two files, `boynames.txt` and `girlnames.txt`, separating the data for the boys and girls.

P8.12 Write a program that reads a file in the same format as `babynames.txt` and prints all names that are both boy and girl names (such as Alexis or Morgan).

P8.13 Write a program that reads the country data in the file `worldpop.txt` (included with the book's source code). Do not edit the file. Use the following algorithm for processing each line. Add non-white space characters to the country name. When you encounter a white space, locate the next non-white space character. If it is not a digit, add a space and that character to the country name. Otherwise unget it and read the number. Print the total of all country populations (excepting the entry for "European Union").

P8.14 Write a program that asks the user for a file name and displays the number of characters, words, and lines in that file. Then have the program ask for the name of the next file. When the user enters a file that doesn't exist (such as the empty string), the program should exit.

P8.15 Write a program `copyfile` that copies one file to another. The file names are specified on the command line. For example,

```
copyfile report.txt report.sav
```

P8.16 Write a program that **concatenates** the contents of several files into one file. For example,

```
catfiles chapter1.txt chapter2.txt chapter3.txt book.txt
```

makes a long file book.txt that contains the contents of the files chapter1.txt, chapter2.txt, and chapter3.txt. The target file is always the last file specified on the command line.

P8.17   *Random monoalphabet cipher.* The Caesar cipher, which shifts all letters by a fixed amount, is far too easy to crack. Here is a better idea. As the key, don't use numbers but words. Suppose the key word is FEATHER. Then first remove duplicate letters, yielding FEATHR, and append the other letters of the alphabet in reverse order:

F E A T H R Z Y X W V U S Q P O N M L K J I G D C B

Now encrypt the letters as follows:

A B C D E F G H I J K L M N O P Q R S T U V W X Y Z
↓ ↓
F E A T H R Z Y X W V U S Q P O N M L K J I G D C B

Write a program that encrypts or decrypts a file using this cipher. For example,

```
crypt -d -kFEATHER encrypt.txt output.txt
```

decrypts a file using the keyword FEATHER. It is an error not to supply a keyword.

P8.18   *Letter frequencies.* If you encrypt a file using the cipher of Exercise P8.17, it will have all of its letters jumbled up, and will look as if there is no hope of decrypting it without knowing the keyword. Guessing the keyword seems hopeless too. There are just too many possible keywords. However, someone who is trained in decryption will be able to break this cipher in no time at all. The average letter frequencies of English letters are well known. The most common letter is E, which occurs about 13 percent of the time. Here are the average frequencies of the letters.

A	8%	H	4%	O	7%	U	3%
B	<1%	I	7%	P	3%	V	<1%
C	3%	J	<1%	Q	<1%	W	2%
D	4%	K	<1%	R	8%	X	<1%
E	13%	L	4%	S	6%	Y	2%
F	3%	M	3%	T	9%	Z	<1%
G	2%	N	8%				

Write a program that reads an input file and displays the letter frequencies in that file. Such a tool will help a code breaker. If the most frequent letters in an encrypted file are H and K, then there is an excellent chance that they are the encryptions of E and T.

Show the result in a table such as the one above, and make sure the columns line up.

P8.19   *Vigenère cipher.* In order to defeat a simple letter frequency analysis, the Vigenère cipher encodes a letter into one of several cipher letters, depending on its position in the input document. Choose a keyword, for example TIGER. Then encode the first letter of the input text like this:

```
A B C D E F G H I J K L M N O P Q R S T U V W X Y Z
↓ ↓ ↓ ↓ ↓ ↓ ↓ ↓ ↓ ↓ ↓ ↓ ↓ ↓ ↓ ↓ ↓ ↓ ↓ ↓ ↓ ↓ ↓ ↓ ↓ ↓
T U V W X Y Z A B C D E F G H I J K L M N O P Q R S
```

The encoded alphabet is just the regular alphabet shifted to start at T, the first letter of the keyword TIGER. The second letter is encrypted according to the following map.

```
A B C D E F G H I J K L M N O P Q R S T U V W X Y Z
↓ ↓ ↓ ↓ ↓ ↓ ↓ ↓ ↓ ↓ ↓ ↓ ↓ ↓ ↓ ↓ ↓ ↓ ↓ ↓ ↓ ↓ ↓ ↓ ↓ ↓
I J K L M N O P Q R S T U V W X Y Z A B C D E F G H
```

The third, fourth, and fifth letters in the input text are encrypted using the alphabet sequences beginning with characters G, E, and R, and so on. Because the key is only five letters long, the sixth letter of the input text is encrypted in the same way as the first.

Write a program that encrypts or decrypts an input text according to this cipher.

P8.20 *Playfair cipher.* Another way of thwarting a simple letter frequency analysis of an encrypted text is to encrypt *pairs* of letters together. A simple scheme to do this is the Playfair cipher. You pick a keyword and remove duplicate letters from it. Then you fill the keyword, and the remaining letters of the alphabet, into a 5 × 5 square. (Since there are only 25 squares, I and J are considered the same letter.)

Here is such an arrangement with the keyword PLAYFAIR.

```
P L A Y F
I R B C D
E G H K M
N O Q S T
U V W X Z
```

To encrypt a letter pair, say AM, look at the rectangle with corners A and M:

```
P L A Y F
I R B C D
E G H K M
N O Q S T
U V W X Z
```

The encoding of this pair is formed by looking at the other two corners of the rectangle, in this case, FH. If both letters happen to be in the same row or column, such as GO, simply swap the two letters. Decryption is done in the same way.

Write a program that encrypts or decrypts an input text according to this cipher.

P8.21 Write a program that edits an image file and reduces the blue and green values by 30 percent, giving it a "sunset" effect.

P8.22 Write a program that edits an image file, turning it into grayscale.

Replace each pixel with a pixel that has the same grayness level for the blue, green, and red component. The grayness level is computed by adding 30 percent of the red level, 59 percent of the green level, and 11 percent of the blue level. (The color-sensing cone cells in the human eye differ in their sensitivity for red, green, and blue light.)

P8.23 *Junk mail.* Write a program that reads in two files: a *template* and a *database*. The template file contains text and tags. The tags have the form |1| |2| |3|… and need to be replaced with the first, second, third, … field in the current database record.

A typical database looks like this:

```
Mr.|Harry|Morgan|1105 Torre Ave.|Cupertino|CA|95014
Dr.|John|Lee|702 Ninth Street Apt. 4|San Jose|CA|95109
Miss|Evelyn|Garcia|1101 S. University Place|Ann Arbor|MI|48105
```

And here is a typical form letter:

```
To:
|1| |2| |3|
|4|
|5|, |6| |7|

Dear |1| |3|:

You and the |3| family may be the lucky winners of $10,000,000 in the C++ compiler
clearinghouse sweepstakes! ...
```

P8.24 Write a program that manipulates three database files. The first file contains the names and telephone numbers of a group of people. The second file contains the names and Social Security numbers of a group of people. The third file contains the Social Security numbers and annual income of a group of people. The groups of people should overlap but need not be completely identical. Your program should ask the user for a telephone number and then print the name, Social Security number, and annual income, if it can determine that information.

P8.25 Write a program that prints out a student grade report. There is a file, classes.txt, that contains the names of all classes taught at a college, such as

classes.txt

```
CSC1
CSC2
CSC46
CSC151
MTH121
...
```

For each class, there is a file with student ID numbers and grades:

csc2.txt

```
11234 A-
12547 B
16753 B+
21886 C
...
```

Write a program that asks for a student ID and prints out a grade report for that student, by searching all class files. Here is a sample report

```
Student ID 16753
CSC2 B+
MTH121 C+
CHN1 A
PHY50 A-
```

Engineering P8.26 After the switch in the figure below closes, the voltage (in volts) across the capacitor is represented by the equation

$$v(t) = B\left(1 - e^{-t/(RC)}\right)$$

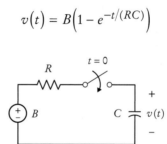

Suppose the parameters of the electric circuit are $B = 12$ volts, $R = 500\ \Omega$, and $C = 0.25\ \mu F$. Consequently

$$v(t) = 12\left(1 - e^{-0.008t}\right)$$

where t has units of μs. Read a file params.txt containing the values for B, R, C, and the starting and ending values for t. Write a file rc.txt of values for the time t and the corresponding capacitor voltage $v(t)$, where t goes from the given starting value to the given ending value in 100 steps. In our example, if t goes from 0 to 1,000 μs, the twelfth entry in the output file would be:

```
110   7.02261
```

Engineering P8.27 The figure below shows a plot of the capacitor voltage from the circuit shown in Exercise P8.26. The capacitor voltage increases from 0 volts to B volts. The "rise time" is defined as the time required for the capacitor voltage to change from $v_1 = 0.05 \times B$ to $v_2 = 0.95 \times B$.

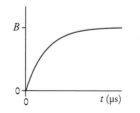

The file rc.txt contains a list of values of time t and the corresponding capacitor voltage $v(t)$. A time in μs and the corresponding voltage in volts are printed on the same line. For example, the line

110   7.02261

indicates that the capacitor voltage is 7.02261 volts when the time is 110 μs. The time is increasing in the data file.

Write a program that reads the file rc.txt and uses the data to calculate the rise time. Approximate B by the voltage in the last line of the file, and find the data points that are closest to $0.05 \times B$ and $0.95 \times B$.

Engineering P8.28 Suppose a file contains bond energies and bond lengths for covalent bonds in the following format:

Single, double, or triple bond	Bond energy (kJ/mol)	Bond length (nm)
C|C	370	0.154
C||C	680	0.13
C|||C	890	0.12
C|H	435	0.11
C|N	305	0.15
C|O	360	0.14
C|F	450	0.14
C|Cl	340	0.18
O|H	500	0.10
O|O	220	0.15
O|Si	375	0.16
N|H	430	0.10
N|O	250	0.12
F|F	160	0.14
H|H	435	0.074

Write a program that accepts data from one column and returns the corresponding data from the other columns in the stored file. If input data matches different rows, then return all matching row data. For example, a bond length input of 0.12 should return triple bond C|||C and bond energy 890 kJ/mol *and* single bond N|O and bond energy 250 kJ/mol.

ANSWERS TO SELF-CHECK QUESTIONS

1. The stream will be in a failed state because there is no file with an empty name.
2. The stream variable is declared as an input stream. It should have been an `ofstream`.
3. The stream parameter variable `in` should be a reference parameter.
4. Initialize `boy_total` and `girl_total` with 10.
5. Add the following code to the beginning of `main`:

   ```
   ofstream out_file;
   out_file.open("output.txt");
   ```

   Change every `cout` to `out_file`.

   Add an `out_file` parameter variable of type `ofstream&` to `process_name`.
6. `number` is 6 because the comma is not recognized as a part of the number. `ch` is `','`.
7. `word` is `"World!"` (including the !) and `ch` is `'W'`.
8.
   ```
   char ch;
   double number;
   string marker;
   in_file >> ch;
   in_file.unget();
   if (isdigit(ch) || ch == '-') { cin >> number; } else { cin >> marker; }
   ```
9. The loop skips a sequence of white space.
10. Some country names (such as `United States`) consist of multiple words.
11. `123456.000000`, because the default precision is 6.
12. `cout << fixed << setprecision(2) << 123456.0;`
13. `00123456`
14. `123456`
15. Because the `setw` manipulator only affects the first output.
16. `123456`
17. `123`
18. `0`
19. `3.3333`. Note that in general format, the precision denotes the total number of digits, not the number of digits after the decimal point.
20.
    ```
    string double_to_string(double x, int digits)
    {
       ostringstream strm;
       strm << fixed << setprecision(digits) << x;
       return strm.str();
    }
    ```
21. `argc` is 3, and `argv` contains the strings `"caesar"`, `"-d"`, and `"encrypt.txt"`.

22.

key	file_count	i	arg
~~3~~	~~0~~	~~1~~	~~-d~~
-3	1	~~2~~	encrypt.txt
		3	

Then the program prints the message

`Usage: caesar [-d] infile outfile`

and exits.

23. FDHVDU

24. It turns them into # characters. The ASCII code for a space is 32, and the # character has code 35.

25. It replaces the initial byte of a file with 0.

26. Change the process function to swap the values of the green and blue arguments. The remainder of the program stays unchanged.

27. You get the original image back.

28. We could have read the header values and pixel data sequentially, but to update the pixels, we had to move backwards.

29. We need 3×100 bytes for each scan line. There is no padding since this number is divisible by 4. The total size $= 3 \times 100 \times 100 + 64 = 30,064$ bytes.

CHAPTER 9

CLASSES

This chapter introduces you to object-oriented programming, an important technique for writing complex programs. In an object-oriented program, you don't simply manipulate numbers and strings, but you work with objects that are meaningful for your application. Objects with the same behavior (such as the windmills to the left) are grouped into classes. A programmer provides the desired behavior by specifying and implementing functions for these classes. In this chapter, you will learn how to discover, specify, and implement your own classes, and how to use them in your programs.

9.1 Object-Oriented Programming

You have learned how to structure your programs by decomposing tasks into functions. This is an excellent practice, but experience shows that it does not go far enough. As programs get larger, it becomes increasingly difficult to maintain a large collection of functions.

To overcome this problem, computer scientists invented **object-oriented programming**, a programming style in which tasks are solved by collaborating objects. Each object has its own set of data, together with a set of functions that can act upon the data. (These functions are called **member functions**).

You have already experienced the object-oriented programming style when you used string objects or streams such as cin and cout. For example, you use the length and substr member functions to work with string objects. The >> and << operators that you use with streams are also implemented as member functions—see Special Topic 9.2 on page 406.

> A class describes a set of objects with the same behavior.

In C++, a programmer doesn't implement a single object. Instead, the programmer provides a **class**. A class describes a set of objects with the same behavior. For example, the string class describes the behavior of all strings. The class specifies how a string stores its characters, which member functions can be used with strings, and how the member functions are implemented.

A class describes a set of objects with the same behavior. For example, a Car class describes all passenger vehicles that have a certain capacity and shape.

You can drive a car by operating the steering wheel and pedals, without knowing how the engine works. Similarly, you use an object through its member functions. The implementation is hidden.

When you develop an object-oriented program, you create your own classes that describe what is important in your application. For example, in a student database you might work with Student and Course classes. Of course, then you must supply member functions for these classes.

When you work with an object, you do not know how it is implemented. You need not know how a string organizes a character sequence, or how the cin object reads input from the console. All you need to know is the **public interface**: the specifications for the member functions that you can invoke. The process of providing a public interface, while hiding the implementation details, is called **encapsulation**.

You will want to use encapsulation for your own classes. When you define a class, you will specify the behavior of the public member functions, but you will hide the implementation details. Encapsulation benefits the programmers who use your classes. They can put your classes to work without having to know their implementations, just as you are able to make use of the string and stream classes without knowing their internal details.

Encapsulation is also a benefit for the implementor of a class. When working on a program that is being developed over a long period of time, it is common for implementation details to change, usually to make objects more efficient or more capable. Encapsulation is crucial to enabling these changes. When the implementation is hidden, the implementor is free to make improvements. Because the implementation is hidden, these improvements do not affect the programmers who use the objects.

> Every class has a public interface: a collection of member functions through which the objects of the class can be manipulated.

> Encapsulation is the act of providing a public interface and hiding implementation details.

> Encapsulation enables changes in the implementation without affecting users of a class.

A driver of an electric car doesn't have to learn new controls even though the car engine is very different. Neither does the programmer who uses an object with an improved implementation—as long as the same member functions are used.

In this chapter, you will learn how to design and implement your own classes in C++, and how to structure your programs in an object-oriented way, using the principle of encapsulation.

SELF CHECK

1. In C++, is cin an object or a class? Is string an object or a class?
2. When using a string object, you do not know how it stores its characters. How can you access them?
3. Describe two possible ways in which a string object might store its characters.
4. Suppose the providers of your C++ compiler decide to change the way that a string object stores its characters, and they update the string member functions accordingly. Which parts of your code do you need to change when you get the new compiler?

Practice It   Now you can try these exercises at the end of the chapter: R9.1, R9.2.

9.2 Specifying the Public Interface of a Class

To define a class, we first need to specify its **public interface**. The public interface of a class consists of all member functions that a user of the class may want to apply to its objects.

Let's consider a simple example. We want to use objects that simulate cash registers. A cashier who rings up a sale presses a key to start the sale, then rings up each item. A display shows the amount owed as well as the total number of items purchased.

In our simulation, we want to carry out the following operations:

Our first example of a class simulates a cash register.

- Add the price of an item.
- Get the total amount of all items, and the count of items purchased.
- Clear the cash register to start a new sale.

The interface is specified in the **class definition**, summarized in Syntax 9.1 on page 393. We will call our class CashRegister. (We follow the convention that the name of a programmer-defined class starts with an uppercase letter, as does each word within the name. This naming convention is called *camel case* because the uppercase letters in the middle of the name look like the humps of a camel.)

Here is the C++ syntax for the `CashRegister` class definition:

```
class CashRegister
{
public:
   void clear();
   void add_item(double price);

   double get_total() const;
   int get_count() const;

private:
   data members—see Section 9.3
};
```

The member functions are declared in the *public section* of the class. Any part of the program can call the member functions. The data members are defined in the *private section* of the class. Only the member functions of the class can access those data members; they are hidden from the remainder of the program.

It is legal to declare the private members before the public section, but in this book, we place the public section first. After all, most programmers reading a class are class users, not implementors, and they are more interested in the public interface than in the private implementation.

The member function declarations look similar to the declarations of regular functions. These declarations do not provide any implementation. You will see in Section 9.4 how to implement the member functions.

There are two kinds of member functions, called **mutators** and **accessors**. A mutator is a function that modifies the data members of the object. The `CashRegister` class

Syntax 9.1   Class Definition

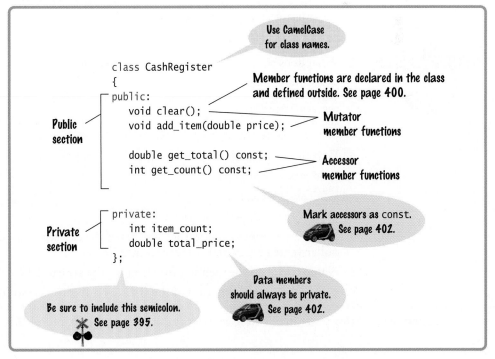

Figure 1 The Interface of the `CashRegister` Class

A mutator member function changes the object on which it operates.

An accessor member function does not change the object on which it operates. Use const with accessors.

has two mutators: `clear` and `add_item`. After you call either of these functions, the total amount and item count are changed.

Accessors just query the object for some information without changing it. The `CashRegister` class has two accessors: `get_total` and `get_count`. Applying either of these functions to a `CashRegister` object simply returns a value and does not modify the object. In C++, you should use the `const` reserved word to mark accessor functions (see Programming Tip 9.2 on page 402), like this:

```
double get_total() const;
```

Member functions are invoked using the dot notation that you have already seen with string and stream functions:

```
CashRegister register1; // Defines a CashRegister object
register1.clear(); // Invokes a member function
```

Now we know *what* a `CashRegister` object can do, but not *how* it does it. Of course, to use `CashRegister` objects in our programs, we don't need to know. We simply use the public interface. Figure 1 shows the interface of the `CashRegister` class. The mutator functions are shown with arrows pointing inside the private data to indicate that they modify the data. The accessor functions are shown with arrows pointing the other way to indicate that they just read the data.

SELF CHECK

5. What does the following code segment print?
```
CashRegister reg;
reg.clear();
reg.add_item(0.95);
reg.add_item(0.95);
cout << reg.get_count() << " " << reg.get_total() << endl;
```

6. What is wrong with the following code segment?
```
CashRegister reg;
reg.clear();
reg.add_item(0.95);
cout << reg.get_amount_due() << endl;
```

7. Declare a member function `get_dollars` of the `CashRegister` class that yields the dollar value of the total amount of the sale.

8. Name two accessor member functions of the `string` class.

9. Is the `get` member function of the `ifstream` class an accessor or a mutator?

Practice It Now you can try these exercises at the end of the chapter: R9.3, R9.7.

Forgetting a Semicolon

Braces { } are common in C++ code, and usually you do not place a semicolon after the closing brace. However, class definitions always end in };. A common error is to forget that semicolon:

```cpp
class CashRegister
{
public:
   ...
private:
   ...
} // Forgot semicolon

int main()
{
   // Many compilers report the error in this line
   ...
}
```

This error can be extremely confusing to many compilers. There is syntax, now obsolete but supported for compatibility with old code, to define class types and variables of that type simultaneously. Because the compiler doesn't know that you don't use that obsolete construction, it tries to analyze the code wrongly and ultimately reports an error. Unfortunately, it may report the error *several lines away* from the line in which you forgot the semicolon.

If the compiler reports bizarre errors in lines that you are sure are correct, check that each of the preceding class definitions is terminated by a semicolon.

9.3 Data Members

> An object holds data members that are accessed by member functions.

An object stores its data in **data members**. These are variables that are declared inside the class.

When implementing a class, you have to determine which data each object needs to store. The object needs to have all the information necessary to carry out any member function call.

Go through all member functions and consider their data requirements. It is a good idea to start with the accessor functions. For example, a CashRegister object must be able to return the correct value for the get_total function. That means, it must either store all entered prices and compute the total in the function call, or it must store the total.

Now apply the same reasoning to the get_count function. If the cash register stores all entered prices, it can count them in the get_count function. Otherwise, you need to have a variable for the count.

Like a wilderness explorer who needs to carry all items that may be needed, an object needs to store the data required for any function calls.

The `add_item` function receives a price as an argument, and it must record the price. If the `CashRegister` object stores an array of entered prices, then the `add_item` function appends the price. On the other hand, if we decide to store just the item total and count, then the `add_item` function updates these two variables.

Finally, the `clear` function must prepare the cash register for the next sale, either by emptying the array of prices or by setting the total and count to zero.

We have now discovered two different ways of representing the data that the object needs. Either of them will work, and we have to make a choice. We will choose the simpler one: variables for the total price and the item count. (Other options are explored in Exercises P9.3 and P9.4.)

> Every object has its own set of data members.

The data members are defined in the private section of the class definition:

```
class CashRegister
{
public:
    // See Section 9.2
private:
    int item_count;
    double total_price;
};
```

Every `CashRegister` object has a separate copy of these data members (see Figure 2).

Because the data members are defined to be private, only the member functions of the class can access them. Programmers using the `CashRegister` class cannot access the data members directly:

```
int main()
{
    ...
    cout << register1.item_count; // Error—use get_count() instead
    ...
}
```

> Private data members can only be accessed by member functions of the same class.

All data access must occur through the public interface. Thus, the data members of an object are effectively hidden from the programmer using the class. While it is theoretically possible in C++ to leave data members unencapsulated (by placing them into the public section), this is very uncommon in practice. We will always make all data members private in this book.

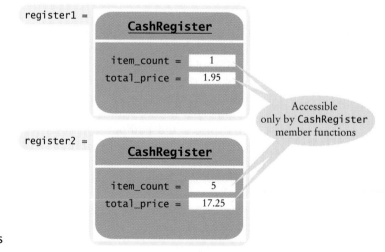

Figure 2
Data Members of CashRegister Objects

These clocks have common behavior, but each of them has a different state. Similarly, objects of a class can have their data members set to different values.

SELF CHECK

10. What is the value of register1.item_count, register1.total_price, register2.item_count, and register2.total_price after these statements?

```
CashRegister register1;
register1.clear();
register1.add_item(0.90);
register1.add_item(0.95);
CashRegister register2;
register2.clear();
register2.add_item(1.90);
```

11. What is wrong with this code segment?

```
CashRegister register2;
register2.clear();
register2.add_item(0.95);
cout << register2.total_price << endl;
```

12. Consider a class Time that represents a point in time, such as 9 A.M. or 3:30 P.M. Give two different sets of data members that can be used for implementing the Time class.

13. Suppose the implementor of the Time class changes from one implementation strategy to another, keeping the public interface unchanged. What do the programmers who use the Time class need to do?

14. Consider a class Grade that represents a letter grade, such as A+ or B. Give two different sets of data members that can be used for implementing the Grade class.

Practice It   Now you can try these exercises at the end of the chapter: R9.16, R9.17, R9.18.

9.4 Member Functions

The definition of a class declares its member functions. Each member function is defined separately, after the class definition. The following sections show how to define member functions.

9.4.1 Implementing Member Functions

Here is the implementation of the add_item function of the CashRegister class.

```
void CashRegister::add_item(double price)
{
   item_count++;
   total_price = total_price + price;
}
```

Use the *ClassName::*
prefix when defining
member functions.

The CashRegister:: prefix makes it clear that we are defining the add_item function of the CashRegister class. In C++ it is perfectly legal to have add_item functions in other classes as well, and it is important to specify exactly which add_item function we are defining. (See Syntax 9.2 on page 400.) You use the *ClassName*::add_item syntax only when *defining* the function, not when calling it. When you call the add_item member function, the call has the form *object*.add_item(...).

When defining an accessor member function, supply the reserved word const following the closing parenthesis of the parameter list. Here is the get_count member function:

```
int CashRegister::get_count() const
{
   return item_count;
}
```

You will find the other member functions with the example program at the end of this section.

9.4.2 Implicit and Explicit Parameters

Whenever you refer to a data member, such as item_count or total_price, in a member function, it denotes the data member *of the object on which the member function was invoked*. For example, consider the call

```
register1.add_item(1.95);
```

The first statement in the CashRegister::add_item function is

```
item_count++;
```

Which item_count is incremented? In this call, it is the item_count of the register1 object. (See Figure 3.)

When an item is added, it affects the data members of the cash register object on which the function is invoked.

① Before the member function call.

register1 =

CashRegister

item_count =   0
total_price =   0

② After the member function call register1.add_item(1.95).

The implicit parameter references this object.

The explicit parameter is set to this argument.

register1 =

CashRegister

item_count =   1
total_price =   1.95

Figure 3   Implicit and Explicit Parameters

> The implicit parameter is a reference to the object on which a member function is applied.

When a member function is called on an object, the **implicit parameter** is a reference to that object.

You can think of the code of the add_item function like this:

```
void CashRegister::add_item(double price)
{
    implicit parameter.item_count++;
    implicit parameter.total_price = implicit parameter.total_price + price;
}
```

In C++, you do not actually write the implicit parameter in the function definition. For that reason, the parameter is called "implicit".

> Explicit parameters of a member function are listed in the function definition.

In contrast, parameter variables that are explicitly mentioned in the function definition, such as the price parameter variable, are called **explicit parameters**. Every member function has exactly one implicit parameter and zero or more explicit parameters.

9.4.3 Calling a Member Function from a Member Function

> When calling another member function on the same object, do not use the dot notation.

When one member function calls another member function *on the same object*, you do not use the dot notation. Instead, you simply use the name of the other function. Here is an example. Suppose we want to implement a member function to add multiple instances of the same item. An easy way to implement this function is to repeatedly call the add_item function:

```
void CashRegister::add_items(int quantity, double price)
{
```

```
      for (int i = 1; i <= quantity; i++)
      {
         add_item(price);
      }
   }
```

Here, the add_item member function is invoked on the implicit parameter.

```
   for (int i = 1; i <= quantity; i++)
   {
      implicit parameter.add_item(price);
   }
```

That is the object on which the add_items function is invoked. For example, in the call

```
   register1.add_items(6, 0.95);
```

the add_item function is invoked six times on register1.

Syntax 9.2   Member Function Definition

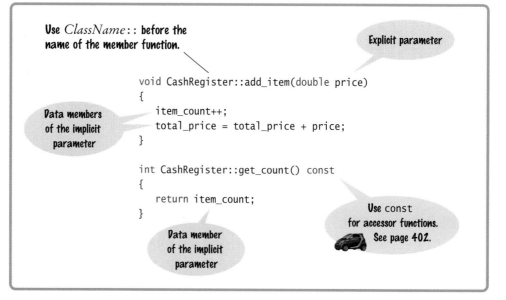

ch09/registertest1.cpp

```
 1  #include <iostream>
 2  #include <iomanip>
 3
 4  using namespace std;
 5
 6  /**
 7     A simulated cash register that tracks the item count and
 8     the total amount due.
 9  */
10  class CashRegister
11  {
12  public:
13     /**
14        Clears the item count and the total.
15     */
16     void clear();
```

```
17
18      /**
19         Adds an item to this cash register.
20         @param price the price of this item
21      */
22      void add_item(double price);
23
24      /**
25         @return the total amount of the current sale
26      */
27      double get_total() const;
28
29      /**
30         @return the item count of the current sale
31      */
32      int get_count() const;
33
34   private:
35      int item_count;
36      double total_price;
37   };
38
39   void CashRegister::clear()
40   {
41      item_count = 0;
42      total_price = 0;
43   }
44
45   void CashRegister::add_item(double price)
46   {
47      item_count++;
48      total_price = total_price + price;
49   }
50
51   double CashRegister::get_total() const
52   {
53      return total_price;
54   }
55
56   int CashRegister::get_count() const
57   {
58      return item_count;
59   }
60
61   /**
62      Displays the item count and total price of a cash register.
63      @param reg the cash register to display
64   */
65   void display(CashRegister reg)
66   {
67      cout << reg.get_count() << " $" << fixed << setprecision(2)
68         << reg.get_total() << endl;
69   }
70
71   int main()
72   {
73      CashRegister register1;
74      register1.clear();
75      register1.add_item(1.95);
76      display(register1);
```

```
77    register1.add_item(0.95);
78    display(register1);
79    register1.add_item(2.50);
80    display(register1);
81    return 0;
82  }
```

Program Run

```
1 $1.95
2 $2.90
3 $5.40
```

SELF CHECK

15. What is wrong with this implementation of the get_total member function?

```
int get_total()
{
    return total_price;
}
```

16. Implement the add_items member function described in Section 9.4.3 without calling add_item.

17. Implement a member function get_dollars of the CashRegister class that yields the amount of the total sale as a dollar value without the cents.

18. Consider the substr member function of the string class. How many parameters does it have, and what are their types?

19. Consider the length member function of the string class. How many parameters does it have, and what are their types?

Practice It   Now you can try these exercises at the end of the chapter: P9.3, P9.4, P9.6.

Programming Tip 9.1

All Data Members Should Be Private; Most Member Functions Should Be Public

It is possible to define data members in the public section of a class, but you should not do that in your own code. Always use encapsulation, with private data members that are manipulated with member functions.

Generally, member functions should be public. However, sometimes you have a member function that is only used as a helper function by other member functions. In that case, you can make the helper function private. Simply declare it in the private section of the class.

Programming Tip 9.2

const **Correctness**

You should declare all accessor functions in C++ with the const reserved word. (Recall that an accessor function is a member function that does not modify its implicit parameter.)

For example, suppose you design the following class:

```
class CashRegister
{
    void display(); // Bad style—no const
    ...
```

```
};
```

When you compile your code, no error is reported. But now suppose that another programmer uses your CashRegister class in a function

```
void display_all(const CashRegister registers[])
{
    for (int i = 0; i < NREGISTERS; i++) { registers[i].display(); }
}
```

That programmer is conscientious and declares the registers parameter variable as const. But then the call registers[i].display() will not compile. Because CashRegister::display is not tagged as const, the compiler suspects that the call registers[i].display() may modify registers[i]. But the function promised not to modify the registers array.

If you write a program with other team members who are conscientious about const, it is very important that you do your part as well. You should therefore get into the habit of using const with all accessor member functions.

9.5 Constructors

A constructor is called automatically whenever an object is created.

A **constructor** is a member function that initializes the data members of an object. The constructor is automatically called whenever an object is created. By supplying a constructor, you can ensure that all data members are properly set before any member functions act on an object.

To understand the importance of constructors, consider the following statements:

```
CashRegister register1;
register1.add_item(1.95);
int count = register1.get_count(); // May not be 1
```

Here, the programmer forgot to call clear before adding items. Therefore, the data members of the register1 object were initialized with random values. Constructors guarantee that an object is always fully initialized when it is defined.

The name of a constructor is the same as the class name.

The name of a constructor is identical to the name of its class. You declare constructors in the class definition, for example:

```
class CashRegister
{
public:
    CashRegister(); // A constructor
    ...
};
```

Constructors never return values, but you do not use the void reserved word when declaring them.

Here is the definition of that constructor:

```
CashRegister::CashRegister()
{
    item_count = 0;
    total_price = 0;
}
```

In the constructor definition, the first CashRegister (before the ::) indicates that we are about to define a member function of the CashRegister class. The second CashRegister is the name of that member function.

A constructor is like a set of assembly instructions for an object.

A default constructor has no arguments.

The constructor that you just saw has no arguments. Such a constructor is called a **default constructor**. It is used whenever you define an object and do not specify any parameters for the construction. For example, if you define

```
CashRegister register1;
```

then the default constructor is called. It sets `register1.item_count` and `register1.total_price` to zero.

A class can have multiple constructors.

Many classes have more than one constructor. This allows you to define objects in different ways. Consider for example a `BankAccount` class that has two constructors:

```
class BankAccount
{
public:
   BankAccount(); // Sets balance to 0
   BankAccount(double initial_balance); // Sets balance to initial_balance
   // Member functions omitted
private:
   double balance;
};
```

The compiler picks the constructor that matches the construction arguments.

Both constructors have the same name as the class, `BankAccount`. But the default constructor has no parameter variables, whereas the second constructor has a `double` parameter variable. (This is an example of *overloading*—see Special Topic 9.2.)

When you construct an object, the compiler chooses the constructor that matches the arguments that you supply. For example,

```
BankAccount joes_account;
   // Uses default constructor
BankAccount lisas_account(499.95);
   // Uses BankAccount(double) constructor
```

Be sure to initialize all number and pointer data members in a constructor.

When implementing a constructor, you need to pay particular attention to all data members that are numbers or pointers. These types are not classes and therefore have no constructors. If you have a data member that is an object of a class (such as a `string` object), then that class has a constructor, and the object will be initialized. For example, all `string` objects are automatically initialized to the empty string.

Consider this class:

```
class Item
{
```

```
public:
    Item();
    // Additional member functions omitted
private:
    string description;
    double price;
};
```

In the `Item` constructor, you need to set `price` to 0, but you need not initialize the `description` data member. It is automatically initialized to the empty string.

If you do not supply any constructor for a class, the compiler automatically generates a default constructor. The default constructor initializes all data members of class type with their default constructors and leaves the other data members uninitialized.

SELF CHECK

20. Provide an implementation for the default constructor of the `BankAccount` class.
21. Provide an implementation for the `BankAccount(double)` constructor.
22. Provide an implementation for the default constructor of the `Item` class.
23. Provide an implementation for the default constructor of the `CashRegister` class that calls the `clear` member function.
24. Which constructor is called in each of the following definitions?

   a. `Item item1;`

   b. `Item item2("Corn flakes");`

   c. `Item item3(3.95);`

   d. `Item item4("Corn flakes", 3.95);`

   e. `Item item5();`

Practice It Now you can try these exercises at the end of the chapter: R9.13, R9.14, P9.5, P9.8.

Common Error 9.2

Trying to Call a Constructor

The constructor is invoked only when an object is first created. You cannot invoke it again. For example, you cannot call the constructor to clear an object:

```
CashRegister register1;
...
register1.CashRegister(); // Error
```

It is true that the default constructor sets a *new* `CashRegister` object to the cleared state, but you cannot invoke a constructor on an *existing* object.

Special Topic 9.1

Initializer Lists

When you construct an object whose data members are themselves objects, those objects are constructed by their class's default constructor. However, if a data member belongs to a class without a default constructor, you need to invoke the data member's constructor explicitly. Here is an example.

This `Item` class has no default constructor:

```
class Item
{
```

```
public:
   Item(string item_description, double item_price);
   // No other constructors
   ...
};
```

This Order class has a data member of type Item:

```
class Order
{
public:
   Order(string customer_name, string item_description, double item_price);
   ...
private:
   Item article;
   string customer;
};
```

The Order constructor must call the Item constructor. That is achieved with an *initializer list*. The initializer list is placed before the opening brace of the constructor. The list starts with a colon and contains names of data members with their construction arguments.

```
Order(string customer_name, string item_description, double item_price)
   : article(item_description, item_price)
{
   customer = customer_name;
}
```

Initializers are separated by commas. The Order constructor can also be written like this:

```
Order(string customer_name, string item_description, double item_price)
   : article(item_description, item_price), customer(customer_name)
{
}
```

Special Topic 9.2

Overloading

When the same function name is used for more than one function, then the name is **overloaded**. In C++ you can overload function names provided the types of the parameter variables are different. For example, you can define two functions, both called print:

```
void print(CashRegister r)
void print(Item i)
```

When the print function is called,

```
print(x);
```

the compiler looks at the type of x. If x is a CashRegister object, the first function is called. If x is an Item object, the second function is called. If x is neither, the compiler generates an error.

It is always possible to avoid overloading by giving each function a unique name, such as print_register or print_item. However, we have no choice with constructors. C++ demands that the name of a constructor equal the name of the class. If a class has more than one constructor, then that name must be overloaded.

In addition to name overloading, C++ also supports **operator overloading**. It is possible to give new meanings to the familiar C++ operators such as +, ==, and <<. This is an advanced technique that we do not discuss in this book.

9.6 Problem Solving: Tracing Objects

You have seen how the technique of hand tracing is useful for understanding how a program works. When your program contains objects, it is useful to adapt the technique so that you gain a better understanding about object data and encapsulation.

Use an index card or a sticky note for each object. On the front, write the member functions that the object can execute. On the back, make a table for the values of the data members.

Here is a card for a CashRegister object:

Write the member functions on the front of a card, and the data member values on the back.

CashRegister reg1		item_count	total_price
clear			
add_item(price)			
get_total			
get_count			

front   *back*

In a small way, this gives you a feel for encapsulation. An object is manipulated through its public interface (on the front of the card), and the data members are hidden in the back.

When an object is constructed, fill in the initial values of the data members.

item_count	total_price
0	0

Whenever a mutator member function is executed, cross out the old values and write the new ones below. Here is what happens after a call to the add_item member function:

Update the values of the data members when a mutator member function is called.

item_count	total_price
~~0~~	~~0~~
1	19.95

If you have more than one object in your program, you will have multiple cards, one for each object:

item_count	total_price
~~0~~	~~0~~
1	19.95

item_count	total_price
~~0~~	~~0~~
1	19.95
2	14.90

These diagrams are also useful when you design a class. Suppose you are asked to enhance the CashRegister class to compute the sales tax. Add a function get_sales_tax to the front of the card. Now turn the card over, look over the data members, and ask yourself whether the object has sufficient information to compute the answer. Remember that each object is an autonomous unit. Any data value that can be used in a computation must be

- A data member.
- A function argument.
- A global constant or variable.

To compute the sales tax, we need to know the tax rate and the total of the taxable items. (Food items are usually not subject to sales tax.) We don't have that information available. Let us introduce additional data members for the tax rate and the taxable total. The tax rate can be set in the constructor (assuming it stays fixed for the lifetime of the object). When adding an item, we need to be told whether the item is taxable. If so, we add its price to the taxable total.

For example, consider the following statements.

```
CashRegister reg2(7.5); // 7.5 percent sales tax
reg2.add_item(3.95, false); // not taxable
reg2.add_item(19.95, true); // taxable
```

When you record the effect on a card, it looks like this:

item_count	total_price	taxable_total	tax_rate
~~0~~	~~0~~	~~0~~	7.5
~~1~~	~~3.95~~		
2	23.90	19.95	

With this information, it becomes easy to compute the tax. It is **taxable_total x tax_rate / 100**. Tracing the object helped us understand the need for additional data members.

SELF CHECK

25. Consider a Car class that simulates fuel consumption in a car. We will assume a fixed efficiency (in miles per gallon) that is supplied in the constructor. There are member functions for adding gas, driving a given distance, and checking the amount of gas left in the tank. Make a card for a Car object, choosing suitable data members and showing their values after the object was constructed.

26. Trace the following member function calls:

```
Car my_car(25);
my_car.add_gas(20);
my_car.drive(100);
my_car.drive(200);
my_car.add_gas(5);
```

27. Suppose you are asked to simulate the odometer of the car, by adding a member function `get_miles_driven`. Add a data member to the object's card that is suitable for computing this member function.

28. Trace the member functions of Self Check 26, updating the data member that you added in Self Check 27.

Practice It   Now you can try these exercises at the end of the chapter: R9.20, R9.21, R9.22.

HOW TO 9.1   Implementing a Class

A very common task is to implement a class whose objects can carry out a set of specified actions. This How To walks you through the necessary steps.

As an example, consider a class `Menu`. An object of this class can display a menu such as

```
1) Open new account
2) Log into existing account
3) Help
4) Quit
```

Then the menu waits for the user to supply a value. If the user does not supply a valid value, the menu is redisplayed, and the user can try again.

Step 1   Get an informal list of the responsibilities of your objects.

Be careful that you restrict yourself to features that are actually required in the problem. With real-world items, such as cash registers or bank accounts, there are potentially dozens of features that might be worth implementing. However, your job is not to faithfully model the real world. You need to determine only those responsibilities that you need for solving your specific problem.

In the case of the menu, you need to

Display the menu.
Get user input.

Now look for hidden responsibilities that aren't part of the problem description. How do objects get created? Which mundane activities need to happen, such as clearing the cash register at the beginning of each sale?

In the menu example, consider how a menu is produced. The programmer creates an empty menu object and then adds options "Open new account", "Help", and so on. There is a hidden responsibility:

Add an option.

Step 2   Specify the public interface.

Turn the list in Step 1 into a set of member functions, with specific types for the parameter variables and the return values. Be sure to mark accessors as const. Many programmers find this step simpler if they write out member function calls that are applied to a sample object, like this:

```
Menu main_menu;
main_menu.add_option("Open new account");
// Add more options
int input = main_menu.get_input();
```

Now we have a specific list of member functions.

- `void add_option(string option)`
- `int get_input() const`

What about displaying the menu? There is no sense in displaying the menu without also asking the user for input. However, `get_input` may need to display the menu more than once if the user provides a bad input. Thus, `display` is a good candidate for a private member function.

To complete the public interface, you need to specify the constructors. Ask yourself what information you need in order to construct an object of your class. Sometimes you will want two constructors: one that sets all data members to a default and one that sets them to user-supplied values.

In the case of the menu example, we can get by with a single constructor that creates an empty menu.

Here is the public interface:

```
class Menu
{
public:
    Menu();
    void add_option(string option);
    int get_input() const
private:
    ...
};
```

Step 3 Document the public interface.

Supply a documentation comment for the class, then comment each member function.

```
/**
    A menu that is displayed on a console.
*/
class Menu
{
public:
    /**
        Constructs a menu with no options.
    */
    Menu();

    /**
        Adds an option to the end of this menu.
        @param option the option to add
    */
    void add_option(string option);

    /**
        Displays the menu, with options numbered starting with 1,
        and prompts the user for input. Repeats until a valid input
        is supplied.
        @return the number that the user supplied
    */
    int get_input() const;
```

```
private:
    ...
};
```

Step 4   Determine data members.

Ask yourself what information an object needs to store to do its job. Remember, the member functions can be called in any order! The object needs to have enough internal memory to be able to process every member function using just its data members and the member function arguments. Go through each member function, perhaps starting with a simple one or an interesting one, and ask yourself what you need to carry out the member function's task. Make data members to store the information that the member function needs.

In the menu example, we clearly need to store the menu options so that the menu can be displayed. How should we store them? As a vector of strings? As one long string? Both approaches can be made to work. We will use a vector here. Exercise P9.7 asks you to implement the other approach.

```
class Menu
{
    ...
private:
    ...
    vector<string> options;
};
```

When checking for user input, we need to know the number of menu items. Because we store them in a vector, the number of menu items is simply obtained as the size of the vector. If you stored the menu items in one long string, you might want to keep another data member that stores the menu item count.

Step 5   Implement constructors and member functions.

Implement the constructors and member functions in your class, one at a time, starting with the easiest ones. For example, here is the implementation of the add_option member function:

```
void Menu::add_option(string option)
{
    options.push_back(option);
}
```

Here is the get_input member function. This member function is a bit more sophisticated. It loops until a valid input has been obtained, and it calls the private display member function to display the menu.

```
int Menu::get_input() const
{
    int input;
    do
    {
        display();
        cin >> input;
    }
    while (input < 1 || input > options.size());
    return input;
}
```

Finally, here is the display member function:

```
void Menu::display() const
{
    for (int i = 0; i < options.size(); i++)
    {
        cout << i + 1 << ") " << options[i] << endl;
    }
```

```
    }
```

The Menu constructor is a bit odd. We need to construct a menu with no options. A vector is a class, and it has a default constructor. That constructor does exactly what we want, namely to construct an empty vector. Nothing else needs to be done:

```
Menu::Menu()
{
}
```

If you find that you have trouble with the implementation of some of your member functions, you may need to rethink your choice of data members. It is common for a beginner to start out with a set of data members that cannot accurately describe the state of an object. Don't hesitate to go back and rethink your implementation strategy.

Once you have completed the implementation, compile your class and fix any compiler errors. (See ch09/menu.cpp in your book's companion code for the completed class.)

Step 6 Test your class.

Write a short tester program and execute it. The tester program should carry out the member function calls that you found in Step 2.

```
int main()
{
    Menu main_menu;
    main_menu.add_option("Open new account");
    main_menu.add_option("Log into existing account");
    main_menu.add_option("Help");
    main_menu.add_option("Quit");
```

Random Fact 9.1 Electronic Voting Machines

In the 2000 presidential elections in the United States, votes were tallied by a variety of machines. Some machines processed cardboard ballots into which voters punched holes to indicate their choices (see photo below). When voters were not careful, remains of paper—the now infamous "chads"—were partially stuck in the punch cards, causing votes to be miscounted. A manual recount was necessary, but it was not carried out everywhere due to time constraints and procedural wrangling. The election was very close, and there remain doubts in the minds of many people whether the election outcome would have been different if the voting machines had accurately counted the intent of the voters.

Subsequently, voting machine manufacturers have argued that electronic voting machines would avoid the problems caused by punch cards or optically scanned forms. In an electronic voting machine, voters indicate their preferences by pressing buttons or touching icons on a computer screen. Typically, each voter is presented with a summary screen for review before casting the ballot. The process is very similar to using an automatic bank teller machine.

It seems plausible that these machines make it more likely that a vote is counted in the same way that the voter intends. However, there has been significant controversy surrounding some types of electronic voting machines. If a machine simply records the votes and prints out the totals after the election has been completed, then how do you know that the machine worked correctly? Inside the machine is a computer that executes a program, and, as you may know from your own experience, programs can have bugs.

In fact, some electronic voting machines do have bugs. There have been isolated cases where machines reported tallies that were impossible. When a machine reports far more or far fewer votes than voters, then it is clear that it malfunctioned. Unfortunately, it is then impossible to find out the actual votes. Over time, one would expect these bugs to be fixed in the software. More insidiously, if the results are plausible, nobody may ever investigate.

Punch Card Ballot

```
    int input = main_menu.get_input();
    cout << "Input: " << input << endl;
    return 0;
}
```

Program Run

```
1) Open new account
2) Log into existing account
3) Help
4) Quit
5
1) Open new account
2) Log into existing account
3) Help
4) Quit
3
Input: 3
```

WORKED EXAMPLE 9.1   **Implementing a Bank Account Class**

This Worked Example shows how to develop a class that simulates a bank account.

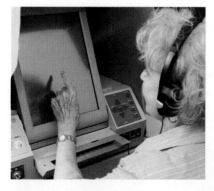

Touch Screen Voting Machine

Many computer scientists have spoken out on this issue and confirmed that it is impossible, with today's technology, to tell that software is error free and has not been tampered with. Many of them recommend that electronic voting machines should employ a voter verifiable audit trail. (A good source of information is http://verifiedvoting.org.) Typically, a voter-verifiable machine prints out a ballot. Each voter has a chance to review the printout, and then deposits it in an old-fashioned ballot box. If there is a problem with the electronic equipment, the printouts can be scanned or counted by hand.

As this book is written, this concept is strongly resisted both by manufacturers of electronic voting machines and by their customers, the cities and counties that run elections. Manufacturers are reluctant to increase the cost of the machines because they may not be able to pass the cost increase on to their customers, who tend to have tight budgets. Election officials fear problems with malfunctioning printers, and some of them have publicly stated that they actually prefer equipment that eliminates bothersome recounts.

What do you think? You probably use an automatic bank teller machine to get cash from your bank account. Do you review the paper record that the machine issues? Do you check your bank statement? Even if you don't, do you put your faith in other people who double-check their balances, so that the bank won't get away with widespread cheating?

At any rate, is the integrity of banking equipment more important or less important than that of voting machines? Won't every voting process have some room for error and fraud anyway? Is the added cost for equipment, paper, and staff time reasonable to combat a potentially slight risk of malfunction and fraud? Computer scientists cannot answer these questions—an informed society must make these tradeoffs. But, like all professionals, they have an obligation to speak out and give accurate testimony about the capabilities and limitations of computing equipment.

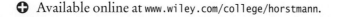

Available online at www.wiley.com/college/horstmann.

9.7 Problem Solving: Discovering Classes

To discover classes, look for nouns in the problem description.

When you solve a problem using objects and classes, you need to determine the classes required for the implementation. You may be able to reuse existing classes, or you may need to implement new ones. One simple approach for discovering classes and member functions is to look for the nouns and verbs in the problem description. Often, nouns correspond to classes, and verbs correspond to member functions.

Concepts from the problem domain, be it science, business, or a game, often make good classes. Examples are

- Cannonball
- CashRegister
- Monster

Concepts from the problem domain are good candidates for classes.

The name for such a class should be a noun that describes the concept. Other frequently used classes represent system services such as files or menus.

What might not be a good class? If you can't tell from the class name what an object of the class is supposed to do, then you are probably not on the right track. For example, your homework assignment might ask you to write a program that prints paychecks. Suppose you start by trying to design a class PaycheckProgram. What would an object of this class do? An object of this class would have to do everything that the homework needs to do. That doesn't simplify anything. A better class would be Paycheck. Then your program can manipulate one or more Paycheck objects.

Another common mistake, particularly by students who are used to writing programs that consist of functions, is to turn an action into a class. For example, if your homework assignment is to compute a paycheck, you may consider writing a class ComputePaycheck. But can you visualize a "ComputePaycheck" object? The fact that "ComputePaycheck" isn't a noun tips you off that you are on the wrong track. On the other hand, a Paycheck class makes intuitive sense. The word "paycheck" is a noun. You can visualize a paycheck object. You can then think about useful member functions of the Paycheck class, such as compute_taxes, that help you solve the assignment.

When you analyze a problem description, you often find that you need multiple classes. It is then helpful to consider how these classes are related. One of the fundamental relationships between classes is the "aggregation" relationship (which is informally known as the "has-a" relationship).

In a class scheduling system, potential classes from the problem domain include Class, LectureHall, Instructor, and Student.

Figure 4 Class Diagram

The **aggregation** relationship states that objects of one class contain objects of another class. Consider a quiz that is made up of questions. Since each quiz has one or more questions, we say that the class Quiz aggregates the class Question. There is a standard notation, called a UML (Unified Modeling Language) class diagram, to describe class relationships. In the UML notation, aggregation is denoted by a line with a diamond-shaped symbol (see Figure 4).

> A class aggregates another if its objects contain objects of the other class.

Finding out about aggregation is very helpful for deciding how to implement classes. For example, when you implement the Quiz class, you will want to store the questions of a quiz as a data member. Since a quiz can have any number of questions, you will choose a vector:

```
class Quiz
{
   ...
private:
   vector<Question> questions;
};
```

In summary, when you analyze a problem description, you will want to carry out these tasks:

- Find the concepts that you need to implement as classes. Often, these will be nouns in the problem description.
- Find the responsibilities of the classes. Often, these will be verbs in the problem description.
- Find relationships between the classes that you have discovered. In this section, we described the aggregation relationship. In the next chapter, you will learn about another important relationship between classes, called inheritance.

A car has a motor and tires. In object-oriented design, this "has-a" relationship is called aggregation.

SELF CHECK

29. What is the rule of thumb for finding classes?

30. Your job is to write a program that plays chess. Might ChessBoard be an appropriate class? How about MovePiece?

31. In an e-mail system, messages are stored in a mailbox. Draw a UML diagram that shows the appropriate aggregation relationship.

32. You are implementing a system to manage a library, keeping track of which books are checked out by whom. Should the Book class aggregate Patron or the other way around?

33. In a library management system, what would be the relationship between classes Patron and Author?

Practice It   Now you can try these exercises at the end of the chapter: R9.23, R9.24, R9.26.

Programming Tip 9.3

Make Parallel Vectors into Vectors of Objects

Sometimes, you find yourself using vectors of the same length, each of which stores a part of what conceptually should be an object. In that situation, it is a good idea to reorganize your program and use a single vector whose elements are objects.

For example, suppose an invoice contains a series of item descriptions and prices. One solution is to keep two vectors:

```
vector<string> descriptions;
vector<double> prices;
```

Each of the vectors will have the same length, and the ith *slice*, consisting of descriptions[i] and prices[i], contains data that needs to be processed together. These vectors are called **parallel vectors** (see Figure 5).

Parallel vectors become a headache in larger programs. The programmer must ensure that the vectors always have the same length and that each slice is filled with values that actually belong together. Moreover, any function that operates on a slice must get all of the vectors as arguments, which is tedious to program.

The remedy is simple. Look at the slice and find the *concept* that it represents. Then make the concept into a class. In this example, each slice contains the description and price of an *item;* turn this into a class.

> Avoid parallel vectors by changing them into vectors of objects.

```
class Item
{
public:
   ...
private:
   string description;
   double price;
};
```

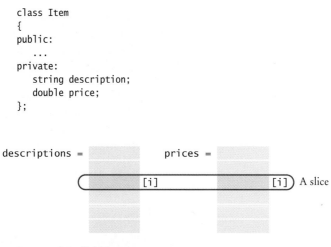

Figure 5   Parallel Vectors

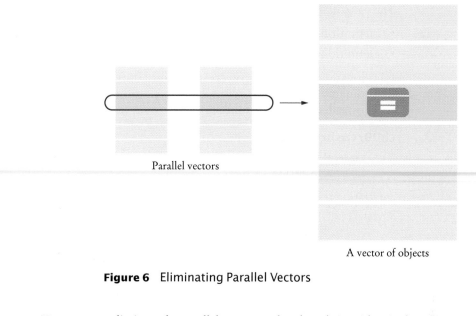

Parallel vectors

A vector of objects

Figure 6   Eliminating Parallel Vectors

You can now eliminate the parallel vectors and replace them with a single vector:

```
vector<Item> items;
```

Each slot in the resulting vector corresponds to a slice in the set of parallel vectors (see Figure 6).

9.8 Separate Compilation

The code of complex programs is distributed over multiple files.

When you write and compile small programs, you can place all your code into a single source file. When your programs get larger or you work in a team, that situation changes. You will want to split your code into separate source files. There are two reasons why this split becomes necessary. First, it takes time to compile a file, and it seems silly to wait for the compiler to keep translating code that doesn't change. If your code is distributed over several source files, then only those files that you change need to be recompiled. The second reason becomes apparent when you work with other programmers in a team. It would be very difficult for multiple programmers to edit a single source file simultaneously. Therefore, the program code is broken up so that each programmer is solely responsible for a separate set of files.

If your program is composed of multiple files, some of these files will define data types or functions that are needed in other files. There must be a path of communication between the files. In C++, that communication happens through the inclusion of **header files**.

A header file contains

Header files contain the definitions of classes and declarations of nonmember functions.

- Definitions of classes.
- Definitions of constants.
- Declarations of nonmember functions.

The source file contains

Source files contain function implementations.

- Definitions of member functions.
- Definitions of nonmember functions.

For the CashRegister class, you create a pair of files, cashregister.h and cashregister.cpp, that contain the interface and the implementation, respectively.

The header file contains the class definition:

ch09/cashregister.h

```
1   #ifndef CASHREGISTER_H
2   #define CASHREGISTER_H
3
4   /**
5       A simulated cash register that tracks the item count and
6       the total amount due.
7   */
8   class CashRegister
9   {
10  public:
11      /**
12          Constructs a cash register with cleared item count and total.
13      */
14      CashRegister();
15
16      /**
17          Clears the item count and the total.
18      */
19      void clear();
20
21      /**
22          Adds an item to this cash register.
23          @param price the price of this item
24      */
25      void add_item(double price);
26
27      /**
28          @return the total amount of the current sale
29      */
30      double get_total() const;
31
32      /**
33          @return the item count of the current sale
34      */
35      int get_count() const;
36
37  private:
38      int item_count;
39      double total_price;
40  };
41
42  #endif
```

You include this header file whenever the definition of the CashRegister class is required. Because this file is not a standard header file, you must enclose its name in quotes, not <...>, when you include it, like this:

```
#include "cashregister.h"
```

Note the set of directives that bracket the header file:

```
#ifndef CASHREGISTER_H
#define CASHREGISTER_H
...
#endif
```

Suppose a file includes two header files: cashregister.h, and another header file that itself includes cashregister.h. The effect of the directives is to skip the file when it is encountered the second time. If we did not have that check, the compiler would complain when it saw the definition for the CashRegister class twice. (Sadly, it doesn't check whether the definitions are identical.)

The source file for the CashRegister class simply contains the definitions of the member functions (including constructors).

Note that the source file cashregister.cpp includes its own header file cashregister.h. The compiler needs to know how the CashRegister class is defined in order to compile the member functions.

ch09/cashregister.cpp

```cpp
1   #include "cashregister.h"
2
3   CashRegister::CashRegister()
4   {
5      clear();
6   }
7
8   void CashRegister::clear()
9   {
10      item_count = 0;
11      total_price = 0;
12   }
13
14   void CashRegister::add_item(double price)
15   {
16      item_count++;
17      total_price = total_price + price;
18   }
19
20   double CashRegister::get_total() const
21   {
22      return total_price;
23   }
24
25   int CashRegister::get_count() const
26   {
27      return item_count;
28   }
```

Note that the function comments are in the header file, because comments are a part of the interface, not the implementation.

The cashregister.cpp file does *not* contain a main function. There are many potential programs that might make use of the CashRegister class. Each of these programs will need to supply its own main function, as well as other functions and classes.

Here is a simple test program that puts the CashRegister class to use. Its source file includes the cashregister.h header file.

ch09/registertest2.cpp

```cpp
1   #include <iostream>
2   #include <iomanip>
3   #include "cashregister.h"
4
5   using namespace std;
6
7   /**
8      Displays the item count and total price of a cash register.
9      @param reg  the cash register to display
10  */
11  void display(CashRegister reg)
12  {
13     cout << reg.get_count() << " $" << fixed << setprecision(2)
14        << reg.get_total() << endl;
15  }
16
17  int main()
18  {
19     CashRegister register1;
20     register1.clear();
21     register1.add_item(1.95);
22     display(register1);
23     register1.add_item(0.95);
24     display(register1);
25     register1.add_item(2.50);
26     display(register1);
27     return 0;
28  }
```

To build the complete program, you need to compile both the registertest2.cpp and cashregister.cpp source files (see Figure 7). The details depend on your compiler. For example, with the Gnu compiler, you issue the command

```
g++ -o registertest registertest2.cpp cashregister.cpp
```

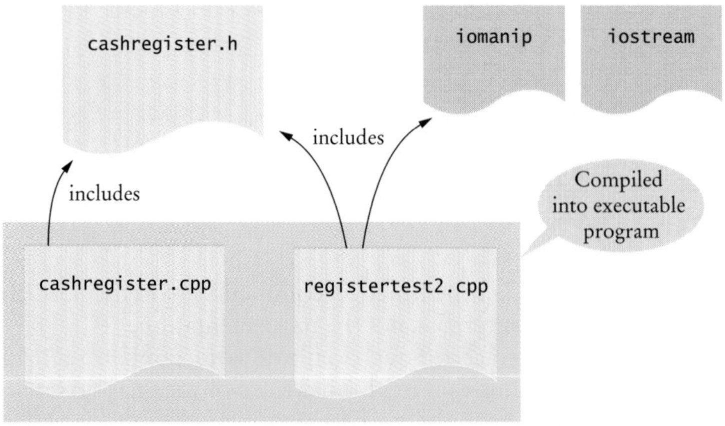

Figure 7 Compiling a Program from Multiple Source Files

You have just seen the simplest and most common case for designing header and source files. There are a few additional technical details that you should know.

- A header file should include all headers that are necessary for defining the class. For example, if a class uses the `string` class, include the `<string>` header as well. Anytime you include a header from the standard library, also include the directive

    ```
    using namespace std;
    ```

    item.h

    ```
    1  #include <string>
    2  using namespace std;
    3
    4  class Item
    5  {
    6     ...
    7  private:
    8     string description
    9  };
    ```

- Place shared constants into a header file. For example,

    volumes.h

    ```
    6  const double CAN_VOLUME = 0.355;
    ```

- To share a nonmember function, place the function declaration into a header file and the definition of the function into the corresponding source file.

    cube.h

    ```
    8  double cube_volume(double side_length);
    ```

    cube.cpp

    ```
    1  #include "cube.h"
    2
    3  double cube_volume(double side_length)
    4  {
    5     double volume = side_length * side_length * side_length;
    6     return volume;
    7  }
    ```

SELF CHECK

34. Suppose the cash register is enhanced to carry out direct debits from bank accounts, and a member function `debit(BankAccount&)` is added to the `CashRegister` class. Which header file do you need to include in `cashregister.h`?

35. In the enhancement described in Self Check 34, what additional file do you need to include in `cashregister.cpp`?

36. In the enhancement described in Self Check 34, what additional file do you need to include in the `bankaccount.h` file?

37. Suppose we want to move the `display` function from `registertest2.cpp` to the `cashregister.h` and `cashregister.cpp` files. Explain how those files need to change.

38. Where is the header file located that you include with the `#include <iostream>` directive?

Practice It   Now you can try these exercises at the end of the chapter: R9.28, R9.29, P9.20.

9.9 Pointers to Objects

The following sections discuss how to work with pointers to objects. As you will see in the next chapter, pointers to objects are important when you work with multiple objects from related classes.

9.9.1 Dynamically Allocating Objects

Use the new operator to obtain an object that is located on the heap.

It is common to allocate objects on the heap. As discussed in Section 7.4, you use the new operator to obtain memory from the heap. For example, the call

```
new CashRegister
```

returns a pointer to a CashRegister object. You can also supply construction arguments:

```
new BankAccount(1000)
```

The new operator returns a pointer to the allocated object.

You usually want to store the pointer that the new operator returns:

```
CashRegister* register_pointer = new CashRegister;
BankAccount* account_pointer = new BankAccount(1000);
```

Note that each of these definitions allocates two entities: a pointer variable and an object on the heap—see Figure 8.

When a heap object is no longer needed, use the delete operator to reclaim its memory.

When you no longer need a heap object, be sure to delete it:

```
delete account_pointer;
```

9.9.2 The -> Operator

Because register_pointer is a pointer to a CashRegister object, the value *register_pointer denotes the CashRegister object itself. To invoke a member function on that object, you might call

```
(*register_pointer).add_item(1.95);
```

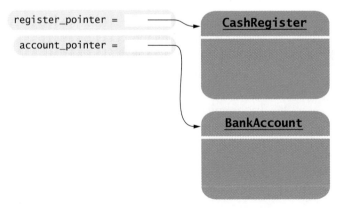

Figure 8 Pointers and the Objects to Which They Point

The parentheses are necessary because in C++ the dot operator takes precedence over the * operator. The expression without the parentheses would be a compile-time error:

```
*register_pointer.add_item(1.95); // Error—you can't apply . to a pointer
```

Because the dot operator has higher precedence than *, the dot would be applied to a pointer, not an object.

Use the -> operator to invoke a member function through a pointer.

Because calling a member function through a pointer is very common, there is an operator to abbreviate the "follow pointer and call member function" operation. That operator is written -> and usually pronounced as "arrow". Here is how you use the "arrow" operator:

```
register_pointer->add_item(1.95);
```

This call means: When invoking the add_item member function, set the implicit parameter to *register_pointer and the explicit parameter to 1.95.

9.9.3 The this Pointer

In a member function, the this pointer points to the implicit parameter.

Each member function has a special parameter variable, called this, which is a pointer to the implicit parameter. For example, consider the CashRegister::add_item function. If you call

```
register1.add_item(1.95)
```

then the this pointer has type CashRegister* and points to the register1 object.

You can use the this pointer inside the definition of a member function. For example, you can implement the add_item function as

```
void CashRegister::add_item(double price)
{
   this->item_count++;
   this->total_price = this->total_price + price;
}
```

Here, the expression this->item_count refers to the item_count data member of the implicit parameter (which is register1.item_count in our example). Some programmers like to use the this pointer in this fashion to make it clear that item_count is a data member and not a variable.

SELF CHECK

39. Write a statement that dynamically allocates a string object and saves the address in a pointer variable str_pointer.
40. Write a statement that deallocates the object that was allocated in Self Check 39.
41. Write a statement that dynamically allocates a string object with contents "Hello" and saves the address in a pointer variable str_pointer.
42. Write a statement that invokes the length member function on the object that was allocated in Self Check 41 and prints the result.
43. What is the type of this when the string::length member function is called?

Practice It   Now you can try these exercises at the end of the chapter: R9.30, P9.21, P9.22.

Destructors and Resource Management

A destructor is a special member function that is automatically executed under two circumstances:

- At the end of the block in which an object variable is defined
- When a heap object is deleted

To understand the need for destructors, consider an implementation of a string class, similar to that of the C++ library. The characters of a string are stored on the heap, and each `String` object contains a pointer to the array holding its characters.

```
class String
{
   ...
private:
   char* char_array;
}
```

The constructor allocates and initializes the character array:

```
String::String(const char initial_chars[])
{
   char_array = new char[strlen(initial_chars) + 1];
   strcpy(char_array, initial_chars);
}
```

It is the job of the destructor to deallocate this memory. The name of the destructor is the ~ character followed by the class name, that is, `~String` in our case. A class can have only one destructor, and the destructor has no arguments.

```
String::~String()
{
   delete[] char_array;
}
```

When a `String` object is no longer needed, the destructor is automatically invoked, and the memory for the characters is properly recycled (see Figure 9):

```
void fun()
{
   String name("Harry"); // ❶ Heap memory is allocated by the constructor
   ...
} // ❷ The destructor is invoked on name, and its heap memory is deallocated
```

As a rule of thumb, if a constructor calls `new`, you should supply a destructor that calls `delete`.

Unfortunately, just supplying a destructor is not enough. Consider this scenario:

```
String name1("Harry");
String name2("Sally");
name1 = name2;
```

The assignment has a very unfortunate effect: The memory for the first `String` has not been deallocated. (The destructor is only called at the end of the block in which `name1` is defined.) And the two `String` objects now share a pointer to the same area of heap memory. Eventually, that memory location will be deleted twice (see Figure 10).

This problem can be overcome by redefining what it means to assign one object to another. In this context, the assignment needs to

- Delete the memory of the `String` object on the left-hand side of the assignment (`name1` in our example).
- Allocate a new memory block to the left-hand side object, and fill it with a copy of the string on the right-hand side.

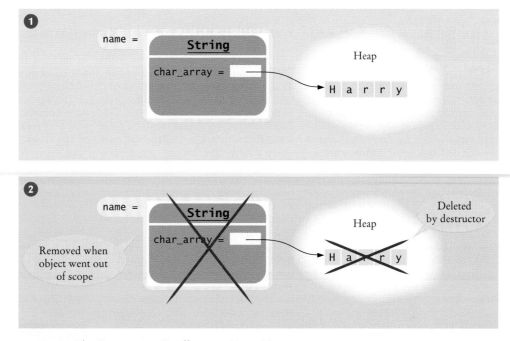

Figure 9   The Destructor Deallocates Heap Memory

In addition, one must also supply a "copy constructor" for making safe copies, for example, when passing an object as a function argument. The destructor, assignment operator, and copy constructor are often called the "big 3" operations of memory management in C++. (See Horstmann & Budd, *Big C++, 2nd Ed.,* Chapter 15, for details.)

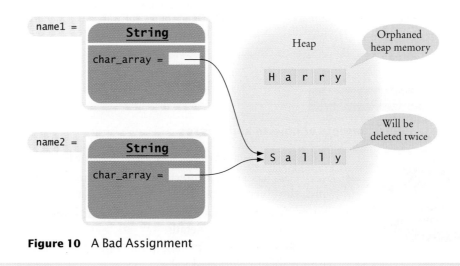

Figure 10   A Bad Assignment

Random Fact 9.2 Open Source and Free Software

Most companies that produce software regard the source code as a trade secret. After all, if customers or competitors had access to the source code, they could study it and create similar programs without paying the original vendor. For the same reason, customers dislike secret source code. If a company goes out of business or decides to discontinue support for a computer program, its users are left stranded. They are unable to fix bugs or adapt the program to a new operating system. Nowadays, some software packages are distributed with "open source" or "free software" licenses. Here, the term "free" doesn't refer to price, but to the freedom to inspect and modify the source code. Richard Stallman, a famous computer scientist and winner of a MacArthur "genius" grant, pioneered the concept of free software. He is the inventor of the Emacs text editor and the originator of the GNU project, which aims to create an entirely free version of a Unix-compatible operating system. All programs of the GNU project are licensed under the *General Public License* or GPL. The GPL allows you to make as many copies as you wish, make any modifications to the source, and redistribute the original and modified programs, charging nothing at all or whatever the market will bear. In return, you must agree that

your modifications also fall under the GPL. You must give out the source code to any changes that you distribute, and anyone else can distribute them under the same conditions. The GPL, and similar open source licenses, form a social contract. Users of the software enjoy the freedom to use and modify the software, and in return they are obligated to share any improvements that they make. Many programs, such as the Linux operating system and the GNU C++ compiler, are distributed under the GPL.

Some commercial software vendors have attacked the GPL as "viral" and "undermining the commercial software sector". Other companies have a more nuanced strategy, producing proprietary software while also contributing to open source projects.

Frankly, open source is not a panacea and there is plenty of room for the commercial software sector. Open source software often lacks the polish of commercial software because many of the programmers are volunteers who are interested in solving their own problems, not in making a product that is easy to use by others. Some product categories are not available at all as open source software because the development work is unattractive when there is little promise of commercial gain. Open source software has been most successful in areas that are

of interest to programmers, such as the Linux operating system, Web servers, and programming tools.

On the positive side, the open software community can be very competitive and creative. It is quite common to see several competing projects that take ideas from each other, all rapidly becoming more capable. Having many programmers involved, all reading the source code, often means that bugs tend to get squashed quickly. Eric Raymond describes open source development in his famous article "The Cathedral and the Bazaar" (http://catb.org/~esr/writings/cathedral-bazaar/cathedral-bazaar/index.html). He writes "Given enough eyeballs, all bugs are shallow".

Richard Stallman, a pioneer of the free source movement.

CHAPTER SUMMARY

Understand the concepts of objects and classes.

- A class describes a set of objects with the same behavior.
- Every class has a public interface: a collection of member functions through which the objects of the class can be manipulated.
- Encapsulation is the act of providing a public interface and hiding implementation details.
- Encapsulation enables changes in the implementation without affecting users of a class.

Formulate the public interface of a class in C++.

- A mutator member function changes the object on which it operates.
- An accessor member function does not change the object on which it operates. Use const with accessors.

Choose data members to represent the state of an object.

- An object holds data members that are accessed by member functions.
- Every object has its own set of data members.
- Private data members can only be accessed by member functions of the same class.

Implement member functions of a class.

- Use the *ClassName*:: prefix when defining member functions.
- The implicit parameter is a reference to the object on which a member function is applied.
- Explicit parameters of a member function are listed in the function definition.
- When calling another member function on the same object, do not use the dot notation.

Design and implement constructors.

- A constructor is called automatically whenever an object is created.
- The name of a constructor is the same as the class name.
- A default constructor has no arguments.
- A class can have multiple constructors.
- The compiler picks the constructor that matches the construction arguments.
- Be sure to initialize all number and pointer data members in a constructor.

Use the technique of object tracing for visualizing object behavior.

- Write the member functions on the front of a card, and the data member values on the back.
- Update the values of the data members when a mutator member function is called.

Discover classes that are needed for solving a programming problem.

- To discover classes, look for nouns in the problem description.
- Concepts from the problem domain are good candidates for classes.
- A class aggregates another if its objects contain objects of the other class.
- Avoid parallel vectors by changing them into vectors of objects.

Separate the interface and implementation of a class in header and source files.

- The code of complex programs is distributed over multiple files.
- Header files contain the definitions of classes and declarations of nonmember functions.
- Source files contain function implementations.

Use pointers to objects and manage dynamically allocated objects.

- Use the new operator to obtain an object that is located on the heap.
- The new operator returns a pointer to the allocated object.
- When a heap object is no longer needed, use the delete operator to reclaim its memory.
- Use the -> operator to invoke a member function through a pointer.
- In a member function, the this pointer points to the implicit parameter.

REVIEW EXERCISES

R9.1 List all classes in the C++ library that you have encountered in this book up to this point.

R9.2 Consider a Date class that stores a calendar date such as November 20, 2011. Consider two possible implementations of this class: by storing the day, month, and year, and by storing the number of days since January 1, 1900. Why might an implementor prefer the second version? How does the choice affect the user of the class?

R9.3 Write a partial C++ class definition that contains the public interface of the Date class described in Exercise R9.2. Supply member functions for setting the date to a particular year, month, and day, for advancing the date by a given number of days, and for finding the number of days between this date and another. Pay attention to const.

R9.4 What value is returned by the calls reg1.get_count(), reg1.get_total(), reg2.get_count(), and reg2.get_total() after these statements?

```
CashRegister reg1;
reg1.clear();
reg1.add_item(0.90);
reg1.add_item(1.95);
CashRegister reg2;
reg2.clear();
reg2.add_item(1.90);
```

R9.5 Consider the Menu class in How To 9.1 on page 409. What is displayed when the following calls are executed?

```
Menu simple_menu;
simple_menu.add_option("Ok");
simple_menu.add_option("Cancel");
int response = simple_menu.get_input();
```

R9.6 What is the *interface* of a class? How does it differ from the *implementation* of a class?

R9.7   What is a member function, and how does it differ from a nonmember function?

R9.8   What is a mutator function? What is an accessor function?

R9.9   What happens if you forget the const in an accessor function? What happens if you accidentally supply a const in a mutator function?

R9.10 What is an implicit parameter? How does it differ from an explicit parameter?

R9.11 How many implicit parameters can a member function have? How many implicit parameters can a nonmember function have? How many explicit parameters can a function have?

R9.12 What is a constructor?

R9.13 What is a default constructor? What is the consequence if a class does not have a default constructor?

R9.14 How many constructors can a class have? Can you have a class with no constructors? If a class has more than one constructor, which of them gets called?

R9.15 What is encapsulation? Why is it useful?

R9.16 Data members are hidden in the private section of a class, but they aren't hidden very well at all. Anyone can read the private section. Explain to what extent the private reserved word hides the private members of a class.

R9.17 You can read the item_count data member of the CashRegister class with the get_count accessor function. Should there be a set_count mutator function to change it? Explain why or why not.

R9.18 Suppose you implement a ChessBoard class. Provide data members to store the pieces on the board and the player who has the next turn.

R9.19 In a nonmember function, it is easy to differentiate between calls to member functions and calls to nonmember functions. How do you tell them apart? Why is it not as easy for functions that are called from a member function?

R9.20 Using the object tracing technique described in Section 9.6, trace the program at the end of Section 9.4.

R9.21 Using the object tracing technique described in Section 9.6, trace the program in Worked Example 9.1.

R9.22 Design a modification of the BankAccount class in Worked Example 9.1 in which the first five transactions per month are free and a $1 fee is charged for every additional transaction. Provide a member function that deducts the fee at the end of a month. What additional data members do you need? Using the object tracing technique described in Section 9.6, trace a scenario that shows how the fees are computed over two months.

R9.23 Consider the following problem description:

> Users place coins in a vending machine and select a product by pushing a button. If the inserted coins are sufficient to cover the purchase price of the product, the product is dispensed and change is given. Otherwise, the inserted coins are returned to the user.

What classes should you use to implement it?

R9.24 Consider the following problem description:

> **Employees receive their biweekly paychecks. They are paid their hourly rates for each hour worked; however, if they worked more than 40 hours per week, they are paid overtime at 150 percent of their regular wage.**

What classes should you use to implement it?

R9.25 Consider the following problem description:

> **Customers order products from a store. Invoices are generated to list the items and quantities ordered, payments received, and amounts still due. Products are shipped to the shipping address of the customer, and invoices are sent to the billing address.**

What classes should you use to implement it?

R9.26 Suppose a vending machine contains products, and users insert coins into the vending machine to purchase products. Draw a UML diagram showing the aggregation relationships between the classes VendingMachine, Coin, and Product.

R9.27 Suppose an Invoice object contains descriptions of the products ordered and the billing and shipping address of the customer. Draw a UML diagram showing the aggregation relationships between the classes Invoice, Address, Customer, and Product.

R9.28 Consider the implementation of a program that plays TicTacToe, with two classes Player and TicTacToeBoard. Each class implementation is placed in its own C++ source file and each class interface is placed in its own header file. In addition, a source file game.cpp contains the code for playing the game and displaying the scores of the players. Describe the contents of each header file, and determine in which files each of them is included.

R9.29 What would happen if the display function was moved from registertest2.cpp to cashregister.h? Try it out if you are not sure.

R9.30 In Exercise P9.22, a MenuItem optionally contains a Menu. Generally, there are two ways for implementing an "optional" relationship. You can use a pointer that may be NULL. Or you may use an indicator, such as a bool value, that specifies whether the optional item is present. Why are pointers required in this case?

PROGRAMMING EXERCISES

P9.1 Implement a class that models a *tally counter*, a mechanical device that is used to count people—for example, to find out how many people attend a concert or board a bus. Whenever the operator pushes a button, the counter value advances by one. Model this operation with a count member function. A physical counter has a display to show the current value. In your class, use a get_value member function instead.

P9.2 Implement a class Rectangle. Provide a constructor to construct a rectangle with a given width and height, member functions get_perimeter and get_area that compute the perimeter and area, and a member function void resize(double factor) that resizes the rectangle by multiplying the width and height by the given factor.

P9.3 Reimplement the CashRegister class so that it keeps track of the price of each added item in a vector<double>. Remove the item_count and total_price data members. Reimplement the clear, add_item, get_total, and get_count member functions. Add a member function display_all that displays the prices of all items in the current sale.

P9.4 Reimplement the CashRegister class so that it keeps track of the total price as an integer: the total cents of the price. For example, instead of storing 17.29, store the integer 1729. Such an implementation is commonly used because it avoids the accumulation of roundoff errors. Do not change the public interface of the class.

P9.5 Add a feature to the CashRegister class for computing sales tax. The tax rate should be supplied when constructing a CashRegister object. Add add_taxable_item and get_total_tax member functions. (Items added with add_item are not taxable.)

P9.6 After closing time, the store manager would like to know how much business was transacted during the day. Modify the CashRegister class to enable this functionality. Supply member functions get_sales_total and get_sales_count to get the total amount of all sales and the number of sales. Supply a member function reset_sales that resets any counters and totals so that the next day's sales start from zero.

P9.7 Reimplement the Menu class so that it stores all menu items in one long string. *Hint:* Keep a separate counter for the number of options. When a new option is added, append the option count, the option, and a newline character.

P9.8 Implement a class StreetAddress. An address has a house number, a street, an optional apartment number, a city, a state, and a postal code. Supply two constructors: one with an apartment number and one without. Supply a print member function that prints the address with the street (and optional apartment number) on one line and the city, state, and postal code on the next line. Supply a member function comes_before that tests whether one address comes before another when the addresses are compared by postal code.

P9.9 Implement a class SodaCan with member functions get_surface_area() and get_volume(). In the constructor, supply the height and radius of the can.

P9.10 Implement a class Portfolio. This class has two data members, checking and savings, of the type BankAccount that was developed in Worked Example 9.1 (ch09/account.cpp in your code files). Implement four member functions:

```
deposit(double amount, string account)
withdraw(double amount, string account)
transfer(double amount, string account)
print_balances()
```

Here the account string is "S" or "C". For the deposit or withdrawal, it indicates which account is affected. For a transfer, it indicates the account from which the money is taken; the money is automatically transferred to the other account.

P9.11 Implement a class Student. For the purpose of this exercise, a student has a name and a total quiz score. Supply an appropriate constructor and functions get_name(), add_quiz(int score), get_total_score(), and get_average_score(). To compute the latter, you also need to store the *number of quizzes* that the student took.

P9.12 Modify the Student class of Exercise P9.11 to compute grade point averages. Member functions are needed to add a grade and get the current GPA. Specify grades as elements of a class Grade. Supply a constructor that constructs a grade from a string, such as "B+". You will also need a function that translates grades into their numeric values (for example, "B+" becomes 3.3).

P9.13 Define a class Country that stores the name of the country, its population, and its area. Using that class, write a program that reads in a set of countries and prints

- The country with the largest area.
- The country with the largest population.
- The country with the largest population density (people per square kilometer or mile).

P9.14 Design a class Message that models an e-mail message. A message has a recipient, a sender, and a message text. Support the following member functions:

- A constructor that takes the sender and recipient and sets the time stamp to the current time
- A member function append that appends a line of text to the message body
- A member function to_string that makes the message into one long string like this: "From: Harry Hacker\nTo: Rudolf Reindeer\n ..."
- A member function print that prints the message text. *Hint:* Use to_string.

Write a program that uses this class to make a message and print it.

P9.15 Design a class Mailbox that stores e-mail messages, using the Message class of Exercise P9.14. Implement the following member functions:

```
void Mailbox::add_message(Message m)

Message Mailbox::get_message(int i) const

void remove_message(int i)
```

P9.16 Implement a VotingMachine class that can be used for a simple election. Have member functions to clear the machine state, to vote for a Democrat, to vote for a Republican, and to get the tallies for both parties. (*Hint:* Use a function in the <cctime> header to get the current date.)

P9.17 Provide a class for authoring a simple letter. In the constructor, supply the names of the sender and the recipient:

```
Letter(string from, string to)
```

Supply a member function

```
void add_line(string line)
```

to add a line of text to the body of the letter. Supply a member function

```
string get_text()
```

that returns the entire text of the letter. The text has the form:

Dear *recipient name*:
blank line
first line of the body
second line of the body
. . .
last line of the body
blank line
Sincerely,

blank line
sender name

Also supply a main function that prints this letter.

```
Dear John:

I am sorry we must part.
I wish you all the best.

Sincerely,

Mary
```

Construct an object of the Letter class and call add_line twice.

P9.18 Write a class Bug that models a bug moving along a horizontal line. The bug moves either to the right or left. Initially, the bug moves to the right, but it can turn to change its direction. In each move, its position changes by one unit in the current direction. Provide a constructor

```
Bug(int initial_position)
```

and member functions

```
void turn()
void move()
int get_position()
```

Sample usage:

```
Bug bugsy(10);
bugsy.move(); // Now the position is 11
bugsy.turn();
bugsy.move(); // Now the position is 10
```

Your main function should construct a bug, make it move and turn a few times, and print the actual and expected positions.

P9.19 Implement a class Moth that models a moth flying in a straight line. The moth has a position, the distance from a fixed origin. When the moth moves toward a point of light, its new position is halfway between its old position and the position of the light source. Supply a constructor

```
Moth(double initial_position)
```

and member functions

```
void move_to_light(double light_position)
double get_position()
```

Your main function should construct a moth, move it toward a couple of light sources, and check that the moth's position is as expected.

P9.20 Implement classes Person and StreetAddress. Each person has a street address. Provide display functions in each class for displaying their contents. Distribute your code over three source files, one for each class, and one containing the main function. Construct two Person objects and display them.

P9.21 Modify the Person class in Exercise P9.20 so that it contains a pointer to the street address. Construct and display two Person objects that share the same StreetAddress object.

P9.22 Reimplement the Menu class from How To 9.1 to support submenus similar to the ones in a graphical user interface.

A menu contains a sequence of menu items. Each menu item has a name and, optionally, a submenu.

Implement classes Menu and MenuItem. Supply a function to display a menu and get user input. Simply number the displayed items and have the user enter the number of the selected item. When an item with a submenu is selected, display the submenu. Otherwise simply print a message with the name of the selected item.

Note that there is a circular dependency between the two classes. To break it, first provide a declaration

```
class Menu;
```

Then define the MenuItem class and finally define the Menu class and the main function.

Engineering P9.23 Define a class ComboLock that works like the combination lock in a gym locker, as shown here. The lock is constructed with a combination—three numbers between 0 and 39. The reset function resets the dial so that it points to 0. The turn_left and turn_right functions turn the dial by a given number of ticks to the left or right. The open function attempts to open the lock. The lock opens if the user first turned it right to the first number in the combination, then left to the second, and then right to the third.

```
class ComboLock
{
public:
    ComboLock(int secret1, int secret2, int secret3);
    void reset();
    void turn_left(int ticks);
    void turn_right(int ticks);
    bool open() const;
```

```
private:
    ...
};
```

Engineering P9.24 Implement a class Car with the following properties. A car has a certain fuel efficiency (measured in miles/gallon) and a certain amount of fuel in the gas tank. The efficiency is specified in the constructor, and the initial fuel level is 0. Supply a member function drive that simulates driving the car for a certain distance, reducing the fuel level in the gas tank, and member functions get_gas_level, to return the current fuel level, and add_gas, to tank up. Sample usage:

```
Car my_hybrid(50); // 50 miles per gallon
my_hybrid.add_gas(20); // Tank 20 gallons
my_hybrid.drive(100); // Drive 100 miles
cout << my_hybrid.get_gas_level() << endl; // Print fuel remaining
```

Engineering P9.25 Write a program that prints all real solutions to the quadratic equation $ax^2 + bx + c = 0$. Read in a, b, c and use the quadratic formula. You may assume that $a \neq 0$. If the *discriminant* $b^2 - 4ac$ is negative, display a message stating that there are no real solutions.

Implement a class QuadraticEquation whose constructor receives the coefficients a, b, c of the quadratic equation. Supply member functions get_solution1 and get_solution2 that get the solutions, using the quadratic formula, or 0 if no solution exists. The get_solution1 function should return the smaller of the two solutions.

Supply a function

```
bool has_solutions() const
```

that returns false if the discriminant is negative.

Engineering P9.26 Design a class Cannonball to model a cannonball that is fired into the air. A ball has

- An x- and a y-position.
- An x- and a y-velocity.

Supply the following member functions:

- A constructor with an x-position (the y-position is initially 0)
- A member function move(double sec) that moves the ball to the next position (First compute the distance traveled in sec seconds, using the current velocities, then update the x- and y-positions; then update the y-velocity by taking into account the gravitational acceleration of -9.81 m/sec^2; the x-velocity is unchanged.) (See Exercise P4.29 for additional details.)
- A member function shoot whose parameters are the angle α and initial velocity v (Compute the x-velocity as $v \cos \alpha$ and the y-velocity as $v \sin \alpha$; then keep calling move with a time interval of 0.1 seconds until the y-position is ≤ 0; display the (x, y) position after every move.)

Use this class in a program that prompts the user for the starting angle and the initial velocity. Then call shoot.

Engineering P9.27 The colored bands on the top-most resistor shown in the photo below indicate a resistance of 6.2 kΩ $\pm 5\%$. The resistor tolerance of $\pm 5\%$ indicates the acceptable variation in the resistance. A 6.2 kΩ $\pm 5\%$ resistor could have a resistance as small as 5.89 kΩ or as large as 6.51 kΩ. We say that 6.2 kΩ is the *nominal value* of the resistance and that the actual value of the resistance can be any value between 5.89 kΩ and 6.51 kΩ.

Write a C++ program that represents a resistor as a class. Provide a single constructor that accepts values for the nominal resistance and tolerance and then determines the actual value randomly. The class should provide public member functions to get the nominal resistance, tolerance, and the actual resistance.

Write a main function for the C++ program that demonstrates that the class works properly by displaying actual resistances for ten 330 Ω ±10% resistors.

Engineering P9.28 In the Resistor class from Exercise P9.27, supply a method that returns a description of the "color bands" for the resistance and tolerance. A resistor has four color bands:

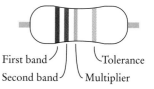

First band / Tolerance
Second band / Multiplier

- The first band is the first significant digit of the resistance value.
- The second band is the second significant digit of the resistance value.
- The third band is the decimal multiplier.
- The fourth band indicates the tolerance.

Color	Digit	Multiplier	Tolerance
Black	0	$\times 10^0$	—
Brown	1	$\times 10^1$	±1%
Red	2	$\times 10^2$	±2%
Orange	3	$\times 10^3$	—
Yellow	4	$\times 10^4$	—
Green	5	$\times 10^5$	±0.5%
Blue	6	$\times 10^6$	±0.25%
Violet	7	$\times 10^7$	±0.1%
Gray	8	$\times 10^8$	±0.05%
White	9	$\times 10^9$	—
Gold	—	$\times 10^{-1}$	±5%
Silver	—	$\times 10^{-2}$	±10%
None	—	—	±20%

For example (using the values from the table as a key), a resistor with red, violet, green, and gold bands (left to right) will have 2 as the first digit, 7 as the second digit, a multiplier of 10^5, and a tolerance of $\pm 5\%$, for a resistance of 2,700 kΩ, plus or minus 5%.

Engineering P9.29 The figure below shows a frequently used electric circuit called a "voltage divider". The input to the circuit is the voltage v_i. The output is the voltage v_o. The output of a voltage divider is proportional to the input, and the constant of proportionality is called the "gain" of the circuit. The voltage divider is represented by the equation

$$G = \frac{v_o}{v_i} = \frac{R_2}{R_1 + R_2}$$

where G is the gain and R_1 and R_2 are the resistances of the two resistors that comprise the voltage divider.

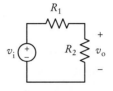

Manufacturing variations cause the actual resistance values to deviate from the nominal values, as described in Exercise P9.27. In turn, variations in the resistance values cause variations in the values of the gain of the voltage divider. We calculate the *nominal value of the gain* using the nominal resistance values and the *actual value of the gain* using actual resistance values.

Write a C++ program that contains two classes, `VoltageDivider` and `Resistor`. The `Resistor` class is described in Exercise P9.27. The `VoltageDivider` class should have two data members that are objects of the `Resistor` class. Provide a single constructor that accepts two `Resistor` objects, nominal values for their resistances, and the resistor tolerance. The class should provide public member functions to get the nominal and actual values of the voltage divider's gain.

Write a `main` function for the program that demonstrates that the class works properly by displaying nominal and actual gain for ten voltage dividers each consisting of 5% resistors having nominal values $R_1 = 250\ \Omega$ and $R_2 = 750\ \Omega$.

ANSWERS TO SELF-CHECK QUESTIONS

1. `cin` is an object, `string` is a class.
2. Through the `substr` member function and the `[]` operator.
3. As a `vector<char>`. As a char array.
4. None. The member functions will have the same effect, and your code could not have manipulated `string` objects in any other way.
5. `2 1.90`
6. There is no member function named `get_amount_due`.
7. `int get_dollars() const;`
8. `length`, `substr`

9. A mutator. Getting a character removes it from the stream, thereby modifying it. Not convinced? Consider what happens if you call the `get` function twice. You will usually get two different characters. But if you call an accessor twice on an object (without a mutation between the two calls), you are sure to get the same result.

10. 2, 1.85, 1, 1.90

11. The code tries to access a private data member.

12. (1) ```
    int hours; // Between 1 and 12
    int minutes; // Between 0 and 59
    bool pm; // True for P.M., false for A.M.
    ```

    (2) ```
    int hours; // Military time, between 0 and 23
    int minutes; // Between 0 and 59
    ```

    (3) ```
    int total_minutes // Between 0 and 60 * 24 - 1
    ```

13. They need not change their programs at all since the public interface has not changed. They need to recompile with the new version of the `Time` class.

14. (1) `string letter_grade; // "A+", "B"`

    (2) `double number_grade; // 4.3, 3.0`

15. (1) The `CashRegister::` is missing. (2) The `const` is missing.

16. ```
    void CashRegister::add_items(int quantity, double price)
    {
        item_count = item_count + quantity;
        total_price = total_price + quantity * price;
    }
    ```

17. ```
    int CashRegister::get_dollars() const
    {
        int dollars = total_price; // Truncates cents
        return dollars;
    }
    ```

18. Three parameters: two explicit parameters of type `int`, and one implicit parameter of type `string`.

19. One parameter: the implicit parameter of type `string`. The function has no explicit parameters.

20. `BankAccount::BankAccount() { balance = 0; }`

21. ```
    BankAccount::BankAccount(double initial_balance)
    {
        balance = initial_balance;
    }
    ```

22. ```
    Item::Item()
    {
        price = 0;
    }
    ```

    Note that the `description` data member need not be initialized.

23. ```
    CashRegister::CashRegister()
    {
        clear();
    }
    ```

24. (a) Default constructor. (b) `Item(string)` or `Item(const char[])`
    (c) `Item(double)` (d) `Item(string, double)` (e) Does not define an object.

25.

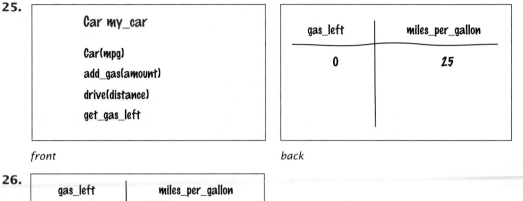

Car my_car		gas_left	miles_per_gallon
Car(mpg)		0	25
add_gas(amount)			
drive(distance)			
get_gas_left			

front   *back*

26.

gas_left	miles_per_gallon
~~0~~	25
~~20~~	
~~16~~	
~~8~~	
13	

27.

gas_left	miles_per_gallon	total_miles
0	25	0

28.

gas_left	miles_per_gallon	total_miles
~~0~~	25	0
~~20~~		
~~16~~		100
~~8~~		200
13		

29. Look for nouns in the problem description.

30. Yes (ChessBoard) and no (MovePiece).

31.

Mailbox ◇——— Message

32. Typically, a library system wants to track which books a patron has checked out, so it makes more sense to have Patron aggregate Book. However, there is not always one true answer in design. If you feel strongly that it is important to identify the patron who had checked out a particular book (perhaps to notify the patron to return it because it was requested by someone else), then you can argue that the aggregation should go the other way around.

33. There would be no relationship.

34. The header file that defines the `BankAccount` class, probably named `bankaccount.h`.

35. None. The `cashregister.cpp` file includes `cashregister.h`, which includes `bankaccount.h`.

36. None. The bank account need not know anything about cash registers.

37. Add the following line to `cashregister.h`:

    ```
    void display(CashRegister reg);
    ```

    Add the implementation of the `display` function to `cashregister.cpp`.

38. The answer depends on your system. On my system, the file is located at `/usr/include/c++/4.2/iostream`.

39. `string* str_pointer = new string;`

40. `delete str_pointer;`

41. `string* str_pointer = new string("Hello");`

    or

    ```
    string* str_pointer = new string;
    *str_pointer = "Hello";
    ```

42. `cout << str_pointer->length();`

43. `string*`, or more accurately, `const string*` because `length` is an accessor function.

INHERITANCE

Objects from related classes usually share common behavior. For example, shovels, rakes, and clippers all perform gardening tasks. In this chapter, you will learn how the notion of inheritance expresses the relationship between specialized and general classes. By using inheritance, you will be able to share code between classes and provide services that can be used by multiple classes.

10.1 Inheritance Hierarchies

> A derived class inherits data and behavior from a base class.

In object-oriented design, **inheritance** is a relationship between a more general class (called the **base class**) and a more specialized class (called the **derived class**). The derived class inherits data and behavior from the base class. For example, consider the relationships between different kinds of vehicles depicted in Figure 1.

Cars share the common traits of all vehicles, such as the ability to transport people from one place to another. We say that the class Car inherits from the class Vehicle. In this relationship, the Vehicle class is the base class and the Car class is the derived class.

Informally, the inheritance relationship is called the *is-a* relationship. Contrast this relationship with the *has-a* relationship that we discussed in Section 9.7. Every car *is a* vehicle. Every vehicle *has an* engine.

> You can always use a derived-class object in place of a base-class object.

The inheritance relationship is very powerful because it allows us to reuse algorithms with objects of different classes. Suppose we have an algorithm that manipulates a Vehicle object. Because a car is a special kind of vehicle, we can supply a Car object to such an algorithm, and it will work correctly. This is an example of the **substitution principle** that states that you can always use a derived-class object when a base-class object is expected.

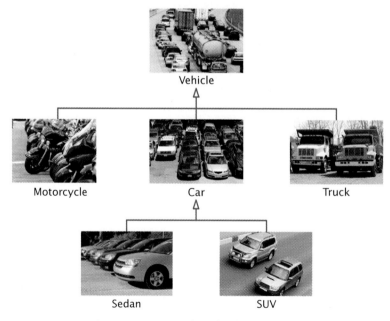

Figure 1 An Inheritance Hierarchy of Vehicle Classes

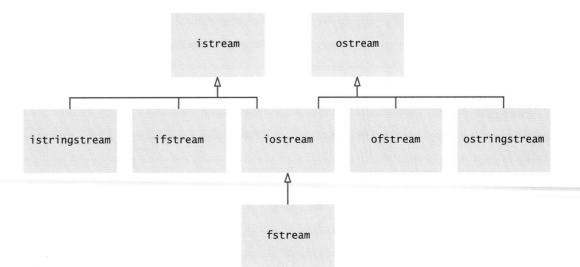

Figure 2 The Inheritance Hierarchy of Stream Classes

The inheritance relationship can give rise to hierarchies where classes get ever more specialized, as shown in Figure 1. The C++ stream classes, shown in Figure 2, are another example of such a hierarchy. Figure 2 uses the UML notation for inheritance where the base and derived class are joined with an arrow that points to the base class.

As you can see, an ifstream (an input stream that reads from a file) is a special case of an istream (an input stream that reads data from any source). If you have an ifstream, it can be the argument for a function that expects an istream.

```
void process_input(istream& in) // Can call with an ifstream object
```

Why provide a function that processes istream objects instead of ifstream objects? That function is more useful because it can handle *any* kind of input stream (such as an istringstream, which is convenient for testing). This again is the substitution principle at work.

In this chapter, we will consider a simple hierarchy of classes. Most likely, you have taken computer-graded quizzes. A quiz consists of questions, and there are different kinds of questions:

- Fill-in-the-blank

- Choice (single or multiple)

- Numeric (where an approximate answer is ok; e.g., 1.33 when the actual answer is 4/3)

- Free response

We will develop a simple but flexible quiz-taking program to illustrate inheritance.

Figure 3 shows an inheritance hierarchy for these question types.

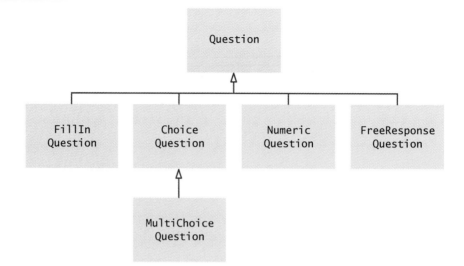

Figure 3 Inheritance Hierarchy of Question Types

At the root of this hierarchy is the Question type. A question can display its text, and it can check whether a given response is a correct answer:

```
class Question
{
public:
    Question();
    void set_text(string question_text);
    void set_answer(string correct_response);
    bool check_answer(string response) const;
    void display() const;
private:
    string text;
    string answer;
};
```

How the text is displayed depends on the question type. Later in this chapter, you will see some variations, but the base class simply sends the question text to cout. How the response is checked also depends on the question type. As already mentioned, a numeric question might accept approximate answers (see Exercise P10.1). In Exercise P10.3, you will see another way of checking the response. But in the base class, we will simply require that the response match the correct answer exactly.

In the following sections, you will see how to form derived classes that inherit the member functions and data members of this base class.

Here is the implementation of the Question class and a simple test program. Note that the Question class constructor needs to do no work because the text and answer fields are automatically set to the empty string. The boolalpha stream manipulator in the main function causes Boolean values to be displayed as true and false instead of the default 1 and 0.

ch10/quiz1/test.cpp

```
1   #include <iostream>
2   #include <sstream>
3   #include <string>
```

```
 4
 5   using namespace std;
 6
 7   class Question
 8   {
 9   public:
10      /**
11         Constructs a question with empty text and answer.
12      */
13      Question();
14
15      /**
16         @param question_text the text of this question
17      */
18      void set_text(string question_text);
19
20      /**
21         @param correct_response the answer for this question
22      */
23      void set_answer(string correct_response);
24
25      /**
26         @param response the response to check
27         @return true if the response was correct, false otherwise
28      */
29      bool check_answer(string response) const;
30
31      /**
32         Displays this question.
33      */
34      void display() const;
35
36   private:
37      string text;
38      string answer;
39   };
40
41   Question::Question()
42   {
43   }
44
45   void Question::set_text(string question_text)
46   {
47      text = question_text;
48   }
49
50   void Question::set_answer(string correct_response)
51   {
52      answer = correct_response;
53   }
54
55   bool Question::check_answer(string response) const
56   {
57      return response == answer;
58   }
59
60   void Question::display() const
61   {
62      cout << text << endl;
63   }
```

```
64
65   int main()
66   {
67      string response;
68      cout << boolalpha; // Show Boolean values as true, false
69
70      Question q1;
71      q1.set_text("Who was the inventor of C++?");
72      q1.set_answer("Bjarne Stroustrup");
73
74      q1.display();
75      cout << "Your answer: ";
76      getline(cin, response);
77      cout << q1.check_answer(response) << endl;
78
79      return 0;
80   }
```

Program Run

```
Who was the inventor of C++?
Your answer: Bjarne Stroustrup
true
```

SELF CHECK

1. Consider classes Manager and Employee. Which should be the base class and which should be the derived class?

2. What are the inheritance relationships between classes BankAccount, Checking-Account, and SavingsAccount?

3. Consider the function do_something(istream& stream). List all stream classes from Figure 2 whose objects can be passed to this function.

4. Consider the function do_something(Car& c). List all vehicle classes from Figure 1 whose objects *cannot* be passed to this function.

5. Should a class Quiz inherit from the class Question? Why or why not?

Practice It Now you can try these exercises at the end of the chapter: R10.1, R10.2, R10.5.

10.2 Implementing Derived Classes

In C++, you form a derived class from a base class by specifying what makes the derived class different. You define the member functions that are new to the derived class. The derived class inherits all member functions from the base class, but you can change the implementation if the inherited behavior is not appropriate.

The derived class automatically inherits all data members from the base class. You only define the added data members.

Here is the syntax for the definition of a derived class:

```
class ChoiceQuestion : public Question
{
public:
    New and changed member functions
private:
    Additional data members
};
```

Like the manufacturer of a stretch limo, who starts with a regular car and modifies it, a programmer makes a derived class by modifying another class.

The : symbol denotes inheritance. The reserved word `public` is required for a technical reason (see Common Error 10.1 on page 449).

A `ChoiceQuestion` object differs from a `Question` object in three ways:

- Its objects store the various choices for the answer.
- There is a member function for adding another choice.
- The `display` function of the `ChoiceQuestion` class shows these choices so that the respondent can choose one of them.

When the `ChoiceQuestion` class inherits from the `Question` class, it needs only to spell out these three differences:

```
class ChoiceQuestion : public Question
{
public:
   ChoiceQuestion();
   void add_choice(string choice, bool correct);
   void display() const;
private:
   vector<string> choices;
};
```

Figure 4 shows the layout of a `ChoiceQuestion` object. It inherits the text and answer data members from the `Question` base object, and it adds an additional data member: the choices vector.

The `add_choice` function is specific to the `ChoiceQuestion` class. You can only apply it to `ChoiceQuestion` objects, not general `Question` objects. However, the `display` function is a redefinition of a function that exists in the base class, to take into account the special needs of the derived class. We say that the derived class **overrides** this function. You will see how in Section 10.3

In the `ChoiceQuestion` class definition you specify only new member functions and data members. All other member functions and data members of the `Question` class are automatically inherited by the `Question` class. For example, each `ChoiceQuestion` object still has text and answer data members, and `set_text`, `set_answer`, and `check_answer` member functions.

> A derived class can override a base-class function by providing a new implementation.

> The derived class inherits all data members and all functions that it does not override.

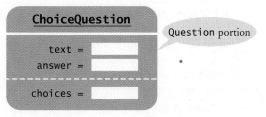

Figure 4 Data Layout of a Derived-Class Object

Syntax 10.1 Derived-Class Definition

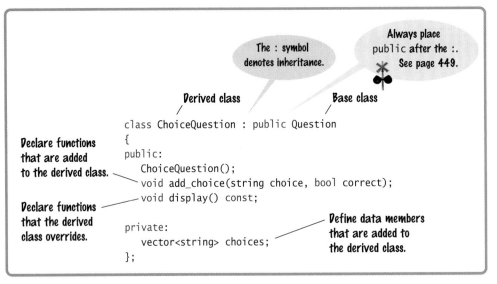

You can call the inherited member functions on a derived-class object:

```
choice_question.set_answer("2");
```

However, the inherited data members are inaccessible. Because these members are private data of the base class, only the base class has access to them. The derived class has no more access rights than any other class.

In particular, the `ChoiceQuestion` member functions cannot directly access the `answer` member. These member functions must use the public interface of the `Question` class to access its private data, just like every other function.

To illustrate this point, let us implement the `add_choice` member function. The function has two parameters: the choice to be added (which is appended to the vector of choices), and a Boolean value to indicate whether this choice is correct. If it is true, set the answer to the current choice number. (We use an `ostringstream` to convert the number to a string—see Section 8.4 for details.)

```
void ChoiceQuestion::add_choice(string choice, bool correct)
{
    choices.push_back(choice);
    if (correct)
    {
        // Convert choices.size() to string
        ostringstream stream;
        stream << choices.size();
        string num_str = stream.str();
        // Set num_str as the answer
        ...
    }
}
```

You can't just access the `answer` member in the base class. Fortunately, the `Question` class has a `set_answer` member function. You can call that member function. On which object? The question that you are currently modifying—that is, the implicit parameter of the `ChoiceQuestion::add_choice` function. As you saw in Chapter 9, if you invoke a member function on the implicit parameter, you don't specify the parameter but just write the member function name:

```
set_answer(num_str);
```

The compiler interprets this call as

```
implicit parameter.set_answer(num_str);
```

SELF CHECK

6. Suppose q is an object of the class Question and cq an object of the class Choice-Question. Which of the following calls are legal?

   a. q.set_answer(response)

   b. cq.set_answer(response)

   c. q.add_option(option, true)

   d. cq.add_option(option, true)

7. Define a class Manager that inherits from the class Employee and adds a data member bonus for storing a salary bonus. Omit the constructor declaration.

8. Suppose the class Employee is defined as follows:

```
class Employee
{
public:
    Employee();
    void set_name(string new_name);
    void set_base_salary(double new_salary);
    string get_name();
    double get_salary() const;
private:
    string name;
    double base_salary;
}
```

   Which data members does the Manager class from Self Check 7 have?

9. Define a class Manager that inherits from the class Employee and overrides the get_salary function.

10. Which member functions does the Manager class from Self Check 9 inherit?

Practice It   Now you can try these exercises at the end of the chapter: P10.2, P10.6.

Common Error 10.1

Private Inheritance

It is a common error to forget the reserved word public that must follow the colon after the derived-class name.

```
class ChoiceQuestion : Question // Error
{
    ...
};
```

The class definition will compile. The ChoiceQuestion still inherits from Question, but it inherits *privately*. That is, only the member functions of ChoiceQuestion get to call member functions of Question. Whenever another function invokes a Question member function on a ChoiceQuestion object, the compiler will flag this as an error:

```
int main()
{
```

```
    ChoiceQuestion q;
    ...
    cout << q.check_answer(response); // Error
}
```

This private inheritance is rarely useful. In fact, it violates the spirit of using inheritance in the first place—namely, to create objects that are usable just like the base-class objects. You should always use public inheritance and remember to supply the `public` reserved word in the definition of the derived class.

Common Error 10.2

Replicating Base-Class Members

A derived class has no access to the data members of the base class.

```
ChoiceQuestion::ChoiceQuestion(string question_text)
{
    text = question_text; // Error—tries to access private base-class member
}
```

When faced with a compiler error, beginners commonly "solve" this issue by adding *another* data member with the same name to the derived class:

```
class ChoiceQuestion : public Question
{
    ...
private:
    vector<string> choices;
    string text; // Don't!
}
```

Sure, now the constructor compiles, but it doesn't set the correct text! Such a ChoiceQuestion object has two data members, both named text. The constructor sets one of them, and the display member function displays the other.

Instead of uselessly replicating a base-class data member, you need to call a member function that updates the base-class member, such as the set_text function in our example.

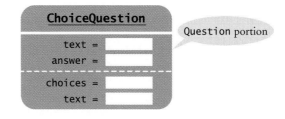

Programming Tip 10.1

Use a Single Class for Variation in Values, Inheritance for Variation in Behavior

The purpose of inheritance is to model objects with different *behavior*. When students first learn about inheritance, they have a tendency to overuse it, by creating multiple classes even though the variation could be expressed with a simple data member.

Consider a program that tracks the fuel efficiency of a fleet of cars by logging the distance traveled and the refueling amounts. Some cars in the fleet are hybrids. Should you create a derived class HybridCar? Not in this application. Hybrids don't behave any differently than other cars when it comes to driving and refueling. They just have a better fuel efficiency. A single Car class with a data member

```
double miles_per_gallon;
```

is entirely sufficient.

However, if you write a program that shows how to repair different kinds of vehicles, then it makes sense to have a separate class HybridCar. When it comes to repairs, hybrid cars behave differently from other cars.

Special Topic 10.1

Calling the Base-Class Constructor

Consider the process of constructing a derived-class object. A derived-class constructor can only initialize the data members of the derived class. But the base-class data members also need to be initialized. Unless you specify otherwise, the base-class data members are initialized with the default constructor of the base class.

> Unless specified otherwise, the base-class data members are initialized with the default constructor.

In order to specify another constructor, you use an initializer list, as described in Special Topic 9.1. Specify the name of the base class and the construction arguments in the initializer list. For example, suppose the Question base class had a constructor for setting the question text. Here is how a derived-class constructor could call that base-class constructor:

```
ChoiceQuestion::ChoiceQuestion(string question_text)
   : Question(question_text)
{
}
```

The derived-class constructor calls the base-class constructor before executing the code inside the { }.

In our example program, we used the default constructor of the base class. However, if a base class has no default constructor, you must use the initializer list syntax.

> The constructor of a derived class can supply arguments to a base-class constructor.

Syntax 10.2   Constructor with Base-Class Initializer

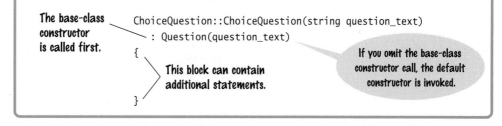

The base-class constructor is called first.

```
ChoiceQuestion::ChoiceQuestion(string question_text)
   : Question(question_text)
{

}
```

This block can contain additional statements.

If you omit the base-class constructor call, the default constructor is invoked.

10.3 Overriding Member Functions

The derived class inherits the member functions from the base class. If you are not satisfied with the behavior of the inherited member function, you can **override** it by specifying a new implementation in the derived class.

A derived class can inherit a function from the base class, or it can override it by providing another implementation.

Consider the `display` function of the `ChoiceQuestion` class. It needs to override the base-class `display` function in order to show the choices for the answer. Specifically, the derived-class function needs to

- **Display the question text.**
- **Display the answer choices.**

The second part is easy because the answer choices are a data member of the derived class.

```cpp
void ChoiceQuestion::display() const
{
   // Display the question text
   ...
   // Display the answer choices
   for (int i = 0; i < choices.size(); i++)
   {
      cout << i + 1 << ": " << choices[i] << endl;
   }
}
```

But how do you get the question text? You can't access the `text` member of the base class directly because it is private.

Instead, you can call the `display` function of the base class.

```cpp
void ChoiceQuestion::display() const
{
   // Display the question text
   display(); // Invokes implicit parameter.display()
   // Display the answer choices
   ...
}
```

However, this won't quite work. Because the implicit parameter of `ChoiceQuestion::display` is of type `ChoiceQuestion`, and there is a function named `display` in the `ChoiceQuestion` class, that function will be called—but that is just the function you are currently writing! The function would call itself over and over.

To display the question text, you must be more specific about which function named `display` you want to call. You want `Question::display`:

```cpp
void ChoiceQuestion::display() const
{
   // Display the question text
   Question::display(); // OK
   // Display the answer choices
   ...
}
```

Use *BaseClass::function* notation to explicitly call a base-class function.

When you override a function, you usually want to *extend* the functionality of the base-class version. Therefore, you often need to invoke the base-class version before extending it. To invoke it, you need to use the *BaseClass::function* notation. However, you have no obligation to call the base-class function. Occasionally, a derived class overrides a base-class function and specifies an entirely different functionality.

Here is the complete program that displays a plain `Question` object and a `Choice-Question` object. (The definition of the `Question` class, which you have already seen, is placed into `question.h`, and the implementation is in `question.cpp`.) This example shows how you can use inheritance to form a more specialized class from a base class.

ch10/quiz2/test.cpp

```cpp
1    #include <iostream>
2    #include <sstream>
3    #include <vector>
4    #include "question.h"
5
6    class ChoiceQuestion : public Question
7    {
8    public:
9       /**
10         Constructs a choice question with no choices.
11      */
12      ChoiceQuestion();
13
14      /**
15         Adds an answer choice to this question.
16         @param choice the choice to add
17         @param correct true if this is the correct choice, false otherwise
18      */
19      void add_choice(string choice, bool correct);
20
21      void display() const;
22   private:
23      vector<string> choices;
24   };
25
26   ChoiceQuestion::ChoiceQuestion()
27   {
28   }
29
30   void ChoiceQuestion::add_choice(string choice, bool correct)
31   {
32      choices.push_back(choice);
33      if (correct)
34      {
35         // Convert choices.size() to string
36         ostringstream stream;
37         stream << choices.size();
38         string num_str = stream.str();
39         set_answer(num_str);
40      }
41   }
42
43   void ChoiceQuestion::display() const
44   {
45      // Display the question text
46      Question::display();
47      // Display the answer choices
48      for (int i = 0; i < choices.size(); i++)
49      {
50         cout << i + 1 << ": " << choices[i] << endl;
51      }
52   }
53
54   int main()
55
56      string response;
57      cout << boolalpha;
58
```

```
59      // Ask a basic question
60
61      Question q1;
62      q1.set_text("Who was the inventor of C++?");
63      q1.set_answer("Bjarne Stroustrup");
64
65      q1.display();
66      cout << "Your answer: ";
67      getline(cin, response);
68      cout << q1.check_answer(response) << endl;
69
70      // Ask a choice question
71
72      ChoiceQuestion q2;
73      q2.set_text("In which country was the inventor of C++ born?");
74      q2.add_choice("Australia", false);
75      q2.add_choice("Denmark", true);
76      q2.add_choice("Korea", false);
77      q2.add_choice("United States", false);
78
79      q2.display();
80      cout << "Your answer: ";
81      getline(cin, response);
82      cout << q2.check_answer(response) << endl;
83
84      return 0;
85  }
```

Program Run

```
Who was the inventor of C++?
Your answer: Bjarne Stroustrup
true
In which country was the inventor of C++ born?
1: Australia
2: Denmark
3: Korea
4: United States
Your answer: 2
true
```

SELF CHECK

11. What is wrong with the following implementation of the display function?

```
void ChoiceQuestion::display() const
{
    cout << text << endl;
    for (int i = 0; i < choices.size(); i++)
    {
        cout << i + 1 << ": " << choices[i] << endl;
    }
}
```

12. What is wrong with the following implementation of the display function?

```
void ChoiceQuestion::display() const
{
    this->display();
    for (int i = 0; i < choices.size(); i++)
    {
```

```
        cout << i + 1 << ": " << choices[i] << endl;
      }
   }
```

13. Look again at the implementation of the `add_choice` function that calls the `set_answer` function of the base class. Why don't you need to call `Question::set_answer`?

14. In the `Manager` class of Self Check 9, override the `get_name` function so that managers have a `*` before their name (such as `*Lin, Sally`).

15. In the `Manager` class of Self Check 9, override the `get_salary` function so that it returns the sum of the salary and the bonus.

Practice It Now you can try these exercises at the end of the chapter: R10.12, P10.1.

Common Error 10.3

Forgetting the Base-Class Name

A common error in extending the functionality of a base-class function is to forget the base-class name. For example, to compute the salary of a manager, get the salary of the underlying `Employee` object and add a bonus:

```
double Manager::get_salary() const
{
   double base_salary = get_salary();
      // Error—should be Employee::get_salary()
   return base_salary + bonus;
}
```

Here `get_salary()` refers to the `get_salary` function applied to the implicit parameter of the member function. The implicit parameter is of type `Manager`, and there is a `Manager::get_salary` function, so that function is called. Of course, that is a recursive call to the function that we are writing. Instead, you must specify which `get_salary` function you want to call. In this case, you need to call `Employee::get_salary` explicitly.

Whenever you call a base-class function from a derived-class function with the same name, be sure to give the full name of the function, including the base-class name.

10.4 Virtual Functions and Polymorphism

In the preceding sections you saw one important use of inheritance: to form a more specialized class from a base class. In the following sections you will see an even more powerful application of inheritance: to work with objects whose type and behavior can vary at run time. This variation of behavior is achieved with **virtual functions**. When you invoke a virtual function on an object, the C++ run-time system determines which actual member function to call, depending on the class to which the object belongs.

In the following sections, you will see why you need to use pointers to access objects whose class can vary at run-time, and how a virtual function selects the member function that is appropriate for a given object.

10.4.1 The Slicing Problem

In this section, we will discuss a problem that commonly arises when you work with a collection of objects that belong to different classes in a class hierarchy.

If you look into the main function of quiz2/test.cpp, you will find that there was some repetitive code to display each question and check the responses. It would be nicer if all questions were collected in an array and one could use a loop to present them to the user:

```
const int QUIZZES = 2;
Question quiz[QUIZZES];
quiz[0].set_text("Who was the inventor of C++?");
quiz[0].set_answer("Bjarne Stroustrup");
ChoiceQuestion cq;
cq.set_text("In which country was the inventor of C++ born?");
cq.add_choice("Australia", false);
...
quiz[1] = cq;

for (int i = 0; i < QUIZZES; i++)
{
   quiz[i].display();
   cout << "Your answer: ";
   getline(cin, response);
   cout << quiz[i].check_answer(response) << endl;
}
```

The array quiz holds objects of type Question. The compiler realizes that a Choice-Question is a special case of a Question. Thus it permits the assignment from a choice question to a question:

```
quiz[1] = cq;
```

However, a ChoiceQuestion object has three data members, whereas a Question object has just two. There is no room to store the derived-class data. That data simply gets *sliced away* when you assign a derived-class object to a base-class variable (see Figure 5).

If you run the resulting program, the options are not displayed:

```
Who was the inventor of C++?
Your answer: Bjarne Stroustrup
true
In which country was the inventor of C++ born?
Your answer:
```

When converting a derived-class object to a base class, the derived-class data is sliced away.

This problem is very typical of code that needs to manipulate objects from a mixture of classes in an inheritance hierarchy. Derived-class objects are usually bigger than base-class objects, and objects of different derived classes have different sizes. An array of objects cannot deal with this variation in sizes.

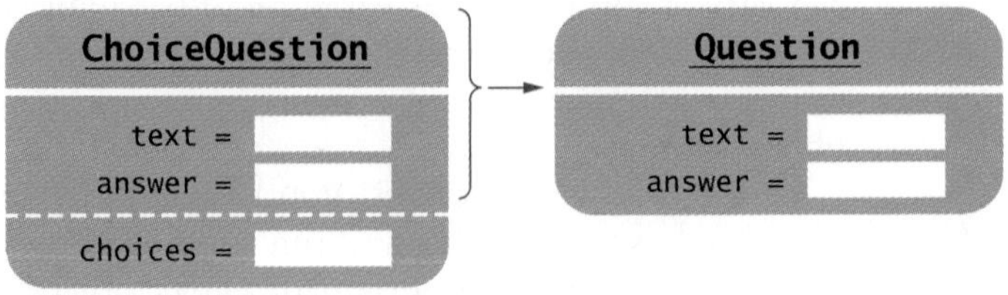

Figure 5 Slicing Away Derived-Class Data

Instead, you need to store the actual objects elsewhere and collect their locations in an array by storing pointers. We will discuss the use of pointers in the next section.

10.4.2 Pointers to Base and Derived Classes

To access objects from different classes in a class hierarchy, use pointers. Pointers to the various objects all have the same size—namely, the size of a memory address—even though the objects themselves may have different sizes.

Here is the code to set up the array of pointers (see Figure 6):

```
Question* quiz[2];
quiz[0] = new Question;
quiz[0]->set_text("Who was the inventor of C++?");
quiz[0]->set_answer("Bjarne Stroustrup");
ChoiceQuestion* cq_pointer = new ChoiceQuestion;
cq_pointer->set_text("In which country was the inventor of C++ born?");
cq_pointer->add_choice("Australia", false);
...
quiz[1] = cq_pointer;
```

As the highlighted code shows, you simply define the array to hold pointers, allocate all objects by calling new, and use the -> operator instead of the dot operator.

Note that the last assignment assigns a derived-class pointer of type ChoiceQuestion* to a base-class pointer of type Question*. This is perfectly legal. A pointer is the starting address of an object. Because every ChoiceQuestion is a special case of a Question, the starting address of a ChoiceQuestion object is, in particular, the starting address of a Question object. The reverse assignment—from a base-class pointer to a derived-class pointer—is an error.

> A derived-class pointer can be converted to a base-class pointer.

The code to present all questions is

```
for (int i = 0; i < QUIZZES; i++)
{
    quiz[i]->display();
    cout << "Your answer: ";
    getline(cin, response);
    cout << quiz[i]->check_answer(response) << endl;
}
```

Again, note the use of the -> operator because quiz[i] is a pointer.

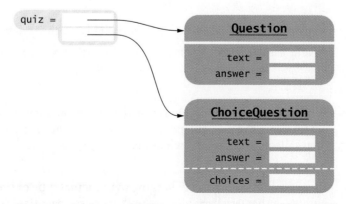

Figure 6 An Array of Pointers Can Store Objects from Different Classes

10.4.3 Virtual Functions

When you collect objects of different classes in a class hierarchy, and then invoke a member function, you want the appropriate member function to be applied. For example, when you call the `display` member function on a `Question*` pointer that happens to point to a `ChoiceQuestion`, you want the choices to be displayed.

For reasons of efficiency, this is not the default in C++. By default, a call

```
quiz[i]->display();
```

always calls `Question::display` because the type of `quiz[i]` is `Question*`.

However, in this case you really want to determine the actual type of the object to which `quiz[i]` points, which can be either a `Question` or a `ChoiceQuestion` object, and then call the appropriate function. In C++, you must alert the compiler that the function call needs to be preceded by the appropriate function selection, which can be a different one for every iteration in the loop. You use the `virtual` reserved word for this purpose:

```
class Question
{
public:
   Question();
   void set_text(string question_text);
   void set_answer(string correct_response);
   virtual bool check_answer(string response) const;
   virtual void display() const;
private:
   ...
};
```

The `virtual` reserved word must be used in the *base class*. All functions with the same name and parameter variable types in derived classes are then automatically virtual. However, it is considered good taste to supply the `virtual` reserved word for the derived-class functions as well.

```
class ChoiceQuestion : public Question
{
public:
   ChoiceQuestion();
   void add_choice(string choice, bool correct);
   virtual void display() const;
private:
   ...
};
```

You do not supply the reserved word `virtual` in the function definition:

```
void Question::display() const // No virtual reserved word
{
   cout << text << endl;
}
```

When a virtual function is called, the version belonging to the actual type of the implicit parameter is invoked.

Whenever a virtual function is called, the compiler determines the type of the implicit parameter in the particular call at run time. The appropriate function for that object is then called. For example, when the `display` function is declared virtual, the call

```
quiz[i]->display();
```

always calls the function belonging to the actual type of the object to which `display[i]` points—either `Question::display` or `ChoiceQuestion::display`.

In the same way that vehicles can differ in their method of locomotion, polymorphic objects carry out tasks in different ways.

10.4.4 Polymorphism

Polymorphism (literally, "having multiple shapes") describes objects that share a set of tasks and execute them in different ways.

The `quiz` array collects a mixture of both kinds of questions. Such a collection is called **polymorphic** (literally, "of multiple shapes"). Objects in a polymorphic collection have some commonality but are not necessarily of the same type. Inheritance is used to express this commonality, and virtual functions enable variations in behavior.

Virtual functions give programs a great deal of flexibility. The question presentation loop describes only the general mechanism: "Display the question, get a response, and check it". Each object knows on its own how to carry out the specific tasks: "Display the question" and "Check a response".

Using virtual functions makes programs *easily extensible*. Suppose we want to have a new kind of question for calculations, where we are willing to accept an approximate answer. All we need to do is to define a new class `NumericQuestion`, with its own `check_answer` function. Then we can populate the `quiz` array with a mixture of plain questions, choice questions, and numeric questions. The code that presents the questions need not be changed at all! The calls to the virtual functions automatically select the correct member functions of the newly defined classes.

Here is the final version of the quiz program, using pointers and virtual functions. When you run the program, you will find that the appropriate versions of the virtual functions are called. (The files `question.cpp` and `choicequestion.cpp` are included in your book's companion code.)

ch10/quiz3/question.h

```
1   #ifndef QUESTION_H
2   #define QUESTION_H
3
4   #include <string>
5
6   using namespace std;
7
8   class Question
9   {
10  public:
11     /**
12        Constructs a question with empty question and answer.
13     */
14     Question();
15
```

```
16     /**
17        @param question_text the text of this question
18     */
19     void set_text(string question_text);
20
21     /**
22        @param correct_response the answer for this question
23     */
24     void set_answer(string correct_response);
25
26     /**
27        @param response the response to check
28        @return true if the response was correct, false otherwise
29     */
30     virtual bool check_answer(string response) const;
31
32     /**
33        Displays this question.
34     */
35     virtual void display() const;
36  private:
37     string text;
38     string answer;
39  };
40
41  #endif
```

ch10/quiz3/choicequestion.h

```
1   #ifndef CHOICEQUESTION_H
2   #define CHOICEQUESTION_H
3
4   #include <vector>
5   #include "question.h"
6
7   class ChoiceQuestion : public Question
8   {
9   public:
10     /**
11        Constructs a choice question with no choices.
12     */
13     ChoiceQuestion();
14
15     /**
16        Adds an answer choice to this question.
17        @param choice the choice to add
18        @param correct true if this is the correct choice, false otherwise
19     */
20     void add_choice(string choice, bool correct);
21
22     virtual void display() const;
23  private:
24     vector<string> choices;
25  };
26
27  #endif
```

ch10/quiz3/test.cpp

```cpp
1   #include <iostream>
2   #include "question.h"
3   #include "choicequestion.h"
4
5   int main()
6   {
7      string response;
8      cout << boolalpha;
9
10     // Make a quiz with two questions
11     const int QUIZZES = 2;
12     Question* quiz[QUIZZES];
13     quiz[0] = new Question;
14     quiz[0]->set_text("Who was the inventor of C++?");
15     quiz[0]->set_answer("Bjarne Stroustrup");
16
17     ChoiceQuestion* cq_pointer = new ChoiceQuestion;
18     cq_pointer->set_text(
19        "In which country was the inventor of C++ born?");
20     cq_pointer->add_choice("Australia", false);
21     cq_pointer->add_choice("Denmark", true);
22     cq_pointer->add_choice("Korea", false);
23     cq_pointer->add_choice("United States", false);
24     quiz[1] = cq_pointer;
25
26     // Check answers for all questions
27     for (int i = 0; i < QUIZZES; i++)
28     {
29        quiz[i]->display();
30        cout << "Your answer: ";
31        getline(cin, response);
32        cout << quiz[i]->check_answer(response) << endl;
33     }
34
35     return 0;
36  }
```

16. Why did the test program introduce the variable `cq_pointer` instead of directly calling `quiz[1]->add_choice("Australia", false)`?

17. Which of the following statements are legal?

a. `ChoiceQuestion q;`
`Question a = q;`

b. `ChoiceQuestion b = a;`

c. `a.add_choice("Yes", true);`

d. `b.add_choice("No", false);`

18. Which of the following statements are legal?

a. `Question* p = new ChoiceQuestion;`

b. `ChoiceQuestion* q = p;`

c. `p->add_choice("Yes", true);`

d. `q->add_choice("No", false);`

19. What is displayed as the result of the following statements?

```
ChoiceQuestion* p = new ChoiceQuestion;
p->set_text("What is the answer?");
p->add_choice("42", true);
p->add_choice("Something else", false);
Question q = *p;
q.display();
```

20. Suppose check_answer was not declared virtual in question.h. How would the behavior of test.cpp change?

Practice It Now you can try these exercises at the end of the chapter: R10.14, R10.15, P10.11, P10.12.

Programming Tip 10.2

Don't Use Type Tags

Some programmers build inheritance hierarchies in which each object has a tag that indicates its type, commonly a string. They then query that string:

```
if (q->get_type() == "Question")
{
    // Do something
}
else if (q->get_type() == "ChoiceQuestion")
{
    // Do something else
}
```

This is a poor strategy. If a new class is added, then all these queries need to be revised. In contrast, consider the addition of a class NumericQuestion to our quiz program. *Nothing* needs to change in that program because it uses virtual functions, not type tags.

Whenever you find yourself adding a type tag to a hierarchy of classes, reconsider and use virtual functions instead.

Common Error 10.4

Slicing an Object

In C++ it is legal to copy a derived-class object into a base-class variable. However, any derived-class information is lost in the process. For example, when a Manager object is assigned to a variable of type Employee, the result is only the employee portion of the manager data:

```
Manager m;
...
Employee e = m; // Holds only the Employee base data of m
```

Any information that is particular to managers is sliced off, because it would not fit into a variable of type Employee. To avoid slicing, you can use pointers.

The slicing problem commonly occurs when a function has a polymorphic parameter (that is, a parameter that can belong to a base class or a derived class). In that case, the parameter variable must be a pointer or a reference. Consider this example:

```
void ask(Question q) // Error
{
```

```
      q.display();
      cout << "Your answer: ";
      getline(cin, response);
      cout << q.check_answer(response) << endl;
   }
```

If you call this function with a `ChoiceQuestion` object, then the parameter variable `q` is initialized with a copy of that object. But `q` is a `Question` object; the derived-class information is sliced away. The simplest remedy is to use a reference:

```
   void ask(const Question& q)
```

Now only the *address* is passed to the function. A reference is really a pointer in disguise. No slicing occurs, and virtual functions work correctly.

Special Topic 10.2

Virtual Self-Calls

Suppose we add the following function to the `Question` class:

```
   void Question::ask() const
   {
      display();
      cout << "Your answer: ";
      getline(cin, response);
      cout << check_answer(response) << endl;
   }
```

Now consider the call

```
   ChoiceQuestion cq;
   cq.set_text("In which country was the inventor of C++ born?");
   ...
   cq.ask();
```

Which `display` and `check_answer` function will the `ask` function call? If you look inside the code of the `Question::ask` function, you can see that these functions are executed on the implicit parameter:

```
   void Question::ask() const
   {
      implicit parameter.display();
      cout << "Your answer: ";
      getline(cin, response);
      cout << implicit parameter.check_answer(response) << endl;
   }
```

The implicit parameter in our call is `cq`, an object of type `ChoiceQuestion`. Because the `display` and `check_answer` functions are virtual, the `ChoiceQuestion` versions of the functions are called automatically. This happens even though the `ask` function is defined in the `Question` class, which has *no knowledge* of the `ChoiceQuestion` class.

As you can see, virtual functions are a very powerful mechanism. The `Question` class supplies an ask function that specifies the common nature of asking a question, namely to display it and check the response. How the displaying and checking are carried out is left to the derived classes.

Developing an Inheritance Hierarchy

When you work with a set of classes, some of which are more general and others more specialized, you want to organize them into an inheritance hierarchy. This enables you to process objects of different classes in a uniform way.

As an example, we will consider a bank that offers its customers the following account types:

- A savings account that earns interest. The interest compounds monthly and is computed on the minimum monthly balance.

- A checking account that has no interest, gives you three free withdrawals per month, and charges a $1 transaction fee for each additional withdrawal.

The program will manage a set of accounts of both types, and it should be structured so that other account types can be added without affecting the main processing loop. Supply a menu

```
D)eposit  W)ithdraw  M)onth end  Q)uit
```

For deposits and withdrawals, query the account number and amount. Print the balance of the account after each transaction.

In the "Month end" command, accumulate interest or clear the transaction counter, depending on the type of the bank account. Then print the balance of all accounts.

Step 1   List the classes that are part of the hierarchy.

In our case, the problem description yields two classes: SavingsAccount and CheckingAccount. To express the commonality between them, we will introduce a class BankAccount.

Step 2   Organize the classes into an inheritance hierarchy.

Draw a UML diagram that shows base and derived classes. Here is the diagram for our example:

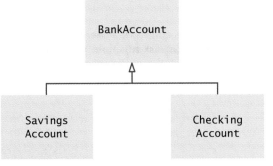

Step 3   Determine the common responsibilities.

In Step 2, you will have identified a class at the base of the hierarchy. That class needs to have sufficient responsibilities to carry out the tasks at hand. To find out what those tasks are, write pseudocode for processing the objects:

```
For each user command
    If it is a deposit or withdrawal
        Deposit or withdraw the amount from the specified account.
        Print the balance.
    If it is month end processing
        For each account
            Call month end processing.
            Print the balance.
```

From the pseudocode, we obtain the following list of common responsibilities that every bank account must carry out:

> **Deposit money.**
> **Withdraw money.**
> **Get the balance.**
> **Carry out month end processing.**

Step 4   Decide which functions are overridden in derived classes.

For each derived class and each of the common responsibilities, decide whether the behavior can be inherited or whether it needs to be overridden. Declare any functions that are overridden as `virtual` in the root of the hierarchy.

Getting the balance is common to all account types. Withdrawing and end of month processing are different for the derived classes, so they need to be declared `virtual`. Because it is entirely possible that some future account type will levy a fee for deposits, it seems prudent to declare the `deposit` member function virtual as well.

```cpp
class BankAccount
{
public:
   virtual void deposit(double amount);
   virtual void withdraw(double amount);
   virtual void month_end();
   double get_balance() const;
private:
   ...
};
```

Step 5   Define the public interface of each derived class.

Typically, derived classes have responsibilities other than those of the base class. List those, as well as the member functions that need to be overridden. You also need to specify how the objects of the derived classes should be constructed.

In this example, we need a way of setting the interest rate for the savings account. In addition, we need to specify constructors and overridden functions.

```cpp
class SavingsAccount : public BankAccount
{
public:
   /**
       Constructs a savings account with a zero balance.
   */
   SavingsAccount();

   /**
       Sets the interest rate for this account.
       @param rate the monthly interest rate in percent
   */
   void set_interest_rate(double rate);

   virtual void withdraw(double amount);
   virtual void month_end();
private:
   ...
};

class CheckingAccount : public BankAccount
{
```

```
public:
   /**
      Constructs a checking account with a zero balance.
   */
   CheckingAccount();

   virtual void withdraw(double amount);
   virtual void month_end();
private:
   ...
};
```

Step 6 Identify data members.

List the data members for each class. If you find a data member that is common to all classes, be sure to place it in the base of the hierarchy.

All accounts have a balance. We store that value in the BankAccount base class:

```
class BankAccount
{
   ...
private:
   double balance;
};
```

The SavingsAccount class needs to store the interest rate. It also needs to store the minimum monthly balance, which must be updated by all withdrawals:

```
class SavingsAccount : public BankAccount
{
   ...
private:
   double interest_rate;
   double min_balance;
};
```

The CheckingAccount class needs to count the withdrawals, so that the charge can be applied after the free withdrawal limit is reached:

```
class CheckingAccount : public BankAccount
{
   ...
private:
   int withdrawals;
};
```

Step 7 Implement constructors and member functions.

The member functions of the BankAccount class update or return the balance:

```
BankAccount::BankAccount()
{
   balance = 0;
}

void BankAccount::deposit(double amount)
{
   balance = balance + amount;
}

void BankAccount::withdraw(double amount)
{
   balance = balance - amount;
}
```

```
double BankAccount::get_balance() const
{
   return balance;
}
```

At the level of the BankAccount base class, we can say nothing about end of month processing. We choose to make that function do nothing:

```
void BankAccount::month_end()
{
}
```

In the withdraw member function of the SavingsAccount class, the minimum balance is updated. Note the call to the base-class member function:

```
void SavingsAccount::withdraw(double amount)
{
   BankAccount::withdraw(amount);
   double balance = get_balance();
   if (balance < min_balance)
   {
      min_balance = balance;
   }
}
```

In the month_end member function of the SavingsAccount class, the interest is deposited into the account. We must call the deposit member function since we have no direct access to the balance data member. The minimum balance is reset for the next month:

```
void SavingsAccount::month_end()
{
   double interest = min_balance * interest_rate / 100;
   deposit(interest);
   min_balance = get_balance();
}
```

The withdraw function of the CheckingAccount class needs to check the withdrawal count. If there have been too many withdrawals, a charge is applied. Again, note how the function invokes the base-class function, using the BankAccount:: syntax:

```
void CheckingAccount::withdraw(double amount)
{
   const int FREE_WITHDRAWALS = 3;
   const int WITHDRAWAL_FEE = 1;

   BankAccount::withdraw(amount);
   withdrawals++;
   if (withdrawals > FREE_WITHDRAWALS)
   {
      BankAccount::withdraw(WITHDRAWAL_FEE);
   }
}
```

End of month processing for a checking account simply resets the withdrawal count:

```
void CheckingAccount::month_end()
{
   withdrawals = 0;
}
```

Step 8   Allocate objects on the heap and process them.

For polymorphism (that is, variation of behavior) to work in C++, you need to call virtual functions through pointers. The easiest strategy is to allocate all polymorphic objects on the heap, using the new operator.

In our sample program, we allocate 5 checking accounts and 5 savings accounts and store their addresses in an array of bank account pointers. Then we accept user commands and execute deposits, withdrawals, and monthly processing.

```cpp
int main()
{
   cout << fixed << setprecision(2);

   // Create accounts
   const int ACCOUNTS_SIZE = 10;
   BankAccount* accounts[ACCOUNTS_SIZE];
   for (int i = 0; i < ACCOUNTS_SIZE / 2; i++)
   {
      accounts[i] = new CheckingAccount;
   }
   for (int i = ACCOUNTS_SIZE / 2; i < ACCOUNTS_SIZE; i++)
   {
      SavingsAccount* account = new SavingsAccount;
      account->set_interest_rate(0.75);
      accounts[i] = account;
   }

   // Execute commands
   bool more = true;
   while (more)
   {
      cout << "D)eposit  W)ithdraw  M)onth end  Q)uit: ";
      string input;
      cin >> input;
      if (input == "D" || input == "W")   // Deposit or withdrawal
      {
         cout << "Enter account number and amount: ";
         int num;
         double amount;
         cin >> num >> amount;

         if (input == "D") { accounts[num]->deposit(amount); }
         else { accounts[num]->withdraw(amount); }

         cout << "Balance: " << accounts[num]->get_balance() << endl;
      }
      else if (input == "M")   // Month end processing
      {
         for (int n = 0; n < ACCOUNTS_SIZE(); n++)
         {
            accounts[n]->month_end();
            cout << n << " " << accounts[n]->get_balance() << endl;
         }
      }
      else if (input == "Q")
      {
         more = false;
      }
   }

   return 0;
}
```

See ch10/accounts.cpp for the complete program.

WORKED EXAMPLE 10.1 **Implementing an Employee Hierarchy for Payroll Processing**

This Worked Example shows how to implement payroll processing that works for different kinds of employees.

Random Fact 10.1 The Limits of Computation

Have you ever wondered how your instructor or grader makes sure your programming homework is correct? In all likelihood, they look at your solution and perhaps run it with some test inputs. But usually they have a correct solution available. That suggests that there might be an easier way. Perhaps they could feed your program and their correct program into a "program comparator", a computer program that analyzes both programs and determines whether they both compute the same results. Of course, your solution and the program that is known to be correct need not be identical—what matters is that they produce the same output when given the same input.

How could such a program comparator work? Well, the C++ compiler knows how to read a program and make sense of the classes, functions, and statements. So it seems plausible that someone could, with some effort, write a program that reads two C++ programs, analyzes what they do, and determines whether they solve the same task. Of course, such a program would be very attractive to instructors, because it could automate the grading process. Thus, even though no such program exists today, it might be tempting to try to develop one and sell it to universities around the world.

However, before you start raising venture capital for such an effort, you should know that theoretical computer scientists have proven that it is impossible to develop such a program, *no matter how hard you try*.

There are quite a few of these unsolvable problems. The first one, called the *halting problem*, was dis-covered by the British researcher Alan Turing in 1936. Because his research occurred before the first actual computer was constructed, Turing had to devise a theoretical device, the *Turing machine*, to explain how computers could work. The Turing machine consists of a long magnetic tape, a read/write head, and a program that has numbered instructions of the form: "If the current symbol under the head is x, then replace it with y, move the head one unit left or right, and continue with instruction n" (see figure on the next page). Interestingly enough, with just these instructions, you can pro-gram just as much as with C++, even though it is incredibly tedious to do so. Theoretical computer scientists like Turing machines because they can be described using nothing more than the laws of mathematics.

Alan Turing

Expressed in terms of C++, the halt-ing problem states: "It is impossible to write a program with two inputs, namely the source code of an arbi-trary C++ program P and a string I, that decides whether the program P,

when executed with the input I, will halt without getting into an infinite loop". Of course, for some kinds of programs and inputs, it is possible to decide whether the programs halt with the given input. The halting problem asserts that it is impossible to come up with a single decision-making algo-rithm that works with all programs and inputs. Note that you can't simply run the program P on the input I to settle this question. If the program runs for 1,000 days, you don't know that the program is in an infinite loop. Maybe you just have to wait another day for it to stop.

Such a "halt checker", if it could be written, might also be useful for grad-ing homework. An instructor could use it to screen student submissions to see if they get into an infinite loop with a particular input, and then not check them any further. However, as Turing demonstrated, such a program cannot be written. His argument is ingenious and quite simple.

Suppose a "halt checker" program existed. Let's call it H. From H, we will develop another program, the "killer" program K. K does the following com-putation. Its input is a string contain-ing the source code for a program R. It then applies the halting checker on the input program R and the input string R. That is, it checks whether the program R halts if its input is its own source code. It sounds bizarre to feed a program to itself, but it isn't impos-sible. For example, the C++ compiler is written in C++, and you can use it to compile itself. Or, as a simpler exam-ple, you can use a word count program to count the words in its own source code. *(continued)*

When *K* gets the answer from *H* that *R* halts when applied to itself, it is programmed to enter an infinite loop. Otherwise *K* exits. In C++, the program might look like this:

```
int main()
{
    string r = read program input;
    HaltChecker checker;
    if (checker.check(r, r))
    {
        while (true) { }
        // Infinite loop
    }
    else
    {
        return 0;
    }
}
```

Now ask yourself: What does the halt checker answer when asked if *K* halts when given *K* as the input? Maybe it finds out that *K* gets into an infinite loop with such an input. But wait, that can't be right. That would mean that checker.check(r,r) returns false when r is the program code of *K*. As you can plainly see, in that case, the main function returns, so *K* didn't get into an infinite loop. That shows that *K* must halt when analyzing itself, so checker.check(r, r) should return true. But then the main function doesn't terminate—it goes into an infinite loop. That shows that it is logically impossible to implement a program that can check whether every program halts on a particular input.

It is sobering to know that there are limits to computing. There are prob-lems that no computer program, no matter how ingenious, can answer.

Theoretical computer scientists are working on other research involving the nature of computation. One important question that remains unsettled to this day deals with problems that in practice are very time-consuming to solve. It may be that these problems are intrinsically hard, in which case it would be pointless to try to look for better algorithms. Such theoretical research can have important practi-cal applications. For example, right now, nobody knows whether the most common encryption schemes used today could be broken by discover-ing a new algorithm (see Random Fact 8.1 for more information on encryp-tion algorithms). Knowing that no fast algorithms exist for breaking a par-ticular code could make us feel more comfortable about the security of encryption.

Program

Instruction number	If tape symbol is	Replace with	Then move head	Then go to instruction
1	0	2	right	2
1	1	1	left	4
2	0	0	right	2
2	1	1	right	2
2	2	0	left	3
3	0	0	left	3
3	1	1	left	3
3	2	2	right	1
4	1	1	right	5
4	2	0	left	4

Control unit

Read/write head

Tape

A Turing Machine

CHAPTER SUMMARY

Explain the notions of inheritance, base class, and derived class.

- A derived class inherits data and behavior from a base class.
- You can always use a derived-class object in place of a base-class object.

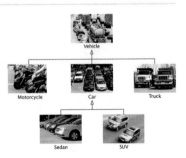

Implement derived classes in C++.

- A derived class can override a base-class function by providing a new implementation.
- The derived class inherits all data members and all functions that it does not override.
- Unless specified otherwise, the base-class data members are initialized with the default constructor.
- The constructor of a derived class can supply arguments to a base-class constructor.

Describe how a derived class can override functions from a base class.

- A derived class can inherit a function from the base class, or it can override it by providing another implementation.
- Use *BaseClass::function* notation to explicitly call a base-class function.

Describe virtual functions and polymorphism.

- When converting a derived-class object to a base class, the derived-class data is sliced away.
- A derived-class pointer can be converted to a base-class pointer.
- When a virtual function is called, the version belonging to the actual type of the implicit parameter is invoked.
- Polymorphism (literally, "having multiple shapes") describes objects that share a set of tasks and execute them in different ways.

REVIEW EXERCISES

R10.1 Identify the base class and the derived class in each of the following pairs of classes.

    a. Employee, Manager

    b. Polygon, Triangle

    c. GraduateStudent, Student

    d. Person, Student

    e. Employee, Professor

    f. BankAccount, CheckingAccount

    g. Vehicle, Car

    h. Vehicle, Minivan

    i. Car, Minivan

    j. Truck, Vehicle

R10.2 An object-oriented traffic simulation system has the following classes:

Vehicle	PickupTruck
Car	SportUtilityVehicle
Truck	Minivan
Sedan	Bicycle
Coupe	Motorcycle

Draw a UML diagram that shows the inheritance relationships between these classes.

R10.3 What inheritance relationships would you establish among the following classes?

Student	Professor
Employee	Secretary
Person	Janitor
DepartmentChair	

R10.4 Draw a UML diagram that shows the inheritance and aggregation relationships between the classes:

Person	Instructor
Student	Lecture
Course	Lab

R10.5 Consider a program for managing inventory in a small appliance store. Why isn't it useful to have a base class SmallAppliance and derived classes Toaster, CarVacuum, TravelIron, and so on?

R10.6 Which data members does the CheckingAccount class in How To 10.1 on page 464 inherit from its base class? Which data members does it add?

R10.7 Which functions does the SavingsAccount class in How To 10.1 on page 464 inherit from its base class? Which functions does it override? Which functions does it add?

R10.8 Design an inheritance hierarchy for geometric shapes: rectangles, squares, and circles. Draw a UML diagram. Provide a virtual function to compute the area of a shape. Provide appropriate constructors for each class. Write the class definitions but do not provide implementations of the member functions.

R10.9 Continue Exercise R10.8 by writing a main function that executes the following steps:

> Fill a vector of shape pointers with a rectangle, a square, and a circle.
> Print the area of each shape.
> Deallocate all heap objects.

R10.10 Can you convert a base-class object into a derived-class object? A derived-class object into a base-class object? A base-class pointer into a derived-class pointer? A derived-class pointer into a base-class pointer? If so, give examples. If not, explain why not.

R10.11 Consider a function process_file(ostream& str). Objects from which of the classes in Figure 2 can be passed as parameters to this function?

R10.12 What does the following program print?

```cpp
class B
{
public:
    void print(int n) const;
};

void B::print(int n) const
{
    cout << n << endl;
}

class D : public B
{
public:
    void print(int n) const;
};

void D::print(int n) const
{
    if (n <= 1) { B::print(n); }
    else if (n % 2 == 0) { print(n / 2); }
    else { print(3 * n + 1); }
}

int main()
{
    D d;
    d.print(3);
    return 0;
}
```

Determine the answer by hand, not by compiling and running the program.

R10.13 Suppose the class D inherits from B. Which of the following assignments are legal?

```cpp
B b;
D d;
B* pb;
D* pd;
```

a. b = d;
b. d = b;
c. pd = pb;
d. pb = pd;
e. d = pd;
f. b = *pd;
g. *pd = *pb;

R10.14 Suppose the class Sub is derived from the class Sandwich. Which of the following assignments are legal?

```cpp
Sandwich* x = new Sandwich();
Sub* y = new Sub();
```

a. x = y;
b. y = x;
c. y = new Sandwich();

d. x = new Sub();

e. *x = *y;

f. *y = *x;

R10.15 What does the program print? Explain your answers by tracing the flow of each call.

```cpp
class B
{
public:
   B();
   virtual void p() const;
   void q() const;
};

B::B() {}
void B::p() const { cout << "B::p\n"; }
void B::q() const { cout << "B::q\n"; }

class D : public B
{
public:
   D();
   virtual void p() const;
   void q() const;
};

D::D() {}
void D::p() const { cout << "D::p\n"; }
void D::q() const { cout << "D::q\n"; }

int main()
{
   B b;
   D d;
   B* pb = new B;
   B* pd = new D;
   D* pd2 = new D;

   b.p(); b.q();
   d.p(); d.q();
   pb->p(); pb->q();
   pd->p(); pd->q();
   pd2->p(); pd2->q();
   return 0;
}
```

R10.16 Using the Employee class from Worked Example 10.1 (ch10/salaries.cpp in your companion code), form a subclass Volunteer of Employee and provide a constructor Volunteer(string name) that sets the salary to 0.

R10.17 In the accounts.cpp program of How To 10.1, would it be reasonable to make the get_balance function virtual? Explain your reasoning.

R10.18 What is the effect of declaring the display member function virtual only in the ChoiceQuestion class?

PROGRAMMING EXERCISES

P10.1   Add a class NumericQuestion to the question hierarchy of Section 10.1. If the response and the expected answer differ by no more than 0.01, then accept it as correct.

P10.2   Add a class FillInQuestion to the question hierarchy of Section 10.1. Such a question is constructed with a string that contains the answer, surrounded by _ _, for example, "The inventor of C++ was _Bjarne Stroustrup_". The question should be displayed as

```
The inventor of C++ was _____
```

Provide a main function that demonstrates your class.

P10.3   Modify the check_answer member function of the Question class so that it does not take into account different spaces or upper/lowercase characters. For example, the response " bjarne stroustrup" should match an answer of "Bjarne Stroustrup".

P10.4   Add a class MultiChoiceQuestion to the question hierarchy of Section 10.1 that allows multiple correct choices. The respondent should provide any one of the correct choices. The answer string should contain all of the correct choices, separated by spaces.

P10.5   Add a class ChooseAllCorrect to the question hierarchy of Section 10.1 that allows multiple correct choices. The respondent should provide all correct choices, separated by spaces.

P10.6   Add a member function add_text to the Question base class and provide a different implementation of ChoiceQuestion that calls add_text rather than storing a vector of choices.

P10.7   Change the CheckingAccount class in How To 10.1 so that a $1 fee is levied for deposits or withdrawals in excess of three free monthly transactions. Place the code for computing the fee into a private member function that you call from the deposit and withdraw member functions.

P10.8   Derive a class Programmer from Employee. Supply a constructor Programmer(string name, double salary) that calls the base-class constructor. Supply a function get_name that returns the name in the format "Hacker, Harry (Programmer)".

P10.9   Implement a base class Person. Derive classes Student and Instructor from Person. A person has a name and a birthday. A student has a major, and an instructor has a salary. Write the class definitions, the constructors, and the member functions display for all classes.

P10.10   Derive a class Manager from Employee. Add a data member named department of type string. Supply a function display that displays the manager's name, department, and salary. Derive a class Executive from Manager. Supply a function display that displays the string Executive, followed by the information stored in the Manager base object.

P10.11   Implement a base class Account and derived classes Savings and Checking. In the base class, supply member functions deposit and withdraw. Provide a function daily_interest that computes and adds the daily interest. For calculations, assume that every month has 30 days. Checking accounts yield interest of 3 percent annually on balances over $1,000. Savings accounts yield interest of 6 percent annually on the entire balance. Write a test program that makes a month's worth of deposits and withdrawals and calculates the interest every day.

P10.12 Implement a base class `Appointment` and derived classes `Onetime`, `Daily`, `Weekly`, and `Monthly`. An appointment has a description (for example, "see the dentist") and a date and time. Write a virtual function `occurs_on(int year, int month, int day)` that checks whether the appointment occurs on that date. For example, for a monthly appointment, you must check whether the day of the month matches. Then fill a vector of `Appointment*` with a mixture of appointments. Have the user enter a date and print out all appointments that happen on that date.

P10.13 Improve the appointment book program of Exercise P10.12. Give the user the option to add new appointments. The user must specify the type of the appointment, the description, and the date and time.

P10.14 Improve the appointment book program of Exercises P10.12 and P10.13 by letting the user save the appointment data to a file and reload the data from a file. The saving part is straightforward: Make a virtual function save. Save out the type, description, date, and time. The loading part is not so easy. You must first determine the type of the appointment to be loaded, create an object of that type with its default constructor, and then call a virtual `load` function to load the remainder.

P10.15 Use polymorphism to carry out image manipulations such as those described in Exercises P8.10 and P8.11. Design a base class `Effect` and derived classes `Sunset` and `Grayscale`. Use a virtual function `process`. The file processing part of your program should repeatedly call `process` on an `Effect*` pointer, without having to know which effect is applied.

Engineering P10.16 In this problem, you will model a circuit consisting of an arbitrary configuration of resistors. Provide a base class `Circuit` with a member function `get_resistance`. Provide a derived class `Resistor` representing a single resistor. Provide derived classes `Serial` and `Parallel`, each of which contains a `vector<Circuit*>`. A `Serial` circuit models a series of circuits, each of which can be a single resistor or another circuit. Similarly, a `Parallel` circuit models a set of circuits in parallel. For example, the following circuit is a `Parallel` circuit containing a single resistor and one `Serial` circuit.

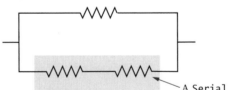

A `Serial` circuit

Use Ohm's law to compute the combined resistance.

Engineering P10.17 Part (a) of the figure below shows a symbolic representation of an electric circuit called an *amplifier*. The input to the amplifier is the voltage v_i and the output is the voltage v_o. The output of an amplifier is proportional to the input. The constant of proportionality is called the "gain" of the amplifier.

Parts (b), (c), and (d) show schematics of three specific types of amplifier: the *inverting amplifier*, *noninverting amplifier*, and *voltage divider amplifier*. Each of these three amplifiers consists of two resistors and an op amp. The value of the gain of each amplifier depends on the values of its resistances. In particular, the gain, g, of the inverting amplifier is given by $g = -\dfrac{R_2}{R_1}$. Similarly the gains of the noninverting amplifier and voltage divider amplifier are given by $g = 1 + \dfrac{R_2}{R_1}$ and $g = \dfrac{R_2}{R_1 + R_2}$, respectively.

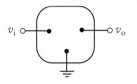

(a) Amplifier

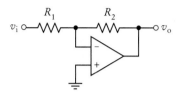

(b) Inverting amplifier

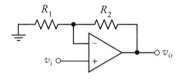

(c) Noninverting amplifier

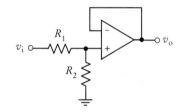

(d) Voltage divider amplifier

Write a C++ program that represents the amplifier as a base class and represents the inverting, noninverting, and voltage divider amplifiers as derived classes. Give the base class two virtual functions, get_gain and a get_description function that returns a string identifying the amplifier. Each derived class should have a constructor with two arguments, the resistances of the amplifier.

The derived classes need to override the get_gain and get_description functions of the base class.

Write a main function for the C++ program that demonstrates that the derived classes all work properly for sample values of the resistances.

Engineering P10.18 Resonant circuits are used to select a signal (e.g., a radio station or TV channel) from among other competing signals. Resonant circuits are characterized by the frequency response shown in the figure below. The resonant frequency response is completely described by three parameters: the resonant frequency, ω_o, the bandwidth, B, and the gain at the resonant frequency, k.

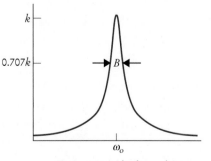

Frequency (rad/s, log scale)

Two simple resonant circuits are shown in the figure below. The circuit in (a) is called a *parallel resonant circuit*. The circuit in (b) is called a *series resonant circuit*. Both resonant circuits consist of a resistor having resistance R, a capacitor having capacitance C, and an inductor having inductance L.

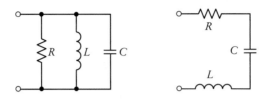

(a) Parallel resonant circuit   (b) Series resonant circuit

These circuits are designed by determining values of R, C, and L that cause the resonant frequency response to be described by specified values of ω_0, B, and k. The design equations for the parallel resonant circuit are:

$$R = k, \quad C = \frac{1}{BR}, \text{ and } \quad L = \frac{1}{\omega_0^2 C}$$

Similarly, the design equations for the series resonant circuit are:

$$R = \frac{1}{k}, \quad L = \frac{R}{B}, \text{ and } \quad C = \frac{1}{\omega_0^2 L}$$

Write a C++ program that represents ResonantCircuit as a base class and represents the SeriesResonantCircuit and ParallelResonantCircuit as derived classes. Give the base class three private data members representing the parameters ω_0, B, and k of the resonant frequency response. The base class should provide public member functions to get and set each of these members. The base class should also provide a display function that prints a description of the resonant frequency response.

Each derived class should provide a function that designs the corresponding resonant circuit. The derived classes should also override the display function of the base class to print descriptions of both the frequency response (the values of ω_0, B, and k) and the circuit (the values of R, C, and L).

All classes should provide appropriate constructors.

Write a main function for the C++ program that demonstrates that the derived classes all work properly.

ANSWERS TO SELF-CHECK QUESTIONS

1. Because every manager is an employee but not the other way around, the Manager class is more specialized. It is the derived class, and Employee is the base class.

2. CheckingAccount and SavingsAccount both inherit from the more general class BankAccount.

3. istream, istringstream, ifstream, iostream, fstream

4. Vehicle, Truck, Motorcycle

5. It shouldn't. A quiz isn't a question; it *has* questions.

6. a, b, d

7. ```
class Manager : public Employee
{
private:
    double bonus;
}
```

8. name, base_salary, and bonus

9. ```
class Manager : public Employee
{
public:
    double get_salary() const;
}
```

10. get_name, set_name, set_base_salary

11. The function is not allowed to access the text member from the base class.

12. The type of the this pointer is ChoiceQuestion*. Therefore, the display function of ChoiceQuestion is selected, and the function calls itself.

13. Because there is no ambiguity. The derived class doesn't have a set_answer function.

14. ```
string Manager::get_name() const
{
    return "*" + Employee::get_name();
}
```

15. ```
double Manager::get_salary() const
{
    return Employee::get_salary() + bonus;
}
```

16. The type of quiz[1] is Question*, and the Question class has no member function called add_choice.

17. a and d are legal.

18. a and d are legal.

19. Only the question text, not the choices. The choices are sliced away when *p is assigned to the object q.

20. It wouldn't change. The function is never overridden in the classes used in our test program.

C++ LANGUAGE CODING GUIDELINES

Introduction

This coding style guide is a simplified version of one that has been used with good success both in industrial practice and for college courses. It lays down rules that you must follow for your programming assignments.

A style guide is a set of mandatory requirements for layout and formatting. Uniform style makes it easier for you to read code from your instructor and classmates. You will really appreciate the consistency if you do a team project. It is also easier for your instructor and your grader to grasp the essence of your programs quickly.

A style guide makes you a more productive programmer because it *reduces gratuitous choice*. If you don't have to make choices about trivial matters, you can spend your energy on the solution of real problems.

In these guidelines a number of constructs are plainly outlawed. That doesn't mean that programmers using them are evil or incompetent. It does mean that the constructs are of marginal utility and can be expressed just as well or even better with other language constructs.

If you have already programmed in C or C++, you may be initially uncomfortable about giving up some fond habits. However, it is a sign of professionalism to set aside personal preferences in minor matters and to compromise for the benefit of your group.

These guidelines are necessarily somewhat long and dull. They also mention features that you may not yet have seen in class. Here are the most important highlights:

- Tabs are set every three spaces.
- Variable and function names are lowercase.
- Constant names are uppercase. Class names start with an uppercase letter.
- There are spaces after reserved words and between binary operators.
- Braces must line up.
- No magic numbers may be used.
- Every function must have a comment.
- At most 30 lines of code may be used per function.
- No goto, continue, or break is allowed.
- At most two global variables may be used per file.

A note to the instructor: Of course, many programmers and organizations have strong feelings about coding style. If this style guide is incompatible with your own preferences or with local custom, please feel free to modify it. For that purpose, this coding style guide is available in electronic form on the companion web site for this book.

Source Files

Each program is a collection of one or more files or modules. The executable program is obtained by compiling and linking these files. Organize the material in each file as follows:

- Header comments
- `#include` statements
- Constants
- Classes
- Functions

It is common to start each file with a comment block. Here is a typical format:

```
/**
   @file invoice.cpp
   @author Jenny Koo
   @date 2012-01-24
   @version 3.14
*/
```

You may also want to include a copyright notice, such as

```
/* Copyright 2012 Jenny Koo */
```

A valid copyright notice consists of

- the copyright symbol © or the word "Copyright" or the abbreviation "Copr."
- the year of first publication of the work
- the name of the owner of the copyright

(Note: To save space, this header comment has been omitted from the programs in this book as well as the programs on disk so that the actual line numbers match those that are printed in the book.)

Next, list all included header files.

```
#include <iostream>
#include "question.h"
```

Do not embed absolute path names, such as

```
#include "c:\me\my_homework\widgets.h"  // Don't !!!
```

After the header files, list constants that are needed throughout the program file.

```
const int GRID_SIZE = 20;
const double CLOCK_RADIUS = 5;
```

Then supply the definitions of all classes.

```
class Product
{
   ...
};
```

Order the class definitions so that a class is defined before it is used in another class.

Finally, list all functions, including member functions of classes and nonmember functions. Order the nonmember functions so that a function is defined before it is called. As a consequence, the `main` function will be the last function in your file.

Functions

Supply a comment of the following form for every function.

```
/**
    Explanation.
    @param parameter variable₁   explanation
    @param parameter variable₂   explanation
    ...
    @return explanation
*/
```

The introductory explanation is required for all functions except `main`. It should start with an uppercase letter and end with a period. Some documentation tools extract the first sentence of the explanation into a summary table. Thus, if you provide an explanation that consists of multiple sentences, formulate the explanation such that the first sentence is a concise explanation of the function's purpose.

Omit the `@param` comment if the function has no parameter variables. Omit the `@return` comment for `void` functions. Here is a typical example:

```
/**
    Converts calendar date into Julian day. This algorithm is from Press
    et al., Numerical Recipes in C, 2nd ed., Cambridge University Press, 1992.
    @param year the year of the date to be converted
    @param month the month of the date to be converted
    @param day the day of the date to be converted
    @return the Julian day number that begins at noon of the given
    calendar date
*/
long dat2jul(int year, int month, int day)
{
    ...
}
```

Parameter variable names must be explicit, especially if they are integers or Boolean.

```
Employee remove(int d, double s); // Huh?
Employee remove(int department, double severance_pay); // OK
```

Of course, for very generic functions, short names may be very appropriate.

Do not write `void` functions that return exactly one answer through a reference. Instead, make the result into a return value.

```
void find(vector<Employee> c, bool& found); // Don't!
bool find(vector<Employee> c); // OK
```

Of course, if the function computes more than one value, some or all results can be returned through reference parameters.

Functions must have at most 30 lines of code. (Comments, blank lines, and lines containing only braces are not included in this count.) Functions that consist of one long `if/else/else` statement sequence may be longer, provided each branch is 10 lines or less. This rule forces you to break up complex computations into separate functions.

Local Variables

Do not define all local variables at the beginning of a block. Define each variable just before it is used for the first time.

Every variable must be either explicitly initialized when defined or set in the immediately following statement (for example, through a >> instruction).

```
int pennies = 0;
```

or

```
int pennies;
cin >> pennies;
```

Move variables to the innermost block in which they are needed:

```
while (...)
{
    double xnew = (xold + a / xold) / 2;
    ...
}
```

Do not define two variables in one statement:

```
int dimes = 0, nickels = 0; // Don't
```

When defining a pointer variable, place the * with the type, not the variable:

```
Link* p; // OK
```

not

```
Link *p; // Don't
```

Constants

In C++, do not use #define to define constants:

```
#define CLOCK_RADIUS 5 // Don't
```

Use const instead:

```
const double CLOCK_RADIUS = 5; // The radius of the clock face
```

You may not use magic numbers in your code. (A magic number is an integer constant embedded in code without a constant definition.) Any number except 0, 1, or 2 is considered magic:

```
if (p.get_x() < 10) // Don't
```

Use a const variable instead:

```
const double WINDOW_XMAX = 10;
if (p.get_x() < WINDOW_XMAX) // OK
```

Even the most reasonable cosmic constant is going to change one day. You think there are 365 days per year? Your customers on Mars are going to be pretty unhappy about your silly prejudice.

Make a constant

```
const int DAYS_PER_YEAR = 365;
```

so that you can easily produce a Martian version without trying to find all the 365's, 364's, 366's, 367's, and so on in your code.

Classes

Lay out the items of a class as follows:

```
class ClassName
{
public:
    constructors
    mutators
    accessors
private:
    data
};
```

All data fields of classes must be private.

Control Flow

The for Statement

Use for loops only when a variable runs from somewhere to somewhere else with some constant increment/decrement.

```
for (i = 0; i < a.size(); i++)
{
    cout << a[i] << endl;
}
```

Do not use the for loop for weird constructs such as

```
for (xnew = a / 2; count < ITERATIONS; cout << xnew) // Don't
{
    xold = xnew;
    xnew = xold + a / xold;
    count++;
}
```

Make such a loop into a while loop, so the sequence of instructions is much clearer.

```
xnew = a / 2;
while (count < ITERATIONS) // OK
{
    xold = xnew;
    xnew = xold + a / xold;
    count++;
    cout << xnew;
}
```

Nonlinear Control Flow

Don't use the switch statement. Use if/else instead.

Do not use the break, continue, or goto statement. Use a bool variable to control the execution flow.

Lexical Issues

Naming Conventions

The following rules specify when to use upper- and lowercase letters in identifier names.

1. All variable and function names and all data fields of classes are in lowercase, sometimes with an underscore in the middle. For example, first_player.

2. All constants are in uppercase, with an occasional underscore. For example, CLOCK_RADIUS.

3. All class names start with uppercase and are followed by lowercase letters, with an occasional uppercase letter in the middle. For example, BankTeller.

Names must be reasonably long and descriptive. Use first_player instead of fp. No drppng f vwls. Local variables that are fairly routine can be short (ch, i) as long as they are really just boring holders for an input character, a loop counter, and so on. Also, do not use ctr, c, cntr, cnt, c2 for five counter variables in your function. Surely each of these variables has a specific purpose and can be named to remind the reader of it (for example, ccurrent, cnext, cprevious, cnew, cresult).

Indentation and White Space

Use tab stops every three columns. Save your file so that it contains no tabs at all. That means you will need to change the tab stop setting in your editor! In the editor, make sure to select "3 spaces per tab stop" and "save all tabs as spaces". Every programming editor has these settings. If yours doesn't, don't use tabs at all but type the correct number of spaces to achieve indentation.

Use blank lines freely to separate logically distinct parts of a function.

Use a blank space around every binary operator:

```
x1 = (-b - sqrt(b * b - 4 * a * c)) / (2 * a); // Good
x1=(-b-sqrt(b*b-4*a*c))/(2*a); // Bad
```

Leave a blank space after (and not before) each comma, semicolon, and reserved word, but not after a function name.

```
if (x == 0) ...
f(a, b[i]);
```

Every line must fit in 80 columns. If you must break a statement, add an indentation level for the continuation:

```
a[n] = ................................................
   + ................;
```

Braces

Opening and closing braces must line up, either horizontally or vertically.

```
while (i < n) { cout << a[i] << endl; i++; }  // OK
while (i < n)
{
   cout << a[i] << endl;
   i++;
}  // OK
```

Some programmers don't line up vertical braces but place the { *behind* the `while`:

```
while (i < n) {   // Don't
   cout << a[i] << endl;
   i++;
}
```

This style saves a line, but it is difficult to match the braces.

Always use braces with `if`, `while`, `do`, and `for` statements, even if the body is only a single statement.

```
if (floor > 13)
{              // OK
   floor--;
}
if (floor > 13)
   floor--;   // Don't
```

Unstable Layout

Some programmers take great pride in lining up certain columns in their code:

```
class Employee
{
   ...
private:
   string   name;
      int   age;
   double   hourly_wage;
};
```

This is undeniably neat, and we recommend it if your editor does it for you, but *don't* do it manually. The layout is not *stable* under change. A data type that is longer than the pre-allotted number of columns requires that you move *all* entries around.

Some programmers like to format multiline comments so that every line starts with **:

```
/* This is a comment
** that extends over
** three source lines
*/
```

Again, this is neat if your editor has a command to add and remove the asterisks, and if you know that all programmers who will maintain your code also have such an editor. Otherwise, it can be a powerful method of *discouraging* programmers from editing the comment. If you have to choose between pretty comments and comments that reflect the current facts of the program, facts win over beauty.

APPENDIX B

RESERVED WORD SUMMARY

Reserved Word	Description	Reference Location
bool	The Boolean type	Section 3.7
break	Break out of a loop or switch	Special Topic 3.3, 4.2
case	A label in a switch statement	Special Topic 3.3
char	The character type	Section 7.3
class	Definition of a class	Section 9.2
const	Definition of a constant value, reference, member function, or pointer	Section 2.1.5, Special Topic 5.2, Special Topic 6.4, Section 9.2
default	The default case of a switch statement	Special Topic 3.3
delete	Return a memory block to the heap	Section 7.4
do	A loop that is executed at least once	Section 4.4
double	The double-precision, floating-point type	Section 2.1.2
else	The alternative clause in an if statement	Section 3.1
false	The false Boolean value	Section 3.7
float	The single-precision, floating-point type	Special Topic 2.1
for	A loop that is intended to initialize, test, and update a variable	Section 4.3
if	The conditional branch statement	Section 3.1
int	The integer type	Section 2.1
long	A modifier for the int and double types that indicates that the type may have more bytes	Special Topic 2.1
namespace	A name space for disambiguating names	Section 1.5
new	Allocate a memory block from the heap	Section 7.4
private	Features of a class that can only be accessed by this class and its friends	Section 9.2

Reserved Word	Description	Reference Location
public	Features of a class that can be accessed by all functions	Section 9.2
return	Returns a value from a function	Section 5.4
short	A modifier for the int type that indicates that the type may have fewer bytes	Special Topic 2.1
static_cast	Convert from one type to another	Special Topic 2.3
struct	A construct for aggregating items of arbitrary types into a single value	Section 7.7
switch	A statement that selects among multiple branches, depending upon the value of an expression	Special Topic 3.3
this	The pointer to the implicit parameter of a member function	Section 9.9.3
true	The true value of the Boolean type	Section 3.7
unsigned	A modifier for the int and char types that indicates that values of the type cannot be negative	Special Topic 2.1
using	Importing a name space	Section 1.5
virtual	A member function with dynamic dispatch	Section 10.4
void	The empty type of a function or pointer	Section 5.5
while	A loop statement that is controlled by a condition	Section 4.1

The following reserved words are not covered in this book:

asm	explicit	operator	template	union
auto	export	protected	throw	volatile
catch	extern	register	try	wchar_t
const_cast	friend	reinterpret_cast	typedef	
continue	goto	signed	typeid	
dynamic_cast	inline	sizeof	type_info	
enum	mutable	static	typename	

OPERATOR SUMMARY

The operators are listed in groups of decreasing precedence in the table below. The horizontal lines in the table indicate a change in operator precedence. For example, z = x - y; means z = (x - y); because = has a lower precedence than - .

The prefix unary operators and the assignment operators associate right-to-left. All other operators associate left-to-right. For example, x - y - z means (x - y) - z because - associates left-to-right, but x = y = z means x = (y = z) because = associates right-to-left.

Operator	Description	Reference Location
::	Scope resolution	Section 9.4.1
.	Access member	Section 2.5.4, Section 7.7.2
->	Dereference and access member	Section 9.9
[]	Vector or array subscript	Section 6.1
()	Function call	Section 5.1
++	Increment	Section 2.2.2
--	Decrement	Section 2.2.2
!	Boolean NOT	Section 3.8
~	Bitwise NOT	Appendix G
+ (unary)	Positive	Section 2.2.1
- (unary)	Negative	Section 2.2.1
* (unary)	Pointer dereferencing	Section 7.1
& (unary)	Address of variable	Section 5.9, Section 7.1
new	Heap allocation	Section 7.4
delete	Heap recycling	Section 7.4
sizeof	Size of variable or type	Appendix F
(*type*)	Cast	not covered

Operator	Description	Reference Location
.*	Access pointer to member	not covered
->*	Dereference and access pointer to member	not covered
*	Multiplication	Section 2.2.1
/	Division or integer division	Section 2.2.1, Section 2.2.3
%	Integer remainder	Section 2.2.3
+	Addition	Section 2.2.1
-	Subtraction	Section 2.2.1
<<	Output	Section 1.5, Section 2.3.2, Appendix G
>>	Input	Section 2.3.1, Appendix G
<	Less than	Section 3.2
<=	Less than or equal	Section 3.2
>	Greater than	Section 3.2
>=	Greater than or equal	Section 3.2
==	Equal	Section 3.2
!=	Not equal	Section 3.2
&	Bitwise and	Appendix G
^	Bitwise xor	Appendix G
|	Bitwise or	Appendix G
&&	Boolean *and*	Section 3.7
||	Boolean *or*	Section 3.7
? :	Selection	Special Topic 3.1
=	Assignment	Section 2.1.4
+= -= *= /= %= &= |= ^= >>= <<=	Combined operator and assignment	Special Topic 2.4
,	Sequencing of expressions	not covered

CHARACTER CODES

These escape sequences can occur in strings (for example, "\n") and characters (for example, '\'').

Escape Sequence	Description
\n	Newline
\r	Carriage return
\t	Tab
\v	Vertical tab
\b	Backspace
\f	Form feed
\a	Alert
\\	Backslash
\"	Double quote
\'	Single quote
\?	Question mark
$\backslash x h_1 h_2$	Code specified in hexadecimal
$\backslash o_1 o_2 o_3$	Code specified in octal

Table 1 ASCII Code Table

Dec. Code	Hex Code	Char-acter	Dec. Code	Hex Code	Char-acter	Dec. Code	Hex Code	Char-acter	Dec. Code	Hex Code	Char-acter
0	00	\0	32	20	Space	64	40	@	96	60	`
1	01		33	21	!	65	41	A	97	61	a
2	02		34	22	"	66	42	B	98	62	b
3	03		35	23	#	67	43	C	99	63	c
4	04		36	24	$	68	44	D	100	64	d
5	05		37	25	%	69	45	E	101	65	e
6	06		38	26	&	70	46	F	102	66	f
7	07	\a	39	27	'	71	47	G	103	67	g
8	08	\b	40	28	(	72	48	H	104	68	h
9	09	\t	41	29	)	73	49	I	105	69	i
10	0A	\n	42	2A	*	74	4A	J	106	6A	j
11	0B	\v	43	2B	+	75	4B	K	107	6B	k
12	0C	\f	44	2C	,	76	4C	L	108	6C	l
13	0D	\r	45	2D	-	77	4D	M	109	6D	m
14	0E		46	2E	.	78	4E	N	110	6E	n
15	0F		47	2F	/	79	4F	O	111	6F	o
16	10		48	30	0	80	50	P	112	70	p
17	11		49	31	1	81	51	Q	113	71	q
18	12		50	32	2	82	52	R	114	72	r
19	13		51	33	3	83	53	S	115	73	s
20	14		52	34	4	84	54	T	116	74	t
21	15		53	35	5	85	55	U	117	75	u
22	16		54	36	6	86	56	V	118	76	v
23	17		55	37	7	87	57	W	119	77	w
24	18		56	38	8	88	58	X	120	78	x
25	19		57	39	9	89	59	Y	121	79	y
26	1A		58	3A	:	90	5A	Z	122	7A	z
27	1B		59	3B	;	91	5B	[	123	7B	{
28	1C		60	3C	<	92	5C	\	124	7C	|
29	1D		61	3D	=	93	5D	]	125	7D	}
30	1E		62	3E	>	94	5E	^	126	7E	~
31	1F		63	3F	?	95	5F	_	127	7F	

C++ LIBRARY SUMMARY

Standard Code Libraries

<cmath>

- `double sqrt(double x)`

  Function: Square root, $\sqrt{x}$

- `double pow(double x, double y)`

  Function: Power, x^y. If $x > 0$, y can be any value. If x is 0, y must be > 0. If $x < 0$, y must be an integer.

- `double sin(double x)`

  Function: Sine, $\sin x$ (x in radians)

- `double cos(double x)`

  Function: Cosine, $\cos x$ (x in radians)

- `double tan(double x)`

  Function: Tangent, $\tan x$ (x in radians)

- `double log10(double x)`

  Function: Decimal log, $\log_{10}(x)$, $x > 0$

- `double fabs(double x)`

  Function: Absolute value, $|x|$

<cstdlib>

- `int abs(int x)`

  Function: Absolute value, $|x|$

- `void exit(int n)`

  Function: Exits the program with status code n.

- `int rand()`

  Function: Random integer

- `void srand(int n)`

  Function: Sets the seed of the random number generator to n.

<cctype>

- `bool isalpha(char c)`

  Function: Tests whether c is a letter.

- `char` **`isalnum`**`(char c)`

  Function: Test whether `c` is a letter or a number.
- `bool` **`isdigit`**`(char c)`

  Function: Tests whether `c` is a digit.
- `bool` **`isspace`**`(char c)`

  Function: Tests whether `c` is white space.
- `bool` **`islower`**`(char c)`

  Function: Tests whether `c` is lowercase.
- `bool` **`isupper`**`(char c)`

  Function: Tests whether `c` is uppercase.
- `char` **`tolower`**`(char c)`

  Function: Returns the lowercase of `c`.
- `char` **`toupper`**`(char c)`

  Function: Returns the uppercase of `c`.

`<ctime>`

- `time_t` **`time`**`(time_t* p)`

  Function: Returns the number of seconds since January 1, 1970, 00:00:00 GMT. If `p` is not `NULL`, the return value is also stored in the location to which `p` points.

`<string>`

- `istream&` **`getline`**`(istream& in, string s)`

  Function: Gets the next input line from the input stream `in` and stores it in the string `s`.

Class `string`

- `int string::`**`length`**`() const`

  Member function: Returns the length of the string.
- `string string::`**`substr`**`(int i) const`

  Member function: Returns the substring from index `i` to the end of the string.
- `string string::`**`substr`**`(int i, int n) const`

  Member function: Returns the substring of length `n` starting at index `i`.
- `const char* string::`**`c_str`**`() const`

  Member function: Returns a `char` array with the characters in this string.

`<iomanip>`

- **`boolalpha`**

  Manipulator: Causes Boolean values to be displayed as true and false instead of the default 1 and 0.
- **`fixed`**

  Manipulator: Selects fixed floating-point format, with trailing zeroes.

Standard Code Libraries

- `left, right`
  Manipulator: Left- or right-justifies values if they are shorter than the field width.
- `scientific`
  Manipulator: Selects scientific floating-point format, such as 1.729000e+03.
- `setfill(char c)`
  Manipulator: Sets the fill character to the character c.
- `setprecision(int n)`
  Manipulator: Sets the precision of floating-point values to n digits after the decimal point in fixed and scientific formats.
- `setw(int n)`
  Manipulator: Sets the width of the next field.

<iostream>

Class istream

- `bool istream::fail() const`
  Function: True if input has failed.
- `istream& istream::get(char& c)`
  Function: Gets the next character and places it into c.
- `istream& istream::unget()`
  Function: Puts the last character read back into the stream, to be read again in the next input operation; only one character can be put back at a time.
- `istream& istream::seekg(long p)`
  Function: Moves the get position to position p.
- `long istream::tellg()`
  Function: Returns the get position.

Class ostream

- `ostream& ostream::seekp(long p)`
  Function: Moves the put position to position p.
- `long ostream::tellp()`
  Function: Returns the put position.

<fstream>

Class ifstream

- `void ifstream::open(const char n[])`
  Function: Opens a file with name n for reading.

Class ofstream

- `void ofstream::open(const char n[])`
  Function: Opens a file with name n for writing.

Class fstream

- `void fstream::`**`open`**`(const char n[])`

  Function: Opens a file with name n for reading and writing.

Class fstreambase

- `void fstreambase::`**`close`**`()`

  Function: Closes the file stream.

  Notes:
  - fstreambase is the common base class of ifstream, ofstream, and fstream.
  - To open a binary file both for input and output, use f.open(n, ios::in | ios::out | ios::binary)

\<strstream>

Class istringstream

- `istringstream::`**`istringstream`**`(string s)`

  Constructs a string stream that reads from the string s.

Class ostringstream

- `string ostringstream::`**`str`**`() const`

  Function: Returns the string that was collected by the string stream.

  Notes:
  - Call istrstream(s.c_str()) to construct an istrstream.
  - Call s = string(out.str()) to get a string object that contains the characters collected by the ostrstream out.

\<vector>

Class vector\<T>

- `int vector<T>::`**`size`**`() const`

  Function: Returns the number of elements in the container.
- `vector<T>::`**`vector`**`(int n)`

  Function: Constructs a vector with n elements.
- `void vector<T>::`**`push_back`**`(const T& x)`

  Function: Inserts x after the last element.
- `void vector<T>::`**`pop_back`**`()`

  Function: Removes (but does not return) the last element.
- `T& vector<T>::`**`operator`**`[](int n)`

  Function: Accesses the element at index n.
- `T& vector<T>::`**`at`**`(int n)`

  Function: Accesses the element at index n, checking that the index is in range.

GLOSSARY

Accessor function A function that accesses an object but does not change it.

Address A value that specifies the location of a variable in memory.

Aggregation relationship The "*has-a*" relationship between classes.

Algorithm An unambiguous, executable, and terminating specification to solve a problem.

ANSI/ISO C++ Standard The standard for the C++ language that was developed by the American National Standards Institute and the International Standards Organization.

Argument A parameter value in a function call, or one of the values combined by an operator.

Array A collection of values of the same type, each of which can be accessed by an integer index.

Arrow operator The -> operator. p->m is the same as (*p).m.

ASCII code The American Standard Code for Information Interchange, which associates code values between 0 and 127 to letters, digits, punctuation marks, and control characters.

Assignment Placing a new value into a variable.

Base class A class from which another class is derived.

Binary file A file in which values are stored in their binary representation and cannot be read as text.

Binary search A fast algorithm for finding a value in a sorted array. It narrows the search down to half of the array in every step.

Bit Binary digit; the smallest unit of information, having two possible values, 0 and 1. A data element consisting of n bits has 2^n possible values.

Black Box A device with a given specification but unknown implementation.

Block A group of statements bracketed by {}.

Boolean operator See **Logical operator**.

Boolean type A type with two values, true and false.

Boundary test case A test case involving values that are at the outer boundary of the set of legal values. For example, if a function is expected to work for all nonnegative integers, then 0 is a boundary test case.

Bounds error Trying to access an array element that is outside the legal range.

break statement A statement that terminates a loop or switch statement.

Byte A number between 0 and 255 (eight bits). Essentially all currently manufactured computers use a byte as the smallest unit of storage in memory.

Capacity The number of values that a data structure such as an array can potentially hold, in contrast to the size (the number of elements it currently holds).

Case-sensitive Distinguishing upper- and lowercase characters.

Cast Converting a value from one type to a different type. For example, the cast from a floating-point number x to an integer is expressed in C++ by the static cast notation, static_cast<int>(x).

Character A single letter, digit, or symbol.

Class A programmer-defined data type.

Command line The line you type when you start a program in a command window. It consists of the program name and the command line arguments.

Command line arguments Additional strings of information provided at the command line that the program can use.

Comment An explanation to make the human reader understand a section of a program; ignored by the compiler.

Compiler A program that translates code in a high-level language such as C++ to machine instructions.

Compile-time error See **Syntax error**.

Concatenation Placing one string after another.

Constant A value that cannot be changed by the program. In C++, constants are marked with the reserved word const.

Constructor A function that initializes a newly allocated object.

CPU (Central Processing Unit) The part of a computer that executes the machine instructions.

Dangling pointer A pointer that does not point to a valid location.

Data member A variable that is present in every object of a class.

Debugger A program that lets a user run another program one or a few steps at a time, stop execution, and inspect the variables in order to analyze the program for bugs.

Declaration A statement that announces the existence of a variable, function, or class but does not define it.

Default constructor A constructor that can be invoked with no parameters.

Definition A statement or series of statements that fully describes a variable, a function and its implementation, a type, or a class and its properties.

delete operator The operator that recycles memory to the heap.

Derived class A class that modifies a base class by adding data members, adding member functions, or redefining member functions.

Directory A structure on a disk that can hold files or other directories; also called a folder.

Dot notation The notation *object.function*(*parameters*) used to invoke a member function on an object.

Element A storage location in an array.

Encapsulation The hiding of implementation details.

Escape character A character in text that is not taken literally but has a special meaning when combined with the character or characters that follow it. The \ character is an escape character in C++ strings.

Exception A condition that prevents a program from continuing normally.

Executable file The file that contains a program's machine instructions.

Explicit parameter A parameter of a member function other than the object on which the function is invoked.

Expression A syntactical construct that is made up of constants, variables, and/or function calls, and the operators combining them.

Extension The last part of a file name, which specifies the file type. For example, the extension .cpp denotes a C++ file.

Failed stream state The state of a stream after an invalid operation has been attempted, such as reading a number when the next stream position yielded a non-digit, or reading after the end of file was reached.

File A sequence of bytes that is stored on disk.

File pointer The position within a file of the next byte to be read or written. It can be moved so as to access any byte in the file.

Floating-point number A number with a fractional part.

Folder Directory.

Function A sequence of statements that can be invoked multiple times, with different values for its parameter variables.

Global variable A variable whose scope is not restricted to a single function.

Header file A file that informs the compiler of features that are available in another module or library.

Heap A reservoir of storage from which memory can be allocated when a program runs.

IDE (Integrated Development Environment) A programming environment that includes an editor, compiler, and debugger.

Implicit parameter The object on which a member function is called. For example, in the call x.f(y), the object x is the implicit parameter of f.

#include directive An instruction to the preprocessor to include a header file.

Index The position of an element in an array.

Inheritance The "*is-a*" relationship between a general base class and a specialized derived class.

Initialization Setting a variable to a well-defined value when it is created.

Integer A number without a fractional part.

Integer division Taking the quotient of two integers and discarding the remainder. In C++, the / symbol denotes integer division if both arguments are integers. For example, 11 / 4 is 2, not 2.75.

Interface The set of functions that can be applied to objects of a given type.

Lexicographic ordering Ordering strings in the same order as in a dictionary, by skipping all matching characters and comparing the first nonmatching characters of both strings. For example, "orbit" comes before "orchid" in the lexicographic ordering. Note that in C++, unlike a dictionary, the ordering is case-sensitive: Z comes before a.

Library A set of precompiled functions that can be included in programs.

Linker The program that combines object and library files into an executable file.

Local variable A variable whose scope is a single block.

Logic error An error in a syntactically correct program that causes it to act differently from its specification.

Logical operator An operator that can be applied to Boolean values. C++ has three logical operators: &&, ||, and !.

Loop A sequence of instructions that is executed repeatedly.

Loop and a half A loop whose termination decision is neither at the beginning nor at the end.

Machine code Instructions that can be executed directly by the CPU.

Magic number A number that appears in a program without explanation.

main function The function that is called first when a program executes.

Member function A function that is defined by a class and operates on objects of that class.

Memory The circuitry that stores code and data in a computer.

Memory leak Memory that is dynamically allocated but never returned to the heap manager. A succession of memory leaks can cause the heap manager to run out of memory.

Modulus operator The % operator that yields the remainder of an integer division.

Mutator function A member function that changes the state of an object.

Nested block A block that is contained inside another block.

Nested loop A loop that is contained in another loop.

new operator The operator that allocates new memory from the heap.

Newline The '\n' character, which indicates the end of a line.

Object-oriented programming A programming style in which tasks are solved by collaborating objects.

Off-by-one error A common programming error in which a value is one larger or smaller than it should be.

Opening a file Preparing a file for reading or writing.

Operator A symbol denoting a mathematical or logical operation, such as + or &&.

Operator precedence The rule that governs which operator is evaluated first. For example, in C++ the && operator has a higher precedence than the || operator. Hence a || b && c is interpreted as a || (b && c).

Overloading Giving more than one meaning to a function name or operator.

Overriding Redefining a function from a base class in a derived class.

Parallel arrays Arrays of the same length, in which corresponding elements are logically related.

Parameter variable A variable in a function that is initialized with the argument value when the function is called.

Pointer A value that denotes the memory location of an object.

Polymorphism Selecting a function among several functions with the same name, by comparing the actual types of the parameters.

Prompt A string that prompts the program user to provide input.

Prototype The declaration of a function, including its parameter types and return type.

Pseudocode A mixture of English and C++ used when developing the code for a program.

Pseudorandom numbers A number that appears to be random but is generated by a formula.

Public interface The features of a class that are accessible to all clients.

Random access The ability to access any value directly without having to read the values preceding it.

Recursive function A function that can call itself with simpler values. It must handle the simplest values without calling itself.

Reference parameter A parameter that is bound to a variable supplied in the call. Changes made to the parameter within the function affect the variable outside the function.

Relational operator An operator that compares two values, yielding a Boolean result.

Reserved word A word that has a special meaning in a programming language and therefore cannot be used as a name by the programmer.

Return value The value returned by a function through a return statement.

Roundoff error An error introduced by the fact that the computer can store only a finite number of digits of a floating-point number.

Run-time error See **Logic error**.

Scope The part of a program in which a variable is defined.

Selection sort A sorting algorithm in which the smallest element is repeatedly found and removed until no elements remain.

Sentinel A value in input that is not to be used as an actual input value but to signal the end of input.

Sequential access Accessing values one after another without skipping over any of them.

Slicing an object Copying an object of a derived class into a variable of the base class, thereby losing the derived-class data.

Source file A file containing instructions in a programming language.

Stepwise refinement Solving a problem by breaking it into smaller problems and then further decomposing those smaller problems.

Stream An abstraction for a sequence of bytes from which data can be read or to which data can be written.

String A sequence of characters.

Structure A construct for aggregating items of arbitrary types into a single value.

Stub A function with no or minimal functionality.

Substitution principle The rule that states that you can use a derived-class object whenever a base-class object is expected.

Syntax Rules that define how to form instructions in a particular programming language.

Syntax error   An instruction that does not follow the programming language rules and is rejected by the compiler.

Tab character   The '\t' character, which advances the next character on the line to the next one of a set of fixed screen positions known as tab stops.

Test coverage   The instructions of a program that are executed when a set of test cases are run.

Text file   A file in which values are stored in their text representation.

Trace message   A message that is printed during a program run for debugging purposes.

Type   A named set of values and the operations that can be carried out with them.

Unary operator   An operator with one argument.

Unicode   A standard code that assigns values consisting of two bytes to characters used in scripts around the world.

Uninitialized variable   A variable that has not been set to a particular value. It is filled with whatever "random" bytes happen to be present in the memory location that the variable occupies.

Unit test   A test of a function by itself, isolated from the remainder of the program.

Value parameter   A function parameter whose value is copied into a parameter variable of a function. If a variable is passed as a value parameter, changes made to the parameter variable inside the function do not affect the original variable outside the program.

Variable   A storage location that can hold different values.

Vector   The standard C++ template for a dynamically-growing array.

Virtual function   A function that can be redefined in a derived class. The actual function called depends on the type of the object on which it is invoked at run time.

void   A reserved word indicating no type or an unknown type.

Walkthrough   Simulating a program or a part of a program by hand to test for correct behavior.

White space   A sequence consisting of space, tab, and/or newline characters.

INDEX

Page references followed by *t* indicate material in tables. Functions and classes from the C++ library are included by name. For functions and classes created for application examples, refer to the program listed under the main heading "applications."

Symbols

( ) (parentheses)
    order of arithmetic operations, 40
    unbalanced, 42
& (ampersand)
    address operator, 309
    reference parameter indicator, 222, 266
-> (arrow operator), 337, 422–423
* (asterisk)
    indirection operator, 309
    multiplication operator, 40, 105*t*
\ (backslash)
    displaying as a literal, 14
    escape sequence, 14, 493*t*
&& (Boolean AND)
    confusing with || (OR), 107
    description, 105*t*
    inverting, 108
    short-circuit evaluation, 108
! (Boolean NOT)
    description, 105*t*
    inverting conditions, 108
|| (Boolean OR)
    confusing with && (AND), 107
    description, 105*t*
    inverting, 108
    short-circuit evaluation, 108
= (equal sign)
    vs. ==, equality relational operator, 83
    assignment operator, 34–35
>> (extraction operator)
    assigning values to variables, 48
    reading input from a screen, 48
    reading numbers from binary files, 373
    reading strings from the console, 58
<< (insertion operator)
    displaying to the screen, 12
    ending displayed output, 14
    formatting printed output, 51*t*
    starting a new line, 15
    syntax, 13
- (minus sign)
    subtraction operator, 40
    unary negative operator, 105*t*
    unary operator, spaces in, 46

+ (plus sign)
    addition operator, 40, 105*t*
    concatenation operator, 57
    unary positive operator, 105*t*
"..." (quotation marks)
    displaying as literals, 14, 493*t*
    string indicators, 13
/ (slash)
    division operator, 40, 105*t*
: (colon), inheritance indicator, 447
. (dot), dot operator, 337
/*...*/, multiline comments, C++ code, 36
/**...*/, multiline comments, Java style, 199
{ } (braces)
    coding guidelines, 487
    in if statements, 79–80, 98
? : (question mark, colon), selection
    operator, 81
\" (backslash, double quote), double quote
    escape sequence, 493*t*
\? (backslash, question mark), question
    mark escape sequence, 493*t*
\' (backslash, quote), single quote escape
    sequence, 493*t*
== (equal signs), equality operator
    vs. = (equal sign), assignment operator, 83
    Boolean operations, 105*t*
    description, 83*t*
    equality testing, 83
!= (exclamation, equal), not equal operator,
    83*t*, 105*t*
> (greater than), relational operator, 83*t*, 105*t*
>= (greater than or equal), relational opera-
    tor, 83*t*, 105*t*
- (hyphen), in option names, 365
< (less than), relational operator, 83*t*, 105*t*
<= (less than or equal), relational operator,
    83*t*, 105*t*
- (minus sign), subtraction operator, 105*t*
-- (minus signs), decrement operator, 40,
    105*t*
% (percent sign), modulus operator, 41, 105*t*
++ (plus signs), increment operator, 40, 105*t*
// (slashes), single-line comment
    indicator, 36

CREDITS

Text Credits

Exercises P2.25, P5.32, P5.34: Adapted from *MATLAB: An Introduction with Applications*, Third Edition, Amos Gilat (John Wiley & Sons, Inc., 2008) Reprinted with permission of John Wiley & Sons, Inc.

P4.28, P4.30: Adapted from *Introduction to Engineering Programming: Solving Problems with Algorithms*, James P. Holloway (John Wiley & Sons, Inc., 2004) Reprinted with permission of John Wiley & Sons, Inc.

P6.33: Courtesy of Jonathan Tolstedt, North Dakota State University.

Illustration Credits

Preface Page v: iStockphoto.

Chapter 1 Page 1, 2: Sebastian Duda/iStockphoto.
Page 3, 21: Natalia Siverina/iStockphoto.
Page 4: PhotoDisc, Inc./GettyImages.
Page 5: UPPA/Photoshot Holdings Ltd.
Page 6: Courtesy of Bjarne Stroustrup.
Page 7: Stockphoto.
Page 11 (top), 22: Tatiana Popova/iStockphoto.
Page 11 (bottom): Josh Hodge/iStockphoto.
Page 15, 22: Martin Carlsson/iStockphoto.
Page 17: iStockphoto.
Page 19, 22: Claudia DeWald/iStockphoto.
Page 20: David H. Lewis/iStockphoto.
Page 21: Robert Ban/iStockphoto.
Page 24: Mark Massel/PhotoDisc, Inc.
Page 27: Courtesy NASA/JPL-Caltech.

Chapter 2 Page 29, 30 (top): Chad Anderson/iStockphoto.
Page 30 (middle): iStockphoto; travis manley/iStockphoto.
Page 30 (bottom), 62: Javier Larrea/Age Fotostock.
Page 31, 62: Ingenui/iStockphoto.
Page 35: james stedl/iStockphoto.
Page 39: Finn Brandt/iStockphoto.
Page 40: Yunus Arakon/iStockphoto.
Page 41, 62: Michael Flippo/iStockphoto.
Page 43: Joe McDaniel/iStockphoto.
Page 47: Courtesy of Larry Hoyle, Institute for Policy & Social Research, University of Kansas.

Page 49, 62: Rich Koele/iStockphoto.
Page 53: Courtesy NASA/JPL-Caltech.
Page 54: Photos.com/Jupiter Images.
Page 56, 62: jason walton/iStockphoto.
Page 59, 63: Rich Legg/iStockphoto.
Page 61 (left): Paul Vachier/iStockphoto.
Page 61 (top right): Joel Carllet/iStockphoto.
Page 61 (bottom right): iStockphoto.
Page 65: Thomas Stange/iStockphoto.
Page 67: iStockphoto.
Page 68: Steve Snyder/iStockphoto.
Page 70: José Luis Gutiérrez/iStockphoto.
Page 71: TebNad/iStockphoto.

Chapter 3 Page 75, 76: iStockphoto.
Page 76: Oleksandr Gumerov/iStockphoto.
Page 77, 113: Creatas/Media Bakery.
Page 79: Timothy Large/iStockphoto.
Page 81: Photo by Vincent LaRussa/John Wiley & Sons, Inc.
Page 82, 113: iStockphoto.
Page 86 (top): iStockphoto.
Page 86 (bottom), 113: Corbis Digital Stock.
Page 87: iStockphoto.
Page 89: Bob Daemmrich/Getty Images.
Page 90, 113: Kevin Russ/iStockphoto.
Page 93: iStockphoto.
Page 94, 114: iStockphoto.
Page 97: Derek Thomas/iStockphoto.
Page 100: Ekspansio/iStockphoto.
Page 103: Bananastock/Media Bakery.
Page 104 (top), 114: Jon Patton/iStockphoto.
Page 104 (bottom): Catharina van den Dikkenberg/iStockphoto.
Page 108: YouraPechkin/iStockphoto.
Page 109, 114: Tetra Images/Media Bakery.
Page 111: Jean-MariePLUCHON/iStockphoto.
Page 113: Vaughn Youtz/Zuma Press.
Page 120: iStockphoto.
Page 121: iStockphoto.
Page 122: Charles Schultz/iStockphoto.
Page 123 (top): Darko Novakovic/iStockphoto.
Page 123 (bottom): Nancy Louie/iStockphoto.
Page 124: Susan Stevenson/iStockphoto.
Page 125: rotofrank/iStockphoto.
Page 126: Courtesy NASA/JPL-Caltech.

Chapter 4   Page 131, 132 (top): iStockphoto.
Page 132 (middle): Jarek Szymanski/iStockphoto.
Page 132 (bottom), 173: Maco Maccarini/iStockphoto.
Page 137 (top): ohiophoto/iStockphoto.
Page 137 (bottom): Karen Town/iStockphoto.
Page 138: Naval Surface Weapons Center, Dahlgren, VA.
Pages 139–141 (paperclip): Yvan Dubé/iStockphoto.
Page 143, 173: Enrico Fianchini/iStockphoto.
Page 148: iStockphoto.
Page 150, 173: Rhoberazzi/iStockphoto.
Page 155: Courtesy of Martin Hardee.
Page 158: Dietmar Klement/iStockphoto.
Page 159: iStockphoto.
Page 160: matt matthews/iStockphoto.
Page 161: Tommy Ingberg/iStockphoto.
Page 162: Steve Geer/iStockphoto.
Page 164: iStockphoto.
Page 166, 174: david kahn/iStockphoto.
Page 169, 174: Kiyoshi Takahase/iStockphoto.
Page 170: Tim Starkey/iStockphoto.
Page 172: Don Bayley/iStockphoto.
Page 173 (second from top): Derek Thomas/iStockphoto.
Page 179: david franklin/iStockphoto.
Page 180: Anthony Rosenberg/iStockphoto.
Page 181: Eric Isselée/iStockphoto.
Page 184: Charles Gibson/iStockphoto.
Page 185 (top): Michael O Flachra/iStockphoto.
Page 185 (bottom), 186 (top): *Introduction to Engineering Programming: Solving Problems with Algorithms*, James P. Holloway (John Wiley & Sons, Inc., 2004) Reprinted with permission of John Wiley & Sons, Inc.
Page 186 (middle): Mark Kostich/iStockphoto.
Page 186 (bottom): Ziga Cetrtic//iStockphoto.

Chapter 5   Page 193, 194: Joselito Brianes/iStockphoto.
Page 195, 232: Yenwen Lu/iStockphoto.
Page 196: dieter Spears/iStockphoto.
Page 197, 232: Nina Shannon/iStockphoto.
Page 199 (collage), 232: christine balderas/iStockphoto (cherry pie); dieter Spears/iStockphoto (apple pie); Klaudia Steiner/iStockphoto (cherries); iStockphoto (apples).
Page 202, 232: Natalia Bratslavsky/iStockphoto.
Page 204: Holger Mette/iStockphoto.
Page 206, 232: Pelfreth/Dreamstime.com.
Page 209: Lawrence Sawyer/iStockphoto.
Page 210, 232: Rob Belknap/iStockphoto.
Page 211: iStockphoto.

Page 217: iStockphoto.

Page 218 (top): paul kline/iStockphoto.

Page 218 (collage), 233: Joan Champ/iStockphoto (Railway and Main);
Steven Johnson/iStockphoto (Main and N. Putnam); Jeffrey Smith/iStockphoto
(Main and South St.).

Page 222: Winston Davidian/iStockphoto.

Page 226: Janice Richard/iStockphoto.

Page 227, 233: Nicolae Popovici/iStockphoto.

Page 231: Reprint Courtesy of International Business Machine Corporation,
copyright © International Business Machines Corporation.

Page 234: Stacey Newman/iStockphoto.

Page 240: Matjaz Boncina/iStockphoto.

Page 241: Charles Schultz/iStockphoto.

Page 244: Craig Cozart/iStockphoto.

Chapter 6   Page 249, 250: graham kiotz/iStockphoto.

Page 252, 290: Max Dimyadi/iStockphoto.

Page 253, 291: Jarek Szymanski/iStockphoto.

Page 257 (top): matt matthews/iStockphoto.

Page 257 (bottom): Michal Kram/iStockphoto.

Page 258, 291: Yegor Korzh/iStockphoto.

Page 274: Kiyoshi Takahase/iStockphoto.

Page 275 (top), 291: Jennifer Conner/iStockphoto.

Page 275–276 (coins), 305: jamesbenet/iStockphoto; Jorge Delgado/iStockphoto.

Page 277: Claudio Arnese/iStockphoto.

Page 278 (top), 291: Chris Burt/iStockphoto.

Page 278 (bottom): technotr/iStockphoto.

Page 284, 292: Michael Brake/iStockphoto.

Page 290: Topham/The Image Works.

Page 301 (top): Gordon Heeley/iStockphoto.

Page 301 (bottom): Nikki Bidgood/iStockphoto.

➕ Worked Example 6.1: Ryan Ruffatti/iStockphoto.

Chapter 7   Page 307, 308 (top): Suzanne Tucker/iStockphoto.

Page 308 (bottom), 339: Alexey Chuvarkov/iStockphoto.

Page 320, 339: Sven Larsen/iStockphoto.

Page 326, 339: Carrie Bottomley/iStockphoto.

Page 334: Bartosz Liszkowski/iStockphoto.

Page 336 (top): Courtesy of Professor Naehyuck Chang, Computer Systems Lab,
Department of Computer Engineering, Seoul National University.

Page 336 (bottom), 340: Joel Carillet/iStockphoto.

Page 346: TexPhoto/iStockphoto.

Chapter 8   Page 352, 352 (top): Photo courtesy of Erik Vestergard,
http://www.matematiksider.dk/enigma_eng.html.

Page 352 (bottom), 377: iStockphoto.

Page 355: Nancy Ross/iStockphoto.

Page 359, 378: Getty Images.
Page 361, 378: iStockphoto.
Page 363, 378: iStockphoto.
Page 366, 378: iStockphoto.
Page 368: Anna Khomulo/iStockphoto.
Page 369: Oksana Perkins/iStockphoto.
Page 373, 378: iStockphoto.
Page 374: Cay Horstmann.
Page 383, 384: Cay Horstmann.
Page 386: Chris Dascher/iStockphoto.

Chapter 9   Page 389, 390 (top): Stephanie Strathdee/iStockphoto.
Page 390 (bottom), 426: Michael Shake/iStockphoto.
Page 391 (top), 427: Damir Cudic/iStockphoto.
Page 391 (bottom): Christian Waadt/iStockphoto.
Page 392 (top): James Richey/iStockphoto.
Page 392 (bottom): Eric Isselée/iStockphoto.
Page 395, 427: iStockphoto.
Page 397, 427: Mark Evans/iStockphoto.
Page 398: Glow Images.
Page 404, 427: Ann Marie Kurtz/iStockphoto.
Page 409 (top): Hunteerwagstaff/Dreamstime.com.
Page 409 (bottom): Mark Evans/iStockphoto.
Page 412: Peter Nguyen/iStockphoto.
Page 413: Lisa F. Young/iStockphoto.
Page 414, 427: Oleg Prikhodko/iStockphoto.
Page 415, 427: Anastaslya Maksymenko/iStockphoto.
Page 426: Courtesy of Richard Stallman.
Page 430: Jasmin Awad/iStockphoto.
Page 431: Miklas Voros/iStockphoto.
Page 434: Steve Dibblee/iStockphoto.
Page 437: Maria Toutoudaki/iStockphoto.

Chapter 10   Page 441, 442: Lisa Thornberg/iStockphoto.
Page 442, 470: Tony Tremblay/iStockphoto (vehicle); Peter Dean/iStockphoto (motorcycle); nicholas belton/iStockphoto (car); Robert Pernell/iStockphoto (truck); Clay Blackburn/iStockphoto (sedan); iStockphoto (SUV).
Page 443: paul kline/iStockphoto.
Page 447, 471: Ivan Cholavov/iStockphoto.
Page 459, 471: Aleksandr Popov/iStockphoto.
Page 4 (top): Sean Locke/iStockphoto.
Page 4 (bottom): Science Photo Library/Photo Researchers, Inc.
Page 47 : Maria Toutoudaki/iStockphoto.

Chapter 11   ✚ Chapter Opener: Nicolae Popovici/iStockphoto.

Chapter 12   ✚ Chapter Opener: Volkan Ersoy/iStockphoto.

Chapter 13   ✚ Chapter Opener: andrea laurita/iStockphoto.
Stacks and Queues: Photodisc/Punchstock.
Random Fact 13.1: Courtesy of Nigel Tout.

Chapter 14   ✚ Chapter Opener: nicholas belton/iStockphoto.

Icons   Common Error icon: Scott Harms/iStockphoto.
How To icon: Steve Simzer/iStockphoto.
Paperclip: Yvan Dubé/iStockphoto.
Programming Tip icon: Macdaddy/Dreamstime.com.
Random Fact icon: Mishella/Dreamstime.com.
Self Check icon: Nicholas Homrich/iStockphoto.
Special Topic icon: nathan winter/iStockphoto.
Worked Example icon: Tom Horyn/iStockphoto.

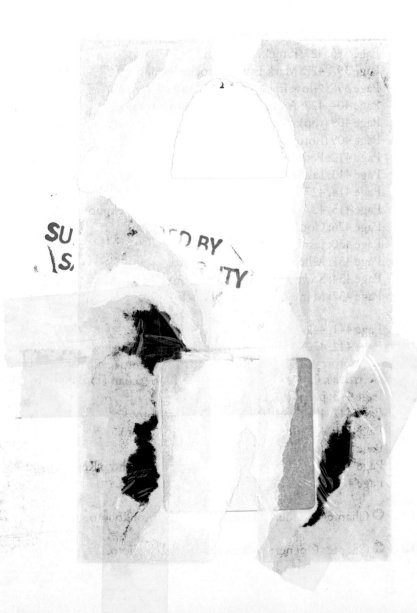